Since the publication of *The Rifles Are There* in 2005, which dealt with the 1st and 2nd Battalions Royal Ulster Rifles in the Second World War, it was felt by many that a follow-up volume dealing with the Korean conflict was overdue. A limited yet competent history had been produced in 1953 by the then Adjutant Captain Hugh Hamill, although this has been long out of print.

A New Battlefield follows the Battalion as it prepares for the first major conflict fought by Britain since the defeat of the Japanese in 1945. During the summer of 1950 the Battalion was stationed at Sobraon Barracks in Colchester, it was in the process of being issued with desert kit for a tour of duty at Khartoum in the Sudan and its numbers were just under four hundred men. For service in Korea these numbers had to be drastically increased and drafts of volunteers and reservists were brought in from various sources. Consequently this 'Irish' Battalion contained men from the Lancastrian Brigade, Welsh Brigade, Mercian Brigade, the Light Infantry and other Battalions of the Irish Brigade. The Irish Brigade also reinforced other regiments, the Royal Inniskilling Fusiliers sending two officers and fifty 'other ranks' to the King's (Liverpool) Regiment. Despite their varied backgrounds all ranks soon coalesced into a professional unit that took the campaign in its stride. From winter temperatures that dropped well below 40°F to a summer heat that rose to 105°F with a humidity to match, these men survived all and dealt with a brave and tenacious enemy.

The Battalion sailed for Korea in October 1950 and fought its first major action in January 1951 at Chaegunghyon, or as it was known to the Rifles, 'Happy Valley'. Here, for the first time, they faced an enemy that often literally fought to the death, despite overwhelming firepower, bombing and widespread use of napalm. Three months later, on the banks of the Imjin River, the Rifles, in conjunction with the remainder of 29 Brigade, faced an army that came in such numbers that running out of ammunition before the enemy ran out of men became a reality. While the Battle of the Imjin is today largely remembered for the last stand fought by the 'Glorious Glosters', research revels that it was the Royal Ulster Rifles that held open the door that allowed the survivors of 29 Brigade to escape annihilation. The media reacts with horror at the loss of life in Afghanistan when it is in single figures, yet during the fighting at 'Happy Valley' the Battalion lost 157 men in one twenty-four hour period.

In the 1950s, with limited television and press coverage, Korea was quite literally on the far side of the world and generated little interest with the population; it remains so to this day. With the current situation in that country its past deserves to be re-examined and reassessed.

Besides numerous photographs there are also appendices including Honours and Awards, Operation 'Spitfire', an Order of Battle for 29 Brigade, and a Nominal Roll, which includes casualties.

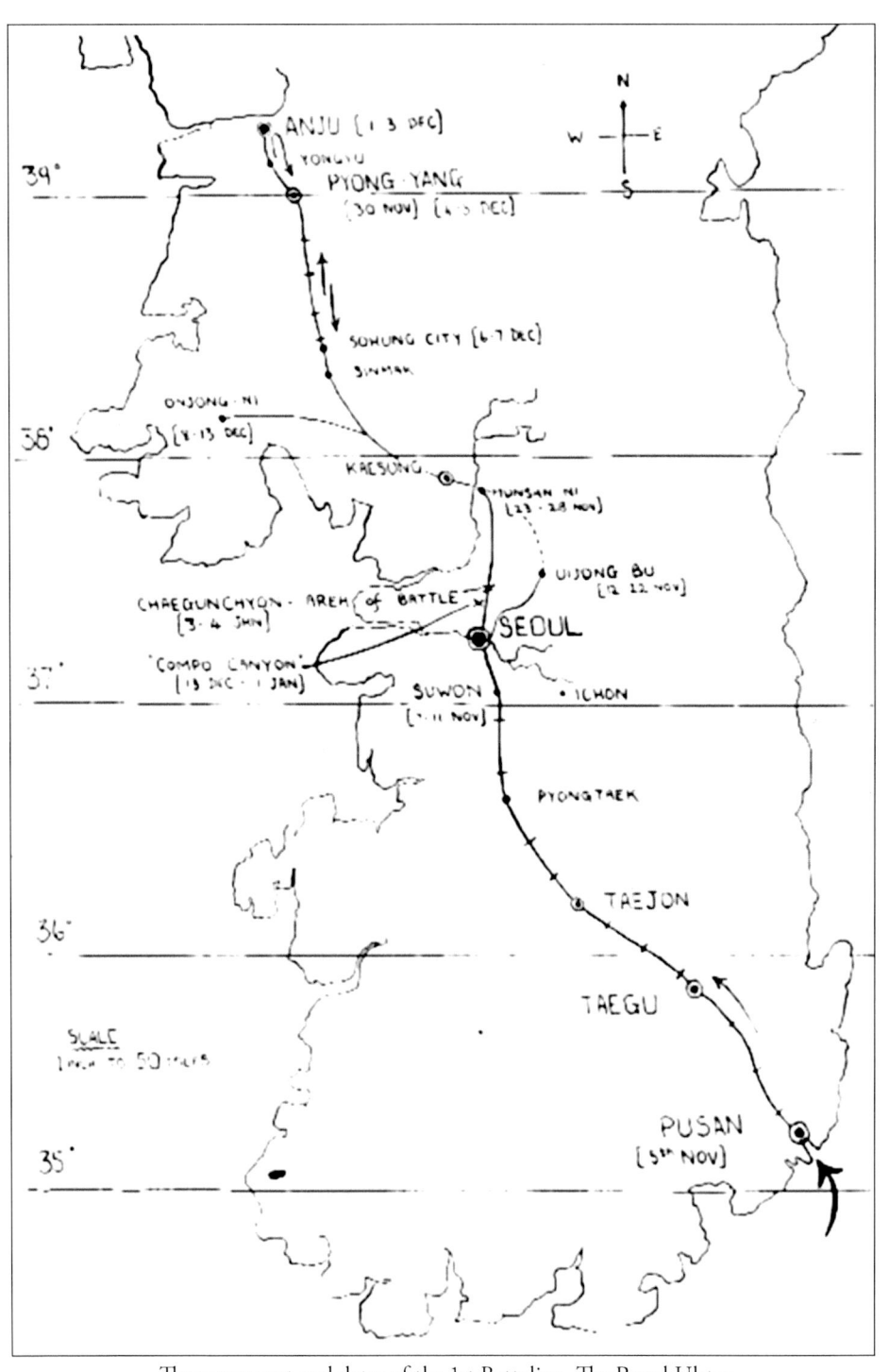

The movement and dates of the 1st Battalion, The Royal Ulster Rifles in Korea. (The Royal Ulster Rifles in Korea, 1953)

A NEW BATTLEFIELD

THE ROYAL ULSTER RIFLES IN KOREA
1950–51

David R. Orr and David Truesdale

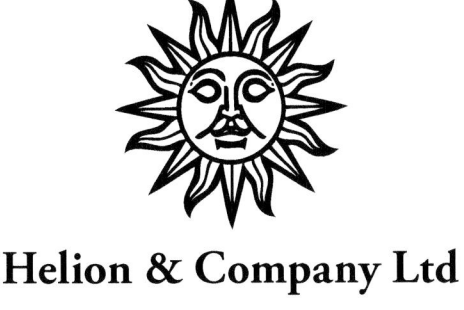

Helion & Company Ltd

Helion & Company Limited
26 Willow Road
Solihull
West Midlands B91 1UE
England
Tel. 0121 705 3393
Fax 0121 711 4075
Email: info@helion.co.uk
Website: www.helion.co.uk
Twitter: @helionbooks
Visit our blog http://blog.helion.co.uk/

Published by Helion & Company 2011
This paperback reprint 2013

Designed and typeset by Farr out Publications, Wokingham, Berkshire
Cover designed by Farr out Publications, Wokingham, Berkshire
Printed by Lightning Source, Milton Keynes, Buckinghamshire

Text © David R. Orr and David Truesdale 2011
Photographs and maps as credited.

Cover illustration: 'The Battle of Imjin, Crash Action' by David Rowlands. On 25th April 1951, Lieutenant John Mole, in command of the remaining section of the Royal Ulster Rifles 3 inch mortars, dismounted in the open and replied with rapid mortar fire on to the slopes from which a hail of machine-gun fire swept the valley floor. The surviving tanks of C Squadron the 8th King's Royal Irish Hussars kept up a heavy fire on the Chinese formations swarming down the valley slopes (David Rowlands & The Royal Irish Regiment).

Every effort has been made to ensure the accuracy of the information presented in this book, and every reasonable effort has been made to trace copyright holders. The publisher will not assume liability for damages caused by inaccuracies in the data, or for any copyright inadvertently breached, and makes no warranty whatsoever expressed or implied.

ISBN 978-1-908916-92-1

British Library Cataloguing-in-Publication Data.
A catalogue record for this book is available from the British Library.

All rights reserved. No part of this publication may be reproduced, stored in a retrieval system,or transmitted, in any form, or by any means, electronic, mechanical, photocopying, recording or otherwise, without the express written consent of Helion & Company Limited.

For details of other military history titles published by Helion & Company Limited contact the above address, or visit our website: http://www.helion.co.uk.

We always welcome receiving book proposals from prospective authors.

Contents

List of Illustrations	vi
List of Maps	xvi
Glossary and List of Abbreviations	xvii
Foreword by Brigadier M.N.S. McCord CBE MC	20
Acknowledgements	22
Introduction by Lt-Col R. Charley OBE JP DL	24
Background	25
1 The Rifles, a brief history	30
2 Preparation	34
3 Sailing to the far side of the world	50
4 Korea	58
5 Advance and withdrawal	73
6 Happy Valley	83
7 Replacements and Prisoners of War	106
8 Reconnaissance and Resupply	125
9 On the Imjin	144
10 The Battle of the Imjin	156
11 The War grinds on	187
12 Checkpoint 'How'	214
13 The Closing Days	223
Epilogue	236
Appendices	
I Order of Battle	244
II Honours and Awards	248
III Nominal Roll	256
IV Operation 'Spitfire'	316
V Korean Lament	317
Bibliography	318
Index	320

List of Illustrations

Brigadier M. McCord, King's Div and ADC to HM the Queen 1981-84, Colonel Royal Irish Rangers 1985-90. (Mervyn McCord)   20
Lt-Col R. Charley CO Queen's University OTC, 1965, aged 41 years. (R. Charley)   26
St Patrick's Barracks, 1940. (RUR Museum)   32
St Patrick's Barracks, The RUR Regimental Depot, Ballymena, Northern Ireland. (RUR Museum)   32
Members of Support Company of the 1st Battalion at Colchester. (RUR Museum)   34
Mortar Section of the 1st Battalion at Colchester. (RUR Museum)   35
Corporal Tommy Cushing, a native of Tipperary, originally joined the US Army in 1926, to see what it was like in the army on the other side of the Atlantic. He stayed for ten years before returning to Tipperary. He re-enlisted and in 1939 went to France with the BEF, but did not get away at Dunkirk. He had long spells in Dachau, Buchenwald and Belsen. When told by an officer he was 'for Korea', he grinned and said "Well I suppose it's just another spot of bother, so let's get it over ….".   36
Adjutant, Captain H. Hamill. (Mervyn McCord/RUR Association)   38
Captain Stuart de Longueil, OC A Echelon and Adjutant wearing a dog skin cap, in Happy Valley. (Mervyn McCord/RUR Association)   40
George Prescott Westcar, John ffrench and Arthur McCallan admire the local 'talent'. (*Quis Separabit*)   41
Grave of 2nd Lieutenant Prescott-Westcar, United Nations Memorial Cemetery, Pusan, Korea. (RUR Association)   41
Lieutenant R. Benson, D Company (RUR Museum)   43
Padre Kelly at 57 Regimental Aid Post, Happy Valley. (Mervyn McCord/RUR Association)   44
Padre Kelly with a Fusilier driver in Happy Valley. (RUR Museum)   44
Officers of the 1st Battalion, The Royal Ulster Rifles with General Steele, taken a day prior to departure for Korea.   45
Back row: ? , ? , Lt Nicholl, ? , Lt Benson, Lt Davies, Lt Prescott-Westcar, Lt Shaw, Frazer.   45
Middle row: Capt Ferrie (MO), Capt Millar, Capt Neely, Capt Dickson, Capt Smith, Capt Ellison, Padre Kelly, Capt Charley, Lt Theobald.   45
Front row: Major de Longueuil, Major Shaw, Major Ryan, Major Blake, General Steele, Lt-Col Carson, Capt Hamill, Major Gaffikin, Major Mulligan (RUR Museum)   45
As the men of the Royal Ulster Rifles bound for Korea waved goodbye pipers of the London Irish Rifles played them away. A crowd sang, *Auld Lang Syne*.   46
Rt Hon John Strachey, Secretary of State for War, visiting the men of the Royal Ulster Rifles before they leave on HMT *Empire Pride*. (RUR Museum)   46

LIST OF ILLUSTRATIONS vii

Boarding the HMT *Empire Pride* at Liverpool with the Liver Building in the background. (RUR Museum)	46
Members of 1st Battalion, The Royal Ulster Rifles preparing to leave for Korea from Liverpool on 1st October 1950. (RUR Museum)	47
Colonel Carson wishing luck to members of 1st Battalion, The Royal Ulster Rifles as they prepare to leave for Korea from Liverpool on 1st October 1950. (RUR Museum)	47
Men of the 1st Battalion, the Royal Ulster Rifles, crowd the side of the troopship *Empire Pride* as she pulls away from the quay at Liverpool en route for Korea.	48
Onboard HMT *Empire Pride*. (RUR Museum)	48
Dinner-time onboard the *Empire Pride*, soon to run out of potatoes. (RUR Museum)	51
Bill McConnell. (Bill McConnell)	51
On board HMT *Empire Pride*, possibly near Suez. (RUR Museum)	52
Five Royal Ulster Rifleman who sailed in the *Empire Pride* for Korea. Left to right – Sergeant F. Nugent, Crumlin Road; Corporal Y. Johnson, Malvern Street; Rifleman J. Addis, Ligioniel; Corporal J. Boyle, York Street and Corporal S. Mark, Drummond Street, Larne. (*Northern Whig*)	53
Riflemen taking a break in Colombo en-route to Korea. (Bill McConnell)	53
Beer duty, Korea, 1951. (William May/RUR Association)	54
B Company, The 1st Battalion at Singapore, 27 October 1950, preparing for a route march. (RUR Museum)	55
The Battalion pipers leading the route march in Singapore. (RUR Museum)	55
The Battalion begins a route march in Singapore, 27 October 1950, after disembarking from the *Empire Pride* to acclimatise the men to the conditions east of Suez. (RUR Museum)	56
HMT *Empire Pride*, Pusan, October 1950. (Mervyn McCord/RUR Association)	57
The US Negro band welcomes 1 RUR to Pusan, October 1950. (Mervyn McCord)	59
Marching from the ship to the train, Pusan 1950. (Mervyn McCord)	59
A Company march to the train, Shaw-Stewart front left. (Mervyn McCord)	60
Suwon from Pusan. (Mervyn McCord)	61
The Han River from the top. (Mervyn McCord)	63
Men of the 1st Battalion, The Royal Ulster Rifles present arms as Lieut-General Sir Horace Robertson leaves the former British Legation in Seoul. The Rifles had been granted the honour of providing the guard at the Legation. The guard seen here consists (from left) of Sergeant H. Campbell, Corporal J. O'Neill, both of Belfast; Lance Corporal K. Joyce of Glassdrummond; Rifleman J. Moore of Belfast; Lance Corporal M. Hickey of Limerick; Rifleman D. Glendon of Durham and Rifleman R. Stewart of Belfast. (*Belfast Telegraph*)	63
Suk Bum Yoon and two other porters, Uijonbu, November 1950. (Mervyn McCord/RUR Association)	64
First deployment, Uijonbu November 1950. RUR Command Post and Suk Bum Yoon in the foreground. (Mervyn McCord/RUR Association)	65

Men of the Royal Ulster Rifles with local Korean children at Uijongbu, Korea. Middle (left) Mark McConnell (right) Jim Rodgers. Back, R to L, Rifleman Riley, Brown. (Mark McConnell)	65
A Battalion jeep sporting the Divisional sign on the windscreen. (Mervyn McCord/RUR Association)	67
Rifleman P. Dolan in the area of Uijongbu, just north of the capital city of Seoul. (RUR Museum)	69
A Royal Ulster Rifles position observing Korean 'traffic' – carts pulled by oxen. (RUR Museum)	70
Leaving Uijongbu for the long journey to Pyongyang. RUR trucks 78RC52 and 19RB77 beside factory shed. The tyres of the trucks have been fitted with snow chains. (Mervyn McCord/RUR Association)	70
Defence Platoon, HQ Company, digging-in at Sinujui, about 80 miles south of the Yalu River (in picture are Corporal McKeown and Rifleman Galway). (RUR Museum)	71
A recce of Seoul, December 1950. (Mervyn McCord)	73
Battle patrol, December 1950.(Mervyn McCord)	74
The Commanders of the two original brigade groups of the 1st Commonwealth Division. Left, Brigadier T. Brodie, 29th British Infantry Brigade; right, Brigadier B.A. Coad, 27th Commonwealth Infantry Brigade. (Public Relations, Headquarters, BCOF)	74
Pyongyang, November 1950. (RUR Association)	75
The 29th British Brigade retreat from Pyongyang (Henry O'Kane)	78
1 RUR 17pdr anti-tank guns at Pyongyang, November 1950. (Mervyn McCord)	79
Lady Mountbatten with Lieutenant-Colonel A.G. Rangaraj (Officer Commanding, 60th Indian Field Ambulance) standing near a type of American helicopter in common use in Korea. (Public Relations, Headquarters, BCOF)	81
Stores in Compo Canyon, Happy Valley, Christmas 1950. (Mervyn McCord/RUR Association)	84
Battalion Headquarters. (RUR Museum)	84
The famous 'Gin Place', also known as Battalion Headquarters, Happy Valley, Christmas 1950. (RUR Museum)	84
(Back row) Sergeant Walker and Rifleman Horrabin, (front row) Rifleman Washer, Mrs O, O's mother and Mr O, who helped with platoon chores. (*Quis Separabit*)	85
RUR Coy positions at Chaegunghyon looking north from 'Cooperforce'. (RUR Association)	85
Captain A.B. 'Beetle' Williams with Colonel Carson, Captain Hamill and Major Blake. (Mervyn McCord/RUR Association)	86
Happy Valley, where 1 RUR spent Christmas 1950.(Mervyn McCord)	86
Lieutenant McCallan, Captain Hamill and Colonel Carson at Compo Canyon. (Mervyn McCord/RUR Association)	86
Major de Longueuil in dog skin cap with Captains Hinde and Hamill in Happy Valley. (RUR Museum)	87
Pipe Major 'Lakari' Woods speaking with a senior officer. (RUR Museum)	88

LIST OF ILLUSTRATIONS ix

Warning orders for January's battle – Captain B. Williams, Bde IO, Colonel Carson (hooded), Captain Hamill and Major Blake. (Mervyn McCord/RUR Association)	92
A British Cromwell tank being loaded onto a rail flat car at Hiro Station, Japan-bound for Divisional Battle School. Six of the OP tanks of 45 Field Regiment under the command of Captain Astley-Cooper were Cromwells. (George Forty)	92
Members of the Royal Ulster Rifles in action in snow-covered country somewhere in Korea, 1951. Note the different styles of headgear. (RUR Museum)	97
CSM Sean Fitzsimons. (Mark McConnell)	101
Captain Majury directing operations of the 3" Mortars. (RUR Museum)	103
Telegram from Majury, January 1951. (Mervyn McCord/RUR Association)	103
Captain James Majury, who had been a prisoner of war during the Korean War. (RUR Association)	104
Major M.D.G.C. Ryan, the senior British officer amongst the captives of January 1951. (RUR Association)	104
Grave of Major C.A.H.B. Blake, United Nations Memorial Cemetery, Pusan, Korea. (RUR Museum)	105
Cromwell OP Tank, 45th RA, Happy Valley. (Henry O'Kane)	105
CSM Joe McCrory, BEM. (Henry O'Kane)	105
The original caption reads: "This North Korean flag makes an interesting addition to The Royal Ulster Rifles regimental museum at the Depot, Ballymena. The flag – red, white and blue stripes with a red star in white circle – was found in a house in Seoul and was sent to Major R.M. Parsons, OC Depot, by Major J.S.C.G. de Longueuil MC. Displaying the flag in this picture are Cpl T.G. Nolan (left) who is in charge of the museum and L/Cpl K. Stowe." (*Belfast Telegraph*)	107
Lance Corporal M. Vance.	107
The original caption reads: "Warmly wrapped up against raw weather, a group of Royal Ulster Rifles who have been in action against the Communist forces, kneel down in the snow as they pose for this picture "somewhere in South Korea". From left to right (front) are Corporal Tom Murray, Wiltshire; Lance Corporal Joe Farrell, Belfast; Major H.M. Gaffikin, Kings Road, Knock, Belfast; Corporal Bill Lorimer, Ballymena and Rifleman Tommy Kelly, Liverpool. At the rear (left to right) Sergeant Nat Kennedy, Belfast; Lieutenant J.A. Beckett, Cheshire; Sergeant Terry Mann, Worcestershire; Rifleman Terry Byrne, Liverpool and Rifleman Jim Greenwood, Somerset." (*Belfast Telegraph*, February 1951)	108
Return to the Imjin – Captain H.D. Miller resting on a US Jeep complete with American carbine – HQ on the banks of the Imjin. (Mervyn McCord/RUR Association)	109
Lieutenant McCord just returned from a four day patrol and told he been awarded the Military Cross. (Mervyn McCord)	109

Rifleman R. Boyd bids farewell to his fiancée, Miss Peggy Glennon, at York Road Railway station. (*Belfast Telegraph*)	109
Rifleman William Lynch, Falls Road and his fiancée, Miss Violet Miller, Oldpark Road, were to have been married but he was sent to Korea so the wedding had to be postponed. Nevertheless their friends gave Lynch a confetti send-off at the York Road Railway Station when he left with his unit. He is pictured here with his fiancée before he joined the train. (*Belfast Telegraph*)	111
Extract from the diary of Corporal W. Massey whilst a POW, circa 1951. (C. Cunningham)	111
Extract from the diary of Corporal W. Massey whilst a POW, circa 1951. (C. Cunningham)	112
Rifleman Clifford, missing in action.	114
John Lane, Max Nichols and Mason stocking up at the PRI which included Lux soap and Heinz beans. (Mervyn McCord/RUR Museum)	117
Centurion Tank with reversed turret advancing towards friendly lines, Korea, 1951. (William May/RUR Association)	118
Brigadier T. Brodie, Commander of the 29th Independent British Brigade, with S Company MG Crew in Korea. (RUR Museum)	119
Rifleman G. Williams returning from an anti-guerilla mountain patrol. (RUR Museum)	120
A foot patrol heading out into the foothills. (Mervyn McCord/RUR Association)	120
Rifleman J. Pratt returning from an anti-guerilla mountain patrol. (RUR Museum)	120
Suk Bum Yoon and a Rifleman. (Mervyn McCord/RUR Association)	122
Colour Sergeant Rainey with Korean porters and Suk Bum Yoon. (Mervyn McCord/RUR Association)	122
Korean porters by a rail siding. (Mervyn McCord/RUR Association)	123
Hills across the Imjin (Henry O'Kane)	126
RUR Recce patrol in action (Henry O'Kane)	127
Sergeant S.J.H. Rankin, missing in action.	130
The cover of a book of prayer for Captain James Majury, made and presented by the many Protestants, No.2 Company, Prisoner of War Camp Number 2, North Korea. (Mervyn McCord/RUR Association)	131
Imjin Patrols (Mervyn McCord)	133
2nd Lieutenant McCord, Anti-Tank Platoon Comander. 17 pdr A/T gun in the background. (Mervyn McCord)	133
RSM Patterson, Major Rickcord and piper, St Patrick's Day, 1951. (Mervyn McCord/RUR Association)	137
Outdoor canteen line, St Patrick's Day 1951. (Mervyn McCord/RUR Association)	137
Captain Ivor Daniels, Major Rickcord and Lieutenant Mervyn McCord, on board the tender to HMS *Belfast*. (Mervyn McCord/RUR Association)	138
McCord, Smyth and Rickcord on a tender from HMS *Belfast*, Inchon 1951. (Mervyn McCord/RUR Association)	139
McCord, Smyth and Rickcord onboard HMS *Belfast*, Inchon 1951. (Mervyn McCord/RUR Association)	140

LIST OF ILLUSTRATIONS xi

HMS *Belfast*'s 6 inch guns bombard Haju, west coast of Korea, Christmas 1951. (Stan Packer)	140
HMS *Belfast* in the Inland Sea for Kure, Japan, 1950-52. (Stan Packer)	141
Three North Korean prisoners captured at Chinnampo, 18 March 1951 on board HMS *Belfast*. The guard on the right is carrying the Sten Gun Mk V. (Stan Packer)	142
"You are crossing the 38th Parallel by courtesy of the Royal Ulster Rifles", the Ulster Crossing, early April 1951. (Mervyn McCord/ RUR Association)	146
Back to the Imjin-Ulster Crossing, early April 1951. Royal Ulster Rifleman with his hand on a jeep with the road winding out behind. (Mervyn McCord/RUR Museum)	146
Battalion objective in the hills leading to the Han River. (RUR Association)	149
Advancing to the Han River. (RUR Association)	150
Onto Fort Nixon - 'B' Company advance towards Hill 194 after the crossing to the Imjin River, supported by Centurions of the 8th King's Royal Irish Hussars. Figures two and four are battalion porters. (RUR Association)	151
Ulster Crossing with Fort Nixon beyond, early April 1951. (Mervyn McCord/RUR Association)	151
Lance Corporal Alberts, wounded by a gunshot, was the first Royal Ulster Rifleman to be evacuated from the battlefield by helicopter casevac. (Mervyn McCord)	152
Evacuating a seriously wounded Rifleman by helicopter. Lance Corporal Alberts was the first of the Battalion to be evacuated in this manner. (RUR Association)	153
RUR crossing the Imjin River on the deck of a Centurion tank. (Mervyn McCord/RUR Association)	153
RUR dismounting from a Centurion tank having crossed the Imjin River, with dry feet. (RUR Museum)	154
Battalion sports 21 April 1951. The battle started 23 April. (Mervyn McCord)	154
The scene at the port of Inchon, Korea, where men of the King's Own Scottish Borderers were piped ashore with the pipers of the 1st Battalion, The Royal Ulster Rifles when they arrived to replace the Argyll and Sutherland Highlanders, who were leaving Korea for their original Far East Station, Hong Kong. (RUR Museum)	157
Men of the King's Own Scottish Borderers were piped ashore with the pipers of the 1st Battalion, The Royal Ulster Rifles when they arrived to replace the Argyll and Sutherland Highlanders. (RUR Museum)	157
Ferrying Oxford carriers across the Imjin. (RUR Association)	159
Medical Section halftrack at the Ulster Crossing. (Mervyn McCord/ RUR Association)	160
45th Field, Regiment of Artillery. (RUR Museum)	160
Checking the papers of a Korean. (Mervyn McCord/RUR Association)	160
Lieutenant Houston Shaw-Stewart gets the MC ribbon. (Mervyn McCord)	164
Major Shaw (*Belfast Telegraph*)	164

NAAFI in Korea. (RUR Museum)	165
Bren Gun in action. (RUR Museum)	167
Hill 398. C and D Coys were at the top. A Coy was on a (hidden) spur running off north-west. (RUR Association)	170
Major John Shaw, Battalion HQ, Imjin on the last morning of the Imjin Battle. He was killed 30 minutes later. (Mervyn McCord/RUR Association)	175
Henry O'Kane. (Henry O'Kane)	176
Grave of Major Shaw, United Nations Memorial Cemetery, Pusan, Korea. (RUR Association)	176
US M40 155mm self propelled guns and Bofors firing in support of the RUR attack, April 1951. (Mervyn McCord)	177
The view north from the B Coy block. The Rifles and RNF were ambushed by the enemy in the hills to the left of the photograph whilst withdrawing south along the valley floor. (RUR Association)	179
Combined 1 RUR/1 RNF/ 170 Bty (4" Mortars) mortar lines on the last morning of the Imjin Battle April 1951 after expending ammo at a rapid rate – the Chinese were on the hills in the background. Mervyn McCord's 'slit' (ammo box riveted) as Signals Officer. (Mervyn McCord)	181
Expending mortar ammunition on the last morning of the Imjin battle. (Mervyn McCord)	181
Rifleman Chris Spiers.	182
A scene during the concluding stages of the Imjin River battle. Men of the 29th British Brigade rest by the roadside during the withdrawal on 25 April 1951. (RUR Museum)	184
Destroyed Bren Carrier. (RUR Museum)	185
Ulster Crossing to Fort Nixon. (Mervyn McCord)	185
Shown here shortly after the battle of the Imjin River, in which they played an active part are six Belfastmen, who all served with 1st Battalion, The Royal Ulster Rifles. From left they are - Rifleman David Kielty, Western Street, Shankill Road; David Fisher, Downing Street, Shankill Road; Sergeant Jack Simpson, Divis Street, Falls Road and Rifleman Robert Church, Little Sackville Street, Shankill Road. Kneeling are, George McClare, Grove Street East, Beersbridge Road and Samuel Elliott, Rockland Street, Donegall Road.	188
The Mortar Platoon dug-in. (RUR Museum)	190
Lieutenant Gordon Potts in Korea, September 1951. (*Quis Separabit*)	192
Members of the RUR Association Comforts' Fund Committee making up parcels of books and woollens. L to R - Miss June Charley, Mrs Cussans, Mrs H.R. Charley and Mrs Emily Reade.	194
Bivouacs at Line Kansas 1951. (Mervyn McCord/RUR Association)	198
The Royal Ulster Rifles Command Post on Line 'Kansas'. (RUR Museum)	198
Destroyed Chinese artillery in the Imjin. (RUR Association)	201
The River Imjin, showing two bridges built by American engineers, over which the Commonwealth Division was mainly supplied – the low-level bridge in use and the high-level bridge under construction.	

It should be noted that the river was exceptionally low when the photograph was taken. (Public Relations, Headquarters, BCOF)	202
Representatives of all Commonwealth countries who provided units in the 1st Commonwealth Division; L to R, India, Wales, Canada, England, Australia, New Zealand, Northern Ireland and Scotland. (Public Relations, Headquarters, BCOF)	202
The memorial and view looking north towards Chaegunghyon, which gives an excellent indication of the type of terrain which the Battalion fought over. (RUR Association)	204
The Royal Ulster Rifles Memorial on the heights above Happy Valley at its dedication. (Mervyn McCord/RUR Association)	205
Colonel Carson and Brigadier Brodie at the dedication of the Memorial above Happy Valley, 1951. (William May/RUR Museum)	205
Father Ryan and Lieutenant John Mole at the dedication of the Royal Ulster Rifles Memorial in Korea. (Mervyn /McCord/RUR Association)	206
Colonel Carson, Major Rickcord, DSO and CO 8th Hussars (centre) in conversation at the dedication service of the Royal Ulster Rifles Memorial, 1951. (RUR Museum)	206
Imjin Pontoon Bridge, Korea, 1951. (William May/RUR Association)	207
Korea, summer 1951. (RUR Museum)	207
RUR C Coy POWs – No 1 Camp, Intercamp Olympics, Korea. (Mervyn McCord/RUR Association)	208
POWs playing cards during the winter of 1952 (Henry O'Kane)	208
US Diamond T towing what appear to be two damaged Carriers. (RUR Museum)	209
Presentation of awards to the men of the 29th Brigade accompanied by the 1st Battalion, The Royal Ulster Rifles Pipe Band. (RUR Museum)	209
Inter-Company Sports at 'Somme Stadium', Korea. (RUR Museum)	210
An 'Elephant House' position for a Centurion on Yong Dong. (George Forty)	211
Mortar Platoon dug-in. (Mervyn McCord/RUR Association)	215
A jeep patrol returning to base. (Mervyn McCord/RUR Association)	215
Two Rifleman digging in, in the winter. (RUR Museum)	216
Two Riflemen examine a well believed to be the resting place of a missionary. (Mervyn McCord/RUR Association)	217
Patrol briefing, Korea, 1951. (William May/RUR Association)	218
Battalion vehicles, Korea, 1951. (William May/RUR Association)	218
Bren Carriers, Korea, 1951. (William May/RUR Association)	219
Machine Gun post, Korea, 1951. (William May/RUR Association)	219
Group and tank, Korea, 1951 (William May/RUR Association)	221
'Doc' Halliday. (RUR Museum)	221
Captain de Longueil, OC A Echelon in Happy Valley. (Mervyn McCord/RUR Association)	224
Front, L to R: Paddy Maher, Tom McCann, Bertie McIlwaine. Rear: Tommy Maher. Tommy McIlwaine is holding a stripped Thompson SMG. (Mark McConnell)	225
Captured the same day, taught Communism in the same Korean school, released by the enemy at the same time, these three British soldiers	

were still together at the BCOF hospital Kure, Japan. Left to right, Gunner Hill Slade, Wimbledon, London, Sergeant Jimmy Rankine, Belfast and Lance Corporal Stan Harris, Liverpool. Sister Ranson of Australia is distributing the tea. (RUR Museum) 227

This street scene in Hiroshima gives a good impression of the fascinating things to be seen while on R&R in Japan. (George Forty) 228

The Colonel of the regiment, General Steele, welcoming home members of the 1st Battalion, The Royal Ulster Rifles who had served in Korea. (RUR Museum) 228

The Boxing Team, Hong Kong, 1951. (William May/RUR Association) 229

Range practice in Hong Kong. (RUR Museum) 229

Pipe practice at Battalion Headquarters. (Mervyn McCord/RUR Association) 230

HMT *Empire Halladale*, used as a troopship to take the Royal Ulster Rifles to Hong Kong from Korea, 1951. (Roger Gladin) 230

Bunks onboard HMT *Empire Halladale*. (Roger Gladin) 231

Killing time, playing cards on board HMT *Empire Halladale*. (Roger Gladin) 231

A 'Girls' Opera' at Takarazuka, Japan 1951, playing to the biggest stage in the world. (Stan Packer) 232

A wet night in Hong Kong, all the servicemen are sheltering in the bars! 232

This Victorian silver biscuit barrel in the shape of a drum was originally presented by the 1st Battalion of the Royal Ulster Rifles to HMS *Belfast* at her launching in March 1938. There are four silver statuettes of Royal Ulster Rifles personnel, a mounted Officer on the lid and on the base stand a Drummer, a Bugler and a Rifleman. (Mervyn McCord) 233

Main street of Sasebo, Japan during the Korean war, 1950-52. (Stan Packer) 233

The Freedom of Belfast, band and bugles of the 1st Battalion, The Royal Ulster Rifles. (Henry O'Kane) 234

HMS *Belfast* at Hong Kong, Christmas 1950. The white building at the stern of the ship is the 'Old China Fleet Club'. (Stan Packer) 236

September 1953, Sergeant Ted Balfour being flown back from Korea to Japan after being a POW for two years and eight months. (RUR Association) 237

Ex-POWs celebrate on their way home: Reg Budden, Glosters, Henry O'Kane, RUR, Ben Baough, 8th Irish Hussars, Stan Lea, Glosters, Gerry Hassett, RUR. (Henry O'Kane) 237

General Sir James Steele, Colonel of the Regiment, laying a wreath at the Ballymena War Memorial on Remembrance Day 1953. (RUR Museum) 238

The Memorial at St Patrick's Barracks, Ballymena. (Mervyn McCord) 238

Between 23-30 July 2003 a party of The Royal Ulster Rifles, Korean War Veterans attended the Korean War Armistice commemorations in Korea. They were Major Joe Lavery, Thomas McConkey, Martin Vance and Henry Kane, who all served as prisoners of war at No.5 Camp Pyucyon. The group are seen here photographed outside the Korean National War Memorial in Seoul. (*Quis Separabit*) 240

'Morning Calm' – a 'fish eye' view of the Korean War Monument commemorating the 50th Anniversary of the signing of the armistice

agreement. The monument was unveiled on 27 July 2003 in the pouring rain, but no mud. (Derek M. Slattery/RUR Museum)	240
The band of The Royal Irish Regiment lead the parade at the rededication of Korea Memorial, Belfast City Hall, 25 April 2010. (David R. Orr)	241
Colonel Robin Charley (left) and Sergeant Joe Farrell in front of the memorial at Belfast City Hall, 4 January 2009. (*Belfast Telegraph*)	241
Veterans parade after the rededication of Korea Memorial, Belfast City Hall, 25 April 2010. (David R. Orr)	242
Spencer McWhirter at the rededication of the Korea Memorial, Belfast City Hall, 25 April 2010. (Mark Ramsay)	242
The Korea Memorial adorned with wreaths following the rededication at Belfast City Hall, 25 April 2010. (David R. Orr)	242
Korean Memorial Garden, National Arboretum. (Mervyn McCord)	243
Major Sir C.J. Nixon, Bart, MC and Sergeant J. Knight in conversation in 'A' Company Area at Pyontaek. (RUR Museum)	253
Korea Medal 1950–53. (RUR Museum)	254
The United Nations Korea Service Medal 1950–54. (RUR Museum)	255
Corporal Tommy Cushing.	313
Rifleman Francis Crilly, missing in action.	313
Lieutenant G. Fitz-Gibbon, killed in action.	313
Rifleman McNabb, missing in action.	313
Rifleman Lodge, missing in action.	313
Rifleman Graham, missing in action.	313
Rifleman J. Stevenson, missing in action.	313
Rifleman Thomas Beattie McHaffey, missing in action.	313
Rifleman Andrew Aicken, missing in action.	313
Rifleman T. Kennedy.	314
Rifleman William Sinclair.	314
Corporal W. Mills returning from an anti-guerilla patrol. (RUR Museum)	314
Rifleman Desmond Henry Johnston.	314
Corporal E. Phillips, captured by the Chinese. (RUR Museum)	314
Rifleman A. Ryan returning from an anti-guerilla patrol. (RUR Museum)	314
Rifleman Thomas Wright.	314
Sergeant J. Talbot, Chinese prisoner. (RUR Museum)	314
Rifleman T. Agnew (*Belfast Telegraph*)	314
Rifleman S.H. Greer.	315
Rifleman Joseph Davison.	315
Rifleman Thomas W. Lorimer.	315
Rifleman B. Canavan.	315
Rifleman McCormick at Sinujui about 80 miles south of Yalu River. Rifleman McCormick was later missing presumed killed during the Battle of the Imjin. (RUR Museum)	317

List of Maps

The movement and dates of the 1st Battalion, The Royal Ulster Rifles in
    Korea. (The Royal Ulster Rifles in Korea, 1953)   ii
Map of Korea showing its position in the region. (Courtesy *Belfast Telegraph*)   50
1st Battalion, The Royal Ulster Rifles battle area 1–4 January 1951.
    (Crown Copyright)   90
Map of the Battle of 'Happy Valley', Chaegunghyon, January 1951,
    amended by Brig. M. McCord. (Brig. M. McCord)   91
The Battle of Chaegunghyon, January 1951. (*The Royal Ulster Rifles in Korea*, 1953)   100
The action at Chunghung Dong. (Barclay, *The First Commonwealth Division*)   102
Map showing location of main POW camps in North Korea (Cyril
    Cunningham. Reproduced courtesy of Pen & Sword Publishers)   129
Areas occupied by the 27th Commonwealth and 29th British Infantry
    Brigades on 22 April 1951, just before the battles of the Imjin and
    Kapyong Rivers. (Barclay, *The First Commonwealth Division*)   156
The Battle of the Imjin River, 22-25 April 1951. (Barclay, *The First
    Commonwealth Division*)   163
Battle of the Imjin River, April 1951. (RUR Association)   178
Battle of the Imjin River, April 1951. (Mervyn McCord)   180
Chong-Song prisoner of war camp. (Henry O'Kane)   191
Operations 'Minden' and 'Commando'. The advance of the 1st
    Commonwealth Division from the line of the Imjin River, 8
    September to 8 October 1951. (Barclay, *The First Commonwealth Division*)   203

Glossary and List of Abbreviations

ACC	Army Catering Corps.
AGSM	African General Service Medal.
ARV	Armoured Recovery Vehicle.
AVRE	Armoured Vehicle Royal Engineers.
AWOL	Absent without leave.
B Echelon	The battalion supply column off base.
Bailey Bridge	Of British design, the Bailey Bridge is a temporary structure that, in only a matter of hours, can be erected to span a river and be strong enough to support the immense weight of a tank. The bridge can be broken down into assorted parts and carried in transport vehicles.
Battalion	An infantry unit containing between 500-800 men, and commanded by a Lieutenant-Colonel.
BEM	British Empire Medal.
Bofors	Light anti aircraft gun of 40mm calibre.
Bren Carrier	See Universal Carrier.
Bren Gun	A Light Machine Gun.
Brigade Group	A Brigade with attached support units; e.g. medical staff, engineers and anti-tank gunners.
Brigade	A formation of two or more Battalions acting together under the overall command of a Brigadier.
CBE	Commander of the Order of the British Empire.
CCF	Chinese Communist Forces.
Chopper	Slang for helicopter.
CO	Commanding Officer.
Company	A subdivision of a Battalion, commanded by a Major and consisting of approximately 120 men.
Cpl	Corporal.
CQMS	Company Quartermaster Sergeant.
CSM	Company Sergeant-Major, the leading Sergeant in a Company.
DAA	Deputy Assistant Adjutant.
DCM	Distinguished Conduct Medal.
DSO	Distinguished Service Order.
dwt	dry weight tonnage.
FDL	Forward Defence Line.
FOO	Forward Observation Officer.
GCB	Grand Cross in the Order of the Bath.
GSM	General Service Medal.
IO	Intelligence officer.
JRHU	Joint Replacement Holding Unit.

KBE	Knight Commander of the Order of the British Empire.
KIA	Killed in action.
Lee Enfield MkIV	The standard British infantry rifle.
LMG	Light machine gun, in the British Army the Bren gun.
M.A.S.H.	Mobile Army Surgical Hospital.
Maj	Major.
MBE	Member, Order of the British Empire.
MC	Military Cross.
MID	Mentioned in Despatches.
MM	Military Medal.
MMG	Medium machine gun, in the British Army the .303 Vickers.
MO	Medical Officer.
MSR	Main Supply Route.
MT	Motor Transport.
MTO	Motor Transport Officer.
NAAFI	Navy, Army and Airforce Institute.
NCO	Non Commissioned Officer, such as warrant officers, sergeants or corporals.
OCTU	Officer Cadet Training Unit.
O-Group	Order Group. A commander may order an O-Group to assemble all of his subalterns to give them their orders.
OP	Observation Post.
PIAT	Projector Infantry Anti-Tank. A hand-held weapon that fires an armour-piercing projectile, most adept at dealing with lightly armoured vehicles.
Platoon	Four platoons existed within an infantry battalion, and each was commanded by a Lieutenant. Platoons could consist of as many as sixty men.
Pontoon Bridge	See Bailey Bridge.
QM	Quartermaster.
QMG	Quartermaster General.
R and R	Rest and Recreation.
RA	Royal Artillery.
RAC	Royal Armoured Corps.
RAF	Royal Air Force.
RAMC	Royal Army Medical Corps.
RAOC	Royal Army Ordnance Corps.
RAP	Regimental Aid Post.
RASC	Royal Army Service Corps.
RCR	Royal Canadian Regiment.
RCT	Regimental Combat Team.
RE	Royal Engineers.
REME	Royal Electrical and Mechanical Engineers.
Rfm	Rifleman.
RHU	Replacement Holding Unit.
ROK	Republic of Korea. South Korea.

RSM	Regimental Sergeant-Major, the most senior Warrant Officer in a battalion, in battle he was responsible for the re-supply of ammunition.
RTO	Road Transport Officer.
Sapper	A private of the Royal Engineers.
Self-Propelled (SP) Gun	A large artillery gun, mounted on its own vehicle like a tank, unlike the static artillery guns that were towed behind jeeps or lorries.
Sgt	Sergeant.
Slit trench	The name given to a one-man trench that infantrymen dig with the shovels they carry. Providing the ground is soft, a trench can be quickly dug so that a single man can place his body as much beneath the level of earth as possible. Not only does this make the man a harder target during firefights, but it greatly reduces the chance of injury from artillery bombardment. Known as foxholes in the American and Canadian Armies.
Sten	Sub-machine gun, usually carried by British officers and NCOs, not very reliable.
Universal Carrier	A tracked and lightly armoured vehicle used by the British for, as its name implies, a number of duties from transport of men and supplies, to a weapons platform for mortars or mounting a Bren light machine gun.
Very light	A cartridge fired from a flare pistol, providing light at night or a signal during daylight hours
WIA	Wounded in action.

Foreword by
Brigadier M.N.S. McCord CBE MC

Brigadier M. McCord, King's Div and ADC to HM the Queen 1981-84, Colonel Royal Irish Rangers 1985-90. (Mervyn McCord)

In 1950 the 1st Battalion, which had amalgamated with the 2nd Battalion in 1948, were in Colchester preparing to go to Khartoum. Sport played a large part in fitness training. The Cross Country and Boxing teams were Army finalists. Henry Cooper and his twin brother were amongst the opponents. With the exception of a few National Service officers, the rest of the battalion were Regulars.

When the Korean War broke out few knew where it was. There was an influx of reservists, many of whom had only recently left. They came from all parts of Ireland, the other Irish regiments and the North of England. The authors described in *The Rifles Are There* how quickly new arrivals absorbed the élan and tradition of the Rifles – history repeated itself.

Many of those mentioned in their first book appear again, led by Colonel "Hank" Carson, who commanded from D-Day to the Rhine Crossing, and Major Gerald Rickord, who commanded from the Rhine to the Baltic. All the company commanders and senior NCOs had similar wartime experience which they quickly used to instill the *esprit de corps* of the Rifles and meld the reinforcements into a very effective fighting force.

Colonel Carson and his Adjutant, Captain Hugh Hamill, remained in post throughout the campaign. On arrival in Hong Kong Captain Hamill handed over and was relieved of all duties to write *The Royal Ulster Rifles in Korea* – our official history. Based on the War Diary, for which he was responsible, this has been widely acclaimed as one of the best and most accurate accounts of a unit's tour in Korea

Since then many more details have come to light and many tales have been told; of minor incidents and of life as Prisoners of War. David Truesdale and David Orr have met and talked to many of the veterans and have widely researched the books published in more recent years. Amongst these Rifleman Henry *O'Kane's Korea* is a classic, to be compared with *The Letters of Rifleman Wheeler* and *The Recollections of Private Harris* in the Peninsular War. It deserves to be more widely read.

The Rifles are proud to claim that they did not lose any ground to the massed onslaughts of the Chinese. The Belgian Battalion, who fought the Imjin battle from Fort Nixon, were full of praise for our preparations of the position and for the extra ammunition and grenades we handed over to them. We successfully fought two major rearguard actions and did not yield to the enemy. Our major losses were incurred when we had to withdraw to conform to the general dispositions of the UN Forces. This meant leaving well-prepared defences and running the gauntlet of surrounding Chinese masses.

Once again we are indebted to David Truesdale and David Orr for giving us another very readable account of the exploits of the Rifles and the soldiers with whom we have been privileged to serve.

Quis Separabit.

M.N.S. McCord October 2010

Acknowledgements

In writing this history various sources and individuals were consulted, in particular the archives of the Royal Ulster Rifles Museum, including the Battalion War Diary for the relevant period and the Royal Ulster Rifles Association.

Individuals:
Mr Robin Bruford-Davies, ex-RUR Korea
Colonel (Ret) Robin Charley, ex-RUR, Korea
Mr A.C. Craig, former Fleet Air Arm Korea
Mrs Mary Cunningham (Widow of Cyril Cunningham)
Mrs Heather Curran, Bangor Museum, County Down
Major (Ret) Jack Dunlop, Royal Inniskilling Fusiliers Museum, Enniskillen
Stuart Eastwood, Border Regiment & King's Own Royal Border Regiment Museum, Carlisle
Ruth Evans, Royal Inniskilling Fusiliers Museum, Enniskillen
Mr George Forty, author of *At War In Korea*
Mr Roger Gladin
Martin Hill, Group Editorial Executive, Independent News & Media (NI)
Mr Peter Jordan, Museum Curator, Britain's Small Wars
Mr Noel Kane, Somme Museum
Capt (Ret) Jaki Knox, RUR Museum, Belfast
Ruth Kusionowicz, Archive/Information Manager, *Soldier Magazine*
Leanne Macey-Lillie, Somme Museum, Newtownards
Jonathan Maguire
Mr William 'Bill' McConnell, MBE ex-RUR Korea
Mr Mark McConnell ex-RUR Korea
Lt. Col. Andrew McCord
Brigadier M.N.S. McCord ex-RUR Korea
Mr Bob McKinley, Somme Museum Newtownards
Mr Spencer McWhirter, ex-RUR Korea
Mr John Mole, ex-RUR Korea
Amanda Moreno BA, Royal Irish Fusiliers Museum, Armagh
Mr Terence Nelson, RUR Museum, Belfast
Dr Kathy Neoh, for explaining in layman's terms such things as filariasis
Mr Stanley N Packer
Mr Richard Parkinson, Somme Museum, Newtownards
Mark Ramsey, for local newspaper research
Mr Harry Pegg, ex-RUR
Mr David Rowlands for permission to reproduce his painting 'Crash Action'
Mr Chris Spiers ex-RUR Korea
Darwin Templeton, Editor, *Belfast News Letter*
Carol Walker, Somme Museum, Newtownards

ACKNOWLEDGEMENTS

Major (Ret) Roy Walker, RUR Museum, Belfast
National Archives, Kew
Bangor Spectator
Belfast Telegraph
Daily Telegraph
News Letter
Northern Whig
Archives Royal Inniskilling Fusiliers Museum, Enniskillen
Archives Royal Irish Fusiliers Museum, Armagh
Archive Royal Ulster Rifles Museum, Belfast
Audio interviews, held in the Royal Ulster Rifles Museum, Belfast:
  Lance Corporal Erreagar, 8th King's Royal Irish Hussars
  Captain John Lane, 2IC A Company RUR on the Imjin
  Second Lieutenant Mervyn McCord RUR
  Sir Christopher Nixon RUR
  Rifleman Henry O'Kane, C Company RUR on the Imjin
  RSM Patterson RUR
  Major Gerald Rickcord, A/CO, RUR on the Imjin
  Rifleman Tyas RUR on the Imjin

Introduction by Colonel W.R.H. Charley OBE JP DL

Lt-Col R. Charley CO Queen's University OTC, 1965, aged 41 years. (R. Charley)

In 2008 I was invited to write the foreword to *Duty Without Glory*, the history of the Ulster Home Guard. Now, three years later, in what are perilous times in Korea and elsewhere, I have been asked to write a few words on this history of the 1st Battalion, Royal Ulster Rifles in the conflict known as the Korean War.

In the ranks of the 'Rifles' were many veterans of the Second World War, Reservists, 'K' Volunteers and National Servicemen. It says much for the organisational power of the Regiment that these men were quickly absorbed into the ranks and were soon functioning as a cohesive unit.

On the battlefield, in defence or attack, the Battalion operated in a thoroughly professional manner and despite extreme weather conditions, from freezing winter to the high humidity of summer, humour was rarely absent.

I had been acting in the role of ADC on the outbreak of the War and as there were no vacancies for a Captain with the Battalion, I dropped a rank and was fortunate to serve with B Company in Korea.

For too long Korea has been a forgotten war and this timely history will hopefully bring home to the reader the valiant part played by a unique body of men in a unique Regiment.

Quis Separabit

W.R.H. Charley

Background

Korea is a peninsula to the east of the Chinese mainland that is bounded on three sides by water. To the west is the Yellow Sea, to the East the Sea of Japan, while its southern tip lies within the Tsushima Strait. The Chinese had added Korea to their empire in 1637 and it remained so until its independence under the Treaty of Shimonoseki in 1895.

Korea was the catalyst for the Russo-Japanese War of 1904-05, the first major conflict of the 20th Century. On land the battles were dominated by artillery, machine guns and barbed wire, resulting in no decisive victories for either side. At sea however, Japan emerged triumphant with superior seamanship and naval gunnery and on 2 January 1905, the Russians were forced to surrender.

In November 1905 Japan took control of Korea and began settling Japanese families in the country. By 1932, a Korean guerrilla group led by Kim II-Sung came into being and over the next ten years launched a series of attacks against the occupying Japanese. During the Second World War Japan sent troops to Korea in large numbers and Kim was forced to take shelter in the Soviet Union.

On 4 February 1945 the Yalta Conference was held in the Crimea and after discussion between the 'Big Three', Roosevelt, Churchill and Stalin, an agreement was reached between the Allies that Soviet and American troops would occupy Korea after the War. The country was divided at the 38th Parallel and in 1948 the Soviet Union established a People's Democratic Republic in North Korea, while the United States assisted in establishing the Republic of South Korea.[1]

At the end of the War Soviet Russian and American forces took the surrender of the Japanese in Korea; the Soviets to the north of the 38th Parallel and the Americans to the south. Agreement on the independent rule of Korea could not be agreed on despite attempts of the United Nations to organise elections in the Soviet Zone. As a consequence the Republic of Korea was formed in the South in 1948 under President Syngman Rhee. As a direct result the North declared itself the Democratic People's Republic of Korea, led by Kim Il Sung.

After the Second World War Syngman Rhee emerged as the main right-wing politician in South Korea and in 1947 he received the unofficial support of the United States. The following year Rhee became the first president of South Korea and soon developed a reputation for autocratic rule.

In June 1949 the United States Army began to withdraw from South Korea. Statements made by General Douglas McArthur and US Secretary of State Dean Acheson, suggested that the United States did not consider the area as being of prime importance. Acheson argued that if South Korea was attacked, "The initial reliance must be on the people attacked to resist it and then upon the commitments of the entire civilised world under the Charter of the United Nations." Kim II-Sung, now communist dictator of North Korea became convinced that the people in the south would welcome

---

1 Wheal & Pope, *Macmillan Dictionary of the Second World War*, London, 1989.

the reunification of Korea. Consequently, at dawn on 25 June 1950, the North Korean army launched a surprise attack across the northern border.

With an order of battle similar to the Soviet Union, the Chinese High Command placed their divisions directly under the Army command, thus dispensing with Corps command. Consequently a Chinese Communist Forces (CCF) Army would consist of three infantry divisions with a total strength of between 20,000 and 32,000 men. In turn a division consisted of three regiments, each of which averaged 2,700 men, sub-divided into three battalions, each of three rifle companies and a support company containing the heavy weapons. The vast majority of men in a Chinese Division were 'bayonets', combat soldiers; and while numerically inferior to either an American or British Division, it did field more 'bayonets'.

Three days later, communist forces captured the South Korean capital, Seoul. The Security Council of the United Nations recommended that troops should be sent to defend South Korea. As the Soviet Union was boycotting the Security Council at the time, it was unable to veto this decision. Fifteen nations sent troops to Korea, where they were organised under the command of General Douglas MacArthur, who had emerged from the Second World War with a reputation for success. The element of surprise had enabled the North Koreans to occupy the South, except for the area around the port of Pusan where a defensive perimeter was held. On 15 September, MacArthur landed both American and South Korean Marines at Inchon, 200 miles behind the North Korean lines, in Operation Chromite. The following day he launched a counter-attack from the south. When the North Koreans retreated, MacArthur's forces carried the war northwards at a rapid rate, reaching the Yalu River, the frontier between Korea and China, on 24 October 1950.

MacArthur was ordered to limit the war to Korea. He disagreed, favouring an attack on Chinese forces. He began to make inflammatory statements indicating his disagreements with the United States government; there was even a hint that nuclear weapons could be used against China if necessary. MacArthur gained support from right-wing members of the Senate such as the rabid anti-communist Senator Joe McCarthy. In April 1951, President Harry Truman, fearing escalation to nuclear war, removed MacArthur from command of the United Nations forces in Korea. His place was taken by Lieutenant General Matthew B. Ridgway, a veteran of both World Wars and the planner of the first successful Allied airborne assault, part of Operation Husky, the invasion of Sicily in 1943.

The Chinese government deployed 180,000 'volunteers' to assist North Korea. These reinforcements enabled North Korean forces to take Seoul for a second time in January 1951. UN troops eventually managed to halt the invasion sixty miles south of the 38th parallel. A counter-offensive at the end of January gradually recovered lost ground. Once in control of South Korea, representatives of the UN began peace talks with the North Korean government on 8 July 1951. An armistice agreement, maintaining the divided Korea, was signed at Panmunjom on 27 July 1953.

The United Nations Security Council at this stage was being vetoed by the Soviet delegate because the Council refused to grant communist China membership, however the Council ordered the NKPA to withdraw from South Korea and the following day still with the Soviet veto absent agreed to "…furnish such assistant to the Republic of

Korea as may be necessary to repel the armed attack and to restore international peace and security in the area." Sixteen nations promised aid to South Korea.[2]

On 29 June 1949, General McArthur had been instructed to use the naval and air elements of the Far East Command to support South Korean forces. However, he was to restrict the employment of the army to essential communications. The first shots of the coming war were fired on 2 July and came not from American or South Korean forces, but by the Royal Navy. HMS *Jamaica* and HMS *Black Swan* had been attacked by six North Korean torpedo boats. The action was brief, with all but one of the enemy craft being sunk. Although described as a 'police action' Britain was once again at war.[3]

During the last week of June 1950 the British Cabinet agreed the resolution that it was the "clear duty of the United Kingdom Government to do everything in their power, in concert with other members of the United Nations, to help South Korea to resist this aggression." They also agreed that the British Far East Fleet should join in any offensive action against North Korea. Under the command of Rear-Admiral Andrews, the first ships sailed to join the American Forces; the light fleet carrier *Triumph*; the cruisers, *Belfast* and *Jamaica* and the destroyers *Cossack* and *Consort*.

On 1 July 1950 the Lord Mayor of Belfast sent a telegram to the Secretary of the Admiralty, London, "On behalf of the citizens of Belfast the Lord Mayor wishes God speed and safe keeping to the Captain and ship's company of HMS *Belfast* as they join the American Force in the Pacific in the present emergency."[4]

In Korea the war was going badly for the Americans and their South Korean allies. The United Nations was forced to appeal for additional forces and Britain immediately dispatched two infantry brigades from her garrison in Hong Kong. Almost immediately after this an announcement was made that a further 'composite and self contained' Brigade group was to be posted to Korea. This had come about as a result of a top secret minute dated 17 August and sent from the War Office to the Prime Minister, Clement Attlee. Two infantry battalions would be sent from the Hong Kong garrison after it had first been reinforced to preclude any possible incursion by the People's Republic of China, who might be tempted to take back the colony. Consequently the 1st Battalion the Wiltshire Regiment and a squadron of the 4th Hussars, equipped with armoured cars, moved in as the 1st Argyll and Sutherland Highlanders and 1st Middlesex moved out. These two battalions became 27 Brigade and were commanded by Brigadier Aubrey Coad, an infantry officer of vast experience who had served with the 5th Battalion the Dorset Regiment during the Second World War. Both battalions were under strength, with three-quarters of their personnel national servicemen who had never been under fire before and were paid £1.62 a week by a grateful nation for risking their lives. Due to the ad-hoc way in which the Brigade was able to achieve the necessary arms, ammunition, uniform and equipment they gained the unfortunate nickname of the "Woolworth's Brigade". The Brigade set sail on the light fleet aircraft carrier *Unicorn* and the cruiser *Ceylon*, escorted by an Australian destroyer. The Brigade arrived at Pusan in the "Land of the Morning Calm" on 29 August 1950. They would later be renamed 27th

---

2   Catchpole, "The Commonwealth in Korea", *History Today*, November 1998.
3   Lowe, *The Origins of the Korean War*, London, 1986.
4   *Belfast Telegraph*, 1 July 1950.

Commonwealth Infantry Brigade when they were joined by the all-volunteer Australian 3rd Infantry Battalion.⁵

British Commanders were worried about the American rank and file in battle and their officers' ability to direct them correctly. General Leslie Mansergh, a veteran British officer who had fought in the Far East as an infantry commander reported, "I doubt whether any British really think that the war in Korea will be brought to a successful conclusion. The reason for this is primarily because of the lack of American determination and their inability to stand and fight … I would judge that American morale is low and in some units thoroughly bad". His concerns were essentially summed up in three areas – The Americans didn't want to be in Korea, they had lost most of their regular officers, and in an Army which followed the Patton principle of attack, they had never been taught the need to defend. However the British officers were unanimous in their praise of the US Marines and the American gunners who fired most of the artillery support for the British brigades.⁶ Mansergh's rather jaundiced view would be disproved on many occasions and the Rifles would benefit from American assistance when required. In one field the Americans did find difficulty and that was in estimating damage and casualties in particular operations. In one instance, a raid on the airfield of Sinuiju, American pilots claimed thirty five enemy aircraft destroyed in one attack. Subsequent photographic reconnaissance showed one destroyed and one damaged. For an attack on a hill position General James A. Van Fleet estimated that it would cost two hundred casualties to achieve a successful attack. In fact about six thousand UN soldiers were killed or wounded and the hill was never taken.⁷

Many of us have watched the events of the Korean War depicted in the American situation comedy *M*A*S*H*, and could be forgiven for thinking that only the Americans made a significant contribution to the conflict in south-east Asia. However one fact is very accurate, that conditions on the front were horrific and even those veterans of the Battle of the Bulge, fought in the Ardennes in the winter of 1944-45, the worst winter in Europe for a quarter of a century, had never encountered anything like it. Even a slight wound could prove fatal if it wasn't for the speedy evacuation to one of the seven MASH (Mobile Army Surgical Hospital) centres which often relied on the new concept of 'chopper' evacuations, though even the helicopters couldn't fly during the snowstorms.

Korea was the first and to date the largest deployment of United Nations troops. As well as America and Britain, troops from Australia, Belgium, Canada, Columbia, Cuba, Ethiopia, France⁸, Greece, Luxembourg, Netherlands, New Zealand, Philippines, Thailand and Turkey took part, either on land, sea or in the air.

In the Second World War the various battalions of the Royal Ulster Rifles had never served East of Suez, their battlefields had been France, Germany, Sicily and the Italian

---

5   Catchpole, *The Korean War*, London, 2000.
6   Whiting, *Battleground Korea, The British in Korea*, Stroud, 1999.
7   Bailey, *The Korean Armistice*, Basingstoke, 1992.
8   Post 9/11 it has become common currency among some people to ridicule the fighting ability of the French. In Korea the Bataillon Francais de l'ONU (BF-ONU), a force of volunteers, was attached to the US 23rd Infantry Regiment, 2nd Division, serving with distinction in several actions including Heartbreak Ridge in 1951. The reader should also remember that France was at this time engaged in a war in Indochina against the Vietminh, something the United States would soon experience. The Americans should also remember that during their 'revolution', without Count Rochambeau and his 8,300 French soldiers Yorktown would never have fallen and the entire 'revolution' may well have failed.

mainland. Korea was to be a different war. The country was one of extremes. The summer heat could rise to 105° F with equally high humidity, while in the winter the temperature would drop to minus 40° F with horrific winds blowing down from Siberia. The terrain was mountainous with rocky hills rising to over 3,000 feet, their lower slopes covered in thick shrubs and stunted trees making movement in the summer difficult, higher up they were generally bereft of any cover at all. Roads and tracks were few and far between and were usually of poor construction. Other obstructions to vehicles were numerous paddy fields that covered the valley floors. Added to all this were the plagues of malarial mosquitoes and rats that carried and spread all sorts of other diseases. Locally produced foodstuffs had to be carefully prepared due to the widespread use of human faeces as a fertiliser. A Rifles officer recalled that in the soaring heat of high summer, the entire countryside had a "widespread odour of putrefaction", while a corporal remembered "the stench of shit everywhere". This was Korea, this was their new battlefield.

1

The Rifles, a brief history

The year 1793 saw war declared between Britain and France. With the need for more troops in the British Army the 83rd Regiment of Foot was raised by Colonel William Fitch in the city of Dublin.

The Regiment was to see its first action in the West Indies during the Maroon War of 1795, while part of the Regiment was engaged at St. Domingo. On the cessation of hostilities the Regiment remained as garrison troops for the next seven years. During this time they, in common with all other regiments on such service, lost more men to disease than to enemy action. After the Peace of Amiens the Regiment returned to Ireland where it raised a second battalion to meet the expansion of the Army as a result of the Napoleonic Wars. In 1805, the 1st Battalion landed at Cape Town in South Africa and quickly overran the small Dutch garrison. The Battalion would remain there until 1818.

In 1809, the 2nd Battalion became part of Wellington's Peninsula Expeditionary Army in Portugal. For the following five years they marched and counter-marched the length and breadth of Spain and Portugal, until finally crossing into France. In that time they gained twelve battle honours. Of these two deserve particular mention. The action at Talavera was fought on 28 July 1809. The Battalion suffered over 50% casualties including their commanding officer, Colonel Alexander Gordon. Such were the officer casualties in the Battalion that Sergeant Major Joseph Swinburne was granted an Ensigncy for his distinguished service and was appointed Adjutant. Joseph Swinburne was one of the few men in Wellington's army to rise from the rank of Private to Brevet Lieutenant Colonel. He received the Peninsula War medal with ten clasps and served for forty-four years as an officer before retiring in 1853 with a Major's full pay.

At Badajoz on 25 March 1812, Wellington ordered an assault against Fort Picurina, part of the defences of the town. A 'forlorn hope' of five hundred men included two officers and fifty men from the Battalion. A hero of the assault was Sergeant Thomas Hazlehurst, responsible for saving the life of Captain Powys who fell wounded in the breach and would have been bayoneted to death but for the actions of the determined Sergeant.

The 86th Foot was raised in the County of Shropshire by General Cornelius Cuyler and went by the name 'Cuyler's Shropshire Volunteers'. Recruiting initially proved difficult, with more men wanting to work on the land than take the 'King's Shilling'. Therefore the regiment moved to Ireland and was allotted the province of Leinster as a new recruiting area, which proved eminently successful. The 86th had their first taste of action while serving as marines and were engaged in several actions against the French. A detachment of six companies accompanied the expedition to Egypt in June 1801. They carried out an epic march of some eighty miles from Suez to Cairo, the whole time under a blazing sun. During this time there were no provisions and the column's water supply had become polluted with maggots. The men were dressed in the heavy scarlet coats of the time, but despite this only seventeen stragglers were reported, of these eight died of sunstroke. This campaign saw the end of Napoleon's dream of an Egyptian empire in the sun. By Royal Authority the emblem of the Sphinx, inscribed 'Egypt' was added to the regimental crest.

Both the 83rd and 86th Regiments were involved in the Indian Mutiny. They took part in many of the actions, perhaps the most famous was the assault on the city of Jhansi on 3 April 1858. The garrison at the time of the assault was unknown, but was estimated at no less than 13,000 men, supported by some forty pieces of artillery crewed by well trained gunners. The assault was both fierce and bloody; the storming party surmounted the walls despite a terrible fire from enemy musketry and cannon. There was bitter hand-to-hand fighting and many casualties were sustained, but eventually resistance was crushed and victory went to the British.

Three Victoria Crosses were awarded to the 86th. These were Lieutenant H.E. Jerome, and Privates Byrne and Pearson. Jerome had been born 'in the regiment' and would later be promoted to Brevet Major; his brother also served with the 86th and was later its commanding officer. James Byrne came from County Wicklow, survived to old age and died in Dublin in 1872. James Pearson, from Queen's County, Ireland died in India in 1900.

In 1881 the 83rd and 86th Regiments amalgamated to form the Royal Irish Rifles, 1st and 2nd Battalions respectively. The Royal North Downshire Militia formed the 3rd Battalion, the Antrim Militia the 4th, the Royal South Down Light Infantry the 5th and the Louth Rifles Militia the 6th.

The 2nd Battalion was mobilised for duty in the South African War on 9 October 1899. Of the 704 men called to the colours only nine failed to appear. As none of these men were ever heard of again, evidence would point to the fact that they had died prior to the call up. The Battalion left Victoria Barracks, Belfast on 25 October and travelled south by train to Queenstown. From here they embarked on the SS *Britannic* for South Africa, arriving in Cape Town on 13 November. Throughout the War the Battalion served at Cape Colony, Orange Free State, Belfast (SA), Ladysmith, Paardeberg, The Transvaal and Tugela Heights. They were also present at Stormberg on 10 December 1899, the anniversary of which is commemorated to this day at the City Hall in Belfast, Northern Ireland. No Victoria Crosses were earned in the conflict, but three DSOs and ten Distinguished Conduct Medals reflected the service and valour of both officers and men.

In a brief introduction such as this there is little space to record the heroism and devotion displayed by the Rifles in the Great War. The 2nd Battalion formed part of the British Expeditionary Force that fought at Mons, during the Retreat and subsequent battles of the Marne and the Aisne, prior to moving north into Flanders. In the ensuing trench warfare the 1st and 2nd Battalions served throughout the War, losing many times their number in casualties. The 6th Battalion served with 10th (Irish) Division at Gallipoli, in Macedonia and Palestine. A further fifteen battalions of the Rifles were formed, all but one of which served on the Western Front, mostly with 36th (Ulster) Division.

In 1921 came another change of title when, with the partition of Ireland, they became the Royal Ulster Rifles. (Actually as a result of a War Office decision to mark the province of Ulster with a regiment, Leinster, Connaught and Munster already having

St Patrick's Barracks, 1940. (RUR Museum)

St Patrick's Barracks, The RUR Regimental Depot,
Ballymena, Northern Ireland. (RUR Museum)

regiments.) At Parkhurst Barracks the 1st Battalion held a 'funeral' for the Royal Irish Rifles, erecting a suitably inscribed headstone. (RIR R.I.P RUR). When the Barracks later became a prison the headstone was transferred to the Regimental Museum in Belfast. Present at this occasion was the father of Lieutenant, later Brigadier McCord, who served in Korea.

With partition the British Army lost the services of the Royal Dublin Fusiliers, Royal Munster Fusiliers, Connaught Rangers, the Leinster Regiment, the Royal Irish Regiment and the South Irish Horse.

In 1937, the London Irish Rifles joined the Regiment as a Territorial Army battalion. The London Irish had been formed in 1859 as a 'Corps of Irish Gentlemen at Arms', subsequently becoming a Volunteer Corps. They had served in the South African War and in the Great War as part of the London Regiment. They had seen service in the Second World War in the Middle East, Sicily and Italy.

At the beginning of 1939, both Battalions of the Royal Ulster Rifles were serving abroad. The 2nd Battalion was in Palestine and by the time it left to return to the United Kingdom a total of five awards of the Military Cross, four Military Medals and eighty-seven Mentions in Despatches had been awarded. The 1st Battalion was at Razani on the North West Frontier of India. In June 1940 they sailed from Bombay aboard the SS *Karanja*. The ship had been at sea for six stormy days when at 0400hrs on 10 June smoke was seen pouring from the aft hold. A volunteer fire fighting party was assembled. This consisted of Captains Otway and Ridgeway, twelve 'other ranks' from the Battalion, the ship's chief officer, a cadet and several Lascar sailors. The first job was to break into the hold. The railings around the hatch covers were cut away with axes and the covers, by now red hot, were lifted clear. Water was then hosed onto the lower deck to make it cool enough to stand on. When this was done the party descended to repeat the process all over again. The fire was successfully extinguished and Captain Otway was awarded the Military Cross for his actions. Otway would go on to lead the famous attack on the Merville Battery on D-Day.

During the Second World War the 1st Battalion took on an Airborne role landing in Normandy by glider on D-Day. During the Battle of the Ardennes they fought as conventional infantry before returning to gliders for Operation Varsity, the crossing of the Rhine in March 1945.

The 2nd Battalion served with the British Expeditionary Force in France in 1940 and were successfully evacuated from Dunkirk. Almost as a foretaste of things to come, the Battalion was in such a position as to 'hold the door' as an almost surrounded Battalion of Gloucesters made their escape from the Germans. They returned to the Continent landing on the 'Queen Red' part of Sword Beach on D-Day and fighting throughout the Normandy campaign and on into Germany in 1945, ending the War on the Baltic coast.

2

Preparation

With the outbreak of the War in Korea, the 1st Battalion Royal Ulster Rifles had been preparing to proceed to Khartoum, the capital of the Sudan and arrangements were in hand to move the relevant families on 5 October. The change of destination to Korea caused a degree of apprehension among certain members of the Regiment. They were about to undertake a Colonial War very different from that experienced in the Great War (1914-1918) and the Second World War (1939-1945). In the days of Empire, Colonel Cardwell devised a Regimental system of two battalions, which enabled seventy-five regiments to police one-third of the world. This was achieved by having one battalion serve abroad, while the second remained in the United Kingdom and provided a steady supply of trained reinforcements. However since the end of the Second World War more than one battalion per regiment was a rarity indeed. Now the men preparing to move were poorly equipped, poorly clothed for the winter to come and lacked the reinforcements that a second depot battalion would provide in the event of casualties.

During the summer of 1950, the Battalion had been engaged in the normal routine of a Field Service Battalion and had its home at Sobraon Barracks in Colchester. At this time the Battalion was at the 'lower establishment' of 367 'other ranks'. To bring the Battalion up to 'high establishment' some thirty volunteers (Type K) were expected along with reservists from the following: North Irish Brigade 240, Lancastrian Brigade 390, Greenjackets 67, Light Infantry 66, Mercian Brigade 12, Welsh Brigade 12. Men

Members of Support Company of the 1st Battalion at Colchester. (RUR Museum)

Mortar Section of the 1st Battalion at Colchester. (RUR Museum)

from the North Irish Brigade also reinforced other regiments, an immediate draft of fifty 'other ranks' and two officers were sent to the King's (Liverpool) Regiment.

The Battalion was part of 29 Independent Infantry Brigade, a unit which at this time seemed to exist more in the minds of military planners as opposed to troops and equipment on the ground. Brigade Headquarters was situated in Colchester, as was the 45 Field Regiment Royal Artillery, along with the recently arrived 1st Battalion, Gloucestershire Regiment, while the Centurion tanks of the 8th King's Royal Irish Hussars were to be found at Tidworth.

The third battalion of the Brigade, 1st Battalion Royal Northumberland Fusiliers, was yet to join, while the Royal Engineers, Royal Army Medical Corps, Royal Army Service Corps and other units of the Brigade Group were yet to be formed. The Brigade didn't comprise any of the fashionable regiments but was instead full of ordinary provincial men who later nicknamed the formation the "Frozen Rectum" Brigade after their Brigade patch of a white circle on a base of a black square which some suggested represented their bare behinds sitting on thunder boxes in the temperatures of minus forty degrees in the biting Korea winter wind.[1]

By the autumn of 1950, The Royal Ulster Rifles and the other units in their paper formation had become a reality and was titled the 29 Independent Brigade Group, with command going to Brigadier Tom Brodie, CBE, DSO, a former Chindit who had fought the Japanese in the Second World War. Within the Rifles the reinforcements had settled down after a somewhat bewildered beginning and all ranks were adapting to their new role. After some rapid training and a brief spell of leave the Battalion made ready to leave Colchester for their new battlefield.

---

1 Whiting, *Battleground Korea, The British in Korea*, Stroud, 1999.

Corporal Tommy Cushing, a native of Tipperary, originally joined the US Army in 1926, to see what it was like in the army on the other side of the Atlantic. He stayed for ten years before returning to Tipperary. He re-enlisted and in 1939 went to France with the BEF, but did not get away at Dunkirk. He had long spells in Dachau, Buchenwald and Belsen. When told by an officer he was 'for Korea', he grinned and said "Well I suppose it's just another spot of bother, so let's get it over ….".

On 21 August 1950 the *Belfast Telegraph* reported that the first batch of Northern Ireland volunteers for active service Korea passed through the recruiting offices in Omagh and Belfast. All of the five men were under 30 years of age with a minimum of 18 months previous service, being demobilised subsequent to January 1946. Attested in Belfast were J.C. McClelland aged 28, Thomas Gorman, aged 23 both from Belfast and John Doran aged 28 from Newcastle, County Down. McClelland and Gorman had previously been employed at the Admiralty Maintenance Yard, Sydenham at Belfast and were sent to Ballykinlar to attend a short refresher course before being posted to a unit for service abroad. During the Second World War McClelland had served with the Royal Ulster Rifles, from April 1941 to October 1946. Gorman served with the Irish Guards from January 1945 until January 1948. Doran had served in the General Service Corps and Royal Engineers from 1943 until 1947. He was to spend some time at a Royal Engineer Depot before being sent out to Korea. John Stewart, aged 23 from Enniskillen and William J. Cowan, from Londonderry attested at Omagh and also attended Ballykinlar from a period of preliminary training. Stewart had previously served in the RAOC and Cowan in the Royal Armoured Corps.[2]

On 30 September 1950, General Sir James Steele, GCB, KBE, the Colonel of the Regiment visited the Battalion prior to their departure for Korea. In his speech to the men he reminded them that they were taking part in a United Nations operation, which

---

2 *Belfast Telegraph*, 21 August 1950.

was something new in the annals of the British Army. The General had come to the end of thirty-six years of service just a few days previously and remarked that he could not resist feeling of envy for those who were just beginning on this new enterprise.

General Steele paid a visit to the town of Ballymena in County Antrim on 1 July 1950. During the visit he commented that whilst the number of men joining the Army from Northern Ireland was better than the rest of the United Kingdom,

> We still have to rely on the absorption of some National Servicemen from England and we try to draft those with Irish associations in order to keep the Regiment up to strength. I cannot regard that as satisfactory from a long-term point of view. I think we ought to make it our pride, boast and target to make The RUR self-contained from its own kith and kin.[3]

The men of the Battalion who sailed for Korea came from all parts of the British Isles and Ireland and consisted of regulars, reservists and volunteers. Some had only just managed to get small businesses going since the end of the Second World War, other were recently married, some were well past the first flush of youth and had been looking forward to a more settled future. What all ranks had in common was a high degree of physical fitness. Sport played a big part in fitness training and both the boxing and cross-country running teams were Army Finalists, Andy McNab, a heavyweight, had fought the later to be famous Henry Cooper, who at the time still had amateur status. It goes without saying that not all turned up for duty. One man did arrive, closely followed by a wife and two children and stated in language of a colourful nature "You better have these as well."[4] One well known 'character' of the Battalion immediately went absent, he would later rejoin at Liverpool much against his will.

To the veterans of the previous conflict the Battalion organisation had not changed. There was a Battalion Headquarters, Headquarter Company, four rifle companies, numbered A, B, C, D and a Support Company. That listed below is taken from Army Form B 158A, dated 26 November 1950; however changes occurred almost immediately after landing in Korea.

Battalion Headquarters

Command of the Battalion went to Lieutenant Colonel Robert John Heyworth 'Hank' Carson. Carson had been born in India in 1909, the son Major Robert Carson, Royal Artillery, who was killed in the Great War while serving with the 139th Heavy Battery.[5] Educated at Charterhouse and then at The Royal Military College Sandhurst, Carson was commissioned into the Royal Ulster Rifles in 1929. Before the War he served in Aldershot, Belfast, Palestine, Egypt, Hong Kong, the Isle of Wight and later Armagh and Ballymena. From 1942 to 1943 he commanded 70th (Young Soldiers) Battalion RUR. Carson had assumed command of the Battalion at Chilton Foliat in 1943. He

---

3 *Belfast Telegraph*, 1 July 1950.
4 RUR Museum Archives.
5 Major Robert Carson, 139th Heavy Battery, Royal Garrison Artillery, killed on 24 August 1916, the son of William and Isabella Carson of Carnalea, County Down and husband of Helen B. Carson of Broadwater, East Malling, Kent, he is buried in Martinsart War Cemetery, Grave 1.A.8. *Blackthorn Magazine* No 19, 1983.

Adjutant, Captain H. Hamill. (Mervyn McCord/RUR Association)

continued to lead the Battalion in the Normandy campaign, into Germany and the end of the War. He was badly wounded during operation 'Varsity', the crossing of the Rhine, in March 1945, something that would have a telling effect concerning his service in the coming campaign. Carson was considered to be a competent officer, he was shy and reserved in his off duty manner and not normally given to the more raucous Mess pastimes.

The Battalion second-in-command was Major C.A.H.B. Blake. Charles Anthony Howell Bruce Blake had been born in County Wicklow and had joined the Rifles in 1931, serving in Egypt, Hong Kong, Shanghai and India. In 1938 he had gone to Russia to attend a course and was completing his studies in Warsaw when the Germans invaded in 1939. He escaped after many adventures and eventually made his way to Romania and then home. He had served as an instructor at OCTU, as an Intelligence Officer at the War Office and in the Middle East, then with the Russian Liaison Group and for a time was attached to the 1st Polish Independent Parachute Brigade Group. He served as Brigade Major with the 1st Airlanding Brigade of 1st Airborne Division at Arnhem in September 1944 and was one of the fortunate survivors to escape across the Rhine after the battle.

The Battalion Adjutant was Captain Hugh Hamill, who had been promoted from Lieutenant on 22 July 1951. The Assistant Adjutant was Lieutenant E.W. Pigot, who was on secondment from the Royal Irish Fusiliers. Captain J.E.D.'O. Hinde was the Intelligence Officer; he had rejoined the Battalion at Sobraon Barracks in January 1950, after service with the Parachute Regiment in Germany. Captain A.M. 'Sandy' Ferrie was the Medical Officer and became so enthused with the Battalion that he changed his

RAMC cap to that of the Rifles caubeen. In Korea he would have to deal with a variety of diseases and health risks. There was malaria from mosquitoes, encephalitis, a type of sleeping sickness, and filariasis, a specific worm disease carried by mosquitoes. Added to this was the risk of infection from fleas, flies, rats, ticks, and lice. There was also the risk of contracting smallpox, cholera, typhus, dysentery and venereal disease. It would be to Ferrie's credit that apart from one short sharp outbreak of ringworm, the Battalion would have a clean bill of health in Korea, apart from wounds suffered by enemy action.

Headquarters Company
Headquarters Company was commanded by Major J.C.S.G. de Longueuil, MC. Stuart, as he was known to his brother officers, was the younger brother to the eleventh Baron de Longueuil, the only title in the Peerage of Canada, which was created by Louis XIV in 1700 and received recognition by Queen Victoria in 1880. Stuart was born in California, and educated in France and Guernsey before attending Sandhurst in 1937. He was commissioned in The Royal Ulster Rifles in 1938 and joined the 2nd Battalion at Parkhurst Barracks, Isle of Wight, on their return from Palestine. He was appointed Carrier Platoon Commander and took part in the campaign leading up to the evacuation from Dunkirk. As officer commanding C Company he landed in Normandy on D Day and led his Company during the campaign in France, Belgium, Holland and Germany. He was awarded the Military Cross for gallantry during the crossing of the Meuse-Escaut Canal on the night of 18-19 September 1944, for showing coolness and drive when organising the boat parties under heavy fire, before accompanying the leading flights across. On landing they were attacked by a strong enemy patrol that killed Captain Laving, the second-in-command. de Longueuil immediately organised a counter-attack and forced the enemy to withdraw. He acted as second-in-command of the 2nd Battalion for a time during operations in Belgium and Holland in early 1945 and on conclusion of the war joined the British Military Mission to Greece. He subsequently came to the Depot where he was Adjutant for a year before joining the 1st Battalion as officer commanding HQ Company in Ballykinlar where he did a lot as their President to revitalise their Pipe Band. During the severe winter campaign in Korea he was a distinctive figure in his massive fur coat and dog skin cap.

Captain Ken Neely, MBE, was the Signals Officer. He had served with the London Irish in North Africa and Italy, becoming Brigade Major of the 38th (Irish) Brigade by the end of the War. Lieutenant J. Mason, on secondment from the Lancashire Fusiliers, with which he had served in India, was the Assistant Signals Officer and a fluent speaker of Italian![6] Captain Tom Smith from Newtownards, County Down was a veteran of the Second World War, had been commissioned in the field and was an outstanding Quartermaster. It was mainly due to his efforts that the Battalion was ably supplied with what comforts were available. Lieutenant J.A. Beckett from the Lancashire Regiment was the Motor Transport Officer and along with Sergeant William 'Bill' McConnell, ensured that all the Battalion's vehicles were kept up to scratch. Bill McConnell, like many of his generation, had lied about his age when he enlisted in the Rifles in 1941. He was posted to the 1st (Airborne) Battalion and landed by glider in Normandy on D-day.[7]

---

6 Later Sir John Mason, an outstanding diplomat.
7 Bill McConnell would continue to serve until 1969. He was awarded the MBE in 2003 for his work in raising memorials to the 1st and 2nd Battalions at Longueval and Cambes-en-Plaine, Normandy.

Captain Stuart de Longueil, OC A Echelon and Adjutant wearing a dog skin cap, in Happy Valley. (Mervyn McCord/RUR Association)

A Company
Major M.D.G.C. Ryan commanded A Company, with Captain C.J. Sir Nixon Bt, MC, as his second-in-command. Sir Christopher's father was Professor of Anatomy and Physiology at the University of Dublin. The Baronetcy had been created in 1906 in his honour. Lieutenant H.M. Shaw-Stewart, a National Serviceman who had volunteered for Korea, commanded No 1 Platoon, Lieutenant J. Chapman, on secondment from the Loyals, commanded No 2 Platoon, while No 3 Platoon was commanded by Lieutenant J.B. Lane.

B Company
Major J.H.W. Mulligan, who would later be the first Regimental Secretary of the Royal Irish Rangers, commanded B Company, with Lieutenant W.R.H. Charley as his second-in-command. Robin Charley had been acting as a General's aide-de-camp when he was told of the move to Korea and as there were no vacancies for a Captain, he dropped a rank in order to go. Lieutenant B. St Alcock, from the Royal Inniskilling Fusiliers commanded No 4 Platoon, No 5 Platoon was led by Lieutenant J.J. Mole. Mole was the son of a Rifles officer who had been killed in November 1944 and had always been determined to follow a military career.[8] Mole would soon transfer to the Mortar Platoon under Captain Majury and would be heavily involved in the battle of the Imjin.

---

8   Brigadier Gerald Herbert Leo Mole, 129th Infantry Brigade, killed 14 November 1944, buried in Brunssum War Cemetery.

George Prescott Westcar, John ffrench and Arthur McCallan
admire the local 'talent'. (*Quis Separabit*)

Grave of 2nd Lieutenant Prescott-Westcar, United Nations
Memorial Cemetery, Pusan, Korea. (RUR Association)

C Company

Major I.A. May, who had served as Brigadier 'Shan' Hackett's Brigade Major during the Second World War, commanded C Company, with Captain H.D. Miller as his second-in- command. Lieutenant Max Nichols commanded No 7 Platoon, No 8 Platoon was commanded by Second Lieutenant George Prescott-Westcar. The son of a Rifle Brigade officer and a Sandhurst graduate, Prescott-Westcar had joined the Battalion at Colchester in 1949. He was a first class shot and had represented the Battalion at Bisley. He is well remembered within the Battalion for his meeting with General Ridgway. Ridgway was on one of his tours of inspection of the Brigade when he approached the Lieutenant's Platoon and introduced himself with the words, "I'm General Matthew Bunker Ridgway", to which the Lieutenant replied, "Hello, I'm Second Lieutenant George Villiers Beeston Prescott-Westcar". Lieutenant A. Axeford, on secondment from the Manchester Regiment, commanded No 9 Platoon. Also in C Company was Mark McConnell, brother of Bill. Mark had enlisted in 1943 and had volunteered for Airborne Forces, doing his training at Tatton Park. However, an injury during this time had seen his transferred to the 1st Battalion of the Rifles, joining them post D-day.

D Company

D Company was commanded by Major H.M. Gaffikin. The son of a Belfast JP and former pupil of Campbell College, he was a veteran of the Second World War. As his second-in-command he had Captain J.R.M. ffrench with Lieutenant E.R. Bruford-Davies, son of 'Trotsky' Davies, commanding No 10 Platoon, Second Lieutenant R. Benson No 11 Platoon and Second Lieutenant C. MacNicol commanding No 12 Platoon.

Support Company

Support Company did just that, it supported the Battalion with its medium machine-guns and mortars as and when required. It was commanded by Major John Kirkpatrick Hay Shaw MC, an officer of exceptional ability. Shaw had been born at Simla, India in 1916 and after being educated at Boxgrave Preparatory School and Malvern College, attended Sandhurst, being commissioned in the Rifles in 1936. The following year he was posted to the 1st Battalion at Rawalpindi and saw service on the North West Frontier. On 1 April 1940, he was promoted to Captain and returned to the UK with the Battalion. In 1941, he transferred to the 18th Battalion, Royal Fusiliers and saw action with Paiforce[9] in Iraq. When the Battalion was converted to the 100 Light Anti-aircraft Regiment he was promoted to Acting Major in December 1941. A desire for a more active role saw him accompanying another Rifles' officer, Lieutenant Colonel 'Trotsky' Davies to Force 133, a commando unit operating in the Mediterranean and Albania, and for his actions here he was awarded the Military Cross. Later still he was part of Force 136 in Burma where he remained until the surrender of the Japanese.

The 3" mortar could also be found in the support companies. It fired a 10-pound high explosive or smoke bomb out to 1,600 yards and was man portable, being broken down into three loads, base plate, bipod and barrel. At Arnhem in September 1944 a bomb from a 3" mortar had destroyed one of the much-vaunted Tiger tanks.[10] The mortar usually had a crew of three men, but often extra men known as 'mules' were attached to

---

9 Persia and Iraq Force.
10 Kershaw, *It Never Snows In September*, Shepperton, 1994.

Lieutenant R. Benson, D Company (RUR Museum)

carry ammunition. The Mortar Platoon, consisting of six 3" mortars, was commanded by Captain J.H.S. Majury. Majury came from County Antrim and had been educated at Ballymena Academy, RBAI and McCrea and Magee College, Derry. He had enlisted in 1940 and was seconded to the Indian Army, serving in the South Wazirean Scouts, reaching the rank of Major. He had been commissioned into the Regular Army in June 1941 and joined the RUR in 1947. Lieutenant A.E. Hill was his second-in-command. Among the 'other ranks' of the Mortar Platoon was Corporal Joseph Lavery of Dewey Street, Belfast. Lavery had just completed a five year Regular engagement when war broke out in Korea and his discharge was deferred. Five days before embarking on the *Empire Pride* he had married Miss Georgina Thompson

The Medium Machine Gun Platoon, consisting of six Vickers machine-guns, was commanded by Captain A.J. McCallan, another 'son' of the Regiment. The Vickers was a tripod mounted, water-cooled weapon that required four men to operate properly. It had an effective range of 2,000 yards and fired at 600 rounds per minute, being fed from a 250 round fabric ammunition belt. In hot weather or prolonged firing the water would boil and had to be replenished on a regular basis. Should there be a shortage of water the crew were expected to provide their own! In the Bitter Korean winter it was necessary to fill the water jackets with antifreeze. It was a very dependable gun and while manufacture had stopped in 1945, it would continue in service until 1965.

Second Lieutenant Mervyn McCord commanded the Anti-Tank Platoon, which consisted of 17pdr anti-tank guns towed by Oxford Carriers. The Oxford was a heavier version of the British Universal Carrier, more commonly known as the 'Bren' Carrier. With the need for a towing vehicle for the heavier anti-tank guns and other weapons, the Oxford was introduced in 1946; it was powered by a Cadillac five litre V8 engine giving 110 horsepower, weighed six tonnes and was more than capable of towing the 17pdr. In Korea it would have a more exciting employment.

Padre Kelly at 57 Regimental Aid Post, Happy Valley. (Mervyn McCord/RUR Association)

Padre Kelly with a Fusilier driver in Happy Valley. (RUR Museum)

Captain Cocksedge commanded the Assault Pioneer Platoon with Lieutenant R.S. Gill, on secondment from the Manchester Regiment, as his second-in-command. The role of the Platoon was to assist in constructing field defences such as bunkers, firing positions and where necessary the ability to cross both natural and man-made obstacles. They were skilled in the use of demolitions, the laying and lifting of landmines and booby traps and normal infantry duties when required. One of the weapons issued to the Platoon was the Second World War vintage No 75 (Hawkins) Grenade. This was named after its designer and was first issued in 1941, being approved for general issue in 1942. It is perhaps inappropriate to call it a grenade, as it was in fact a small anti-tank mine resembling a flat screw-topped talcum powder tin. Designed to be laid flat under the tracks of a tank, or if attached to a piece of cord, pulled across the path of an advancing vehicle, it could also be thrown, but not with any accuracy.[11]

---

11 Individual weaponry had changed little since 1945; the standard rifle was the bolt-action Lee Enfield .303, an accurate weapon in trained hands, although its slow rate of fire would often see the Rifleman at a disadvantage in close-quarter fighting. In the field each man was usually issued with fifty rounds per rifle, in Korea the minimum issue would be one hundred and fifty or sometime more. The Bren gun remained as the Section light machine-gun and was again extremely effective when handled properly, usually firing short bursts of three to five rounds. Due to its very light recoil it was extremely accurate and acted as a superb support weapon. It fired the same cartridge as the .303 rifle from a thirty-round top-loaded box magazine at a rate of 500 rounds per minute and while it could be used by one man, it was most effective with a crew of two. Unfortunately there was also still the Sten gun and despite it being the Mk V version, this had improved little since its introduction during the Second World

Officers of the 1st Battalion, The Royal Ulster Rifles with General Steele, taken a day prior to departure for Korea.
Back row: ?, ?, Lt Nicholl, ?, Lt Benson, Lt Davies, Lt Prescott-Westcar, Lt Shaw, Frazer.
Middle row: Capt Ferrie (MO), Capt Millar, Capt Neely, Capt Dickson, Capt Smith, Capt Ellison, Padre Kelly, Capt Charley, Lt Theobald.
Front row: Major de Longueuil, Major Shaw, Major Ryan, Major Blake, General Steele, Lt-Col Carson, Capt Hamill, Major Gaffikin, Major Mulligan (RUR Museum)

Religious comfort for the Battalion was supplied by two Padres, Father Ryan ministered to the Roman Catholics, while Padre Kelly saw to the needs of the C of E and other dominations. There is an old saying that 'there are no atheists in foxholes', which may well be true, however the strain of combat can give rise to what some might consider strange behaviour on the battlefield. One man, a Protestant, was given a set of rosary beads by Father Kelly, which he wore throughout the campaign and beyond, refusing to take them off even when he returned home, wearing them until his death some years ago.[12]

War. With a calibre of 9mm it was fitted with a side-mounted magazine holding 32 rounds and fired at 550 rounds per minute. A simple blow-back action held in a pressed steel housing, it was cheap to produce; more than two million had seen service in the Second World War, being issued to both elite paratroopers and rag tag resistance fighters. Nevertheless, it was dangerous in untrained hands and accidents were plentiful. Thankfully in Korea it would be possible to replace a number of them with other weapons including the American Thompson sub-machine-gun and the M1 Carbine. A new weapon to the Battalion was the bazooka, an American-designed shoulder-fired rocket launcher of the Second World War. Originally with a calibre of 2.36" this had been replaced by one of 3.7", which was capable of dealing with the Russian-supplied T34/85 tanks, thankfully something the Rifles never had to face. Nevertheless, the bazooka would prove useful in the coming conflict as an anti-personnel weapon. It was a replacement for the PIAT of Second World War vintage, which, while it had the advantage of not having a back blast, being spring operated, was not capable of dealing with the heavier Russian-supplied tanks.

12 Interview with Mark McConnell.

As the men of the Royal Ulster Rifles bound for Korea waved goodbye pipers of the London Irish Rifles played them away. A crowd sang, *Auld Lang Syne*.

Boarding the HMT *Empire Pride* at Liverpool with the Liver Building in the background. (RUR Museum)

Rt Hon John Strachey, Secretary of State for War, visiting the men of the Royal Ulster Rifles before they leave on HMT *Empire Pride*. (RUR Museum)

Members of 1st Battalion, The Royal Ulster Rifles preparing to leave for Korea from Liverpool on 1st October 1950. (RUR Museum)

Colonel Carson wishing luck to members of 1st Battalion, The Royal Ulster Rifles as they prepare to leave for Korea from Liverpool on 1st October 1950. (RUR Museum)

Men of the 1st Battalion, the Royal Ulster Rifles, crowd the side of the troopship *Empire Pride* as she pulls away from the quay at Liverpool en route for Korea.

Onboard HMT *Empire Pride*. (RUR Museum)

Few photographs of the Battalion in Korea show men wearing steel helmets, although these were issued and various reasons are given for this – too cold in winter, too warm in summer and most men seemed to prefer either the woollen cap comforter, the traditional Korean dog skin cap, or later the American 'baseball' style cap.[13] It should be noted that when it came to the wearing of the caubeen, those men from the old 1st Airborne Battalion pulled the headgear down to the right, while the 2nd Battalion pulled theirs down to the left. This was a result of a parade held in front of the King, when he remarked that the 2nd Battalion's badge was much more clearly seen during the march past![14]

As darkness fell on 1 October 1950, the Battalion entrained for Liverpool and their transport to the Far East, HMT *Empire Pride*. Built in 1941 as a troopship, the *Empire Pride* was managed for the Ministry of War Transport [MOWT] by the Bibby Line and was capable of carrying 1,600 troops. She remained as a troopship until 1954 when she was sold, renamed *Charlton Pride*, and converted to a cargo ship, which she remained until being scrapped in Hong Kong, 1964.[15] [16]

The second day of October saw officers and men engaged in loading equipment on board the troopship. When the last of the numerous bits and pieces that accompany a battalion to war were loaded into the hold the men lined the ships rail to wave goodbye. While the crew made ready to cast off the mooring lines a familiar face was spotted in the crowd on the quay. A Rifleman, recently reported as AWOL, was seen gaily waving up at the ship. The RSM, Alex Patterson and the Provost Sergeant quickly assembled a 'snatch squad' and within a few minutes had the offender on board just before the ship sailed.[17]

The Rt. Hon. John Strachey, 'a gaunt black coated figure' and the Labour Secretary of State for War, along with General Steele, had seen off the ship, wishing all aboard "God's speed", along with the usual political platitudes spoken at these times. At 1945hrs, the troopship cast off from Prince's Landing Stage, Liverpool, loaded with the 1st Battalion Royal Ulster Rifles, 31 CPO, 10th Infantry Workshops, REME, 26 Field Ambulance and elements of 4 Ordnance Base Depot.

As the Pipes and Drums of the Battalion rendered the evening air with familiar tunes the troopship passed the myriad lights along the quay and disappeared into the dusk. To those men from the Shankill Road the *Sash* raised a cheer and a rousing chorus, to those men from the Potteries, the Black Country and the Welsh valleys it met with looks of bemusement. Added to the repertoire were other favourites such as *Wish Me Luck* and *Roll A Silver Dollar*.

---

13 The helmet issued was the British Mk IV.
14 Colonel Robin Charley.
15 http://www.rafseletar.co.uk/troopships.html.
16 http://www.openwriting.com/archives/2007/06/11_the_empire_p_1.php.
17 This man was identified to the authors by Brigadier McCord, who requested it be kept anonymous.

3

Sailing to the far side of the world

The voyage eastwards was largely uneventful, for the men some training was organised, but it was mostly recreation. In the first class lounge the officers had mounted a large map of Korea on the wall and the progress of the war was updated on a regular basis. To all intents and purposes the war appeared to be winding down. Prior to sailing Lieutenant Colonel Carson had given a radio interview in which he had stated that it appeared all the Battalion would be required to do was provide garrison troops and engage in some anti-guerrilla work.

Between 3 and 7 October there was no training on board due to the heavy weather as the ship crossed the Bay of Biscay and many of the Battalion suffer from seasickness,

Map of Korea showing its position in the region. (Courtesy *Belfast Telegraph*)

Bill McConnell. (Bill McConnell)

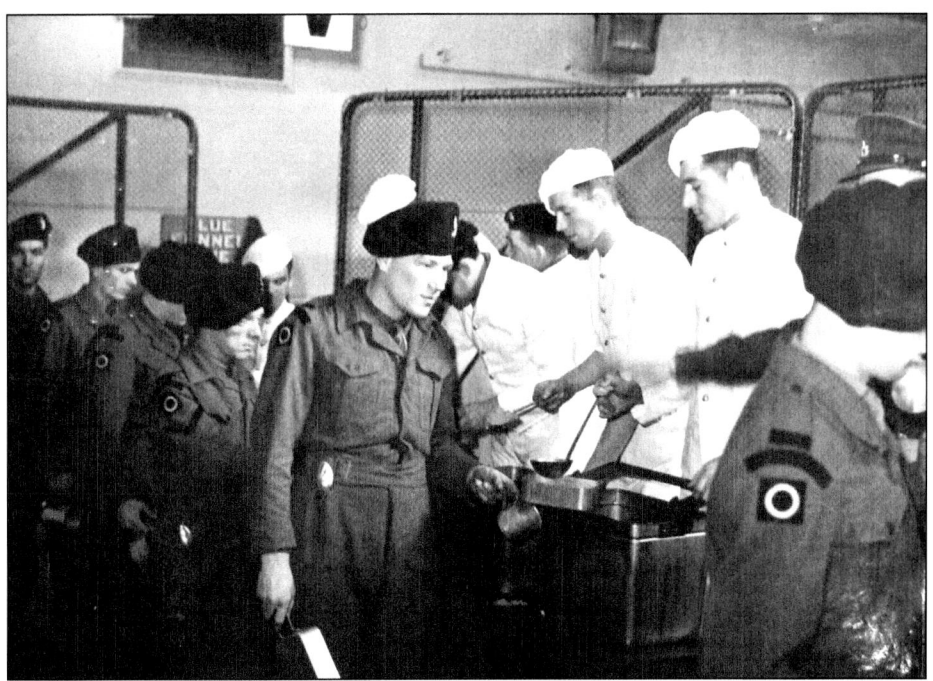

Dinner-time onboard the *Empire Pride*, soon to run out of potatoes. (RUR Museum)

On board HMT *Empire Pride*, possibly near Suez. (RUR Museum)

although the McConnell brothers and others from the Province were content to down a fried breakfast without any ill effects. The first casualty of the Brigade was not destined to die in Korea. As the ship rolled in the heavy seas a Private of 26 Field Ambulance jumped or more likely fell overboard. Life belts were thrown into the sea and a follow up search lasting some two hours failed to find any trace of the body. An accident would also cause the first death to the Battalion in Korea.[1] The following morning, a Sunday, there was a good congregation at all services, giving thanks for surviving the previous storm. The next day training recommenced with physical training on deck, training films below deck and the firing of small arms at targets aft of the ship.

On 10 October at 1730hrs, the ship reached Port Said; the Battalion Pipes played the ship into harbour and the galley staff breathed a sigh of relief. The ability of Ulstermen to consume potatoes and beer had been vastly underestimated and a catering crisis was only avoided when a fresh supply of both was brought on board at Suez.[2]

The following day the ship passed through the Suez Canal with a halt for two hours in the Great Bitter Lakes. To pass the time and give the men some exercise races took place using the ship's lifeboats. These were powered by two men utilizing a set of levers that were attached to a propeller, so it was a matter of muscle power as opposed to skill with oars that won the day for a team from No 3 Deck. For the remainder of the voyage the high humidity prohibited physical training and this continued to be the case for some time.

On 15 October the *Empire Pride* entered Aden dropping anchor at 0730hrs. Aden was an excellent anchorage and had served as a coaling station of the British Empire for many years. Shore leave was granted to the men until 1200hrs, the exception being those men who had refused to be inoculated. The humidity was still a problem and a planned route march was cancelled on the advice of the Medical Officer. The ship sailed at 1630hrs and on calling the roll it was discovered that two men had failed to return and were marked AWOL.[3] This may have been due to the instruction for all ranks to maintain a high fluid intake with beer being substituted for water. Four Riflemen who did overindulge somehow made their way on to a buoy in the harbour and proceeded to

---

1   *Quis Separabit*, 1950.
2   Unpublished manuscript by Derrick Gibson-Harries.
3   Absent Without Leave.

Five Royal Ulster Rifleman who sailed in the *Empire Pride* for Korea. Left to right – Sergeant F. Nugent, Crumlin Road; Corporal Y. Johnson, Malvern Street; Rifleman J. Addis, Ligioniel; Corporal J. Boyle, York Street and Corporal S. Mark, Drummond Street, Larne. (*Northern Whig*)

Riflemen taking a break in Colombo en-route to Korea. (Bill McConnell)

54   A NEW BATTLEFIELD

Beer duty, Korea, 1951. (William May/RUR Association)

regale passing vessels with various remarks and hand signals. When a patrol of the RAF Police arrived there was a scuffle which saw the Police coming off the worst and being ducked into the harbour. All the while there was huge supportive cheering from the decks of the *Empire Pride*. This incident caused quite an uproar among the higher ranks and resulted in the ship following being prohibited from granting shore leave.

As the Battalion sailed out of Aden the *Empress of India* was sighted for the first time. Aboard this troopship was the entire Brigade Headquarters staff and 45 Field Regiment, Royal Artillery.

Six days later the troopship docked at Colombo at 0830hrs. The Battalion, less fatigue parties and defaulters, disembarked for a three-mile route march. This was followed by shore leave from 1300hrs until 1700hrs and resulted in a further three absentees. Sergeant Bill McConnell and some of his MT Platoon took the opportunity to go shopping and avail themselves of the bargains on offer and numerous parcels were despatched back to Northern Ireland containing everything from tea to complete tea sets. While ashore some of the officers took the opportunity to go surfing at the Galle Face Hotel. While at dinner it was decided that an eating contest should be held and dish after dish was ordered from the menu, the declared champion was George Prescott-Westcar. This was followed by an unseemly rush to get back to the ship on time and at 2200hrs, the ship sailed for Singapore.

B Company, The 1st Battalion at Singapore, 27 October 1950, preparing for a route march. (RUR Museum)

The Battalion pipers leading the route march in Singapore. (RUR Museum)

56 A NEW BATTLEFIELD

The Battalion begins a route march in Singapore, 27 October 1950, after disembarking from the *Empire Pride* to acclimatise the men to the conditions east of Suez. (RUR Museum)

Singapore was reached at 1000hrs on 26 October, although it was the following day before it tied up at the quayside. As this was being done the Pipes played on the aft deck, while the band of the Cameronians played on the dock. Mail that had been flown out from the UK was distributed and this was followed at 1430hrs by a route march of approximately three miles. Shore leave was granted from 1700hrs until 2359hrs, this time without absentees. Captain ffrench, Captain Hinde and Lieutenant McCallan joined the ship. While in Singapore the officers were invited to a cocktail party hosted by Humphrey Gore, who was serving on the Staff at Singapore. After the party the officers headed for the famous Raffles Hotel where Sir Christopher Nixon promptly took command of the orchestra piano and began to bang out some favourite tunes. Despite protests from the management that the concert was being broadcast the singing continued into the late hours of the night. The following morning a headline in the *Straits Times* stated "Merriest Regiment for years prepares for Korea". It was also at Singapore that the Battle Inoculation Party, headed by Major Shaw, met up with the Battalion and briefed them on the remainder of their journey and on conditions in Korea.

Unfortunately as the days passed there came the need to add more red symbols to the officers' war map, marking the position and advances of the 'Chinese Communist Forces'. Two days prior to their arrival at the port of Pusan, it became obvious to all that the general tenor of the war had changed and this was to be no picnic.

This view was reinforced on 7 October when the United Nations passed a resolution preparing for the establishment of a unified Government in Korea and inviting the people of both north and south to co-operate in the restoration of peace. This was not to be the case, and during the second half of October a total of nine Chinese armies had been assembling in the hills of North Korea to the south of the Yalu River.

HMT *Empire Pride*, Pusan, October 1950. (Mervyn McCord/RUR Association)

On the morning of 5 November the mountainous coastline of Korea became visible through driving squalls of rain. The Battalion was going to face an enemy of unknown calibre, but the weather so far remained familiar, but not the smell, which was forever etched into the memories of all Riflemen who served there. By mid-morning the *Empire Pride* had anchored in Pusan harbour and curious Riflemen lined the decks, not in the least impressed by the foul water, bleak squalid town and dark ragged mountains that seemed to stretch over the horizon. At noon the men began to go ashore and Major John Shaw, who had flown out previously with the advance party, briefed Colonel Carson on the current situation.

4

Korea

The Riflemen were greeted by music from the 56th Band of the US Eighth Army. This band, dressed in smart uniforms and wearing highly polished steel helmets, was composed entirely of Negro soldiers and was led by a dancing seven foot tall Drum Major. Those members of the Battalion from both Ulster and the Republic of Ireland commented on never having seen so many black people in one place before. The combination of Sousa marches and 'hot' jazz tunes, alternating with tunes from the Battalion pipes, lifted the spirits as the Battalion waited several hours for the march to the railway station. As each man disembarked he was met at the foot of the gangplank by a shy Korean girl and handed an apple.[1] Their arrival at Pusan marked the first unit to arrive from England to join the United Nations force in Korea. It wouldn't be long before they would join in the advance on Pyongyang.[2]

> "Korea is predominantly a rough mountainous country.
> Her highest peaks rise to more than 8,700 feet."
> *The Korean Handbook* as issued by the Department of the Army Office, Washington D.C.

An understatement to say the least and the Riflemen would climb many of them more than once! On a map the distance between point A and point B may be measured at five miles. On foot it would come out more like twenty-five as you made your way up hill and down dale, so to speak.

In the railway station goods yard the men milled about as they were sorted out into the various carriages. Battalion stores in the shape of cookers, food, ammunition, petrol, rations, water and all the paraphernalia necessary for the two-hundred mile journey to Suwon, the Battalion's destination, was supposed to have been loaded prior to the arrival of the men. Unfortunately the stores could not be found and it was only with the assistance of an American soldier and his 'deuce and a half' truck that the stores were discovered after a frantic search through a strange town in near total darkness.

Captain (Quartermaster) Tom Smith surveyed the scene and to his trained eye this amount of chaos at the very beginning of a campaign brought home the thought that the Battalion would have to be self sufficient with regard to creature comforts. It was obvious that the British supply organisation was as yet not working and only limited assistance could be expected from the Americans, who had more than enough on their plate. His future liaison with a Quartermaster of the US 25th Infantry Division would make life a little more comfortable for all concerned and give the Americans a taste for British rum!

---

1   O'Kane, *O'Kane's Korea*, Kenilworth, 1988.
2   http://www.bkva.co.uk/ulster_mem.htm.

The US Negro band welcomes 1 RUR to Pusan, October 1950. (Mervyn McCord)

Marching from the ship to the train, Pusan 1950. (Mervyn McCord)

A Company march to the train, Shaw-Stewart front left. (Mervyn McCord)

Close to midnight the train, one of five in a long convoy, steamed out of the station bound for Suwon, a journey of four to five days, if all went well. During the hours of darkness information was received from an American RTO[3] that a guerrilla ambush was expected as the troop train passed through a tunnel a few miles further on to the north.

Captain Robin Charley ordered his men to line the windows, weapons ready and facing outwards. Sir Christopher Nixon and another Rifles officer got to ride on the footplate of the engine, outwardly to prevent the engineers from deserting their post, but at the same time fulfilling a lifetime ambition to act as 'engine drivers'. A North Korean suspected of being an 'enemy' was arrested and tied to the top of the tender for the journey. The train passed through the tunnel without incident and was swiftly followed by the other four. During one of the frequent stops Pipe Major Woods had set up an oven on the platform and was attempting to cook some food for the men. In the middle of this the train whistle sounded and with a clatter the carriages began to slowly move along the platform. There was a mad scramble by the Pipe Major and his helpers ran alongside the train attempting to get all the equipment back on board before they ran out of platform – this happened on more than one occasion.

With the exception of the supposed ambush the remainder of the journey was quite boring and by 1000hrs on 7 November the Battalion detrained at Suwon and,

---

3   RTO – Road Transport Officer.

Suwon from Pusan. (Mervyn McCord)

headed by the Pipes and Drums, marched the half-mile to their new billets at the Suwon Agricultural School and Laboratory. This was a former silkworm factory that also went under the title Suwon Sericulture College. Here Battalion HQ and Headquarters Company were billeted in the factory, while the companies settled into the surrounding buildings. An advance party under the command of Major Tom Smith and his Colour Sergeants had made everything very comfortable, despite some local difficulties.

The following day at Pusan the Koreans laid on a civic reception complete with garlands of flowers, schoolchildren, apples and 'local belles'. However, the only members of the Regiment still in the port were Sergeant McConnell and the MT drivers, who had spent the night aboard, waiting for their vehicles to be unloaded from the SS *Stratidore* and getting as much rest as possible given the long hours and hazardous road conditions they were going to face. The *Stratidore* also carried the Battalion's six 17pdr anti-tank guns and 971 dwt of ammunition. The Battalion had almost one hundred vehicles available for transport, ranging from jeeps to the Bedford QLD, a general service cargo truck, more commonly known as the 'three tonner', due to its payload. Over 52,000 of these had been built from 1941-1945 and while a dependable vehicle it would find Korean roads heavy going. A number of motorcycles were also on the Battalion strength, but these proved totally unsuitable for the terrain and were left behind in Pusan. In order to assist in keeping the various vehicles in running order Sergeant Dixon of the REME was on attachment to the Rifles and would remain with them throughout their tour.

The majority of the Drivers within the MT Platoon were Z Reservists and proved to be capable of dealing with the many hazards offered by Korean roads.

Over the next few days the Battalion's heavy baggage and stores arrived and was distributed to the various companies. The SS *Statidore* carrying the Battalion vehicles had yet to dock at Pusan and this work was mostly carried out by manpower. To hurry things along a party under the command of Captain H.D. Miller and Lieutenant Alan Hill were dispatched to the port to bring the vehicles up immediately they arrived. This would also prevent other units 'borrowing' them. Of particular interest to Battalion Headquarters was a vehicle that had first appeared in front of the Orderly Room Block at Sobraon Barracks, Colchester, some time earlier.

This vehicle, described as a 'gin palace', was a Bedford QLD converted to a mobile office with folding table along each side and interior electric lights – the Adjutant was very proud. There were those who thought otherwise and attention was drawn to its height above ground and what a good target it would make. However, in Korea, it would be the lack of good roads that would prove its undoing and relegation to B Echelon. In times of emergency Battalion Headquarters would operate out of any location, including, on at least one occasion, a hole in the ground. At B Echelon Captain Tom Smith and his stalwarts provided a 'leave centre' for both the officers and men. Here all ranks could enjoy 48 hours rest in peace and comfort, with hot baths, clean clothing and good food. Tom Smith's well concealed friendship with the Quartermaster of the US 25th Infantry Division did a great deal to make life more comfortable for all concerned, although how the rum account was balanced has never been explained.

At Suwon, a fairly large town by Korean standards, the troops were put through their paces on the 'nursery slopes' of the nearby hills, and the time spent on board ship necessitated some brisk physical training to bring the Battalion back to the peak of fitness. The town had been badly damaged in the earlier fighting and the streets were strewn with knocked out Russian T34 tanks and other vehicles. The Main Supply Route ran through the town and by the roadside the wrecks had been bulldozed to the sides. Close to the town was an airfield and the roar of jet fighters taking off and landing was a near continuous sound.

Since the beginning of hostilities UN Forces had made rapid advances, mostly along the very few roads. Therefore, immense tracts of mountainous countryside remained to be swept for the enemy. It was known that many guerrilla bands had formed, were well armed and organised and were a constant threat to the lines of communication.

On 11 November the morning was spent unloading a supply train at Suwon station. At 1230hrs the Bugles sounded 'All Officers' across the town and from various locations and directions the officers were summoned to a briefing and informed of suspected enemy action to the north of Seoul. The Battalion was put on short notice to move out on anti-guerrilla operations. They were still waiting for their transport and many of the support weapons had yet to arrive. Nevertheless, at 2200hrs, Battalion Headquarters and four rifle companies set out in trucks supplied and driven by the men of 57 Company, Royal Army Service Corps.

Colonel Carson had gone ahead for a briefing from Headquarters Eighth Army and when the Battalion arrived in Seoul he in turn briefed them. The Battalion was tasked with establishing a firm base at the village of Uijongbu, situated about fifteen miles north east of Seoul. This village straddled the main railway line and road running north from

The Han River from the top. (Mervyn McCord)

Men of the 1st Battalion, The Royal Ulster Rifles present arms as Lieut-General Sir Horace Robertson leaves the former British Legation in Seoul. The Rifles had been granted the honour of providing the guard at the Legation. The guard seen here consists (from left) of Sergeant H. Campbell, Corporal J. O'Neill, both of Belfast; Lance Corporal K. Joyce of Glassdrummond; Rifleman J. Moore of Belfast; Lance Corporal M. Hickey of Limerick; Rifleman D. Glendon of Durham and Rifleman R. Stewart of Belfast. (*Belfast Telegraph*)

Suk Bum Yoon and two other porters, Uijonbu, November 1950. (Mervyn McCord/RUR Association)

Seoul towards Chorwon and Kumwha. Once in position the Battalion was to carry out aggressive patrolling in the area to deter any incursion from the roving guerrilla bands.

The journey from Seoul met with some difficulty. Just after midnight the convoy began to move across the Han River in weather that was described as horrifically cold. As the trucks reached the halfway point on the 300 foot long pontoon bridge that spanned the river it became marooned as an exceptionally high tide displaced the pontoons stranding the vehicles on a sandbank. It took two hours for the tide to go out and the bridge to settle down into its original position.

At 0200hrs on 12 November the convoy eventually arrived at Uijongbu, the men almost frozen from the long sit in the unheated vehicles. The view was hardly inspiring, a town in ruins lying in a north-facing mile-wide valley of flat and frozen paddy fields, walled in on the east and west by steep-sided and wood-covered mountains. Once they had dismounted they were placed into a defensive perimeter; no easy task when working from a map in pitch darkness on ground not previously reconnoitred. Lieutenant Robin Bruford-Davies and his No 11 Platoon were allotted the railway-bridge and by 0300hrs had managed to dig defensive positions. Shortly afterwards a group of Koreans were stopped and questioned, it being well after curfew. The Lieutenant had difficulty in deciding if the men were soldiers or police, or even if they were from the north or south. All were searched and passed back to Headquarters for further questioning.[4] B Company

---

4 *Newsletter of The Royal Ulster Rifles Officers' Club* 2003/2004, p.35.

First deployment, Uijonbu November 1950. RUR Command Post and Suk Bum Yoon in the foreground. (Mervyn McCord/RUR Association)

Men of the Royal Ulster Rifles with local Korean children at Uijongbu, Korea. Middle (left) Mark McConnell (right) Jim Rodgers. Back, R to L, Rifleman Riley, Brown. (Mark McConnell)

first met the enemy here, Lieutenant Gill and his No 6 Platoon met up with some 80 men of the North Korean Army who promptly surrendered without resistance.[5]

Later in the day there was the first issue of the Battalion News-Sheet *The Harp*, resurrected from the Second World War, along with much needed winter clothing. The winter in Korea shared one attribute with the summer, in that both were unbearable. A wind blew in from Manchuria that brought the temperature down to –15°C. On going to sleep it was advisable to keep one's head under the blankets and always wear a cap comforter. On waking it was not unusual to find that the blanket had frozen solid, especially where the moisture from breath had accumulated. It generally took between five and ten minutes to put on a pair of boots. Apart from the leather having frozen, each time the lace was inserted into the eyehole a minute was spent in thawing out frozen fingers. It was found that if you stuffed two sand bags with straw and then placed your feet inside it helped insulate your boots from the freezing ground. Vehicles had to have special oil and anti-freeze and to ensure they would start when required their engines were packed with straw. Added to this they were run on an hourly basis throughout the day and night. A supply of antifreeze captured from the enemy, of Russian manufacture, proved useless and froze almost immediately it was poured into vehicle radiators.[6] Considering the experience the Russians had in winter warfare this seems strange and it could be assumed that somewhere along the supply route the antifreeze had been diluted.

All weapons were treated with a special lubricant, but still many firing pins snapped with the cold and the oil froze. It proved more efficient to keep weapons almost dry. The Vickers machine-guns had their water jackets filled with anti-freeze to ensure that they could be brought into action immediately, while for the Bren guns a solution was found that involved constructing a small fireplace in each trench under where the gun usually rested, keeping the Bren clear of ice and providing a little warmth for the men.

The eating and cooking of rations also proved a problem. Attempts to fry eggs, when they were available, often resulted in the egg freezing between being cracked and hitting the pan, with the dreaded sound of a 'pong' as opposed to a sizzle frequently heard. If not careful eating utensils would freeze in the hand, tearing off strips of skin, and shaving was an absolute nightmare. It was eventually decided that shaving should be done at midday as this was the time of day that it was as warm as it was likely to get. While it was a point of both principle and pride to be clean-shaven each morning, a deliberate counterpoint to American forces, perhaps under these severe conditions an element of facial hair would have helped. The heating of liquids on the British-supplied cookers was a problem in that it almost one and a half hours to boil two pints of water in winter conditions. Battalion Headquarters received a plum cake from one of the various comfort funds; an axe was required to slice it. Beer would often freeze in the bottle or when being poured into the mug or glass leaving crispy foam on top that could be eaten. Men who crouched in their trench to sleep froze into that position and had to be forcibly straightened out when they awoke. However, casualties from 'cold exhaustion' were few in the Battalion and in almost every case these were reinforcements sent out from Japan.

B Company again made contact with the enemy and captured a group of twelve armed North Koreans, although to describe them as 'armed' was somewhat of an overstatement. Between them they had one Russian-manufactured rifle, a few rounds

---

5 *Quis Separabit*, 1951, p.27.
6 Barclay, *The First Commonwealth Division*, Aldershot, 1954.

A Battalion jeep sporting the Divisional sign on the windscreen. (Mervyn McCord/RUR Association)

of ammunition and two hand grenades. By 1000hrs a total of 129 North Koreans had been taken, these men, although armed, proved to be friendly and after stacking their arms at Battalion Headquarters, were kept under observation while advice was sought as to what to do with them.

The following day all platoons improved their positions where possible. Windproof smocks were delivered, which did little to protect the men from the biting cold wind. Makeshift windbreaks were constructed from brushwood and these helped, but it was still terribly cold and sleep was almost impossible.

During the day an order was received from Major Lawson, US Army KMAG (Korean Military Advisory Group) that the group of 129 men taken the previous day were to be rearmed and released provided they left the area.[7] Apparently it had been ascertained that they belonged to something called the 'Korean Youth Organisation' and were to be considered allies. The phrase 'not to be trusted as far as they could be thrown' was muttered by some of those present.

Lieutenant Bruford-Davies recalled that on 14 November the Battalion received its first issue of American field rations (K Rations). While some of the food was tasty, too spicy for some, they made a change from 'bully' beef. However, there was one vital ingredient missing, tea! Nevertheless, there was twelve degrees of frost that night, and the freezing weather proved 'good sauce' when it came to a variation of diet and soon

---

7   Translated by American troops as "Kiss My Ass Goodbye" – Halberstam, *The Coldest Winter*, Oxford, 2008.

steaming mugs of coffee were being brewed at any given opportunity. A hot drink was good for morale, but nothing lifted men's spirits like receiving letters from home.[8]

Brigadier Brodie, along with Lieutenant General Sir Horace Robertson, Commander Commonwealth Forces in Korea, came to visit the Battalion and made several speeches to both officers and men. Everyone felt much better when they departed at 1530hrs. That night the wind dropped a little, but there was still twelve degrees of frost.

An intelligence report was received on the morning of 16 November from the South Korean police that a village near Kapyong, some twenty miles to the north east of Uijongbu, was under threat from a force of some 150 armed guerrillas. Captain R. Sinclair MC, the RUR Liaison Officer with 29 Brigade, arrived from Eusak with orders for a patrol to go to Kapyong and investigate. This patrol consisted of Major Gaffikin's D Company along with the Intelligence Section. Artillery support was provided by 116 Battery RA, who also sent out two relay stations to ensure no loss of wireless communication.

Major Gaffikin had commanded D Company from the beginning of the war, he along with his CSM Andrew McConville and CQMS Byrne, were veterans of the Second World War; in fact, Gaffikin and McConville had been together since the campaign in France in 1940. The grandiosely named 'Gaffcol' left camp in trucks supplied by 57 Company, Royal Army Service Corps. Sleet began to fall and under dark cloudy skies the column proceeded towards the objective.

They returned at 2130hrs to report that a group of enemy soldiers numbering 100-150 men had been observed around Kapyong and were moving in the direction of Seoul. Their intention appeared to be to attack Kapyong and the viaduct at Kuam-Ni. No contact was made with the enemy. On returning to camp the truck carrying Lieutenant Bruford-Davies and his platoon was slowly making its way along a narrow dirt track. Suddenly the vehicle skidded on a patch of ice and tumbled into the ditch ending up on its roof. Bruford-Davies and the driver were covered in hot engine oil, but otherwise unharmed. In the back of the truck Riflemen, Cooper, Stewart, Horribin, Street and McCullough, were injured. All five men were taken to the Military Hospital in Seoul, but only Cooper was detained.

At dawn patrols were sent out to all villages within a ten-mile radius. Information gleaned from South Korean police and the villagers, while not 100% accurate, indicated that the groups of guerrillas were moving south towards Seoul. The patrol commanded by Lieutenant Nichols, No 7 Platoon C Company, arrived back at base at 2110hrs, having gone beyond the patrol objectives.

During the day elements of Support Company had arrived at the base, these included the 3" mortars and Vickers machine-guns. The anti-tank guns were due to arrive later. After a night of torrential rain the sun came out and the men were able to dry both uniforms and equipment. The Royal Engineers repaired the Railway Bridge being guarded by No 11 Platoon and there was the opportunity to build shacks for shelter.

---

8 Mail was usually flown out from the United Kingdom three times a week and took approximately six days to arrive from posting, although this was subject to weather conditions. Newspapers, packages and parcels were sent by sea and these took up to six weeks. In both cases the times quoted are for delivery to Korea, to the front line could take a lot longer. Men serving with the Commonwealth Brigades were issued with buff-coloured envelopes which were posted free, while they could also send letters air mail at a concessionary rate of 3d. From home families could also post letters by airmail for 6d, if the envelope was marked 'On Active Service'.

Rifleman P. Dolan in the area of Uijongbu, just north of the capital city of Seoul. (RUR Museum)

It was later discovered that the guerrillas, who had waited for D Company to depart, burned the village of Kapyong.

At 1930hrs the next day, 20 November, the sound of small arms fire was heard from the hills to the south; it lasted for about thirty minutes. Later patrols from A and B Companies found North Korean dead in the assumed position of the firing. The weather had turned very cold. The dawn patrols returned to base with nothing to report and at 1030hrs Colonel Carson sent out a fighting patrol consisting of C Company – no contact was made with the enemy, nor could it be ascertained who had killed the North Koreans. Robin Charley recalled that on patrols the commander and sergeant major moved at the rear so that in the event of coming into contact the commander was best placed to oversee the disposition of his men.

Two days later the Battalion was ordered into Munsan-Ni to defend the road and rail bridges across the Imjin against guerrilla attack. C Company went in first, supported by the Mortar and Machine Gun Platoons. The digging of weapon pits and trenches proved to be backbreaking with the ground rock hard from the severe frost. The stunted fir trees and coarse brown scrub offering nothing in the away of shelter. The following day the remainder of the Battalion, less D Company, were ferried across the river.

The Battalion deployed A Company in the area of the railway bridge, C Company was located at the pontoon bridge, which carried the main road, while the remainder of the Battalion, less D Company, moved into Musan-Ni itself. D Company remained in Uijongbu to maintain a secure base and prevent a repetition of Kapyong. There was an unfortunate incident when a South Korean policeman negligently fired his carbine and

A Royal Ulster Rifles position observing Korean 'traffic' – carts pulled by oxen. (RUR Museum)

Leaving Uijongbu for the long journey to Pyongyang. RUR trucks 78RC52 and 19RB77 beside factory shed. The tyres of the trucks have been fitted with snow chains. (Mervyn McCord/RUR Association)

Defence Platoon, HQ Company, digging-in at Sinujui, about 80 miles south of the Yalu River (in picture are Corporal McKeown and Rifleman Galway). (RUR Museum)

hit Rifleman O'Keefe in the legs. O'Keefe was immediately taken to hospital, while the unfortunate policeman was summarily dealt with by the Military Police attached to the Battalion. Three days later D Company lost another man when Rifleman Mainwaring accidentally shot himself in the knee.

Artillery support was provided by the 25pdrs of 176 Battery, 45 Field Regiment RA, which was now part of the Brigade, as 116 Battery had moved off for pastures new. Major Archie Braithwaite of 176 Battery advised the men of the Battalion on how to make the best use of the winter clothing, which had at last been issued. A string vest, quite a novelty, was worn next to the skin, which was covered by heavy woollen underwear. Battle dress trousers were worn, but not the blouse, which was found to be too constricting, instead the 'jersey heavy wool' was substituted. On the feet were worn oiled wool socks and frost proof ski type boots known as KP Boots, rumoured to have initially been destined for use by the 'Archangel Expedition' of 1919. They only lasted a short while as the rubber soles, which had perished with age, eventually fell off. The Battalion had two men of the ACC suffer from frostbitten toes and they had to be evacuated to Japan. Over all this was worn a loose windproof suit. This was of a light very closely woven camouflaged material. The trousers were tied close at the ankles and waist by cords: the jacket was similarly pulled tight at the hips, buttoned close at the wrists, and had a hood, the rim of which could be drawn tight round the face. It was, in fact, windproof and, if worn properly, kept one fairly warm in the sub-zero temperatures now prevalent. But, as it later proved, it was not rain and snow proof and was only really effective in dry cold. Major Braithwaite was also the first man to adopt the local form of winter head dress, a fur-lined dog skin cap, complete with peak and ear flaps. These soon became very popular within the Battalion, until replaced by an American ski cap with similar attributes. Despite his headgear Major Braithwaite became the first man to be evacuated from the Brigade suffering from frostbite. He was soon followed by several of the Reservists and Colonel Carson decreed that those remaining with the Battalion should be found positions that were not as exposed to the weather, possibly in the rear echelons. However, these transfers could only take place if volunteers were found to take their places in the rifle companies. One such volunteer was Henry O'Kane, a former Royal Inniskilling Fusilier from Londonderry who served in C Company.

As late as 24 November General MacArthur launched his 'Home for Christmas' offensive which resulted in the Allies reaching as far as the Yalu River, apparently oblivious to the fact that approximately two hundred thousand Red Chinese troops were in Korea deploying for a massive counter-offensive.[9]

---

9   Cunningham, *No Mercy, No Leniency*, London, 2000.

5

Advance and withdrawal

This counter-offensive began the following day when Chinese and North Korean troops launched a massive attack against the United Nations positions. This surprise attack had been possible due to the fact that the Chinese Army was a relatively low technology force. There were few radios, which meant there was little monitoring to be done by UN Intelligence and the Chinese sent most of their messages by runner, many of whom were horse mounted. Supplies for the front line troops were brought forward by long columns of porters moving on foot, therefore no evidence to tyre tracks could be seen from air reconnaissance, a bullock cart could just as easily have belonged to a farmer carrying his produce to market as opposed to carrying ammunition for a mortar platoon.

On 27 November the Dingo scout car of the Signals Platoon crashed and Lance Corporal Cruickshank was killed, the first death to the Battalion in Korea. He was buried in the United Nations Cemetery at Kaesong the following day. Captain Miller arrived from Pusan with the remainder of the Battalion's vehicles, including the Oxford Carriers and 17pdr anti-tank guns. Orders were received for the remainder of the Battalion to move north by train to Pyongyang, the North Korean capital. This involved frantic packing by all concerned. The Battalion was loaded into goods wagons in weather that was cold with deep thick snow. As the Battalion was then to go further north to

A recce of Seoul, December 1950. (Mervyn McCord)

Battle patrol, December 1950.(Mervyn McCord)

The Commanders of the two original brigade groups of the 1st Commonwealth Division. Left, Brigadier T. Brodie, 29th British Infantry Brigade; right, Brigadier B.A. Coad, 27th Commonwealth Infantry Brigade. (Public Relations, Headquarters, BCOF)

ADVANCE AND WITHDRAWAL 75

Pyongyang, November 1950. (RUR Association)

a town called Anju it was felt prudent to send an advance party. This was composed of Major Blake, Captain Hinde and Lieutenant Pigot, each travelling in a separate jeep with a driver.

The main body of the Army was still heading fast for the Manchurian border and in fact one regiment had already reached the banks of the Yalu River in the central sector by 28 November. The 27th Brigade, under the command of the US 187th Airborne Regimental Combat Team, was moving up the main west coast route with all speed and had already passed through Sinanju, about sixty or seventy miles south of the border. Brigadier Brodie was champing at the bit lest the 29th Brigade should not be in at the kill and he was not alone in this; consequently, the order to move, which was received on 28 November, came as no surprise.

At about 2200 hours the train carrying the Battalion steamed north on the way to Pyongyang, the North Korean capital. Support Company and the MT column moved by road the same night and it is doubtful whether they in their 180 mile drive in the bitter cold over villainous roads, or the remainder of the Battalion in their unlighted and unheated cattle trucks, had the more arduous journey. The original order had been for the Battalion to move to Anju, about sixty miles north of Pyongyang. On arrival at Pyongyang, where a road detour was necessary owing to the destruction by the enemy of the rail bridges over the Taedong River, a Liaison Officer met the Battalion and Colonel Carson was ordered to move by road to Yongyu, about halfway between Pyongyang and Anju, where the 29th Brigade, until then scattered over South Korea, was assembling in reserve to the US 1st Corps.

At Yongyu, as the men were debussing from the troop carriers there were two accidents, one fatal and both involving the Sten gun. Corporal Gibson of D Company had just jumped down from the truck when his Sten gun discharged and he was fatally wounded. It is believed that the butt of his weapon hit the ground. This caused the breech block to move backwards cocking the weapon, and as it came forward it chambered a round and fired. Later as the Battalion settled down between rows of parked vehicles Corporal Johnston accidentally shot himself with his Sten gun, a not infrequent occurrence with this weapon. In all cases where a unit goes to war, the first deaths are usually the result of an accident. In this case these were no doubt exacerbated by exhaustion and cold.

Arriving at the railway bridge at Taedong on 29 November, it was found to have been demolished and the Battalion had to proceed north by road. Just prior to this the Indian Field Ambulance, recently arrived in Korea and now attached to the 27th Brigade, had managed to stop the American troops from burning a US Medical Train that was stuck in Pyongyang. Having borrowed a steam engine the Indians coupled it to the carriages and managed to bring it south just before the bridge was blown up.

It was about 1600hrs and in the gathering dusk outside the station a column of lorries from 57 Company RASC and American troop carrying vehicles was waiting. These Americans were the 'Wags Truckers', a black unit, so called after their commanding officer, Captain Wagner, a man huge in both build and personality. The Battalion just had time for a quick hot meal before transferring to the trucks and moving off in the darkness through the battered city and across the remaining Taedong Bridge. This last part of the journey was no less exhausting than the earlier stages. The night was once again bitterly cold and, as the trucks ground their way north, they were continually slowed or halted by the increasing volume of southbound traffic. It was beginning to be apparent that the Battalion, and behind it the rest of the 29th Brigade, were going north alone, for it seemed that the whole Army and hordes of refugees were moving southward as fast as they could go. This, in fact, was the truth. The United Nations forces, operating under a divided command, had been met, checked, and split apart by the Chinese counteroffensive. Both the British 27th Brigade and the Turkish Brigade were fighting a desperate rearguard action in the Chongchon river area, while the remainder of US 1st and US 9th Corps was in full retreat, having suffered severe losses.

The complete picture of what was happening was not revealed to the Battalion until about midnight when Colonel Carson was briefed by Major Eastwood, DAA and QMG of 29 Brigade. Eastwood suggested that in view of the changing situation it might be best to harbour for the remainder of the night at a position a few miles further north. Here a Platoon of 57 Company, RASC had leaguered in a field to the side of the road. With no opportunity to reconnoitre their own harbour area Carson agreed and soon the Battalion had virtually formed a square around the parked vehicles.

At dawn on 30 November the Colonel departed for Brigade Headquarters for fresh orders, while the Rifles slowly thawed out in the morning sun. By mid-morning the MT column had arrived and the Battalion was now complete, with the exception of a small party under Major Blake, Captain Hinde and Lieutenant Pigot. This group had gone ahead to carry out a reconnaissance of a harbour area in the vicinity of Anju, which had been the Battalion's original destination.

On learning the truth of what was happening, Major Blake and his party made all haste back to the Battalion, having achieved the distinction of being closer to the Manchurian border than any other unit in 29 Brigade. At noon Colonel Carson returned to the Battalion and almost immediately the Rifles, along with the Glosters and 8th Hussars, was again on the road moving north against the stream of traffic pouring south. The new orders for 29 Brigade were to take up a blocking position across the main road at Sukchon, about twenty miles south of Anju. While the Brigade was in transit the situation changed again and the Brigade was sent to where the main road crossed a wood-covered ridge at Chai-Ri, ten miles south of Sukchon. As luck would have it the road actually passed through the centre of the Battalion position and the headlong nature of the retreat was all too obvious. Through the hours of daylight and darkness a constant stream of vehicles, tanks, troops and refugees passed southwards, creating a thick pall of dust. The Northumberland Fusiliers, last to arrive in the Brigade position, was the first to meet the enemy. In the early hours of the morning they had been attacked by what was described as 'weak regiment' of North Korean guerrillas at Sibyon-Ri, situated about half way between Seoul and Pyongyang. Fortunately the Fusiliers were behind good defensive positions and casualties were light.

Accurate intelligence of enemy activity was hard to come by and it was only as the traffic thinned and small groups of Turkish troops marched by on foot and plainly battle stained, that there was any indication that action would be imminent.

Early in December the Chinese Red Army had smashed through the Allied lines and fanned out on either side to cut off any chance of retreat. In the north-west the Allied forces were hastily withdrawn intact whilst in the north-east the evacuation through the port of Hungman was not as smooth.[1]

On 2 December the order for 29 Brigade to join in the general retreat came and the Battalion joined the column making its way south. Reconnaissance parties led the way, guiding the Battalion around stalled vehicles and other obstacles. While vehicles within the Battalion had their share of breakdowns, it was a credit to the drivers that none were abandoned for this reason.

As the Battalion arrived they could see that the town of Pyongyang was burning and the roar of exploding ammunition dumps could be heard as these were destroyed; nothing was to be left that would be of any use to the Chinese. After an extremely cold night with snow squalls and driving hail the Battalion took up positions along a line of hills about three miles north of the town. This position dominated the approaches to the North Korean capital and the Battalion, along with the remainder of the Brigade, was tasked with covering the withdrawal of the UN Forces from the town. While the Battalion dug defensive positions on the hills just outside the town, the Glosters deployed around the Taedong Bridges. The Battalion's 17pdrs were positioned at the main road junction and had a clear field of fire towards any oncoming armour.

A daily routine had evolved and all ranks could now be 'on parade' by 0915hrs, having breakfasted and washed, with shaving still being carried out at midday. During the day liaison was made with the various units that were due to pass through the town and an attempt was made to ascertain just which would be the last unit to withdraw. The Brigade had the support of 170 Mortar Battery with their 4.2" mortars, along with 176 Battery and their eight ever-dependable 25pdrs. Additionally a troop of the new Centurion tanks made an appearance courtesy of the 8th King's Royal Irish Hussars. This was to be the first major battlefield outing for the new tank and its 20pdr gun.

---

1   Cunningham, *No Mercy, No Leniency*, London, 2000.

78 A NEW BATTLEFIELD

The 29th British Brigade retreat from Pyongyang (Henry O'Kane)

On 4 December the Battalion made its first contact with the 27th Brigade, the 'Woolworth's Brigade', so named due to their heavy reliance on American forces for most of their needs. A member of the Middlesex Regiment summed up the meeting succinctly:

> Well, here they were at last, caught up in the same stupendous mess-up as ourselves. We were delighted to see them and they gave us a glorious welcome as we passed through them. Pretty well every basic sentiment and rugged epithets were joyfully hurled from one side to the other. The colourful texture of the soldier's vocabulary could not have been better displayed. Englishmen are not as a rule so communicative to each other when they meet in foreign countries. Doctor Livingstone would have been badly shaken. The 29th Brigade looked very smart and business like. They must have appeared a strange contrast to us in our worn and dusty motley of American and British winter clothing.[2]

As the vehicles carrying the troops of the Brigade passed the Battalion's positions heading south, the Rifles passed them handfuls of sweets, chocolate, cigarettes and spare items of clothing that had been recovered from the supply dumps in Pyongyang. These had been prepared for destruction by the US troops, but canny Riflemen had liberated supplies prior to the explosions. Captain Robin Charley drove into the town in one of the Battalion jeeps and arrived at an American supply dump. Here he borrowed a trailer and proceeded to fill both it and the jeep with supplies. Despite the chaos of the retreat the Quartermaster insisted on the items being signed for and handed Captain

---

2 Shipster, *The Die-Hards in Korea*, n.p., 1975.

1 RUR 17pdr anti-tank guns at Pyongyang, November 1950. (Mervyn McCord)

Charley the required paperwork.³ This was duly signed with the name Mickey Mouse and followed by a swift departure. As this was going on some Rifleman had taken one of the Battalion's water bowsers to a local brewery and filled it with beer. All ranks, where possible, made use of abandoned American clothing and boots. Sergeant Campbell of the Anti-Tank Platoon went into Pyongyang and discovered an American 'deuce and a half' loaded with food, including turkeys. This vehicle was brought back and Second Lieutenant McCord immediately placed a guard on it. This cache was going to provide Christmas dinner for the Battalion! It was on this date that Lieutenant Beckett was reported missing from B Echelon as of 1530hrs; he would eventually turn up on 23 December.

At 0200hrs on 5 December, 29 Brigade left its positions and moved south across the river. As the Mortar Platoon waited at the bridge Captain James Majury, the Platoon Commander, was aggrieved at the amount of noise made by the Centurion tanks as they clattered over the river. Marching alongside the tanks was a column of ROK infantry. The track of one tank accidentally caught a marching infantryman and crushed his legs beneath the tracks. At once the vehicle stopped and the commander jumped down to help the injured man. Before he could do anything the ROK officer snatched the pistol out of the commander's holster and shot the injured man through the head. Nothing was going to delay the retreat as far as the South Koreans were concerned.⁴

Major Gaffikin's D Company had been in reserve close to Battalion Headquarters and had scattered detachments out guarding bridges and supply dumps. His No 12 Platoon was the last unit of the Rifles to leave, covering the withdrawal of Battalion Headquarters across the sole remaining bridge. It was discovered that one of the Centurions had broken down and could not be moved. No 12 Platoon was tasked with providing a guard on this vehicle until a piece of secret equipment could be removed.

---

3   The Battalion also received assistance from home, courtesy of Mrs Charley and her Ladies Committee, who supplied all sorts of comforts for the men, including food and clothing.
4   Hastings, *The Korean War*, London, 1987.

This was the gun stabiliser, which allowed the Centurion to fire accurately while on the move and under no circumstances could it be allowed to fall into Communist hands. It took a long time to locate an engineer, but once the stabiliser was safely removed the Platoon was able to withdraw. The Centurion was then destroyed with a demolition charge. Once they were clear the men of the Platoon mounted the Centurion tanks and spent the next sixty miles squatting on the engine deck covers attempting to keep warm in the bitter cold. The only casualty of the withdrawal was Rifleman Davis of C Company, who was wounded in the leg when an aircraft of unknown origin strafed the column. These were the only shots fired on either side during the withdrawal, contrary to the many extravagant reports that appeared in the British press. One man was almost left behind. Rifleman McAlonan, a signaller in Headquarters Company equipped with a No 62 set, had watched as the entire Battalion passed through and waited in vain for someone to return to pick him up. It was an alert tank commander that spotted the signaller taking shelter under a bridge. In a few moments McAlonan and his wireless set were sitting on the engine decking of the Centurion as it continued on its way south.

It was here that Colonel Carson decided that the 17pdrs were too cumbersome for the battlefield and these were ordered back to base. This event in turn led to a superb innovation within the Battalion. The Anti-Tank Platoon was abolished and combined with the Assault Pioneer Platoon to create the newly-formed Battle Patrol. Command went to Captain Cocksedge MC and he quickly created an aura of incomparability within the eighty ranks that made up the Patrol. The Patrol was mounted in the Oxford Carriers, these being no longer required to pull the 17pdr guns. The guns were returned to base along with the Battalion's surplus kit. All in all the Oxford was an ideal vehicle for such work, with good road and cross-country speed and the armour would deflect normal small arms fire and was capable of carrying ten fully armed men. American .30 calibre machine-guns were acquired from the Americans and these were mounted on the vehicles. The members of the 'Battle Patrol' soon coined the motto 'Go anywhere and do anything'. Henry O'Kane saw them move out on their first patrol and considered that the Administration Staff must have handpicked every hard drinking, hard fisted troublemaker in the Battalion and the sooner they all got killed the better it would be! However, most of the men were volunteers and thrived in their new environment and proved themselves to be one of "best compact fighting units in the 29th Brigade, if not in all Korea."[5]

On 8 December a further move was made to the south close to Kaesong, C Company was situated about twelve miles from the remainder of the Battalion, at a village called Tangyong-ni. The Battle Patrol carried out a sweep of the area and discovered a large number of dead bodies, all of whom had been shot. Major Blake carried out an investigation and a report was sent to Divisional Headquarters. Later Lieutenant Alan Hill was travelling between C Company at Tangyoung-ni and the Battalion when his vehicle was sniped from the high ground. It was during this move that Sergeant Bill McConnell came across six American vehicles lying abandoned by the roadside, all were out of fuel. These were the famous GMC 'deuce and a half' trucks, a superb vehicle officially rated to carry 5,000lbs cross country and 10,000lbs on roads, but were more than capable of carrying twice that weight. As such they were an absolute treasure and

---

5 O'Kane, *O'Kane's Korea*, Kenilworth, 1988.

Lady Mountbatten with Lieutenant-Colonel A.G. Rangaraj (Officer Commanding, 60th Indian Field Ambulance) standing near a type of American helicopter in common use in Korea. (Public Relations, Headquarters, BCOF)

Bill McConnell soon had them refuelled and brought into his convoy, the fact that one was loaded with K Rations and another with 50 gallon drums of petrol was an added bonus. One truck was then allocated to each company to help with resupply.[6]

The following day a cold wind brought four first line reinforcements and what was described as two "useless Gooks".[7] As a result of the sniping at Lieutenant Hill's vehicle the previous day a sweep was carried out by the Battle Patrol and during a search of Onjong-Ni village some weapons and hand grenades were recovered. What was more important was the discovery that in the centre of the village was a natural hot spring. This proved to be a great asset and for the next two days the entire Battalion availed themselves of a welcome bath. The following day Lieutenant Bruford-Davies and his Platoon were the first to enjoy a bath in a hot sulphur spring at Onjong-Ni, so hot that it was a matter of in and out with the utmost speed. The Battalion remained at the village preparing defences and carrying out patrolling along the road and tracks to the west.

It was at Onjong-Ni that Lieutenant Ted Pigot, the Assistant Adjutant, was almost killed. On searching a deserted Communist Headquarters he found a large steel safe, which he suspected might contains papers of use to the Intelligence Officer. The safe was then carried to Battalion Headquarters and prepared for opening using plastic explosive. While in the process of doing this it was tactfully suggested that the actual opening be carried out some distance away from the Command Post. This was done and after

---

6 Interview with Bill McConnell.
7 Anon. [Hamill], *The Royal Ulster Rifles in Korea*, Belfast, 1953.

lighting the fuse the Lieutenant stood some distance away. The resulting explosion was so great that pieces of the safe were blown over a hundred yards away. Examination of the remains of the safe revealed that the contents had been about fifty pounds of high explosive.

On the evening of 11 December the Battalion left Onjong-Ni, crossing the 38th Parallel and heading south for Changdon, on the north bank of the Imjin River. Here they were placed in a rest area and there was no requirement for the digging of slit trenches. All ranks got a good night's sleep. During the halt in Changdon there was much talk in the ranks with regard to the danger of 'piles' caused by sitting on cold surfaces. The War Diary reported that Rifleman Gales was wounded, but gave no details.

6

Happy Valley

On 14 December, the Brigade stopped at a dried up riverbed some eight miles north of Seoul and close to the village of Chaegunghyon, which would soon be more commonly known as Happy Valley. Here it was to act as a reserve to the US 1st Corps. The area occupied by the Battalion was named 'Compo Canyon', apparently coined by a member of No 4 Platoon B Company.[1] At first sight this was not an inspiring image. There was a driving snowstorm in progress and it was bitterly cold. The following morning not much had changed, except that now the area was wreathed in a thick fog. The Battalion was placed well to the rear of the Brigade and it was not necessary to have 'stand to'. The Rifles were ordered to carry out a reconnaissance of positions north of Seoul and as result of this the Riflemen found themselves occupying a precipitous location that quickly became known as 'Wuthering Heights', obviously conjured up by someone with a literary bent. Support Company and the Battle Patrol were ordered to carry out a reconnaissance of Seoul, which was practically deserted, although the patrol proved to be both interesting and enjoyable. It was discovered that the Americans had taken over the Chosin Hotel and converted it into an 'Officers Club' and great advantage was taken of this facility during the remainder of the Battalion's time in Compo Canyon. The rain turned to snow during the night of 16 December and continued until 1500hrs. In D Company Captain John ffrench brewed a punch from whiskey, honey and water, while the temperature fell to 0°F.

The withdrawal of the Eighth Army had completely outdistanced the Chinese advance, which had not been contested in any way over a distance of 150 miles. It was then decided that a stand should be made on the Imjin and at once the 1st ROK Division and the US 25th Division, who had already met the enemy at Chongchon, set to preparing a defence line on the southern bank of the river. Between 14 December and the New Year the Chinese gradually closed with the UN defences and there was preliminary skirmishing.

During the general retreat, often hampered by up to three million refugees, British troops had witnessed mass executions by the nervous ROK troops enforcing their government's violent campaign against alleged traitors and spies. The officers and men of the Royal Ulster Rifles were shocked at the execution of men, women and children and protested to the United Nations representatives who in turn made representations of the South Korean President Syngamn Rhee, who gave the assurance that in future victims would be shot individually; and this was the regime the Rifles were here to defend.[2]

From now until the end of the year the Battalion had a reasonably quiet time. On 19 December Brigadier Brodie paid a visit, giving what up-to-date information he had to Colonel Carson, while the most important task for No 1 Platoon was the gathering of firewood. The following day was again quiet and a singsong was held in D Company that

---

1 Known as 'Compo Valley' to other battalions.
2 Cunningham, *No Mercy, No Leniency*, London, 2000.

Stores in Compo Canyon, Happy Valley, Christmas 1950. (Mervyn McCord/RUR Association)

The famous 'Gin Place', also known as Battalion Headquarters, Happy Valley, Christmas 1950. (RUR Museum)

Battalion Headquarters. (RUR Museum)

(Back row) Sergeant Walker and Rifleman Horrabin, (front row) Rifleman Washer, Mrs O, O's mother and Mr O, who helped with platoon chores. (*Quis Separabit*)

RUR Coy positions at Chaegunghyon looking north from 'Cooperforce'. (RUR Association)

86 A NEW BATTLEFIELD

Captain A.B. 'Beetle' Williams with Colonel Carson, Captain Hamill and Major Blake. (Mervyn McCord/RUR Association)

Lieutenant McCallan, Captain Hamill and Colonel Carson at Compo Canyon. (Mervyn McCord/RUR Association)

Happy Valley, where 1 RUR spent Christmas 1950.(Mervyn McCord)

Major de Longueuil in dog skin cap with Captains Hinde
and Hamill in Happy Valley. (RUR Museum)

evening. In No 11 Platoon an inordinate amount of drunkenness was noticed. It was later discovered that the rum ration had been liberated from the Company Quartermaster's tent and added to the beer.

On 23 December an exercise was carried out with the tanks of the Hussars. Radio communication was very good and all went well. All ranks received lots of Christmas mail and Rifleman Westwood was especially happy as he was due to go home the following day. This day also saw the death of General Walton Walker, commander-in-chief of the US Eighth Army. Walker had served as a Corps Commander under General Patton in the North-West Europe campaign in the Second World War and had been rated as brave, but not particularly imaginative. He had done very well in the defence of the Pusan perimeter, but by this time was suffering from sheer exhaustion.[3] He was fatally injured in a road accident, when his jeep was in collision with an army truck travelling in the opposite direction.

On Christmas Eve a carol party was led around the camp by Padre Kelly and seemed to be enjoyed by all, despite engendering some serious bouts of homesickness among the younger members of the Battalion.

Christmas Day and all buglers sounded reveille as the Battalion assembled for its various church services. Just before lunch 'Father Christmas' arrived on a homemade sledge towed by a Bren Carrier. At lunchtime Colonel Carson was piped around the various messes by Pipe Major Woods and found no complaints. Throughout the day there were television cameras in the Battalion area recording the various events. Previously Major Gaffikin, a Bugler and three Riflemen recorded an interview to be shown at home

3 Hastings, *The Korean War*, London 1987.

Pipe Major 'Lakari' Woods speaking with a senior officer. (RUR Museum)

on Christmas Day. For Sergeant Bill McConnell this day brought a major problem, but one that was solved by alcohol! The gearbox of one of the American trucks had seized and a repair was needed urgently. This involved towing the damaged truck to the nearest American camp and as most of the Riflemen were wearing 'borrowed' American clothing they were able to drive in after a courtesy challenge. It was then a matter of finding the Motor Pool and asking for a new gearbox to be fitted, which cost one bottle of Black Bush. This day was also Second Lieutenant McCord's 21st Birthday and he celebrated it in a riverbed with some of his closest subaltern friends and a hamper from Fortnum and Mason, supplied by Houston Shaw-Stewart.

By 26 December the battle front had been re-established along the 38th Parallel and plans were made to the defend Seoul with the Royal Ulster Rifles among the defenders.[4] With the holiday now over the Battalion began to prepare lay back positions for the 1st ROK Division midway between the Imjin and the Han. These were situated some 1,000 yards ahead of 'Compo Canyon' and were dug by civilian labour supervised by members of the Battalion. While this was going on the remainder of the Riflemen continued working on a defence position known as 'Wuthering Heights'. It seemed that the high command was doing little else but make preparations for further withdrawals and there was little effort being made to instil into the troops within the Corps a will to stand and fight. On 31 December advance elements of the enemy crossed the Imjin River at Korangpo-Ri and established a bridgehead, from which they swiftly broke out.

4   Cunningham, *No Mercy, No Leniency*, London, 2000.

Order of the Day

At last after weeks of frustration we have nothing between us and the Chinese. I have no intention that this Brigade Group will retire before the enemy unless ordered by higher authority in order to conform with general movement. If you meet him you are to knock hell out of him with everything you have got. You are only to give ground on my orders.

T. Brodie

Brigadier

(29 Brigade War Diary, 1 January 1951)

The Chinese believed that the Imperialists would 'run like sheep' and with the time quickly approaching the Chinese assault infantry, many of them veterans of the war against the Japanese, smeared warmed-up lard on their feet and legs before starting to wade across the near frozen Imjin River to the north of the allied lines. On 1 January 1951, as wave after wave of infantry moved forward, the Chinese gunners prepared for their first mass artillery bombardment scheduled to start once the initial assault wave was in position. The forty mile front they lined up against was being held by three American Brigades, the British 29th Brigade, two ROK Divisions and a Brigade-strength group of Greek and Filipino troops. At zero hour the sky was lit up by flares, while bugles, whistles and orders to charge echoed along Chinese the lines.[5]

The New Year saw an end to the relative peace of the last few days. At 0330hrs, a warning order was received by the Battalion to the effect that they, along with the remainder of the Brigade, was to prepare to launch a counter-attack in the sector held by 1 ROK Division.

As the news of the North Korean attack came in Colonel Carson was confined to bed, having suffered from ill health for the last few days. Major Blake took command of the Battalion and at an 'O' Group he issued the relevant orders and all available intelligence. Colonel Carson had recovered enough to resume command by mid-morning.

At 1030hrs, the Battalion in concert with the remainder of the Brigade left 'Compo Canyon' and proceeded up the MSR (Main Supply Route), their intention to launch a counter-attack against the enemy when and where they were found. It was discovered that the 1st ROK Division had practically ceased to exist, those surviving soldiers having been scattered and almost all equipment lost. The North Koreans had in turn disappeared into the surrounding hills. Brigadier Brodie considered chasing the enemy through the hills, but quickly altered his plan and the Brigade was ordered to occupy the former ROK positions. For a Brigade to hold a line formerly held by a Division meant that the troops were thin on the ground and the Rifles found themselves holding a front of two miles. The village of Chaegunhhyon was situated in the centre of the line, while the Battalion's right flank rested on a rugged mountain known as Nogo San, some 440 metres high. B and D Companies were allocated the high ground to the west of the valley, while A and C Companies were slightly forward and to the east. Battalion Headquarters and A Echelon were position in and around the mouth of a short railway tunnel, with the Battle Patrol holding a small saddle just to the east of the tunnel. In support of the Battle Patrol were three troops of tanks, this was 'Cooperforce', consisting of a composite unit of Churchill and Cromwell tanks from the Reconnaissance Troop

---

5 Farrar-Hockley, *The British Part in the Korean War Volume II*, London, 1995.

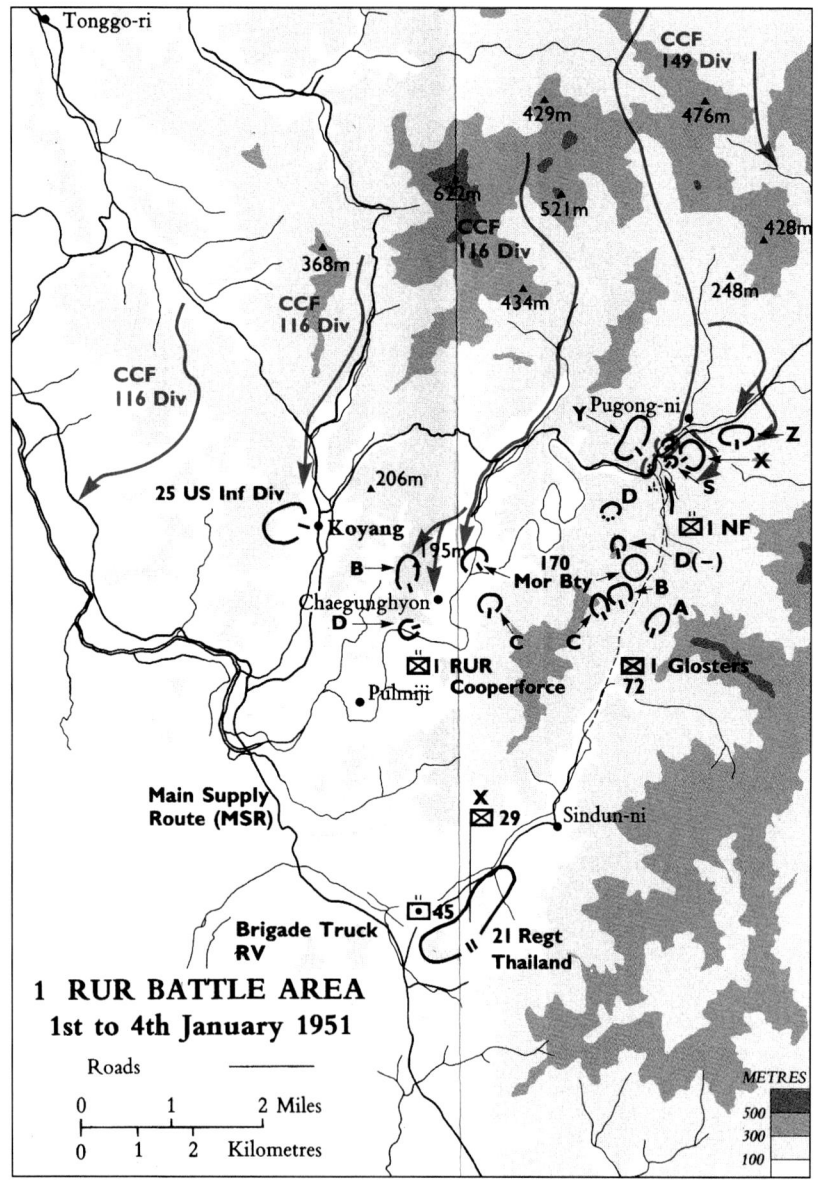

1st Battalion, The Royal Ulster Rifles battle area 1–4 January 1951. (Crown Copyright)

of the Hussars and the six OP tanks of 45 Field Regiment, all under the command of Captain Donald Astley-Cooper, 8th King's Royal Irish Hussars. The Cromwell was a Second World War cruiser tank armed with a 75mm main gun and two Besa machine-guns. It had a crew of five men and was capable of forty miles per hours on a good road, making it an ideal vehicle for reconnaissance, despite the lack of good roads in Korea. No Centurion tanks were made available. It was considered by the American command

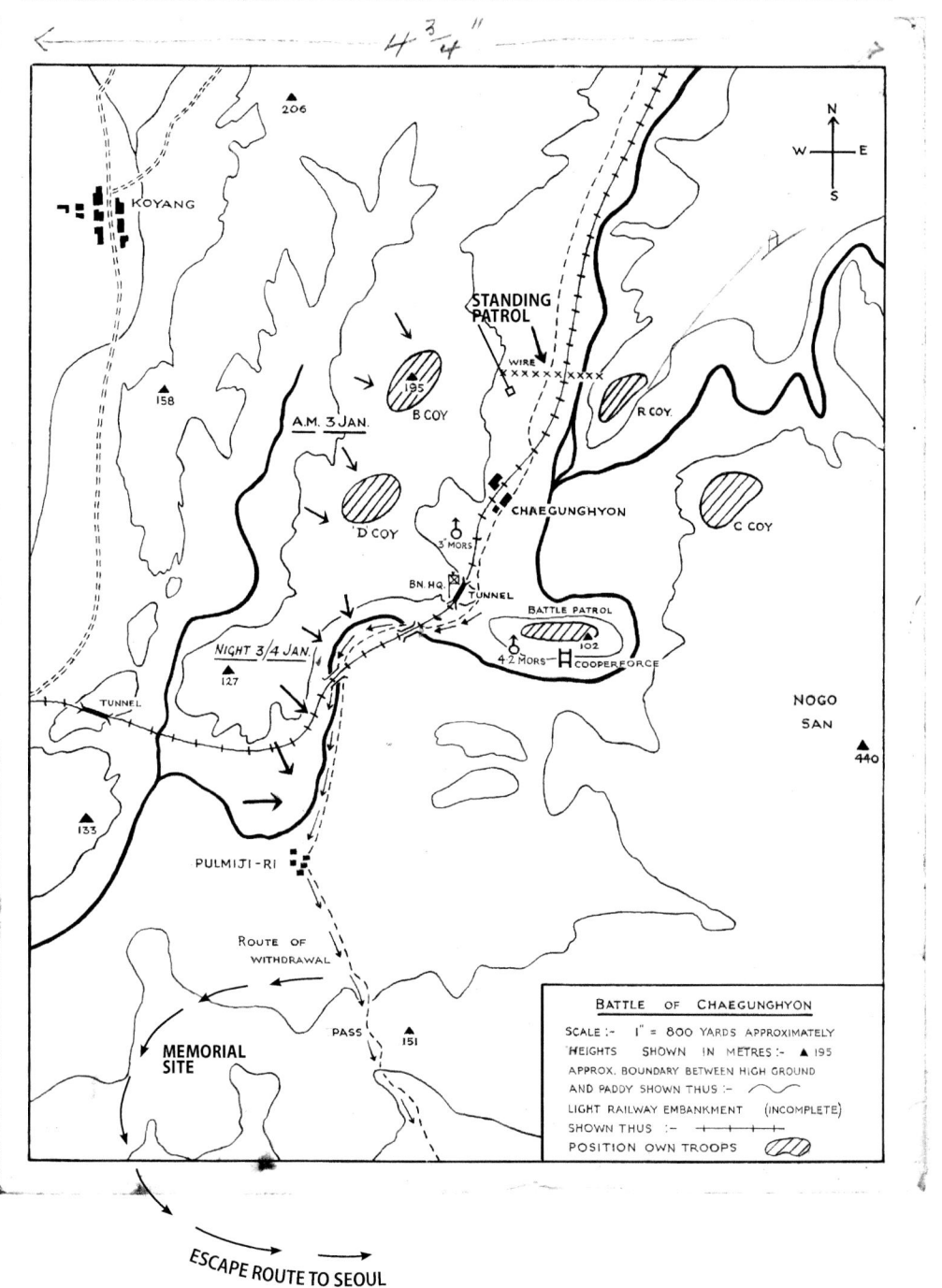

Map of the Battle of 'Happy Valley', Chaegunghyon, January 1951, amended by Brig. M. McCord. (Brig. M. McCord)

Warning orders for January's battle – Captain B. Williams, Bde IO, Colonel Carson (hooded), Captain Hamill and Major Blake. (Mervyn McCord/RUR Association)

A British Cromwell tank being loaded onto a rail flat car at Hiro Station, Japan-bound for Divisional Battle School. Six of the OP tanks of 45 Field Regiment under the command of Captain Astley-Cooper were Cromwells. (George Forty)

that they were too heavy for the few and badly made roads. Consequently all Centurions were deployed south of the Han River.

On the left of the Battalion, deployed across the low hills covering the main Seoul-Kaesong Road, was the 2nd Battalion of the US 35th Infantry Regiment ('The Guys from Hawaii'), its right hand company, E Company, being about a mile from the Rifles left flank. On the right flank of the Rifles were the Glosters and Northumberland Fusiliers, some two miles away and on the far side of Nogo San, which rose to a height of 440 metres. The day was relatively quiet, some American Engineers and a detachment from the 55th Field Squadron, Royal Engineers, arrived and assisted in laying barbed wire across the various positions. A foot patrol from C Company made contact with the Glosters, while the Adjutant paid a visit to the Americans on the left flank. The weather was bright and sunny, but bitterly cold and the ground was covered in snow. The track running south from the American position and on to Brigade Headquarters was ice-covered and the going was extremely difficult. Any vehicle that drove through one of the numerous fords experienced brake failure as these froze immediately on crossing. 'Cooperforce' tanks had managed to use it, but the damage caused was considerable and attempted repairs were underway using a bulldozer.

As darkness approached the Battalion moved into its new positions and proceeded to dig in. This was something well learned in Northern Europe during the last year of the Second World War. The brutal lesson that 'digging saves lives' was equally applicable now on the other side of the world where all three battalions dug-in and established defensive positions. When time and supplies would permit these positions were bolstered by wire, with concrete and timber reinforcements in the forward posts.

By now it was obvious to the Battalion Headquarter officers that Colonel Carson had become too ill to carry on and on the advice of the Medical Officer he was rushed into the ADS (Advanced Dressing Station) of 26 Field Ambulance and command devolved once again to Major Blake, with Major May acting as his second-in-command.

The Battalion made contact with the 2nd Battalion US 35th Regiment on 2 January, both by landline and wireless. From intelligence reports it was gleaned that the main Chinese force were advancing along the Chorwon-Seoul Road, their advance units being within eight miles of Uijongbu. Here the British 27 Brigade was heavily engaged.

The weather was unbearably cold, in the trenches and foxholes the men were standing on sandbags stuffed with rice straw to try and insulate them from the cold. A Platoon of C Company had warm dry feet thanks to their Sergeant who had exchanged his gin/rum ration for a job lot of American boots. Such bartering did not sit well with the authorities, but the men were happy. The cold also saw a rise in the demand of spare boot laces. It was found that the alloy buckles on the jungle green webbing were inclined to snap and boot laces were soon being used to keep equipment together.

Lieutenant Mervyn McCord was another son of a Rifles officer and an ex-Queen's University student. Initially posted to the Anti-Tank Platoon, he was given command of a section of the Battle Patrol and sent north through Koyang to a position some five miles in front of the Forward Defence Lines. From here the patrol was able to observe a wide area and saw no sign of the enemy. After remaining for a time they returned to the Battalion with nothing to report.

Throughout the day stragglers from the 1st ROK Division passed through the Brigade lines and it was obvious that the Division was no longer a combat effective force.

There was also a constant stream of refugees moving south. There were checked by the men of the Battalion before being passed around to the flank and on to the rear. These checks were mainly superfluous, it was impossible for British troops, new to the country, to differentiate between Korean and Chinese and it is fairly certain that a number of enemy troops and agents infiltrated behind the Battalion during the day. By mingling with the civilians these agents were able to gain exact information on the layout of the defences.

By 2200hrs, Brigade Headquarters reported that there was still no contact with the enemy. The following morning at 0200hrs, a foot patrol from D Company met up with their counterparts in Easy Company of the US 35th Regiment. Corporal Joe Farrell remembers these men as being black troops and the two patrols spent some time chatting before some shooting erupted about half a mile away, when both patrols returned to their respective bases. On their way back the men of the patrol could hear Chinese voices in the darkness, Farrell recalls that they "Chattered like a barrel of bloody monkeys". The patrol arrived back in the Battalion lines at the positions held by B Company and a report was passed to Lieutenant Bruford-Davies.

At 0315hrs on 3 January, a message was received via the Liaison Officer at Brigade Headquarters to report the sound of gunfire coming from Koyang, in which there was an outpost of Easy Company of the 35th Regiment. This outpost was quickly pushed back and by 0445hrs, all units were 'stood to'. A wireless message from Easy Company told of the enemy attacking from a position some 2,000 yards to their front. At 0530hrs, A Company observed enemy troops to their front and opened fire. This was swiftly followed by fire from B Company, situated on Point 195, as movement was seen on their right flank. Two reconnaissance patrols from D Company consisting of four Riflemen led by Lieutenant Bruford-Davies and a second comprising of Lieutenant John Mole and a Corporal were sent forward towards Point 158. Mole having been warned by Major Ryan not to 'stick his neck out' went forward for approximately six hundred yards before returning convinced that the enemy was present and in strength.

The foot patrol led by Bruford-Davies consisted of himself, his batman, Rifleman Horribin, who was carrying the No 88 Wireless set and a Bren gun team of two other Riflemen. Aware that the Chinese were masters of camouflage Bruford-Davies led his men carefully down into the valley bottom, their studded boots crunching slowly through the snow. Spotting a light in an isolated farmhouse the Lieutenant attempted to call it in, but discovered that the set was unable to make contact with base.[6] Bruford-Davies reckoned that this was due to the crest of the ridge that prevented a line of sight with his Company. Suddenly there was movement all around the patrol and the Riflemen discovered that they had stumbled into an attacking Korean battalion as it made its way up the hill. There was a flurry of thrown hand grenades and the Bren team managed to get off a few bursts before the patrol was overrun. The Riflemen were then escorted to the rear and as they marched along Bruford-Davies remembered that he had a map in his pocket showing the Company positions. Not wanting this to fall into enemy hands he pretended to stumble and while lying on the ground he managed to bury the map in

---

6   The Wireless Set No 88 was a man-portable transceiver that had been introduced in 1947 to replace the No 38 Set. It was mainly used for short-range infantry communications and fitted into a pouch similar to a Bren gun ammunition pouch, therefore making the operator less conspicuous. The Set had a range of up to two miles in good conditions, which Korea rarely was!

the snow. They were taken to a village that seemed to be some type of headquarters for the North Koreans. The village had previously been strafed and had suffered a degree of damage. To make it appear that it had been completely destroyed cans filled with oil and rags had been set about the streets and set alight, giving the impression of the place being on fire. The patrol was housed in a shed and here ammunition that was still being carried by the men was hidden to prevent it falling into enemy hands.

At 0700hrs, a number of men, one carrying a white flag, approached B Company on Hill 195, walking towards Lieutenant John Mole's No 4 Platoon. They came forward with their hands raised and shouting "South Koreans, we surrender, don't shoot." Suddenly there was a flurry of activity and the 'friendly troops' rushed forward showering the Platoon with previously concealed hand grenades. John Mole found himself firing a Bren gun and for once was wearing a steel helmet. As he exchanged fire with the Chinese his helmet was hit by a bullet and he found himself thrown out of the trench.[7] After a period of what was described as 'confused fighting' and a failed attempt by one of Mole's Corporals to launch a counter-attack, the Platoon was forced to withdraw leaving four casualties behind. This withdrawal was covered in part by the Battalion mortars, allowing Lieutenant Mole to bring his men off the hill without further casualties. As Mole made his way back he found that the hood of his smock contained several bullet holes. One man had been left behind, Rifleman Cain had suffered a broken ankle was unable to move. He was taken prisoner, then quickly escaped, but was later found hiding in the undergrowth. The summit of Hill 195 was now in the hands of the leading elements of the 116 Division, People's Communist Volunteers.

As this was happening D Company was also engaged with the enemy. Major Gaffikin and Lieutenant Benson were wounded at the outset of the fighting. Lieutenant Benson had been exchanging shots with a Chinese soldier on top of the hill armed with a Bren gun. However, the Lieutenant's .303 had been more accurate and fatal, but not before the 'dancing Chinaman' had scored a hit in return, wounding the Lieutenant in the wrist.[8] Lieutenant MacNicol and his No 12 Platoon stopped an attack within yards of their front line. Despite the relatively slow rate of fire of the British .303 rifle, firepower was stopping the Chinese. Major Gaffikin returned to duty immediately after treatment at the RAP, while the Medical Officer, 'Sandy' Ferrie, did a marvellous job continued to treat the wounded with both skill and speed as the situation demanded.

No 11 Platoon was hit from three sides, the advancing Chinese using the numerous scattered bushes as cover, which made it difficult to see them. The sound of them was a different matter; there was the constant blowing of bugles and whistles and shouting, the whole lot appearing like a drunken mob.[9] The Platoon was forced to withdraw, hotly followed by the Chinese. In No 12 Platoon a Bren gun team acquired a good target on the enemy and with several controlled bursts brought down many of the pursuing enemy. Several men saw Sergeant Fowler wave his rifle in the old field signal indicating 'enemy at right in large numbers', which was no exaggeration.

---

7   Mole sent the helmet to his old school, much to the regret of the Regimental Museum.
8   *Quis Separabit*, 1951, p.35.
9   A bugle is an excellent way of controlling troops in darkness or built up areas and has the advantage that all troops hear it at the same time, as opposed to a radio when the message has to be passed from man to man. They were used successfully by troops of a Light Infantry Battalion on the streets of Belfast in 1972.

As dawn broke it became evident that the enemy had made considerable gains. Despite the spirited counter-attack B Company had again been driven off Hill 195, a Chinese bugler in quilted winter uniform and dog skin cap was seen on the summit blowing the victory call just before he was hit by a burst from a machine-gun, while small parties of enemy troops began to make their way along the ridge heading for Battalion Headquarters and the mortar pits. The soldiers of the Chinese 116th Division would seem to have had the upper hand, for now.

In the American sector the Chinese had taken Hill 127 and both hills were then engaged by the Battalion's 3" mortars and the 4.2" mortars of the 170 Mortar Battery. Artillery fire from the supporting tanks and 25pdrs from 175 Battery of 45th Field Regiment, RA, added to the firepower and the Chinese were forced to keep their heads down. Additional firepower was received from the 155mm guns of the American 9th Field Artillery Battalion.[10] Many of the 155mm howitzers were mounted on a fully tracked self-propelled chassis known as the M40. In tandem with the Great War, only disease would kill more than the artillery in Korea.[11]

A Company was withdrawn and held in readiness for any counter-attack, while C Company was engaged in a reconnaissance of A Company positions should it be necessary to take it over. An immediate counter-attack was required to retake Hill 195 and Major Blake ordered A Company to an assembly area just behind Battalion Headquarters, while a platoon of C Company took over their original position. Captain Cocksedge and the ninety men of the Battle Patrol were ordered to move around to the rear and attack from the south end of the ridge to secure a start line for A Company. By 1125hrs, the Battle Patrol, having attacked on foot due to the steep hillside being unsuitable for their carriers, came under fire from the top of the hill and identified some of the weapons as Bren guns.[12] At first thinking this as 'friendly fire' it soon proved otherwise and an airstrike was called in. Almost immediately after laying out the required orange markers four F80 'Shooting Stars' from the US Fifth Air Force Fighter-Bomber Wing arrived and delivered canisters of napalm on the hilltop. Lieutenant McCord recalled being only about thirty yards from the exploding napalm canister and despite he and the remainder of his men feeling the fierce blast of heat, they were thankfully protected by the steepness of the ridge. As the flames died away and the black smoke cleared it became obvious that no counter-attack would be required. On the hill only a few individual enemy could be seen and these were quickly engaged by the Battalion snipers.

It now appeared that the stubbornness of the Battalion's defence assisted by the heavy and accurate fire of the supporting weapons had caused the enemy such casualties that their advance was not only stopped, but the force virtually destroyed. Consequently A Company was ordered to hold fast and B Company was ordered to re-take Hill 195, which they did successfully. Robin Charley maintained that this attack, spearheaded by Lieutenant Ivor Daniels' Platoon, was a near perfect example of how it should be done. With the assault platoon fortified with a tot of rum, supplied by Robin Charley

---

10 Linklater, *Our Men in Korea*, London, 1952.
11 Catchpole, *The Korean War*, London, 2000.
12 The use of such weapons dated back to the Second World War when various groups were equipped with both British and American weapons to fight the Japanese under the Lease Lend Agreement. Added to this there were weapons that had been captured from the Japanese. A Quartermaster's nightmare where ammunition and spare parts were concerned, Lieutenant McCord also noticed that the Chinese Bren gun had a slightly longer barrel.

Members of the Royal Ulster Rifles in action in snow-covered country somewhere in Korea, 1951. Note the different styles of headgear. (RUR Museum)

and CSM Drumgoole and accurate covering fire the attack went 'by the book' and the position was retaken by 1310hrs. In the confusion of the fighting Rifleman Albert Varley found himself lost on a hillside along with his platoon commander and sergeant. A voice called out from the darkness in English "I'm wounded! I'm wounded! Varley found a Chinese soldier lying in the cover of some boulders, he seemed to be seriously injured, and without a thought Varley shot him.

D Company also retook a lost section and by 1335hrs, Major Blake was able to signal to Brigade Headquarters that the situation had been restored. Casualties suffered by the Battalion so far were four killed, twelve wounded and Lieutenant Bruford-Davies with his patrol listed as missing, which was considered 'few' compared to the number of casualties caused to the enemy. It was estimated that the majority of enemy had been killed by mortar fire, with over fifty bodies being counted within the Battalion area. Two wounded Chinese were taken prisoner, but only one survived his wounds to be sent back to Brigade Headquarters for interrogation. From the dead Chinaman, an officer, Lieutenant McCord recovered a bugle and a sword, which were claimed as souvenirs.[13] McCord remembers that many of the enemy looked like Michelin Men in their winter clothing. The afternoon was reasonably quiet and preparations were made for the coming night.

On the Battalion's right flank the Glosters had not been engaged. The Northumberland Fusiliers, lying further east had fought a fierce battle and had for a time been engaged in close-quarter fighting before forcing the enemy to retire.

The Rifles' were content with the outcome of the day's battle. The Chinese, this almost legendary enemy, whose 'hordes' had been responsible for sending the Eighth

---

13 He still has them and they will eventually find their way to the Regimental Museum.

Army into retreat, had been met, fought and defeated, at least for this day. After many days of withdrawal from an enemy they had never seen they now experienced the confident realisation that they, at any rate, were more than a match for their opponents.

At 1740hrs, the Battalion was ordered to withdraw and to be clear by 1830hrs. With only fifty minutes to issue orders and plan routes Major Blake considered that due to the dispersed positions of the Battalion they would be unable to move before 2100hrs. The Division, along with the US 25th Infantry were now to withdraw while in contact with the enemy, not an easy manoeuvre at the best of times. The Americans had received their orders at 1500hrs and began to move an hour later. They, unlike the British, followed the maxim, 'if you can't carry it, dump it'. On the other hand Brodie's men were determined to leave nothing useful for the Chinese. The Northumberland Fusiliers and Glosters had also been ordered out earlier and it was the Rifles who would be acting as the rearguard to the Brigade.

The Brigade was withdrawing south of the Han River and the Battalion was to come down from the hills and to move south as fast as possible to a point six miles back, where transport would be waiting. Speed was of the essence and as the Americans on the left flank had also been ordered back and their route straddled the main road, they were likely to move faster than the Rifles could manage. The route for the Rifles led through a valley overlooked on both sides by hills, with the added complication of a railway line whose bridges and tunnels created more obstacles, as did the small village of Pulmiji-Ri, located near the southern end.

A 'scratch' Battalion of the no longer effective 1st ROK Division had been brought up during the afternoon and placed under command of the Rifles on the southern side of the valley and had begun to dig in. They were ordered to withdraw immediately, as it was considered that their presence during the withdrawal in darkness would be more of a hindrance than a help given their low morale.

Due to a lack of liaison the American unit withdrew between 1740hrs and 1830hrs, leaving the Battalion's left flank open. The Chinese immediately noticed this and soon troops had moved in to flank the main withdrawal route of the Battalion, the track running from Pulmiji-ri to the pass below Point 151. This route, consisting of a narrow, precipitous track covered in frozen ice and snow, to be traversed in darkness, would have been difficult at the best of times. The Chinese would make it nigh impossible.

The route south for the Battalion was to cross a start line just south of Headquarters at 2100hrs, adhering to a strict order of march. This was to consist of B Company in the lead, followed by A Echelon, Main Headquarters, C Company, less one platoon, D Company, A Company, followed by Support Company with the 4.2" Mortar Troop. The tanks of 'Cooperforce', with Lieutenant Prescott-Westcar and No 7 Platoon of C Company mounted on their engine decks would bring up the rear.

A section of the Battle Patrol under Lieutenant McCord, reinforced by a section each of 3" mortars and Vickers machine-guns, was to establish a standing patrol on the track about a thousand yards north of Chaegunghyon to cover the initial movement and then to withdraw at 2230hrs.

The night was bitterly cold with no moon and only faint starlight to illuminate the track as it wound its way across the snow-covered paddy fields. The enemy positions were quiet, the only sound was the crump of exploding bombs as the 3" Mortar Platoon fired off their remaining ammunition into supposed enemy locations. This noise in turn helped disguise the growl of vehicle engines starting up.

The leading section of B Company passed the Regimental Policeman marking the start line at exactly 2100hrs, followed almost immediately by the remainder of the Company. In single file the men made their way down the track, across the ford flowing with ice-cold water and into the valley beyond. Following B Company were the vehicles of A Echelon and Battalion Headquarters, crawling along at walking pace in first gear. The snow made steering and the use of brakes a nightmare as the drivers fought to keep their vehicles on the narrow track. For the next thirty minutes the column snaked its way south, moving slowly but surely towards the rendezvous.

Just as B Company reached the foot of the pass to the south of Pulmiji-Ri the darkness was split apart as flares ignited in the sky above, bathing the entire column in stark white light. This illumination came from American 'Lightning Bugs', converted C47 aircraft that had been adapted to carry 130 Mark 8 flares. The flares ignited at 5,500 feet and burned for approximately five minutes each. They were normally used to light up Chinese targets for B-26 bombers and in fact the 3rd Bombardment Wing would claim a Chinese death toll of 8,000 by the end of this battle.[14] Tonight a number of Riflemen would be added to the score. A message was immediately passed to Brigade to have the aircraft abort, but the C-47's were not under Brigade control and the flares continued.[15]

There were only a few more minutes of quiet before the first Chinese machine-gun opened fire, followed by many more and soon joined by mortars. From this point onwards the situation became one of utter confusion. The main enemy fire had hit the centre of the column, while back at base neither 'Cooperforce' nor McCord's Battle Patrol had begun to move.

The only opportunity for these two units to escape from the trap was for the column to keep moving, as the track was too narrow to permit vehicles to pass. Therefore Major Blake ordered that the Battalion transport should keep moving at all times, not an easy thing for the drivers to accomplish under a rain of machine-gun bullets and exploding mortar bombs. Several vehicles slid off the track and it took enormous effort to get them moving again. Those that could not were unceremoniously pushed clear.

By now it was time for the Battle Patrol to leave and as they came down the track they found the Cromwells of 'Cooperforce' engaging the enemy in the hills with their main armament and Besa machine-guns. Lieutenant McCord ordered the Vickers to open fire from the backs of the Carriers and the enemy were kept busy. McCord then noticed that some of the guns on the Cromwells were not properly 'zeroed'[16] and had caused a number of casualties among the Battle Patrol, including beheading one of the men. The Lieutenant then had to crawl on his belly to get to the tanks and tell them what was happening. Later, when the bodies of these men were being collected, Lieutenant McCord remembers vividly lifting this man's body and having to search for the head.

The fighting was now at close-quarters and many Riflemen had fitted their bayonets. The Chinese had established a machine-gun post in the riverbed in front of Support

---

14 Jackson, *Air War over Korea*, London, 1973.
15 The flares had been dropped to enable friendly aircraft to spot the attacking Chinese.
16 Whereby the guns are aligned with the sights to converge at a set distance.

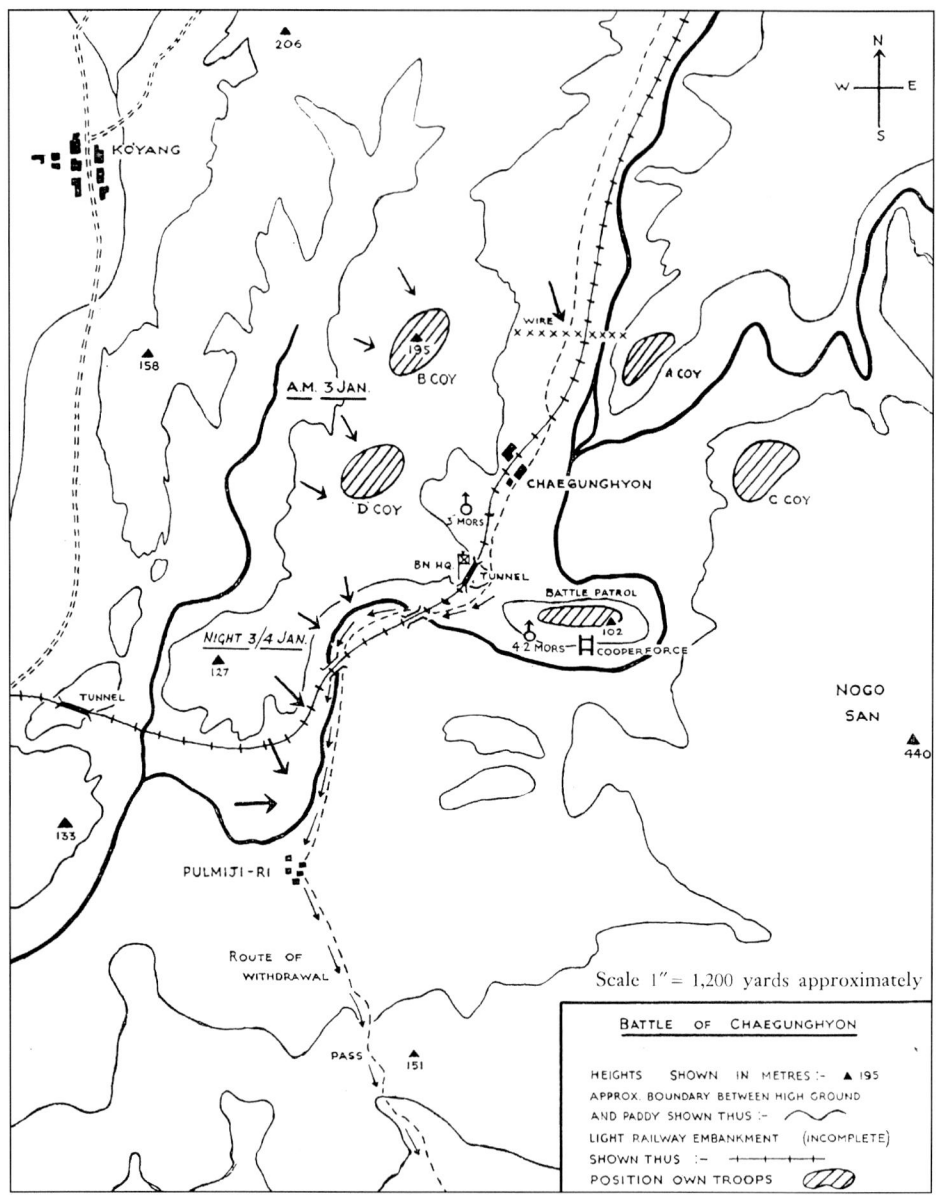

The Battle of Chaegunghyon, January 1951. (*The Royal Ulster Rifles in Korea*, 1953)

Company and as it hosed bullets into the vehicles, hordes of enemy infantry came streaming down the hillside making great use of sub-machine-guns and hand grenades.

Captain Majury and the remnants of his Mortar Platoon were held up at Pulmiji-Ri by a number of burning vehicles that blocked the road. Majury and his men dismounted and fought a close-range action until they ran out of ammunition. At that stage Majury ordered his men to surrender to save further bloodshed and they were taken prisoner.

CSM Sean Fitzsimons. (Mark McConnell)

When fighting the Chinese it was obvious that the British were going to run out of ammunition before the enemy ran out of men.

It was here that Major Blake and Major Ryan were last seen making strenuous efforts to keep the column moving and under control. Lieutenant McCord, with the able assistance of Sergeant Campbell and Corporal Black, came forward with a section of the Battle Patrol and using grenades knocked out the machine-gun post in the riverbed. They then went back to 'Cooperforce' and borrowing a Cromwell came forward to help the main body through the gap thus created.

Captain Astley-Cooper then ordered Lieutenant Geoffrey Alexander and his troop of tanks, with the assistance of No 7 Platoon, to try and break out via the riverbed and head west towards the main road. The Cromwells came under very heavy mortar fire as they moved away – one bomb struck the turret of Lieutenant Alexander's tank and he was killed instantly by a piece of shrapnel to the head. Lieutenant Prescott-Westcar was also hit while attacking an enemy machine-gun post and was not seen again. Some members of No 7 Platoon managed to escape, none of the Cromwells got through. Captain Astley-Cooper's tank lost a track and the crew abandoned the vehicle, attempting to make it out on foot. Astley-Cooper was last seen with fellow crewman Sergeant Farmer making their way along a ditch, but were never seen alive again.[17]

---

17 One Cromwell OP Tank covering the withdrawal of the Rifles was commanded by Major Acton Henry Gordon 'Spud' Gibbon, from a County Fermanagh family. Gibbon was taken prisoner and as a result of his behaviour in the prison camp became the only man to be awarded the George Medal for the Korean conflict.

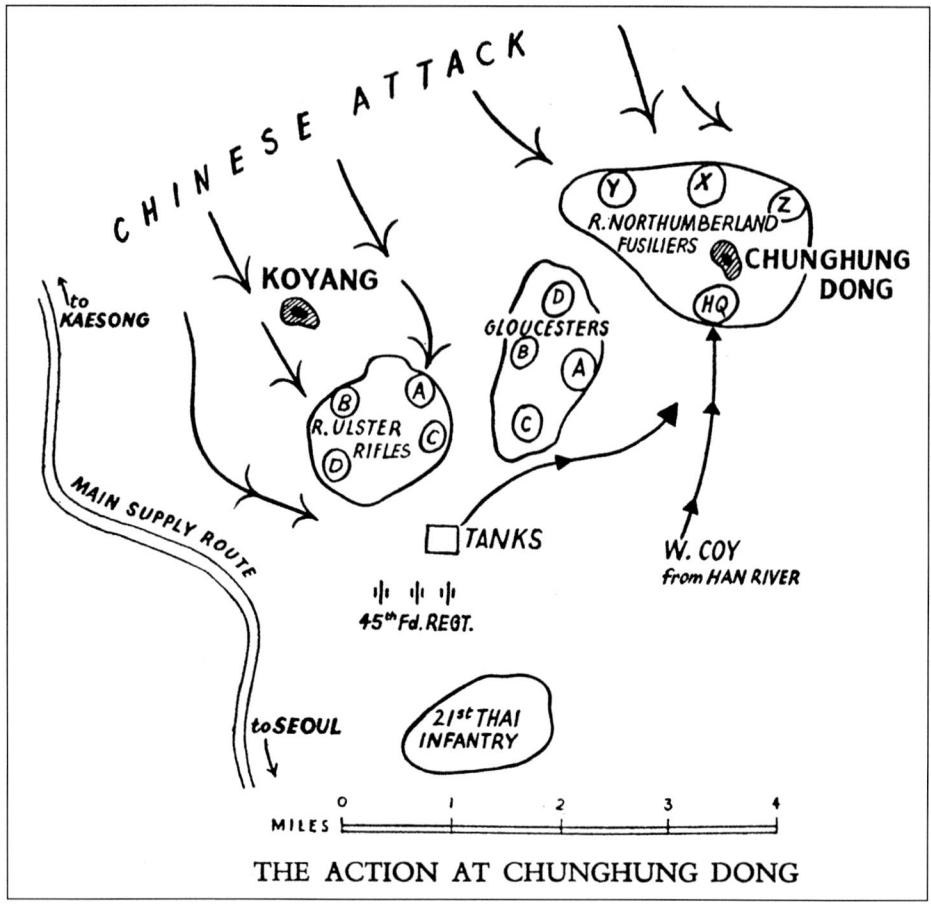

The action at Chunghung Dong. (Barclay, *The First Commonwealth Division*)

Lieutenant McCord and his men became the victims of 'friendly fire' when a Cromwell tank opened up with its 75mm gun on their position. Despite intense mortar and machine-gun fire the Lieutenant crawled to the Cromwell and attempted to use the rear hull mounted telephone. This was damaged and he was forced to climb onto the turret and using language better suited to the barrack room convinced the gunner to cease fire, a tragic incident in a night of tragic incidents. McCord, Sergeant Campbell and the remainder of the Battle Patrol continued down the valley to the next obstacle, a railway bridge. Here the Chinese had ensconced a machine-gun nest among the rocks and this was causing a massive delay as it swept the ground in front. The machine-gun and its crew were summarily dealt with by the two men using hand grenades and the concentrated fire of a Bren gun wielded by McCord. For their actions this night Mervyn McCord received the Military Cross, while Sergeant Harry Campbell was awarded the Military Medal.

Lance Corporal Joe Farrell serving with D Company met his friend Lance Corporal Martin Vance at the valley entrance and advised him to come along. Vance however was a Regimental Policeman and was tasked with guiding the Battalion and others out of

HAPPY VALLEY 103

Captain Majury directing operations of the 3" Mortars. (RUR Museum)

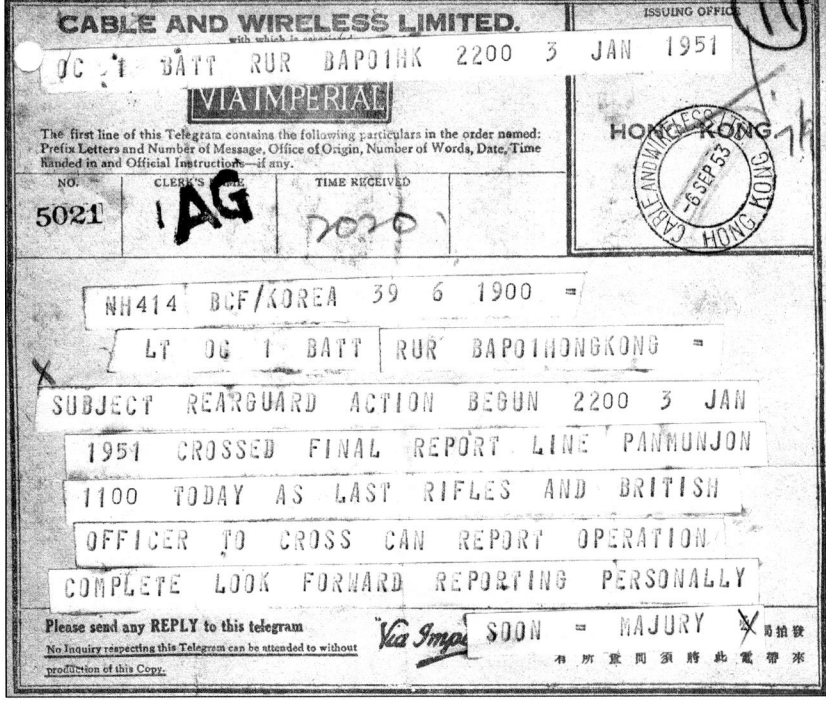

Telegram from Majury, January 1951. (Mervyn McCord/RUR Association)

Captain James Majury, who had been a prisoner of war during the Korean War. (RUR Association)

Major M.D.G.C. Ryan, the senior British officer amongst the captives of January 1951. (RUR Association)

the valley, he refused to leave and was later taken prisoner. As Farrell continued on his way he lost touch with the remainder of D Company and like everyone else got caught by the flares dropped by the 'Lightning Bugs'. As he lay flat on the ground a number of Chinese troops came charging down from the hillside and one actually ran over his back, but without noticing Farrell. As the Lance Corporal got to his feet he heard moaning nearby and found Sergeant 'Hooky' Walker lying with a wound to his head. Getting the injured NCO to his feet both men made their way towards the rear until picked up by a passing truck belonging to the Royal Engineers.

All along the route there was hand-to-hand fighting and as the enemy closed in, Support Company, the last Company to withdraw, was forced to abandon most of the remaining vehicles and take to the mountains, with Major Shaw in command. Shaw also gathered together any other men he could find and by good leadership and sheer determination was able to bring some sixty men over the mountain and in to the assembly area the following morning. To do this required all of Shaw's personality and experience, not to mention the assistance of the last working tank of 'Cooperforce'. Together Riflemen and Cromwell charged through Pulmiji-Ri, by then a mass of burning and destroyed buildings still being fought over by Major Blake and his men. Once through the buildings Shaw took his men into the hills and on south towards the MSR. On approaching the line held by elements of the US 25th Division they came under fire and it was only the strenuous efforts of Major Shaw and Sergeant Campbell that persuaded the Americans that they were shooting British troops. So it was that the last party of the Battalion made it to safety, mounted the two remaining vehicles and drove south.

For Rifleman Henry O'Kane salvation from the battlefield came in the form of 'Wags Truckers'. This gallant Negro trucking company, ably led by Captain Wagner, had come further forward and stayed there longer than anyone had the right to expect. This unit, on permanent attachment to the 29th Brigade, was as happy to see the Riflemen returning as their mothers would have been. O'Kane's group, consisting of men from various companies, stumbled along the track or limped across the paddy fields, the badly wounded being carried by the slightly wounded, for there were few men uninjured. As

Grave of Major C.A.H.B. Blake, United Nations Memorial Cemetery, Pusan, Korea. (RUR Museum)

CSM Joe McCrory, BEM. (Henry O'Kane)

Cromwell OP Tank, 45th RA, Happy Valley. (Henry O'Kane)

they reached the vehicles willing hands helped them aboard and together they jolted in comradeship across the river towards safety.[18]

---

18 Henry O'Kane.

7

Replacements and Prisoners of War

On the morning of 4 January the Battalion assembled at Suwon and the roll was called. It was ascertained that 208 officers and men were shown as killed, wounded or missing. Over the next few days this number dropped to 157 as men made their way back from American hospitals, where they had been receiving treatment, or had been evading in the surrounding countryside. At Pulmiji-Ri a group of men were spotted from the air and an American helicopter pilot flew in to rescue a total of seven men. One of these was the Mortar Platoon store man who had been wounded when his Carrier had crashed on the way out of Happy Valley. Despite being taken prisoner with several other men, he was left behind when the Chinese marched away as he could not walk.

Sergeant Carlin's Provost Section was particularly badly hit, with three men reported missing, of whom two would subsequently die. These were Lance Corporal Vance, who was taken prisoner, Rifleman Bunby, who died as a prisoner of war and Rifleman Michael McSherry who died of wounds on 4 January. During the action there had been few prisoners to guard, but Carlin and his men had performed sterling service in guiding the Battalion from point to point during the battle, as they had done since arriving in Korea.

Sergeant Sean Fitzsimons, who recalled that when you touched metal with your bare hands you left skin behind, had some harsh words about the Sten gun and vowed never to again carry it into battle. The so called 'Arctic Oil' had proved useless and the bolt was either frozen closed, or cocked, but in whatever position it refused to fire. The only totally reliable weapon available to the Rifleman was the .303 Lee Enfield that continued to fire under any conditions. The .303 bullet would easily penetrate the frozen cotton wadding of the Chinese winter uniforms, while in many case the Sten gun's 9mm rounds just seemed to bounce off. The rifle, along with copious numbers of the No 36 hand grenade, were the only weapons the Rifles considered battle worthy.[1] American weapons such as the M1 Carbine and Thompson sub-machine-gun would be eagerly sought out in the coming months, although ammunition and spare parts were always a problem.

The following day the Battalion mounted the engine decks of the Hussars' Centurions and moved about forty miles south to Pyongtaek. Here, along with the remainder of the Brigade, they dug-in on a flat open plain to await the enemy B Company took up positions straddling the railway line south of Osan, which became known as 'Frostbite Alley'. Here they remained for over two weeks. After this short rest for the Company, their next assignment was to act as a 'Porter Company' for the forward companies of the Battalion who were operating in the high ground to the south-east of Seoul on the approaches to the Han River.

---

1   Gibson Harries, *The Royal Ulster Rifles in Korea*, unpublished manuscript.

Lance Corporal M. Vance.

The original caption reads: "This North Korean flag makes an interesting addition to The Royal Ulster Rifles regimental museum at the Depot, Ballymena. The flag – red, white and blue stripes with a red star in white circle – was found in a house in Seoul and was sent to Major R.M. Parsons, OC Depot, by Major J.S.C.G. de Longueuil MC. Displaying the flag in this picture are Cpl T.G. Nolan (left) who is in charge of the museum and L/Cpl K. Stowe." (*Belfast Telegraph*)

In A Company it was confirmed that Major Ryan had been taken prisoner and command passed to Major Sir Christopher Nixon, who had successfully recovered from his wound. To make up for the loss in NCOs Sergeant Byrne from Support Company and Sergeant McGoldrick from D Company were transferred. From JRHU in Japan came Lieutenants Hilton, Moorsom and Potts, the latter from the Royal Inniskilling Fusiliers. Lieutenant Potts and Sergeant Byrne were assigned to No 1 Platoon, while Lieutenant Hilton went to No 3 Platoon. Lieutenant Chapman, who had been wounded commanding No 2 Platoon, was posted to RHU in Japan. The Company also lost CSM McCrory BEM, and Sergeant Cook, two veterans with some forty years service between them; they were posted to the Sergeants' Mess at JRHU. CQMS Gordon was promoted to CSM and Colour Sergeant Lowry became CQMS.

In B Company Lieutenant John Mole moved from No 5 Platoon to be second-in-command of the Mortar Platoon, his place being taken by Lieutenant McCord. The Company lost three of its Platoon Sergeants, Sergeant Copping had been seriously wounded on Hill 195 and been shipped back to England, while Sergeant Killen was sent home on compassionate leave and Sergeant Stafford had been evacuated due to illness. They had been replaced by Sergeants Forrester and Platts from Japan and Sergeant Buckley from the Mortar Platoon. Captain Charley was sent to No 1 Battle Training School as

The original caption reads: "Warmly wrapped up against raw weather, a group of Royal Ulster Rifles who have been in action against the Communist forces, kneel down in the snow as they pose for this picture "somewhere in South Korea". From left to right (front) are Corporal Tom Murray, Wiltshire; Lance Corporal Joe Farrell, Belfast; Major H.M. Gaffikin, Kings Road, Knock, Belfast; Corporal Bill Lorimer, Ballymena and Rifleman Tommy Kelly, Liverpool. At the rear (left to right) Sergeant Nat Kennedy, Belfast; Lieutenant J.A. Beckett, Cheshire; Sergeant Terry Mann, Worcestershire; Rifleman Terry Byrne, Liverpool and Rifleman Jim Greenwood, Somerset." (*Belfast Telegraph*, February 1951)

an instructor on 4 March and was replaced by Captain Daniels from No 5 Platoon.[2] In turn his place was taken by Lieutenant Tony Trevor-Roper from D Company. Probably the most serious change for the Company was losing their commander; Major Mulligan had to return home for compassionate reasons and was replaced by Captain Miller from C Company.

In C Company Captain Miller's place had been taken by Captain Docker, while Lieutenant Moore came in to replace Lieutenant Prescott-Westcar. There had been quite a few replacements within the ranks, with most of these men being Reservists from English units. A new officer was Lieutenant Peter Whitamore, who had previously served with the Loyal North Lancashire Regiment. Whitamore had volunteered for Korea and

---

2   The Battle School was necessary to indoctrinate new arrivals into the ways of fighting in Korea, it also reacclimatised those former wounded released from hospital.

Return to the Imjin – Captain H.D. Miller resting on a US Jeep complete with American carbine – HQ on the banks of the Imjin. (Mervyn McCord/RUR Association)

Lieutenant McCord just returned from a four day patrol and told he been awarded the Military Cross. (Mervyn McCord)

Rifleman R. Boyd bids farewell to his fiancée, Miss Peggy Glennon, at York Road Railway station. (*Belfast Telegraph*)

asked to be posted to the Battalion as he had done his basic training with them on being commissioned.

D Company had lost almost 50% of those men who had sailed on the *Empire Pride* and the majority of these men had become casualties of both the Chinese and the severe winter weather. The ranks were filled with Reservists from the Lancastrian Group, National Servicemen from Gloucestershire and a number of volunteers from the Dorsets, who transferred from garrison duties in Austria. Replacement NCOs came mostly from within the Irish Group. Thankfully most of the officers remained the same, Major Gaffikin and CSM McConville continued the partnership begun in 1940.

The Support Company had suffered badly in the Happy Valley battle. Of the 176 men who had begun the withdrawal ten were killed, thirteen wounded and seventy-three were missing. These losses had largely been made up with Reservists, most of whom were experienced veterans of the Second World War. Captain Majury, commander of the Mortar Platoon, had been taken prisoner and the Company was now commanded by Lieutenant Alan Hill.

The battle earned a number of awards for the Rifles. Major Gaffikin and Major Shaw, MC, were awarded the DSO; Lieutenant McCord received the Military Cross as did Lieutenant Houston Shaw-Stewart. Sergeant Campbell and Sergeant Cooke each received the Military Medal, while Corporal Hunt, Lance Corporal Watkinson and Rifleman Varley were Mentioned in Despatches.

In this, their first major action of the war, during 3/4 January 1951, the Battle of Chaegunghyon (Happy Valley), the Rifles did not lose an inch of ground and successfully covered the withdrawal of the UN forces to the South of the Han River. Eventually when the time came to withdraw from their positions the Chinese were already behind them and the Rifles had to fight their way out.[3]

Those Ulster Riflemen captured during and immediately after the battle suffered exceptionally, not only from the severe winter weather, but also from a lack of organisation by the Chinese regarding their evacuation. There are no published accounts by survivors of this column, but one, believed to be Corporal William Massey, kept a diary of his experiences while a prisoner and he managed to smuggle this out of the camp when he was repatriated. Massey wrote on both sides of a single sheet of rice paper using minute writing and was able to record the names of many of the eighty three other ranks and five officers taken with him, along with details of the hardships they endured. Some of the names included were Major Ryan, Captain Majury, Lieutenant Bruford-Davies, Captain Ferrie the Medical Officer and Captain Gibbon of the Royal Artillery. The initial entry on 3 January records just what happened prior to capture:

> Had great hopes all afternoon. We were moving south of the Han River, but when we went to move at 10.30pm, we were ambushed. We fought it out for four and a half hours. Then we had to surrender. It was a terrible day. I was captured by the Chinese.
>> Over the next three months Massey made entries every few days:
>> 4th January, spent all day in a little room. No food. Moved when it got dark.
>> 5th Spent all day in a big shed.
>> 6th Moved to a new room. Marching all night. Snowing very hard.

---

3 http://www.bkva.co.uk/ulster_mem.htm

Rifleman William Lynch, Falls Road and his fiancée, Miss Violet Miller, Oldpark Road, were to have been married but he was sent to Korea so the wedding had to be postponed. Nevertheless their friends gave Lynch a confetti send-off at the York Road Railway Station when he left with his unit. He is pictured here with his fiancée before he joined the train. (*Belfast Telegraph*)

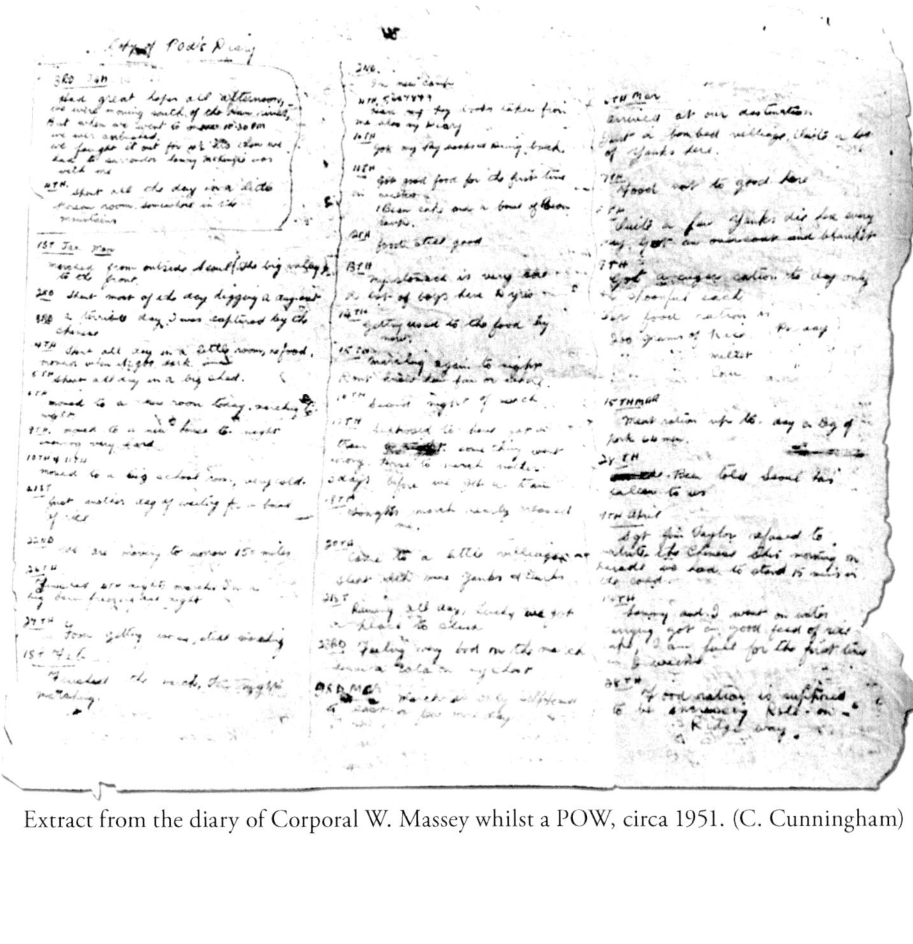

Extract from the diary of Corporal W. Massey whilst a POW, circa 1951. (C. Cunningham)

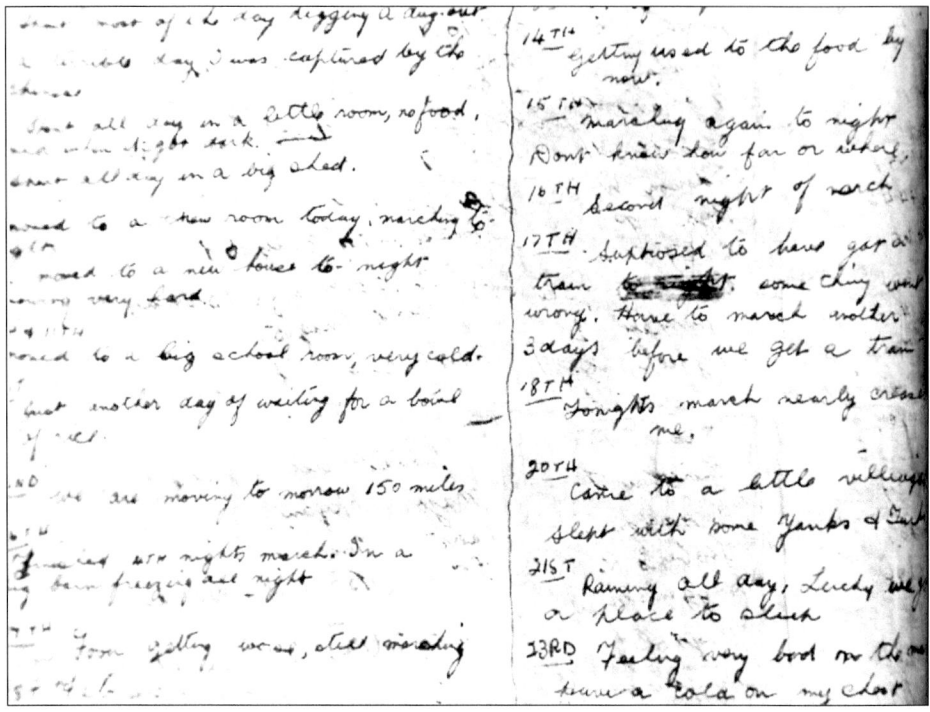

Extract from the diary of Corporal W. Massey whilst a POW, circa 1951. (C. Cunningham)

The creation of a column could take some time with various small groups of British prisoners being rounded up in penny packets. Many of these groups were initially guarded by North Koreans until they were all brought together into the main column, usually under Chinese control. Often non-ambulatory wounded prisoners were abandoned on the battlefield, with the more seriously wounded being shot out of hand. There was a serious lack of medical care available, even for wounded Communist troops. One group of prisoners escorted by Chinese guards reached an assembly area and some of the wounded were loaded on to a train and taken to Pyongyang where they were treated at a Chinese Military Hospital. Quite often it was a different matter for those who were held by the North Koreans. In this case it meant weeks or months of dreadful treatment before being handed over to the Chinese. Rifleman Jim Hibbert spent eighteen months in North Korean hands, being employed for most of the time as slave labour. Other Riflemen, such as J.T. Kelly and J.R. Bartlett, were marched back to the battlefield and worked at clearing the debris and in constructing bunkers and other defences. Others were forced to unload ammunition trains while under American air attack, while some were attached to squads dealing with unexploded bombs and shells. One group of approximately thirty British troops were taken into Pyongyang city and never seen again.[4]

Corporal Massey's column reached 'Bean Camp', a transit camp near Suan, about forty five miles south east of the Korean capital. It was named due to the prisoners' diet,

---

4   Cunningham, *No Mercy, No Leniency*, London, 2000.

mostly beans, sometimes with a little rice or millet. Massey's diary recorded both travel and diet, there are no dates mentioned:

> Just another day waiting for a bowl of rice. Moving tomorrow 150 miles. Finished 4th night marching. In a big barn, freezing all night. Food getting worse. Still marching. Finished the march after ten nights marching. In a new camp. Had my pay book taken from me and also my diary (Pocket Diary). Got my pay book and diary back. Got food for the first time in weeks; 1 bean cake, 1 bowl of bean soup. My stomach very sore. A lot of the boys have dyrio [diarrhoea]. Very bad stomach today. Going to the latrine 30 times a day.

Corporal Massey wasn't the only prisoner to develop dysentery and despite Major Ryan repeatedly requesting contact be made with the International Red Cross for medical and other necessary supplies, he was constantly rebuffed. To both the Chinese and North Koreans the Red Cross was an 'Imperialist spy organisation' and they accused them of using their special status to infiltrate agents into the country. However, Ryan's constant requests achieved some small success and some accommodation with extra fuel for heat was obtained for the sick and wounded. Despite this many prisoners, mostly Americans, but including eight British, died of dysentery, pneumonia and unattended wounds.[5] It would be almost the end of January before the guards considered that the column was far enough north to allow the prisoners to light fires for heat and cooking, although both food and shelter was in short supply.

Rifleman Clifford, another of those captured on 4 January, had eventually ended up in the North Korean interrogation centre known as 'Pak's Palace', located in a brickyard in Pyongyang, although better known to the prisoners as 'Pak's Death House'. Here the interrogation of some prisoners was clearly being aided by Soviet 'advisors' and it was later know that a Colonel Andrep of the MVD had supervised some of the questioning. Clifford had been closely questioned by a European who claimed to be Russian and spoke fluent English.[6]

The remainder of January was a time of reorganisation for the Rifles. Lieutenant Colonel Carson returned to the Battalion from hospital in Japan on 11 January and with Captain Ferrie missing at Happy Valley the Battalion received a new Medical Officer, this was Captain T. Dungavel.

There was near tireless patrolling both on foot and in the available jeeps, however, this was made slightly more bearable with the thought that when the patrols returned to base there were now houses as opposed to slit trenches as billets. A typical Korean house was a single story structure in an L shape or a V with an inside courtyard. Those of peasants were constructed of mud and plaster for the first four feet with the remainder of timber, better off people had houses of masonry in lieu of the mud. In almost all cases the roof was of rice straw, occasionally of tiles. The interior rooms were small and cramped with the floors covered in cheap oilcloth. Furniture was basic, usually small central table and cushions to sit on. Heat for the house was carried under the floors by means of flues fed from an outside fire. Chris Spears recalled coming in from a cold winter patrol, lying fully clothed on such a floor and watching the steam rise off his sodden uniform and

---

5 Cunningham, *No Mercy, No Leniency*, London, 2000.
6 MVD (*Ministerstvo Vnutrennikh Del*, or Ministry of Internal Affairs).

Rifleman Clifford, missing in action.

equipment. When Riflemen were billeted close by or had use of the houses it proved best to allow the Koreans to light the fire. Many Riflemen carried the genes of ship's stokers and when it came to judging the amount of kindling required, were inclined to be over-generous. This usually resulted in the hasty evacuation of all occupants and the complete destruction of the house in question. Some of these houses had belonged to those Koreans involved in the farming of silk worms and many Riflemen found it an unnerving experience to arrive at such a house that had been abandoned only to discover that the silk worms had taken over, with the floor and walls covered in small squirming creatures!

On 5 January Seoul changed hands for the third time in less than six months, falling to an army that was closer to a guerrilla force than an established force. The typical Chinese and North Korean soldier was both tough and cunning. He was capable of marching great distances and quite often would run for the last few miles prior to giving battle. He carried his rations, rice, oatmeal, dried peas and beans, in a cloth bandolier slung across his body and could carry enough food to last him ten days. His intelligence gathering and use of agents was excellent, as was his field craft by day and control of movement by night. He was not well armed, in a section of ten men it was often found, at least in the Happy Valley battle, that only about half the section was armed with a rifles, the remainder carrying only ammunition or grenades, these men being under orders to pick up the weapon of any fallen comrade. He was adequately equipped with machine-guns and mortars, while artillery seemed at times to be scarce and tanks almost non-existent. This was an enemy to be treated with respect in mobile warfare and at night, but in a man-to-man fight the Rifleman considered himself a better soldier.[7]

The fighting so far in Korea was entirely different from that fought previously by veterans of the Second World War in North-West Europe. There were those who compared it to a combination of Burma and the North-West Frontier of India. When in defence the same tactics which had applied in Burma held good in Korea. Companies, Battalions and even Brigades would endeavour to form a closely defended 'box', what with there being no defined front line in the conventional sense. Attacks were expected and did occur from any or all flanks at various times. Infiltration of the lines became common and the best tactic was to sit tight until daylight and then wrinkle the enemy out with fighting patrols and mortar fire.

Prior to the Imjin battle the role of United Nations Troops had been to keep the lines of communications clear and this meant the main road – the mountains were left to the enemy. However, this meant that such lines were constantly under threat of attack and a change was called for.

UN command ordered entire Divisions to sweep the hills in much the same manner as had been carried out in India when 'Tochi' Scouts had carried out a 'Gusht', literally driving the enemy from cover. While these tactics would prove successful they brought their own problems when it came to keeping the units supplied. Initially jeeps were used to bring the supplies forward as far as possible. They were then unloaded and one company per battalion was detailed as porters. This was not practical, available troops were already covering a large amount of ground and an entire company out of the line left many gaps in a defensive position.

On 10 January an announcement from the US Army Press Office imposed censorship on those reporters present in Korea. Reporters were also threatened with arrest and Court Martial if they used words such as 'retreat' as opposed to the phrase 'planned orderly withdrawal'. Such announcements, supposedly coming directly from General MacArthur, made most journalists wonder what colour the sky was in the General's world![8] Throughout the UN Forces in Korea morale was at a low ebb. It is possible that within the ranks of the 27th and 29th and Turkish Brigades, those who had fought and held the Chinese, this was less so, but even they were influenced by the constant talk of retreat and evacuation. However, things were changing. The tragic death of General Walker, C-in-C of the Eighth Army, in a road accident brought a new commander to Korea and a man capable of instilling new spirit into the troops. This was General Matthew B. Ridgway, former commander of the US 82nd Airborne Division and later XVIII Airborne Corps. He was determined to see a reversal of fortune.[9] Ridgway's view was "There are many more Chinese than there are of us; there are therefore many more for us to kill. We will stop thinking in terms of ground lost or won; we will think in terms of casualties inflicted on the enemy; with our single asset, our firepower, we will destroy that of the enemy, his superior numbers." In future all American troops had to parade washed and shaved, with clean equipment and wearing steel helmets. It would appear that the British units had made a deep impression on Ridgway. There was also an insistence that American troops learn to use their feet again and begin to travel cross-

---

7   *Quis Separabit*, 1951.
8   Paraphrased from Reginald Thompson, *Daily Telegraph*.
9   Ryan, *A Bridge Too Far*, London, 1975.

country, as opposed to using their ready supply of trucks on the few Korean roads. This in turn led to basic recruit training back in the United States being made much tougher with the emphasis being on load carrying and route marches. General Ridgway insisted that in future the UN line must roll with the punches, falling back just enough to allow the superiority of artillery and firepower to break up the enemy's superiority in numbers and then immediately counter-attack.

On 12 January a War Office statement was published in the local Northern Ireland press:

> In view of reports that the Royal Ulster Rifles had been wiped out in recent actions in Korea, the War Office states that official reports do not in any way indicate that this is so and in fact, state that all units of the 29th Brigade are still in action and in very good heart, though the Brigade has sustained casualties. Next of kin are being informed as and when casualties are notified to the War Office.

In Korea Captain Balders and Lieutenant Dunlop along with thirty eight 'other ranks' arrived as reinforcements for the Battalion, as it attempted to reorganise after the battle.

On 15 January the US 35th Regiment of the 25th Division advanced through 29th Brigade and advanced northwards to make contact with and harass the enemy. It was also their intention to try and ascertain his strength and intentions for the coming year. The 35th Regiment remained out, operating forward of the Brigade for several days and despite wide sweeping moves found only a protective screen in the area of Osan-Ni. By the end of the week American units of regimental strength were operating forward of the main defence line on a Divisional sector and were beginning to feel their way further north.[10]

At 0830hrs on 20 January Lieutenant Nichols had taken out a jeep patrol to destroy a number of boats on the coast nearby. These boats were suspected of being used to smuggle supplies to Communist guerrillas in the area. The patrol was a failure as due to the prevailing weather conditions it proved impossible to burn the boats. On returning to base it was discovered that Rifleman G. Grace was missing. Grace had enlisted in the Border Regiment in June 1940 and subsequently transferred to the East Lancashire Regiment in April 1942. He seems not to have settled with this unit and deserted in August of the same year. However, records indicate that he later rejoined the Colours and was transferred to the Army Reserve at the end of the Second World War. He was still on the Reserve when called up for service in Korea.

In Belfast, the *Northern Whig* published an accumulated casualty list for the Rifles that listed eleven other ranks killed; three officers and forty five men wounded, five officers and 137 men missing, the vast majority of these from the Happy Valley battle. The article also stated that this number of missing would eventually turn out to have been made prisoner of war. A photograph sent to the press via Peking showed a British prisoner wearing suitable heavy winter clothing, which was supposed to be evidence that prisoners were being well treated – the truth would come later.

On 24 January Colonel Carson received orders for the Battalion to move forward of the Brigade lines and by active patrolling prevent a vacuum forming in the rear of

---

10 An American regiment was the equivalent of a British brigade.

John Lane, Max Nichols and Mason stocking up at the PRI which included Lux soap and Heinz beans. (Mervyn McCord/RUR Museum)

the advancing units of the 25th Division which could be filled by infiltrating Chinese troops. It was suspected that the lacklustre reaction of the enemy might be nothing more than a clever ruse to lure the advancing units into an ambush.

As two roads were involved in the move, the main Suwon Road and a minor road running parallel to it about eight miles to the west, it was decided to split the Battalion into two separate commands. The first, 'Mayforce', consisted of A and B Companies, with two troops of Centurions, two troops of Bofors guns and a 4.2" mortar troop, together with Battalion support weapons, all under the command of Major I.A. May. This force was to establish itself at the village of Sinje on the western route. Battalion Headquarters, C and D Companies and a similar group of supporting arms would comprise 'Coforce', commanded by Colonel Carson, would move to Kyeruji on a lateral track and about half way between the two axis.

The following day 'Mayforce' and 'Coforce' went into action and immediately embarked on a tireless round of patrolling on foot and in jeeps. These patrols kept the two roads and the intervening ground clear of any enemy action from Osan-Ni right up to where the 25th Division was in sporadic contact with the Chinese.

The next day Brigadier Brodie arrived on his usual visit to the Battalion, arriving by helicopter and landing in the back garden of Battalion Headquarters. Although the near-constant patrolling was tiresome in the extreme, training was not ignored and lest the Battalion became too 'defence minded', a set piece attack exercise was laid on by C Company. While all went according to plan the highlight of the exercise was a demonstration of the firepower of the Battalion's supporting arms. The ten minutes of

Centurion Tank with reversed turret advancing towards friendly lines, Korea, 1951. (William May/RUR Association)

'hate' from the Centurions' 20 pounder guns, the 170 Mortars and the Bofors firing in the ground role, was most impressive and inspired great confidence in all who saw it.[11]

While no contact was made with enemy groups during the patrolling period, on 27 January, Sergeant Utting, one of the Battalion snipers, led a patrol from the Defence Platoon out to investigate reports from a local village that a group of suspicious persons was hiding in the neighbourhood. The patrol was a success and a number of deserters from the ROK Army were discovered in a hideout, along with accompanying girlfriends. All were brought back to the Battalion and handed over to the relevant authorities.

On 29 January the Battalion was informed by Brigade that there was widespread typhus among the civilian population and that this had spread to the Chinese troops. All ranks were warned to be on their guard and the relevant medical steps were taken.

The UN front was now moving slowly northwards, the US 25th Division, the newly arrived 3rd Division along with the Turkish Brigade, was inching forward, using a tremendous weight of artillery and air power in the advance. 'Mayforce' closed on the remainder of the Battalion at Kyeruji and both units moved north to concentrate at an area two miles east of Osan-Ni. It was about this time that it was decided to reduce the number of weapons in Support Company. The MMG Platoon was cut down to a single section of two Vickers, while the Mortar Platoon was reduced to two sections, each of two mortars. This meant that the crews made redundant would be able to assist in carrying the weapons and ammunition. Given the terrain that had to be fought across this was often the only way of transporting the weapons.[12]

On 2 February Brigadier Brodie addressed the officers, Warrant Officers and Sergeants of the Battalion, having again arrived by helicopter. The popularity of this machine both for casualty evacuation and the ability for commanders to reach units

---

11 'Hate' in this instance refers to a set period of time that intensive fire is delivered onto a specific target.
12 Anonymous [Capt. H. Hamill], *The Royal Ulster Rifles in Korea*, Belfast, 1953.

REPLACEMENTS AND PRISONERS OF WAR

Brigadier T. Brodie, Commander of the 29th Independent British Brigade, with S Company MG Crew in Korea. (RUR Museum)

quickly was becoming manifest. The Brigadier gave an assessment of the current battle situation and stressed the offensive attitude that was beginning to permeate the Eighth Army under its new commander General Matthew Ridgway. Brodie went on to say that the Divisions were now fighting completely dismounted. When hills were to their front and presenting a barrier they were climbed and supplies of food, water and ammunition were now carried on a man pack basis. It was expected that the 29th Brigade would soon follow suit. This set the Battalion a number of problems to solve and trials and planning began immediately to see how they would be overcome.

In the Rifle Companies the initial question was, how much a Rifleman was expected to carry for a protracted period while marching over hilly countryside and in weather that ranged from tropical to arctic and then fight a battle? For now the weather remained bitterly cold and it was not possible to do away entirely with blankets and heavy winter clothing. After much heated discussion and several practice marches over the surrounding hills the following was agreed on. A soldier was normally dressed in his underclothes, including a string vest, two pairs of socks, a shirt, battle-dress trousers, jersey pullover and heavy frost-proof boots with anklets. In addition he had a fur-lined ski cap, with peak and earflaps. On top of this he wore his web equipment, which held ammunition pouches, water bottle and small pack. This pack contained spare socks, spare felt insoles for the frost-proof boots, shaving kit and mess tins. In his haversack was packed a second heavy woollen pullover and a windproof suit, this being of a lightweight camouflaged material, consisting of trousers and jacket with hood. On top of the haversack was strapped a box of tinned rations, while underneath was slung a lightweight blanket rolled in his poncho. The rations were the American 24-hour combat pack, consisting of tinned beans, meat, spaghetti and fruit. Also included were cigarettes, matches, sugar, coffee and water sterilising tablets. Of course there was no tea, but by now the Rifles were well

Rifleman G. Williams returning from an anti-guerilla mountain patrol. (RUR Museum)

Rifleman J. Pratt returning from an anti-guerilla mountain patrol. (RUR Museum)

used to coffee and any hot drink was better than nothing. While this was an excellent ration there were many men who found the food highly spiced and some existed for a time on just the tinned fruit. Small arms were of course as per normal, with the exception that instead of the normal load of fifty rounds of ammunition the men now carried three times as much, with as many hand grenades as possible.

A foot patrol heading out into the foothills. (Mervyn McCord/RUR Association)

The Rifles had been issued with a superb sleeping bag, this consisted of two separate bags made of quilted kapok and placed one inside the other. However, it was too bulky to carry and was relegated to the A Echelon transport, along with the remainder of the men's kit. This meant that, except in reserve areas, the men were bitterly cold at night, but there was no alternative.

The remaining problem was one of resupply. It was hoped that rations, ammunition and other stores would be brought forward from A Echelon by jeep to a 'jeep head' and from here carried forward by porter. Brigade Headquarters had promised that a local force was being recruited, but in the meantime one rifle company would be allotted to act as porters and the Battalion would operate on a three company basis.

Into being came the 'Battalion Porters'. Under the command of Lieutenant Victor Dunlop, these porters performed superbly during the campaign. The porters 'uniform' consisted of no more than the lid of a 3" mortar bomb container marked with the number 57, this being the Battalion serial number, although in time discarded bits and pieces of uniform were acquired and worn. This disc was worn around the neck on a piece of string. On many occasions a most welcome sight was a Colour Sergeant with a long column of porters strung out behind him loaded with 'C' Rations, water and sometimes mail from home. These loads, quite often heavy were carried with a good humour and little complaint in the most atrocious weather ranging from snow to extreme heat. As well as bringing up much needed supplies the porters would also carry out wounded men.

One such recruit was a fourteen-year-old boy named Suk Bum Yoon. He had twice escaped from Communist-occupied Seoul before being forcibly drafted into the ROK. He, along with many others, was taken by a US Army truck towards the front line and eventually the boy ended up with the Royal Ulster Rifles, after he had been found wandering alongside a railway line by Sergeant Bill McConnell. Here was enlisted into the Battalion Porters, a group of some forty men. His first job was to carry a coil of barbed wire up to the forwards positions, but this proved too much of a load, the boy was weak from malnourishment. The Corporal in charge took the young Korean to RSM Patterson who then detailed him to be a general 'sweeper up' and to do odd jobs in the Rear Echelon.[13] For a time he worked with the MT Section under the watchful eye of Sergeant McConnell, who ensured he had a homemade uniform and received a weekly pay packet.[14] Suk Bum Yoon remained with the Battalion until it left Korea when he then became attached to the Royal Norfolk Regiment.[15]

On 3 February the new second-in-command of the Battalion arrived. This was Major Gerald Rickcord DSO, who had flown directly from the UK to Korea. The son of a naval commander, he had been commissioned into the Rifles in 1934 and served with the 1st Battalion in Egypt, Hong Kong and India. Rickcord returned to the UK in 1939 and was posted to the RUR Depot at Gough Barracks in Armagh. He was then posted to the 10th Battalion Royal East Kent Regiment (The Buffs) as Adjutant, serving from 1040 to 1942. During this time he also commanded a battery of 117 Light

---

13 Hastings, *The Korean War*, London, 1987.
14 Within the Rifles there were such boys, every company had at least one, who made tea and did odd jobs. When the Battalion left Korea for Hong Kong a sum of money was given to an orphanage in Seoul to pay for their keep. (Interview with Bill McConnell)
15 Suk Bum Yoon maintained a close correspondence with RSM Patterson and eventually became a professor of economics and the Dean of Yonsei University in Seoul. *President's Newsletter*, 2000/2001.

Suk Bum Yoon and a Rifleman.
(Mervyn McCord/RUR Association)

Colour Sergeant Rainey with Korean porters and Suk Bum Yoon. (Mervyn McCord/RUR Association)

Anti-Aircraft Regiment during the Luftwaffe air raids on Coventry. This was followed by time at the Senior Officers' School, Brasenose College, Oxford, the Staff College at Camberley and the School of Land Warfare. On returning to his Battalion he took command of B Company, leading it in Normandy and the Ardennes. He took command of the Battalion for Operation 'Varsity', the crossing of the Rhine, until the end of the War. He commanded the 1st Battalion post-war in Palestine, being awarded the DSO in 1945. This was followed by command of the 6th Airborne Division Battle School, before a return to Palestine as Commanding Officer of the 3rd Parachute Battalion. Between Palestine and Korea, he held appointments GS02 HQ N. Ireland District and Brigade Major, 107 (Ulster) Independent Infantry Brigade Group (TA). Prior to leaving for Korea Rickcord's full knowledge of the country came from reading the *Daily Telegraph*, and in this he was not alone. As a bachelor he had done his own packing for the flight and was reluctant to accept from an aunt two pairs of long-johns. Soon after arrival in Korea he was more than glad he had packed them. He also picked up the nickname 'Farmer's Boy', due to his complexion and relaxed manner, although it's doubtful if anyone ever called him that to his face!

A Company had been detached to provide local defence for 45th Field Regiment that was advancing in support of a ROK Regiment of 25th Division to the north of Anyang-Ni. The firepower of the Regiment was, in the parlance of the Americans, 'reinforcing the fires'. On 5 February D Company replaced C Company in defending the Gunners. On returning to the Battalion C Company claimed that their hearing had

REPLACEMENTS AND PRISONERS OF WAR   123

Korean porters by a rail siding. (Mervyn McCord/RUR Association)

been ruined for life. The Companies not employed on reconnaissance of the local roads began training for mountain warfare. This began with short marches over the local hills carrying full equipment. Later this would be extended to carrying extra water, food and ammunition.

On 9 February the Chinese released thirty seven prisoners close to the American front line. As part of a propaganda exercise the men were treated to a party prior to release and among them were six members of the Rifles. These men were able to confirm that the majority of those missing were in fact prisoners. At the same time the Communist authorities in Seoul ordered the civilian population to remain indoors because of a typhus epidemic. This would later form a major point in the propaganda war when the Chinese accused the UN of employing germ warfare. Given the fact that human excrement was used as a fertiliser and the widespread destruction of civil amenities by bombing, it was virtually impossible to prevent such an outbreak.

At noon on 11 February the Battalion left Osan-Ni and was transported by lorry to Suwon, all assuming that they were to remain in Corps Reserve and be billeted in their old home, the silkworm factory. However, when the Battalion arrived it was issued with fresh orders redirecting the Brigade and the Riflemen to Pabalmak, which entailed a long journey via Kumyangjang-Ni. Pabalmak was a sector held by the 1st US Cavalry Division and here the Battalion was to relieve the 5th US Cavalry Regiment. The column of lorries arrived after darkness had fallen and only a few thousand yards from where the Americans were fighting for control of a village. With the entire Brigade strung out over several miles of road, up ahead the Americans continued with their battle and the British troops watched as burning white phosphorous shells exploded on the mountainside.

On the road in front disabled American tanks were towed out of action as flares lit the desolate landscape below.

A preliminary reconnaissance was carried out and as a result the Battalion debussed and formed up on a man pack basis in the bed of a nearby river. At first light, which was 0800hrs on 12 February, the Battalion, less B Company, moved out of Pabalmak and up into the hills via a narrow valley to relieve the American troops, B Company remaining behind to act as porters. By 1430hrs, the relief was complete and the Battalion settled down to occupy the former positions of the Cavalry Regiment. The only casualty during the relief was a Rifleman injured by a splinter from a faulty shell that passed overhead.[16]

The area which the Battalion was now responsible for was mountainous and wild. The only road was that one leading from Pabalmak to the Han River, about twelve miles due north. This road was completely dominated by a long ridge running parallel to it on the eastern side, the main feature of which was Hill 327 on the southernmost tip. At the northern end the ridge rose to a rocky peak about 2,100 feet above the Han. To the west of the road the main ridgeline ran roughly north and south about four miles from the road; between this range and the road was a jumbled mass of hills between 300 and 400 feet high, intersected by deep valleys running eastwards down to the road itself.

---

16 Possibly Private Kelly of the Glosters on attachment to the Rifles.

8

Reconnaissance and Resupply

The task of 29 Brigade was to drive up the axis of the road clearing the hills on both sides as far as the Han. On the right flank the US 24th Regiment of 25th Division was to swing to the east to pin the enemy against the bend of the River. Within the Brigade the Glosters were to advance along the road and clear the hills to the east, while the Rifles were to take the left flank, while keeping contact with the 7th Regiment of the US 3rd Division further to the west. The Northumberland Fusiliers would not be able to deploy on the left until the initial advance was made and there was space for them to sidestep westwards.

The main problem was one of resupply. The Rifle Companies, along with their supporting weapons, were almost 4,000 yards forward of Battalion Headquarters, the intervening countryside was trackless wooded mountainside covered in snow on the higher slopes. The Battalion's A Echelon was another five miles to the south, along a track just about passable for four-wheeled drive vehicles or the Carriers.

On the night of 12 February the first sixty South Korean porters arrived at Headquarters, along with a supply of Everest carrying harnesses. Once instructed in its use they were put to work in moving forward ammunition, rations and wireless batteries to the forward positions, with the men of B Company providing guides and security. Not all the porters liked the supplied harness and many preferred the local Korean version known as a 'Jikkay'. This was a wooden frame shaped like an easel and with it a man, or woman, was capable of carrying a load of some 500lbs, which meant that ten loads equated with the load of a Dakota aircraft.[1] The 'Jikkay' was extensively used by the Chinese and the majority of supplies carried north of the Imjin were carried this way.

The journey was both long and difficult culminating in a climb of 1,300 feet to the various company positions and it as only possible to make one journey in the hours of daylight. Until the MSR, some two miles to the east, could be opened up by the advance of the Glosters, there was apparently no way for vehicles to get closer to the Rifle Companies.

At dawn on the morning of 13 February Major Rickcord and Captain Neely, commanding Headquarters Company, began a thorough reconnaissance of the mountain barrier. They returned that night to report the presence of a goat track that ran from Battalion Headquarters in the valley north over a ridgeline at a saddle some 900 feet high and then down into the village of Oyaso, in the lateral valley immediately behind the Rifle Companies. Major Rickcord believed that this track could be made 'jeepable' and along with Captain Neely, he took immediate steps to organise working parties. This work was all to be done with pick and shovel, the location being totally inaccessible to any form of machines. The men worked throughout the night and by midday on 14 February the first few loaded jeeps set off up the track to try it out. It was

---

1   Barclay, *The First Commonwealth Division*, Aldershot, 1954.

Hills across the Imjin (Henry O'Kane)

accepted that due to the snow and ice on the far side no jeeps would immediately be able to make the return journey.

The climb up the southern slope was relatively easy, the hairpin bends and steep rough gradients being free of snow. At the top, on a level saddle about twenty yards long, they were halted by Captain Neely at a previously established control point with wireless contact both forward to Tactical Headquarters and back to the Main Headquarters in the valley behind. From this point the track fell away steeply into the Oyaso valley, twisting down the mountainside with a gradient in places as much as one in three. Despite the Royal Engineers having strewn pine branches on the snow, the surface was packed firmly and was as slippery as solid ice. At the steepest point, Colour Sergeant Sturgeon of Support Company, with a dozen porters in attendance waited.

The journey down was simple, but terrifying. The jeep began the descent in four-wheel drive and in bottom gear, easing gently on to the slope, with both driver and passenger ready to instantly bale out should it become necessary. The use of brakes was virtually useless, but at the steepest point in the gradient, the porters gamely ran forward, grabbed the jeep at various points and digging in their heels braked it safely down the hill, round the bend and on to a relatively level section of the mountain. Using this method all jeeps made a safe crossing and later that afternoon the Main Headquarters moved over the 'hump' and was re-established with the 'Porter Base' at the village of Oyaso. For the remainder of the day jeeps continued to transport supplies over the mountain and by the following day work on the track had progressed to the extent that un-laden jeeps were able to cross back to A Echelon as well.

No advance was made this day, but reconnaissance patrols revealed considerable traces of enemy activity. During the day Lieutenant Hill, commanding the Mortar Platoon, discovered a number of Chinese anti-tank mines concealed beneath a bed of straw in a river ford on the road running from Oyaso east towards the main road. They were later lifted by members of the Assault Pioneer Platoon. That night an alert sentry

RUR Recce patrol in action (Henry O'Kane)

in A Company heard movement and several hand grenades were thrown out into the darkness. The following morning bloodied tracks in the snow confirmed that at least one enemy casualty had been caused.

Contact was made with the 3rd Battalion of the US 7th Regiment, when a patrol led by Sergeant Campbell of the Battle Patrol arrived in the walled village of Sansong-Ni. The Americans reported no sign of the enemy, although they had been attacked the previous night by a strong force and were still contesting possession of a high hill to the north.

In the early morning of 15 February a Korean civilian was observed approaching the Battalion position from the east. It transpired he came from the village of Pultang-Ni, about a mile from the Battalion Headquarters. The Korean reported that enemy soldiers were in his village, Pultang-Ni, demanding rice. At once the Battle Patrol was alerted and led by Captain Cocksedge set off for the village. On arrival there was a brief skirmish, which saw seven enemy casualties. Two of the Chinese officers and three other ranks were killed, while a wounded Chinese Medial Officer was taken prisoner. The only casualty to the Battle Patrol was Captain Cocksedge, who was shot in the shoulder. As a Section of the Defence Platoon, along with Captain Dungavel, the Rifles' Medical Officer, brought in Captain Cocksedge and the wounded Chinese MO there was another brief skirmish and a further Chinese soldier was killed. Later in the day several more North Korean soldiers who had initially fled the scene surrendered. Subsequent investigations by Captain Hinde, the Intelligence Officer, revealed that the men were from the 8th North Korean Division. This Division had previously made several night incursions against the 7th Regiment, 3rd US Division, which was located on the Battalion's left flank. The objective of the North Koreans was to cause disruption in the rear areas and to destroy various headquarters. In this they had not been successful and when dawn broke they found themselves in the open caught between the entrenched American infantry and a tank battalion.

At dawn Sergeant Kennedy of C Company had taken four Riflemen out on a reconnaissance patrol to investigate a small spur, known as 'Slag Heap Hill', about one mile ahead of the Battalion position. This hill overlooked the road and any Chinese positioned here had complete control of any passing traffic. Sergeant Kennedy posted Rifleman Lyons just beside the road with instructions to make a run for it if anything befell the remainder of the patrol. At a point further on Rifleman Smith was left in a position where he could observe Sergeant Kennedy and Rifleman Pratt as they searched the hilltop. Smith was equipped with a flare pistol and had been instructed to fire it to bring down supporting artillery should there be any enemy interference. As the Sergeant and Rifleman trawled the hilltop they saw a flare arc into the sky. Looking back down the hill they saw Rifleman Lyons surrounded by about a dozen Chinese soldiers. Rifleman Smith was firing at this group and managed to kill two of them before being wounded. When Kennedy and Pratt attempted to get back down the hill the supporting artillery began to fall, some of the shells exploding between them and the road. Unable to get off the hill the two men moved a few hundred yards to one flank and took cover in a stream bed. An Allied spotter aircraft then flew overhead and within a few minutes a hand grenade plopped into the water beside them. As the two men leapt out of the stream they found themselves confronted by an enemy patrol.

These were North Koreans, soldiers with a reputation for being quite ruthless. They quickly searched the two men and removed wristwatches, wallets and papers. Kennedy and Pratt were then forced to kneel and just as a pistol was put to their heads a Chinese patrol arrived on the scene and the officer immediately ordered the North Koreans to stop. They were questioned by the officer who asked them if they were Americans. Kennedy showed his pay book, which bore no trace of anything American and then pointed to their weapons, which were Sten guns. These weapons were familiar to the Chinese as they had been supplied with them during the Second World War in their fight against the Japanese.

There then followed a lecture by the Chinese officer on the evils of American pan-imperialism and the virtues of Chairman Mao's new regime, which was suddenly interrupted by an airstrike, probably called in by the spotter aircraft that had appeared earlier. Within a few seconds both Kennedy, Pratt and the entire contingent of Chinese were back in the stream bed sheltering from bomb fragments. When the aircraft left the patrol collected itself together and prepared to leave. The officer then indicated that Kennedy and Pratt should return to their own lines and warned them that should they be captured again they would be shot! Both groups then went their separate ways, dodging through the artillery shells that were still falling spasmodically.

As night fell Sergeant Kennedy and Rifleman Pratt took shelter in a peasant's hut where they were given some hot water to drink. Most of what happened that afternoon had been observed from C Company's position and it had been proposed that a fighting patrol be sent out to rescue the men. However, this was not permitted at the time as it was felt that more men might be lost in doing so.[2]

The following morning at first light shouts were heard from the front of the Company position and a patrol went out to find both Kennedy and Pratt slowly making their way

---

2   *Quis Separabit*, 1951.

RECONNAISSANCE AND RESUPPLY

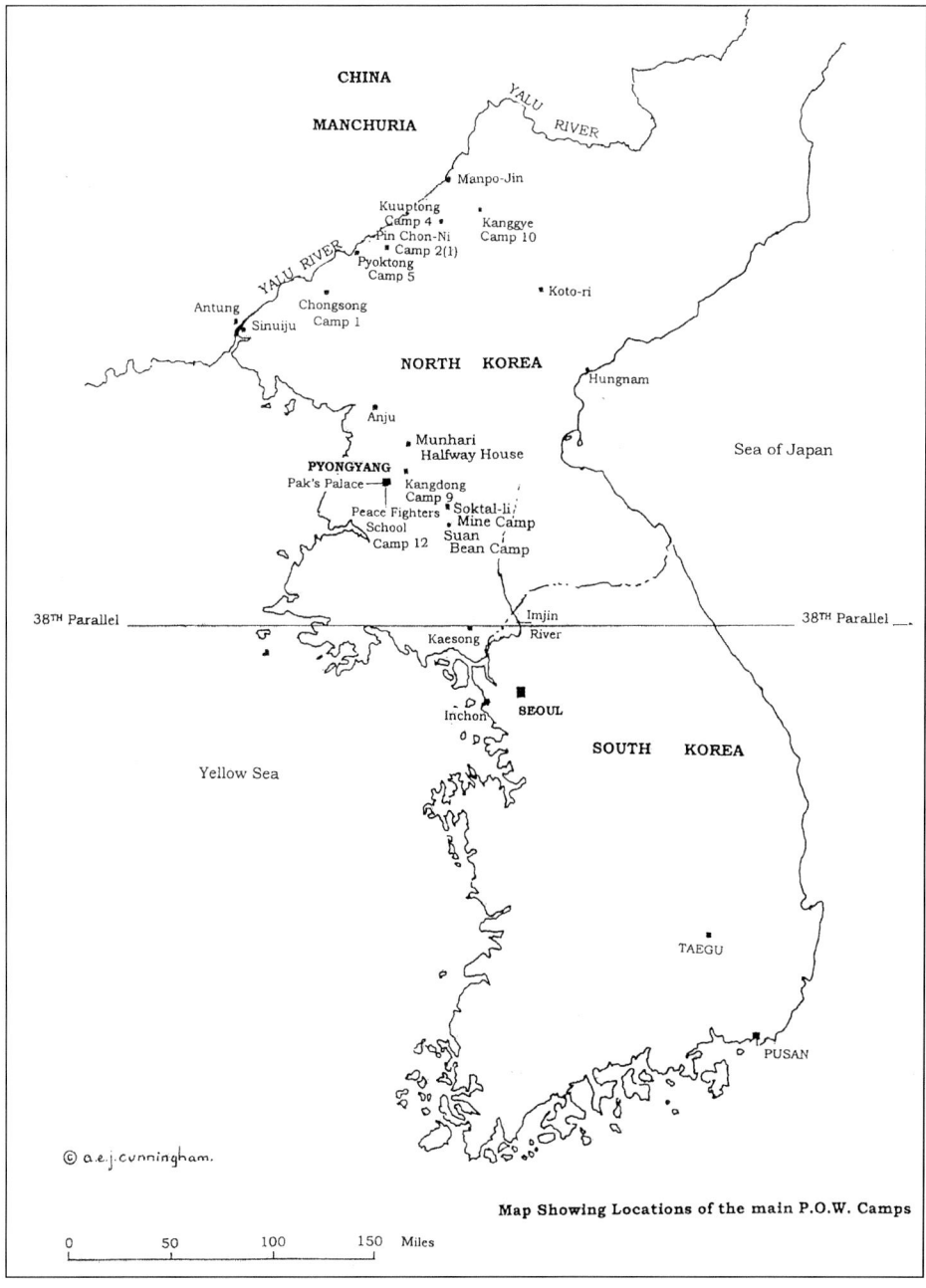

Map showing location of main POW camps in North Korea (Cyril Cunningham. Reproduced courtesy of Pen & Sword Publishers)

Sergeant S.J.H. Rankin,
missing in action.

back to the Company lines. A short time later a Korean peasant arrived with a note from Rifleman Smith. He was in hiding in the valley below with a leg wound, having crawled as far as possible from the site of the previous day's action. He had been left behind by the Chinese as he was unable to walk. When brought back into the Company lines and before being evacuated to hospital, Rifleman Smith was able to confirm that Rifleman Lyons had been taken prisoner by the Chinese.[3] Sergeant Kennedy and Rifleman Pratt were then sent back to B Echelon for a well-deserved rest.

At 0700hrs on 17 February, the Battalion stretched out its frozen limbs to the sound of the Hussars warming up the engines of their Centurions and discovered that the enemy had fled during the night. It seemed that the enemy was making little effort to defend the hills to the west of the main road and was in fact withdrawing on Hill 630, just short of the Han River.

On the same day at 'Bean Camp', Suan, the prisoners prepared to leave on the next stage of their march to the north. Those who were unable to walk or who felt they would not be able to keep up were left behind. For Sergeant S. Rankin, Lance Corporal Harris, Riflemen Griffiths, Akid and Gunner Slade, the fear of immediate execution was paramount and it came as a pleasant surprise when they were released and returned to UN lines. As a feature of the 'Lenient Policy' the prisoners were forced to take propaganda leaflets that called on UN troops to surrender. While these were carefully filed in the nearest rubbish bin, the information that the prisoners could give revealed a lot about how the remaining men were being treated. Sergeant Rankin was able to bring with him a list of those men from the Battalion he had seen in the prison camp. For those who had marched out of 'Bean Camp', Corporal Massey continued to record the journey:

---

3   Rifleman E.B. Lyons, No 14465525, died as a prisoner of war.

The cover of a book of prayer for Captain James Majury, made and presented by the many Protestants, No.2 Company, Prisoner of War Camp Number 2, North Korea. (Mervyn McCord/RUR Association)

Marching again tonight. Don't know where. Supposed to have got a train tonight, but something went wrong. Have to march another three days. Tonight's march nearly creased me. Came to a little village. Slept with some Yanks and Turks.

The column continued to move north and many men died in the snow. Attempts by other prisoners to bury them resulted in threats and curses from the guards. On one occasion Major Ryan and other Riflemen ignored the raised rifles and carried on with a burial, the Major offering a prayer as the dead prisoner was lowered in to his grave.

On 18 February the Rifles moved forward to the lateral ridgeline, once again no opposition was encountered and by nightfall all companies had reached their objectives. Battalion Headquarters and the vehicles of Support Company were now able to move down the Oyaso valley to the main road, at the junction they turned and after a mile and a half turned west up a track in the next re-entrant. For once the severe cold weather was a help rather than a hindrance. As the jeep column cleared the track a Royal Engineers officer arrived and began to dig out several large anti-tank mines that had lain, frozen solid, a mere half inch below the snow in the middle of the track.

Brigadier Brodie ordered a company of the Glosters with a squadron of the Hussars to advance along the road, while the Rifles would follow behind, sweeping the sides of the valley. The Northumberland Fusiliers were tasked with clearing the ridgeline to the west. The remainder of the Glosters were then to act as reserve and to occupy Hills 327 and 248, providing a firm base. As this was happening the 2nd Battalion of the 24th Regiment was to advance on the Brigade's right flank and secure Hill 630.

Throughout the morning of 19 February the advance continued, albeit with little excitement. Things changed at about midday. The Hussars and Glosters reported that they were coming under heavy mortar and small arms fire from enemy positions dug-in on the north-west spurs of Hill 630, near the village of Changu-Ri. As this was within the Rifles' boundary preparations were made to launch an attack and the Battalion was moved up to an assembly area east of the main road and about 800 yards south of the enemy positions. A pre-attack bombardment from the artillery, mortars and Centurion 20 pounders was fired, but shortly afterwards Brigade Headquarters called off the attack as it was thought that not enough daylight remained. It was decided that a full set-piece attack would be carried out the following day.

As dusk fell the Battalion was formed into a secure perimeter on the road with the near vertical wall of Hill 630 on the right flank. Up to this time there was no evidence that the Chinese held the summit of the hill, although continual movement was observed on the spurs. Aerial reconnaissance showed a number of strong bunkers present and considerable enemy activity on the reverse slopes just to the east of Changu-Ri. To the west of the road the Fusiliers had successfully completed their sweep and their forward company was positioned on Hill 127 at the western end of the ridge.

Due to severe resistance the 2nd Battalion US 24th Regiment had made slow progress along the main ridgeline towards Hill 630 and as darkness fell the Battalion was forced to call a halt about a mile short of the peak. Later that evening a Liaison Officer equipped with a wireless set arrived with the Rifles to provide a direct link in the following day's operations.

The plan for 20 February was as follows. The 24th Battalion would continue to advance along the ridge and take Hill 630, A, B, and C Company of the Rifles would work their way up into the west flank of the Hill and then assault along and down the main spur towards the river. Support for this would come from the Rifles' own Support Company, 170 Mortar Battery, a squadron of Centurions, two troops of Bofors guns operating in the ground role and a further squadron of Churchill tanks from the Royal Tank Regiment. As a diversion, the tanks along with the carriers of the Battle Patrol, would drive north along the valley to a position west and slightly north of the enemy position and then engage the reverse slope with fire from all available weapons.

The Battle Patrol diversion moved out at 0800hrs on 20 February, with the main assault force moving up the hill at 1000hrs. Along the road it looked as if the vehicles were on parade with tanks, Bofors and carriers lined up in a row, barely screened by a few trees. The second-in-command was present with the diversionary force and had set up a 'fire control centre' in order to receive wireless messages from the Tactical Headquarters at the foot of the hill.

On Hill 630 the Rifles made a laborious climb over the snow-covered slopes, Meeting no resistance for the first hour. At 1200hrs, A Company, in the vanguard, was pinned down by heavy machine-gun fire from the cliffs above. Rifleman Smith was wounded in the leg by a gunshot, while Rifleman G. Sainsbury was hit in the groin and left hand by shell fragments. Despite the Company's own return fire and support from 170 Mortar Battery, they were unable to resume the advance. In view of this it was decided that the Rifles should hold firm while the 24th Regiment could take the top of the ridge from the south.

Colonel Carson had come forward to meet with Major Nixon to discuss the best way to continue the advance. While both men scanned the rocks above with their binoculars a reflection must have been spotted by one of the Chinese gunners. Suddenly an accurate

RECONNAISSANCE AND RESUPPLY   133

Imjin Patrols (Mervyn McCord)

2nd Lieutentant McCord, Anti-Tank Platoon Comander. 17 pdr
A/T gun in the background. (Mervyn McCord)

burst of machine-gun fire peppered the area and Nixon went down wounded in the side. It was a serious wound and the Major was evacuated down the tortuous slope, being carried by some of the ever-present Battalion Porters.

The Chinese machine-guns were well protected by earthen bunkers and despite every effort were proving impossible to dislodge or silence. An air strike was requested, dangerous with friendly troops so close to the target, but no aircraft were available. The Mortar Battery continued to bomb the hill and the shellfire from the Centurions was extremely accurate, but the field guns were unable to assist as the enemy were in dead ground.

While the Vickers machine-guns were sweeping the hillside, Captain Arthur McCallan, the Platoon Commander, spotted an enemy OP on the summit through his binoculars. Passing this information back to the Adjutant, it was in turn passed to the 'fire control centre' for the attention of the Centurions. Within seconds about twenty rounds of high explosive from the tanks' main armament slammed into the large boulder that helped conceal the OP. At a range of some 2,000 yards it was extremely accurate and the OP ceased to operate. The diversionary force did not get things all its own way and return mortar fire from the Chinese fell close to the vehicles, killing one man and wounding three others of the Battle Patrol.[4] A little later Captain Nigel Balders, on secondment from the Suffolk Regiment, and replacing the previously wounded Captain Cocksedge, was mortally wounded, dying later that night.

By 1400hrs, the US 24th Regiment had successfully captured the 'start line', having had excellent support from the Centurion and Churchill tanks and this allowed the Rifles to advance without further loss. The final one hundred feet of the climb was the hardest the Riflemen had experienced so far and it became increasingly obvious to Colonel Carson that the Battalion's task would not be completed by nightfall.

Brigade Headquarters ordered Carson to hold fast on the summit overnight and complete its sweep the following morning. By 1800hrs it was dark and had become bitterly cold. The men were only lightly dressed, having expected to complete the operation during daylight hours. As they settled down they attempted to dig in, a task not made easier by the ground being covered in snow and the temperature dropping to below freezing. The resupply of rations and ammunition had been promised and was to be delivered by a combined force of Porters, from both the Rifles and Northumberland Fusiliers, at about 2200hrs. Lieutenants Gill and Dunlop were given command and as dusk fell they began to scale the snow-covered hill without benefit of illumination from moon or stars and with no track to follow. By 2300hrs there was no sign of any delivery and contact was made with Battalion Headquarters at the base of the mountain by wireless. The reply was that the Porters had left some time ago and their arrival should be expected at any moment. Therefore the Riflemen settled down to wait for the 'any moment'.[5] By 0200hrs there was still no sign of the Porters and Battalion HQ was again contacted, but could offer no further information. On the mountain top near-frozen men huddled together to keep warm or jumped up and down to increase circulation. At 0300hrs the Battalion was informed that the Porters had returned to base having lost their way in the darkness. For the men on the mountain top it was the longest night in history. However, all was not lost. Captain Mike Glover, one of the Royal Artillery

4   Possibly Rifleman Heward or Rifleman Kelly.
5   *Quis Separabit*, 1951.

Forward Observation officers, had come down the hill a short time earlier and he offered to lead another group of porters to the summit. Lieutenant John Mason immediately rounded up the required number of men, arriving with the men on the summit just before dawn.

Colonel Carson ordered the Rifles forward at 0700hrs on 21 February, the advance down the spur meeting no resistance. By midday the operation was declared complete and it was found that the remaining enemy had crossed the frozen Han River leaving behind only seven dead. The small number of casualties was explained by the fact that during the hours of darkness there had been considerable activity on the hilltop and it was assumed that large numbers of dead and wounded had been carried away.

Despite combat having ceased, there was still the weather to do battle with and heavy rain began, which chilled everyone to the bone. Most of the Battalion were able to find some shelter in a few houses on the lower slopes of the hill. A Company was less fortunate, being positioned on the spur of the main ridge. All ranks had a miserable night and suffered several casualties from exposure.

The following day, 22 February, Major John Shaw and a troop of tanks from 'C' Squadron went out to reconnoitre a large sandbank in the Han River, according to some civilians it was still occupied by the enemy. The patrol found no enemy, but did attract a fair degree of interest from Chinese mortars firing from north of the River. No casualties were sustained and the patrol returned to report no enemy south of the Han.

The Riflemen were relieved from their positions by a battalion of the 24th Regiment on 23 February and returned at 1000hrs for a well-deserved rest in Corps Reserve in the vicinity of Osan-Ni. Here the Battalion was dispersed to various small villages around Osan-Ni. A Company was billeted in a Korean school and within a short time had converted the school yard into a football pitch, which was much in demand by other units. A successful match was played against the Northumberland Fusiliers, the score being one goal to nil. Training was not neglected, the emphasis being on patrolling and anti-ambush drills.

Meanwhile, north of the Imjin, Corporal Massey was again recording his time as a prisoner of war. On or about 23 February he wrote, "Raining all day. Lucky we got a place to sleep. Feeling very bad on the march. Have a cold in my chest. This march is only supposed to last a few more days. Hope I make it." On reaching the various camps prisoners were interviewed by English-speaking Chinese. Here all prisoners were required to provide an autobiographical registration form that gave details of parents, home life, schooling, political leanings and their military service. All men gave their name and number, but as for the other entries these varied widely from corrupted details written in poor handwriting to one man who claimed he was Private 123456, Stalin, Joseph of 1 Kremlin Terrace, Moscow.[6] On the death of Lieutenant Probyn of the Hussars at Suan, Major Ryan was spoken to by a Chinese interpreter who offered his condolences and assured Ryan that such 'unnecessary deaths' would soon come to an end when China and Russia liberated the oppressed workers of the United States and Great Britain. Major Ryan received this with a deathly silence and walked away from his captor.[7] As far as the Chinese were concerned all prisoners were war criminals as they had fought a war of aggression and as such could be executed as stated under the Potsdam Agreement.

---

6   Catchpole, *The Korean War*, London, 2000.
7   Cunningham, *No Mercy, No Leniency*, London, 2000.

However, as part of the Chinese People's Volunteers 'Lenient Policy' this would not be exercised as the soldiers had plainly been hoodwinked by their superiors. As long as prisoners showed a willingness to cooperate they would receive fair treatment. Not all Riflemen proved to be ideal captives. Riflemen J.T. Alexander, J. Shaw and J.J. Buckley were three of the most obstinate. Buckley had managed to conceal a camera despite numerous searches, until he was betrayed by another prisoner. Arrested as a 'spy' he was ordered to confess and when he refused he was beaten around the head with fists and clubs and sent to solitary confinement for two months. On release Buckley returned to the compound, sought out the man who had betrayed him and beat him senseless.

South of the Imjin the Battalion carried on with its regular duties and on 28 February D Company was dispatched to Suwon to take over the defences of the airfield. This would last until 5 March.

On 2 March thirty men were selected from B Company and under the command of Captain Dickie Miller were sent on a most secret operation south of the Han. The weather was absolutely blissful, with orchards in full bloom and the patrol drove about the countryside making noise and creating the impression of a much larger force with the use of increased wireless traffic. On their return on 5 March all was revealed. The Northumberland Fusiliers, with detachments from the other battalions, some tanks and elements from other units, had spent four days simulating a crossing of the Han west of Seoul. This crossing did not, of course, happen, but such was the consternation caused to the Chinese that a proposed crossing designed to outflank Seoul, was cancelled. On 4 March Captain McCallan returned to the Battalion from hospital, fully recovered from the wounds he had received on 3 January.

On 6 March the Battalion was put on orders to move and thanks to the few days rest and recreation all ranks were fit and ready for action. The following day the Battalion moved across country passing through Suwon and Kumyanjang-Ni to Inchon, the furthermost east they had travelled so far in the war.[8] Once again 29 Brigade was allocated to the Army reserve and the Rifles were tasked with a series of counter-attack tasks and reconnaissance; these was immediately carried out over the next two days by the Battalion officers.

North of Inchon the US 24th Division and 27th Commonwealth Brigade had succeeded in securing a crossing on the Han River where it joined the Pukhan River. These bridgeheads were far from secure and it was expected that a Chinese counter-attack would be more than likely.

Corporal Massey and his fellow prisoners had arrived at their new home and his diary recalls the moment:

> 6th March. Arrived at our destination. Just a bombed village. Got no food here. Quite a few Yanks die here every day. Got an overcoat and blanket. Food not good. Sugar ration only one spoonful each. Our food ration is 200gms of rice per day 200gms of millet and 200 of corn.

Massey's new home was Camp 5 and held approximately three hundred American prisoners, there seemed to be no internal discipline exercised by their officers, morale was non-existent and the conditions deplorable. With the arrival of the British contingent

---

8   This town is also spelt as Kumyangjang, which seems to be common factor in books about Korea.

RSM Patterson, Major Rickcord and piper, St Patrick's Day, 1951. (Mervyn McCord/RUR Association)

Outdoor canteen line, St Patrick's Day 1951. (Mervyn McCord/RUR Association)

Major Ryan and the other officers began to try and bring some semblance of order to the camp. This was not an easy task; the American compounds seemed to be controlled by racketeers who ran a thriving black market, which included putting dying prisoners outside in the winter conditions until they died, while their so-called fellow soldiers continued to claim their rations. Within the British prisoners it was decide that they would remain together and look after themselves, continuing their own command structure and discipline. The North Koreans attempted to thwart this by removing the officers to a separate compound, but had not reckoned on the ability of NCOs, who were more than capable of assuming command. Captain Ferrie, the Medical Officer, was permitted to visit the 'other ranks' compound, but without supplies of equipment there was little he could do but issue instruction on basic hygiene. Things improved slightly once the Chinese took control of the camp with a limited issued of medical supplies. However, the Chinese instructions that all men were to be given equal doses meant that those more seriously ill died. Captain Ferrie tried to explain this, but was told that if one man received more than another it was 'undemocratic'. An attempt by the Chinese to establish 'Daily Life' committees within the camp met with only limited success with the Rifles, and while Major Ryan served on such a committee and took on the day-to-day running of the compound, he refused to enter into any political discussion. Rifleman Joe Lavery recalled that apathy was a great danger in the camp, with some men just lying in their own waste and refusing to move for any reason. Despite not being in the best of health Lavery searched the camp for extra food for the sick, forcing them to eat and trying to get them to their feet. With some men it took threats and sometime actual blows to get them to move, but it did help save lives.

Captain Ivor Daniels, Major Rickcord and Lieutenant Mervyn McCord, on board the tender to HMS *Belfast*. (Mervyn McCord/RUR Association)

McCord, Smyth and Rickcord on a tender from HMS *Belfast*, Inchon 1951. (Mervyn McCord/RUR Association)

South of the Imjin the Battalion spent the next few days settling into the new quarters in their various villages, enjoying whatever comforts they could organise for themselves. On 15 March Lieutenant Max Nicholls and his No 8 Platoon of C Company carried out a demonstration of small-arms tactics across the open paddy fields. This demonstration was for the benefit of a large number of officers and NCOs of the Brigade and was a complete success. The afternoon was rounded off with a football game against the Glosters, which the Rifles won four goals to one.

Meanwhile the majority of the Battalion Porters were on loan to the Royal Engineers to assist in keeping the roads under repair – the spring thaw was causing problems with subsidence and threatening the lines of communication. By now the Porters had evolved into a well-organised and efficient body of men. Their strength varied from 100 to 150, depending on sickness and the very occasional case of desertion, but reinforcements were always on hand. The Battalion Porter badge, the identity disc made from the ubiquitous 3" mortar bomb container lid, had now been amended to read '57 Porter'. This not only identified them as belonging to the Rifles, it stopped them being 'press-ganged' by other units, or having them harassed by the ROK Police. Despite the disc being their only article of uniform it was worn with great pride and there was a strong *esprit de corps* within the unit. They became very attached to the Battalion and the Battalion to them, each Company having its own favourites. A Porter Sergeant Major was appointed, as were Porter NCOs and there was even a Porter Colour Sergeant, who issued the daily rice ration. He soon developed all those characteristics that a good Colour Sergeant should have. Overall command of the Porters had devolved to Lieutenant Victor Dunlop, with

McCord, Smyth and Rickcord onboard HMS *Belfast*, Inchon 1951. (Mervyn McCord/RUR Association)

HMS *Belfast*'s 6 inch guns bombard Haju, west coast of Korea, Christmas 1951. (Stan Packer)

RECONNAISSANCE AND RESUPPLY 141

HMS *Belfast* in the Inland Sea for Kure, Japan, 1950-52. (Stan Packer)

the able assistance of Corporal McKeown. Both men put their hearts into what at first seemed a dull job and turned it into a labour of love. It was mainly due to their efforts that the loyalty and efficiency of the Porters was so high throughout the campaign.

The situation on the Han River remained stable and it appeared that the Battalion might be lucky enough to spend St. Patrick's Day in reserve. Preparations were made, a theatre was build and the 29 Brigade concert party were booked. A football match against the 8th Hussars was arranged and invitations to a Sergeants' Mess Smoker and an Officers' Mess Dinner issued.

Things remained quiet and on 17 March, St. Patrick's Day, the sun shone out of a clear blue sky. Brigadier Brodie had virtually promised that he would not move the Battalion if at all possible and he remained true to his word. B Echelon's contribution to the celebrations was without equal. All ranks fed well, if not wisely, with pork, ham and turkey washed down with free beer and Guinness. Luckily the day was quiet and no action required. RSM Patterson and the Sergeants' Mess laid on a successful 'smoker', which impressed the remainder of the Brigade to the extent that 17 March 1952 was immediately ringed in red ink. The only disappointment was the lack of shamrock, apparently it 'died' on the way out from the UK to Korea. However, some comfort was taken in that the final score in the football match saw the Hussars losing five goals to three.

In the early hours of 19 March a signal was received from HMS *Belfast,* then lying off shore at Inchon. An invitation was issued to the officers of the Battalion to pay the cruiser a visit that day. As General Sir Richard Gale was in turn visiting the Battalion at the same time Colonel Carson was unable to accept. Therefore Major Rickcord, the 2ic, Major de Longeuil, Captain Daniels, Lieutenant McCord and Captain Tom Smith quickly got themselves together and made the seventy-five mile drive to the coast. After

Three North Korean prisoners captured at Chinnampo, 18 March 1951 on board HMS *Belfast*. The guard on the right is carrying the Sten Gun Mk V. (Stan Packer)

a short wait on the dockside and with the assistance of an American LCT[9] the four officers were taken from shore to ship and received a warm welcome from Captain Sir Aubrey St. Clair Ford, DSO, RN. As they arrived on board there was an offer to clean their uniforms courtesy of the onboard Chinese-run laundry.[10] Over lunch and several pink gins much was done to further the close relationship between the cruiser and the Regiment, which had existed since the cruiser was first launched. When it was time to leave the officers were played over the side by the Royal Marine band to the tune *Off, Off, Said the Stranger*.

As this was going on General Gale, the Director General of Military Training, had spent the day with the Battalion. Lieutenant Nichols and his No 8 Platoon repeated their 'attack across the paddy field' tactical demonstration, while the Mortar Platoon went through its paces. At the end of the day the General commented favourably on all he saw and left the Battalion feeling well pleased with itself.

Two days later the comfortable stay came to an end and just before midday the Battalion moved to the west coast, once again courtesy of 'Wags Truckers', eventually taking up residence in an old Japanese ordnance depot at Yongdungpo in the southern suburb of Seoul. The advance across the Han had fractured the enemy grip on his river defences and the US 1st Corps had been able to cross in the western sector without serious opposition. The Chinese troops were now withdrawing north to the next river some thirty five miles away, where the Imjin flows into the Han Estuary.

---

9 Landing Craft Tank.
10 It was only some years later that the Rifles officer discovered that due to having lived in the field for so long their uniforms stank to high heaven.

The 1st ROK Division was methodically working its way north along the axis of the Seoul – Musan-Ni Road, while the US 3rd Division moved in concert with it on the Uijongbu axis. 29 Brigade was held in the Seoul area ready to move in whichever direction required. In fact any reinforcement was not required immediately and it was only after an American airdrop failed, through no fault of its own, to fully cut off the escape of the Chinese rearguard at Musan that the Rifles were sent into action.[11] On the eastern flank the US 3rd Division began to meet strong resistance and the Brigade was ordered into the gap between them and the 1st ROK Division north west of Uijongbu.

While at Yongdungpo the Battalion was able to send a burial party back to Happy Valley to bury the dead of 3-4 January. Along with a similar party from the Hussars and 45 Field Regiment, this was successfully carried out, with the vast majority of the bodies being recovered. These were buried in a cemetery created at the head of the pass. On finding the corpse of Lieutenant Prescott-Westcar, it was discovered that his hands and feet had been tied together. This was not unusual – the Chinese had done this with many bodies as it made them easier to drag across the frozen ground to gather them all together. Unfortunately some misguided padre wrote to Prescott-Westcar's parents to tell them this in some detail, which naturally caused a great deal of upset and bitterness. For many years afterwards the parents inserted an acrimoniously worded memorial in both *The Times* and *Daily Telegraph* on the anniversary of the battle.

While passing a stonemason's yard in Seoul Colonel Carson noticed a large piece of pink granite, which he felt was suitable for a memorial. After a degree of haggling by both parties the granite and stonemason accompanied the Battalion on its future travels in Korea.

The Battalion finally moved out at 0400hrs on the morning of 31 March, this time on the trucks of 57 Company RASC, a full reconnaissance having been carried out the previous day by Colonel Carson. The convoy carrying the Battalion crossed the Han River, through the deserted streets of Seoul and on towards Uijongbu. The journey was without incident and by 0900hrs the lorries had driven off the main road for a few miles, ending up in a pleasant valley about twelve miles north of Uijongbu. To the north the men could see an airstrike hitting the summit of Mau San, a 2,000 foot high mountain then under attack by the 7th Regiment of the 3rd US Division. This assault had been underway for the last two days, but neither of the two battalions involved had managed to gain more than a tenacious foothold on the lower slopes. Lying west of Mau San the hills rose in a thickly wooded mountain barrier dominated by Kamak San, 675 metres high. In the foothills of this range the 65th (Puerto Rican) Regiment was steadily pushing forward and it was into this area that the Rifles moved. The 65th, like the US 7th Cavalry Regiment, used *Garry Owen* as one of their marches, a tune well familiar to the Rifles. By nightfall the Rifles were concentrated, with the exception of C Company, in a small valley under the foot of Kamak San. C Company had been ordered to push on up the mountain and they made a gallant effort to do so. However, by 2100hrs, after a nightmare march up a heavily wooded and rocky slope, they were forced to call a halt, as the near complete darkness made any further movement impossible.

---

11 It was intended that the 187 ACT was to parachute in and cut off the escape of the rearguard, but the drop was timed a few hours too late and only some small parties of enemy were captured.

9

On the Imjin

During the night the wireless in Battalion Headquarters was in almost constant use as intelligence reports from Brigade came in. Colonel Carson was informed that it appeared the enemy was not making any effort to defend the ground between the Brigade and the Imjin River, some eight miles to the north. On the right flank the 3rd US Division was going to make a full-scale attack on Mau San, the garrison of which showed signs of weakening.

The Battalion moved off at first light on 1 April, marching into the almost trackless hills, and took over ground previously held by the 65th Regimental Combat Team of the US 3rd Division. Such was the terrain that no wheeled vehicles could be used and all weapons, ammunition, rations and other supplies, including a troop of the 4.2" mortars, had to be carried. The Main Headquarters, which was jeep-borne, and the vehicles of Support Company were sent off to swing round to the east and proceed forward along a suitable track that ran north between Kamak San and Mau San – a track that would no longer be under Chinese control once the American attack had succeeded.

It was during early April that three members of the Battalion held prisoner north of the Imjin attempted an escape. Riflemen Dunne, Moore and Kaye had managed to establish a supply dump on the route they intended to take out of the camp. With the assistance of some trusted fellow prisoners they made a successful breakout, but were forced to return a short time later, unseen and unmissed by the guards. On being questioned why, they revealed that they had forgotten to include matches in their supplies and given the weather conditions, without heat they would not have survived.

The Divisional attack on Mau San was a success and by mid-morning the Battalion's vehicles were able to get forward, moving by bounds up the road. By early evening the Battalion, having completed a gruelling march across country, were in their assigned positions in the hills overlooking the Imjin. As it became dark the jeep convoy and Support Company carriers had arrived in a narrow valley just behind these hills. No contact had been made with the enemy and the American units on the right, having cleared Mau San, were able to push forward to the river in their sector.

With this knowledge making the situation more secure the Battalion settled down for the night. As the various companies began to dig in there was a sudden flurry of activity in Battalion Headquarters, A and B Company. A fire, started by a Signaller in Tactical Headquarters, went out of control and the hillside vegetation, tinder dry after the recent fine weather, caught fire in several places and a rapidly spreading wall of flame ran up the mountainside, destroying about two hundred acres of ground. It was necessary for the companies to move back until the fire had burned itself out and some equipment was lost to the flames. By 1700hrs communications had been opened with the US 3rd Division and both Liaison and Forward Observation Officers were ensconced with the Battalion, which now had the support of the US 39th Field Artillery Battalion, equipped with 105mm guns. While this American method of support was new to the company commanders there were few complaints regarding the weight of fire produced or the delivery of star shells that helped standing patrols ascertain the presence of the enemy, or not!

The 29th Brigade was now dug-in on the hill range south of the Imjin River blocking the route southwards to the Korean capital. They had a clear view of the riverbank below them and were flanked to the west by the 1st ROK Division and, to the east, the US 3rd 'Rock of the Marne' Division, both good infantry units. The position looked stronger than it was as the river, despite being some three hundred yards wide, could be forded at many points, being in reality very shallow. Brigadier Brodie had approximately two and a half thousand rifles to defend a seven and a half mile front.

The sector occupied by the Battalion, located in the foothills of the Kamak San massif, dropped almost down to the river's edge. While the main Battalion positions were about 2,000 yards back from the river, C Company was positioned well forward on Hill 152, which directly overlooked the riverbanks. From here a wide view of the river and a large portion of the far bank could be kept under observation, as could the only know ford in the area, just below the village of Yulp'p-Ri. This position also established C Company as the most forward UN position in Korea.

An intense programme of patrolling began immediately and a reconnaissance in detail was carried towards the river to the Battalion's immediate front. Within these patrols several men wore coloured fluorescent vests to enable supporting aircraft to identify friendly forces. In the event of coming under fire from the nearby hillsides, even from a single sniper, an accompanying air controller, if present, could quickly bring in an airstrike on the suspected position, usually using napalm. The colour of the fluorescent vests were changed every couple of days to prevent the Chinese from copying them.

A small Tactical Headquarters, consisting of Colonel Carson and the Intelligence Officer, Captain Hind, moved up to join C Company and a fighting patrol was ordered out on the night of 2 April. As the reconnaissance was not complete this was postponed for twenty-four hours, but in fact was not carried out until 5 April, due to the difficulty of finding assault boats to carry the men across.

The C Company OP soon became as popular as a box at Ascot and on most days could be found crowded with visitors, armed with binoculars, scrutinising the far hills for any sight of the enemy. At this time the Battalion was supported by the 105mm guns of the 39th US Field Artillery Battalion and anything spotted that could possibly be construed as 'enemy activity' brought down a prompt barrage. If nothing else the enemy was forced to keep his head down and restrict any movement to the hours of darkness. One particular well-concealed machine-gun post caused trouble for a while. It was cleverly dug-into the far bank of the river and took many watchful hours to find. Once spotted the combined fire from the American artillery and the 170 Mortars ensured no further interference.

On 4 April Brigadier Brodie sent out some of the Belgians and a patrol of the 8th Hussars' Centurion tanks to search no-man's land in front of their sector. The joint force bumped into an enemy fighting patrol four miles north of the river. The ensuing firefight, supported by the Centurion's Besa machine-guns, resulted in the Chinese breaking off, leaving behind one of their men subsequently taken prisoner. However when questioned he was able to tell his captors very little of use.

"You are crossing the 38th Parallel by courtesy of the Royal Ulster Rifles", the Ulster Crossing, early April 1951. (Mervyn McCord/RUR Association)

Back to the Imjin-Ulster Crossing, early April 1951. Royal Ulster Rifleman with his hand on a jeep with the road winding out behind. (Mervyn McCord/RUR Museum)

The following day a patrol under the command of Second Lieutenant Derek Gill crossed the river in darkness to carry out a reconnaissance of the village of Tojong, some 800 yards from the far bank. This patrol consisted of Gill, a Corporal, a Rifleman and an interpreter. All ranks were lightly dressed and carried only the minimum of equipment, ammunition pouches and a water bottle, arms were the US M1 Carbine, Sten guns and hand grenades. Rubber PT shoes were worn and as opposed to maps, each man carried a sketch map that had been previously drawn by the individual. The crossing point was covered by snipers from the Battalion and the entire episode was personally controlled by Colonel Carson. Both the crossing and patrol were without incident and there was no evidence of the enemy in or around the village. There was a suspicion that the patrol was followed back to the river, but if there was enemy present they made no attempt to interfere with the patrol or return journey. A further two patrols this time had similar results.

By 8 April, the period of patrolling and reconnaissance along the line of the river showed signs of coming to an end. On the Brigade's right flank the US 3rd Division was beginning its push forward towards the Imjin. At the junction of where the right flank of the 29th Brigade met the 3rd Battalion of the US 7th Regiment, the Imjin turned sharply north, while a tributary, the Hantan, flowed in from the east. The American forces, having successfully patrolled across the Hantan, were now to advance across it in strength and continue their advance to the east bank of the Imjin. As this was happening the 29th Brigade would remain on the south bank of the Imjin, with the exception of the Rifles, who would cross and occupy the vital ground, Hill 194, on which the line would swing, inside the bend of the Imjin on the west bank.

At this time of the year the Imjin was flowing at about eight miles per hour and where the Battalion was to cross it ran deep, approximately twelve feet, with steep banks between thirty and fifty feet high. Any bridgehead that could be established would be under direct observation from Hill 194, which was covered in enemy bunkers and communication trenches. This position would be assaulted by the Rifles in a combined infantry and armour attack. To assist the Battalion in crossing the entire firepower of the Brigade was made available, along with B Squadron of the Hussars. An additional unit provided was a troop of Sappers from the 55th Field Squadron, Royal Engineers.

The first task was to find a suitable crossing place and a reconnaissance party consisting of Major Rickcord, Major Richard Butler of the Hussars and Captain John Page of the Royal Engineers, set off to explore the river banks. Their initial attempt was unsuccessful and drew some sniper fire as they waded in the river to test its depth. The second proved positive and a suitable spot was found approximately one hundred yards up the Hantan. This would involve the Battalion crossing the Hantan and then making a second crossing of the Imjin north of the confluence of the two rivers. However, a ravine on the bank of the Hantan provided a covered approach to the Imjin and on both rivers the fords were suitable for both the Oxford Carriers and tanks of the Hussars. While the Battalion was briefed on the crossing the Sappers brought up their equipment and began to bring up their bridging materials and improve the river approaches.

On the afternoon of 9 April the Northumberland Fusiliers relieved the Battalion and the Riflemen prepared for the crossing, which would take place at first light the following morning. During the night the Sappers constructed footbridges across both rivers, while B Company made themselves familiar with the mounting and dismounting of the Centurions that would carry them across the rivers.

The second hand of various wristwatches had just passed 0600hrs, when a five minute concentration of high explosive fire crashed down on the Battalion's objectives. The Centurion's Rolls Royce Meteor engines roared into life and forged across both waterways to deliver B Company, dry shod, on the north bank of the Imjin. The first footbridge, despite Herculean efforts by the Sappers, was not quite finished and a ten foot gap remained. The men of the Royal Engineers, not to be bested by such a small obstacle, carried the Riflemen men across the gap on their backs, therefore ensuring that men going into battle did not do so soaked in icy water. The second footbridge had to be abandoned when several sections of it were swept away in the strong current. Not to allow delays to endanger the assault, the Centurions and Oxford Carriers then supplied a shuttle service to see the remainder of the Battalion across the two rivers.

As the advance closed in on Hill 194, any suspected enemy position was brought under fire from the supporting artillery and the 20 pounders of the Centurions and then rushed by the infantry. However, no resistance was encountered and when, at 1315hrs, B Company sent up their success signal from the top of Hill 194, it was obvious that the enemy had once again withdrawn out of contact. On the east bank of the Imjin the American forces were driving hard against the Chinese, who were carrying out a fighting withdrawal and now with the Rifles across the river they were outflanked and had no option but to continue to fall back.

The Battalion then reorganised, with Battalion Headquarters, A, B, and C Companies in defensive positions on the Hill, this position was called 'Fort Nixon' in honour of A Company's commander, while D Company occupied a small feature about a thousand yards away, overlooking the village of Majon-Ni. Fort Nixon was just that, a well-defended position on the hilltop well protected by entrenchments, sandbags and bunkers. Within the defences was an adequate supply of food and water, while ammunition was plentiful.

R&R for the Rifles began in early April, with groups of officers and men being flown to Japan for five days in which they could get thoroughly clean, relax and enjoy some of the comforts of civilisation.

The following morning the Battalion felt secure. The slit trenches were protected by barbed wire and trip flares and fields of fire had been cleared. The immediate problem was again one of supplies. The Royal Engineers were of the opinion that with the present current running in the rivers it would take several days to emplace a bridge capable of taking even a jeep. When these were completed there was no track forward to the Battalion position, a distance of over a mile.

Major Rickcord made the following plan. Stores were brought forward to the south bank of the Hantan by jeep and trailer. From here the Battalion Porters carried them across the footbridge to the northern side and a dump was formed. A number of Oxford Carriers would then cross the Imjin, collect the stores and by keeping in the shallows, drive north along the riverbed to a position quite close to Battalion Headquarters. Here they left the river and making their way up the bank arrived at another dump close to Headquarters. From here more Porters would then carry the supplies to the individual companies.

For the next several days this plan worked quite efficiently, until the bridge was completed and a track had been bulldozed up to Battalion Headquarters. Between the Oxfords and the Porters the Battalion was adequately supplied with rations, food and other necessary supplies.

On the right flank the US 3rd Division was meeting determined resistance, but still making progress, while to the front of the 29th Brigade all was quiet. The Rifles were ordered to make deep probing patrols to determine enemy position and, if at all possible, to obtain a prisoner.

On 11 April the Battle Patrol, supported by two troops of B Squadron of the Hussars, made a wide sweep about two miles north of Hill 194 along the river valley. Apart from some spasmodic shooting from the east bank nothing could be found of the enemy. The following day B Company carried out a fighting patrol into the hills to the north-west. About two miles north of the Forward Defence Line (FDL) the Company came under fire from two well-concealed and mutually supporting machine-gun posts. Every attempt to get at the first position was thwarted by enfilade fire from the second, which could not be identified. As the Company's ammunition began to run low they were forced to withdraw under the cover of the artillery. During this action Lance Corporal Alberts was hit in the face by a gunshot, it was a serious wound and he required immediate treatment. Given the distance and terrain involved no vehicle could get to him and he was evacuated by helicopter, the first time that a helicopter ambulance was used by the Battalion. In future operations the helicopter would prove its worth time after time in casualty evacuation and it was a great morale booster to the men to know that in the event of injury they would be spared the carry on a stretcher over rugged countryside, followed by a long, often agonising, ride in an ambulance over rough tracks.

A further sweep by C Company on 13 April failed to find any enemy and it appeared that he had drawn his main line well back and was covering it with a screen of small

Battalion objective in the hills leading to the Han River. (RUR Association)

Advancing to the Han River. (RUR Association)

well-camouflaged posts in depth. Things were not as quiet as they seemed, as anxious as the Rifles were to find the enemy; the enemy was equally as curious about the Rifles.

The following night at 0100hrs, a trip flare erupted at the rear of D Company's position out on the isolated feature to the west of Hill 184. In the light cast by the flare several figures were spotted just below No 12 Platoon and within a few minutes they and the Chinese were exchanging hand grenades at a few yards range. Several of the enemy managed to get over the parapet and into the communications trench between one of the forward sections and Platoon Headquarters. For some time the Chinese troops resisted all efforts to evict them, while at the same time another raiding party came in on the main Company position two hundred yards to the east. This attack was stopped by a volley of grenades and shortly afterwards Second Lieutenant MacNicol got together two of his sections and made a sweep of the Platoon area, again using grenades in preference to small arms. As dawn broke the situation was quiet and No 12 Platoon was still in possession of its hill. A follow up search found three wounded Chinese on the hillside, along with some abandoned weapons. All over the Platoon area were dozens of Chinese stick grenades, it seemed as if a large portion of the grenades used in the attack had been duds. The three prisoners were returned to Battalion Headquarters for interrogation and revealed that they were part of a one hundred man Company, which had been ordered to discover the positions and strength on the hill and if possible to take a prisoner. This action cost D Company one man wounded. As the initial attack had come from the rear of D Company a search of this area was carried out and one dead enemy soldier was found.

A Company then carried out a foot patrol towards the Forward Defence Line, but found no sign of the enemy. The village of Ori-Dong, which the prisoners had revealed was their base of operations, was heavily shelled throughout the day and the following night. The work of wiring and booby trapping the positions continued until 18 April,

Onto Fort Nixon - 'B' Company advance towards Hill 194 after the crossing to the Imjin River, supported by Centurions of the 8th King's Royal Irish Hussars. Figures two and four are battalion porters. (RUR Association)

Ulster Crossing with Fort Nixon beyond, early April 1951. (Mervyn McCord/RUR Association)

Lance Corporal Alberts, wounded by a gunshot, was the first Royal Ulster Rifleman to be evacuated from the battlefield by helicopter casevac. (Mervyn McCord)

when D Company patrolled as far as Ori-Dong. The village was empty, but showed signs of recent occupation by a large force.

On 19 April, the advance party of the Belgian Battalion arrived to carry out a reconnaissance of the positions and the following day the Rifles, along with 26 Field Ambulance, were sent back into Brigade Reserve at Hwangbang-Ni, about five miles south of the Imjin. Here the Battalion had no onerous tasks other than to plan and reconnoitre various counter-attack routes, should they be required. Other than that all ranks enjoyed a well deserved rest and Colonel Carson was at last able to get away to Japan for a few days rest, accompanied by some other officers.

The Belgian United Nations Command (BUNC), a force of 602 men[1] from both Belgium and Luxemburg, was initially commanded by Colonel Albert-Marie Guérisse.[2] The Battalion had been raised from volunteers, of whom some 2,000 had come forward. From these suitable men had been selected, including a platoon of volunteers from the Grand Duchy of Luxembourg. With arms and equipment supplied to them during the Second World War and attired in battledress, three-colour camouflage smocks reminiscent of Second World War Denison smocks but with a design known as 'moon and balls' and wearing a distinct brown beret, the force sailed from Antwerp on board the SS *Kamina*, arriving in Pusan on 31 January 1951. In Korea the Battalion was commanded by Lieutenant Colonel Albert Crahay. Crahay was an artilleryman who

---

1   By the end of the War some 3,498 Belgian troops would serve in Korea, of these 336 were wounded, 99 were killed and five remain missing at the time of writing. One prisoner of war was repatriated.
2   Guerisse had been born in Brussels and served as a Captain with the Medical Branch of the Belgian Army in the Second World War. He was evacuated from Dunkirk and later worked with the Special Operations Executive under the code name 'Pat O'Leary'. Taken prisoner, he survived several concentration camps, including Dachau. Post-war, he rose to the rank of General and received some 35 decorations, including the George Cross.

Evacuating a seriously wounded Rifleman by helicopter. Lance Corporal Alberts was the first of the Battalion to be evacuated in this manner. (RUR Association)

RUR crossing the Imjin River on the deck of a Centurion tank. (Mervyn McCord/RUR Association)

RUR dismounting from a Centurion tank having crossed the
Imjin River, with dry feet. (RUR Museum)

Battalion sports 21 April 1951. The battle started 23 April. (Mervyn McCord)

had dropped a rank to command the Battalion, which he would lead from 21 January until 20 November 1951. The Belgians would appear to have changed commanders on a frequent basis.

Now positioned in Fort Nixon north of the Imjin the Belgian Battalion, with six hundred men, was now defending a position previously held by nine hundred. When the Belgians had moved into the Fort they found it well stocked with rations and with a more than adequate supply of ammunition, especially hand grenades, which proved to be the best weapon for close-range night fighting.

The Rifles themselves were still seriously under strength, not having received adequate reinforcements since the January battles. For now all was quiet, the Regimental Pipes came up to A Echelon and played *Retreat*, while a mobile cinema was requested from the Americans, but most of all the men just rested.

10

The Battle of the Imjin

The soldiers of the Chinese 64th Army that would swarm across the Imjin River were not the undisciplined, mindless mob, high on opium, so often alluded to in history. Organised into three divisions, the 187th, 188th and 189th, these soldiers were in fine physical condition, had been inoculated against cholera, typhus, typhoid and tetanus and were capable of marching impressive distances prior to an attack. Each man wore his winter uniform, sometime with the summer uniform underneath. On his feet he wore leather shoes, fur-lined boots or rubber-soled canvas boot, not dissimilar to baseball boots. He carried seven days' rations, mainly rice and baked wheat cakes and mostly Soviet-supplied small arms.[1] In keeping with the soldiers of other armies, the Chinese soldier also had complaints. His mail from home often took almost a month to arrive, the maps issued were of poor quality and the supplies of ammunition were inadequate. Food was often in short supply and frequent use was made of rations captured from abandoned American stores. In battle each rifleman carried only one hundred rounds, while the sub-machine-gunners were limited to one hundred and fifty and their supply of hand grenades often contained a high percentage of duds. What the 64th Army also lacked at this time was armour. While the Soviets had supplied the

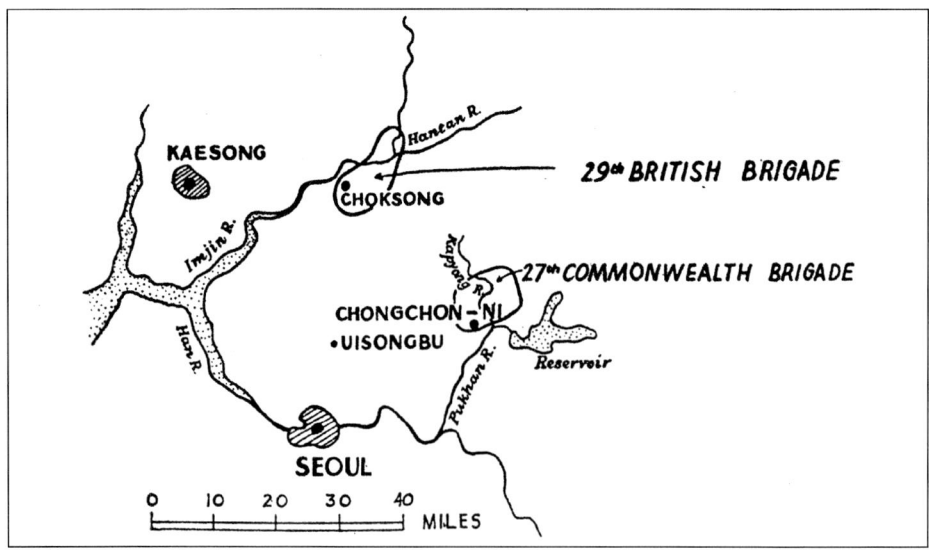

Areas occupied by the 27th Commonwealth and 29th British Infantry Brigades on 22 April 1951, just before the battles of the Imjin and Kapyong Rivers. (Barclay, *The First Commonwealth Division*)

---

1   The Chinese troops also had weapons that had been supplied to them by the British and Americans during the Second World War as well as those captured from the Japanese.

The scene at the port of Inchon, Korea, where men of the King's Own Scottish Borderers were piped ashore with the pipers of the 1st Battalion, The Royal Ulster Rifles when they arrived to replace the Argyll and Sutherland Highlanders, who were leaving Korea for their original Far East Station, Hong Kong. (RUR Museum)

Men of the King's Own Scottish Borderers were piped ashore with the pipers of the 1st Battalion, The Royal Ulster Rifles when they arrived to replace the Argyll and Sutherland Highlanders. (RUR Museum)

excellent T34 tank to the Chinese in limited numbers, none would appear at this battle; in fact, apart from one occasion, for their entire time in Korea the Rifles would only ever see this vehicle lying destroyed or abandoned by the roadside.[2]

Throughout the area controlled by 1st Corps the situation was reported quiet in all sectors. On the left flank the 1st ROK Division was holding the south bank of the Imjin River as far as Munsan-Ni. Further to the east the line was held by the US 3rd Division and ran north along the east bank of the Upper Imjin for a distance of eight miles before curving away to the east towards 25th Division's sector near Yonchon.

In the centre 29 Brigade held a sector some 17,000 yards wide. The Glosters and Northumberland Fusiliers were positioned on the southern bank, while the Belgian Battalion was positioned on Hill 194, on the opposite bank at the point where Upper Imjin turned northwards. The Rifles occupied reserve positions slightly to the rear.

On 29 Brigade's front, as elsewhere, there had been a near constant refusal by the enemy to engage in combat or any other form of contact. Both armoured and infantry patrolling had been carried out up to a depth of 15,000 yards on the north side of the river, but there was no sign of either preparation for an attack by the enemy or his main defence line. Rifleman Dyer, a non-smoker, was one of those picked for night patrols. It was found that being a non-smoker made it easier to find the enemy, who seemed to smoke a great deal. Dyer liked night patrols, they generally lasted between three and five hours and you were given the following day off!

At Brigade Headquarters the intelligence staff could offer no idea as to what would happen in the immediate future, either to hold the line or advance across the Imjin. However, when it was known the word would be sent to all units immediately. Signals within the Brigade were superb with each battalion and its supporting arms connected. All Battalions were in turn netted in on a wireless link connected to the ultra-efficient 45 Field Regiment Royal Artillery, who, on their net, stood for no sloppy wireless procedure under any circumstances.[3]

With regards to defensive positions, 29 Brigade was not in the best positions. While the Imjin River appeared to offer a major obstacle to any force coming south, the recent dry weather had caused it to drop by several feet. There were a number of fords to the Brigade front and the presence of others was suspected, if not identified.

The infantry were spread out over a wide front, none of them actually interconnecting. On the left flank the Glosters occupied a range of low hills facing the main ford, which would subsequently be known as 'Gloster Crossing'. They in turn deployed a standing platoon on the riverbank to give warning of any incursion. Behind the Battalion ran a sinuous track about six miles long, suitable for nothing bigger than a jeep, which ran through a deep ravine until it emerged in a valley that held Brigade Headquarters.

Between the Glosters' right flank and the X Company of the Northumberland Fusiliers was a gap of approximately 4,000 yards. This gap was unoccupied and overlooked by the towering mass of Kamak San, 657 meters high. The Fusiliers were lucky to have been able to dig good defences along a range of foothills that ran along the northern end of the main Brigade axis. They also had a good earthen track between them and Brigade Headquarters known as Route 11. On the right flank was the Belgian

---

2   Mao had described getting military aid from Russian for China as "Like taking meat from the mouth of a tiger" – Halberstam, *The Coldest Winter*, Oxford, 2008.
3   Catchpole, *The Korean War*, London, 2000.

THE BATTLE OF THE IMJIN

Ferrying Oxford carriers across the Imjin. (RUR Association)

Battalion, dug-in on the feature known as Hill 194, on the north bank of the river, ahead of the two bridges now known as 'Ulster Crossing'. The Rifles were concentrated on a small saddle immediately below the south-east shoulder of Kamak San situated on the road about four miles south of the Fusiliers position.

The morning of Saturday 21 April was described as 'warm and balmy' and the situation on the Corps front was reported as being quiet. Within the Battalion time was spent on 'resting', having a bath, cleaning vehicles and carrying out a reconnaissance of counter-attack routes by the company commanders. On the Brigade's left flank the 1st ROK Division defended the southern bank of the Imjin as far as the river mouth at Musan-Ni, the 12th ROK Division was to the south of this, while on the right flank was the US 3rd Division. In the centre the Brigade occupied a frontage of some 17,000 yards with the Glosters and Northumberland Fusiliers on the south bank of the river and the Belgian Battalion to the north just above where the Imjin and Han Rivers met. The Rifles were held in reserve at Hwangbang-ni. With three of its battalions stretched over what would normally have been a divisional front the Brigade was not best placed to fight a defensive battle. The defensive positions, while strong, were widely spaced and there was insufficient barbed wire or mines to fill the gaps. While the Imjin appeared to present a major obstacle to any attacker this was deceptive. The water level had dropped by several feet during the recent dry period and reconnaissance had revealed a number of fords, while the locations of others were suspected.

Medical Section halftrack at the Ulster Crossing. (Mervyn McCord/RUR Association)

Checking the papers of a Korean. (Mervyn McCord/RUR Association)

45th Field, Regiment of Artillery. (RUR Museum)

22 April

From first light on Sunday 22 April all four Battalions had sent forward foot patrols to search out the enemy. The Northumberland Fusiliers were preparing to celebrate St George's Day, in honour of the patron saint of England commemorated on their cap badge. They had hoped to have a modest celebration, however this was not to be and the only indication of the day would be that some men were able to wear roses that had been flown in previously from Tokyo. The 'Gloomies' as the Glosters were known were a little worried that there seemed to be some sort of a 'flap' forming and had established a standing patrol of platoon strength on the river bank at what later became known as Gloster Crossing. To the rear the Rifles were busy strengthening their positions. "The Battalion had a reputation within the Brigade of not being the best disciplined of troops and it was said the 'Micks' were all 'brickies' by trade who took a delight in digging – 'Give them a bag o' cement and they'd turn the bleeding Sahara into a housing estate before yer can say bleeding Jack Robinson!'"[4] This reference to 'brickies' in one history of the Korean War is clearly a direct reference to the role of the Irish as navvies, although this is an unfounded and inaccurate description of the Royal Ulster Rifles, whose members in the Korean conflict came from all parts of the United Kingdom and Ireland. On this morning there had been church services held for both the C of E and RC members of the Battalion. It was also announced that day that Major Shaw and Major Gaffikin had been awarded the DSO and Second Lieutenant Shaw-Stewart the MC for their actions the previous January and an informal party was held in the RHQ Mess. The award of the Military Cross to Mervyn McCord would not be announced until a later date. Colonel Carson and several officers of the Rifles, along with others from the remainder of the Brigade had departed for leave in Japan, while the NAAFI[5] rations had arrived along with a mobile cinema.

At 0945hrs a patrol of the Northumberland Fusiliers was searching some scrub about 2,000 yards from the northern riverbank and just to the west of the Belgian positions when it made contact with the enemy. Later in the afternoon a Belgian patrol, operation out of Fort Nixon on Hill 194, also became involved in a skirmish with the enemy. At Brigade Headquarters reports began to be received from other patrols and air reconnaissance that showed an increase in enemy activity. Small units were reported advancing south from Chorwon and that evening a message from the 25th Division revealed that a captured officer had told of a major attack to be launched that night. This officer was an artillery commander who had been taken while plotting positions along the US 3rd Division front. This information was reinforced when men of the Turkish Brigade captured six members of the Chinese 2nd Motorised Artillery Division.[6]

At Fort Nixon on Hill 194 the Belgian Battalion was well ensconced and liberally supplied with small arms ammunition and hand grenades, courtesy of the Rifles. Earlier in the day a patrol had made contact with the enemy and this had led to the establishment of a listening post, commanded by a Sergeant Leiding, some 1,500 yards forward of the Hill. Due to a false crest the defenders in Fort Nixon did not have a direct line of sight on to Leiding's position. Just after darkness the phone rang and was answered by Sergeant

---

4   Whiting, *Battleground Korea, The British in Korea*, Stroud, 1999 (A book that contains many such unsupported and inaccurate 'facts').
5   Navy, Army and Airforce Institute.
6   Farrar-Hockley, *The British Part in the Korean War Volume II*, London, 1995.

Armand Philips. Over the next few minutes Sergeant Leiding reported a steady stream of enemy passing his position, some armed, others carrying supplies of ammunition.

By 2230hrs, the sky above the Brigade positions was illuminated by numerous star shells and it was plain to see for all defenders that this was a major assault. Hordes of Chinese infantry were swarming across the Imjin, while rafts could be seen ferrying heavy weapons. In front of Sergeant Philips' position the attack was led by a Chinese officer mounted on a small pony, who soon disappeared in a cloud of smoke and dust as the Belgians opened fire.

From the Belgian field kitchen CQMS Andre Van Damme abandoned his cooking and immediately began to bring forward reserve ammunition supplies to the various positions. From C Company the redoubtable CQMS in turn evacuated a number of wounded men, something he would do on numerous occasions throughout the battle. For his action CQMS Van Damme would later be awarded the Bronze Star. As the attacked continued it was only with the ammunition and grenades left by the Rifles that the Belgians were able to keep the Chinese out of the Fort. When the enemy managed to emplace a machine-gun in a position that was particularly dangerous to Sergeant Philips' platoon it was quickly disposed of by an accurate shot from a bazooka.

The Belgians were holding their position and holding it well, but they were now isolated on the north bank of the river.

Throughout the Brigade all units were 'stood to', although it was felt that in keeping with his usual tactics the enemy would take time to initiate probing attacks to try and find weak spots in the defences. This was not the case, and at 2000hrs the enemy flooded across the Imjin, the standing patrol of the Glosters being the first to spot the enemy and open fire. Within the hour both the Fusiliers and Belgians were fighting for their very survival. The left flank of the Belgian position was particularly hard hit and it appeared that the enemy was attempting to force a gap in the Brigade line.

Orders were received by the Rifles to send a force at all speed to secure the bridges at 'Ulster Crossing' and deny them to the enemy. The only unit capable of reaching the crossing in good time was the Battle Patrol and Major Rickcord, acting CO, briefed Lieutenant Hedley Craig, the patrol commander, prior to their leaving at 2359hrs. Craig's orders were to dismount on arrival and dig in, sending the Carriers back to Battalion immediately. If the patrol was hard-pressed they were to withdraw and if unable to do so were to fight their way through to the Belgian position. Lieutenant Craig and the Battle Patrol, fifty Riflemen, plus fourteen men of the 55th Field Squadron Royal Engineers commanded by Lieutenant Eastman, arrived on the southern bank of the Imjin and took up a position overlooking the river. The men also dismounted two 3" mortars and two Vickers machine-guns as added firepower.

Craig had as his second-in-command Lieutenant Patrick Kavanagh, who had only arrived with the Battalion the previous day from Japan. Kavanagh was the son of Ted Kavanagh, the ITMA script writer and had volunteered for service in Korea.[7] While docked in Suez Kavanagh had searched in vain for Egypt's infamous 'dirty postcards'. It was to no avail, vendor after vendor assured the luckless Lieutenant that King Farouk ruled a very moralistic kingdom.[8]

---

7   ITMA, 'It's That Man Again', a popular BBC wireless comedy programme that ran from 1939-1949. The title referred to the number of times that Hitler's name appeared in pre-War newspapers.
8   Hastings, *The Korean War*, London, 1987.

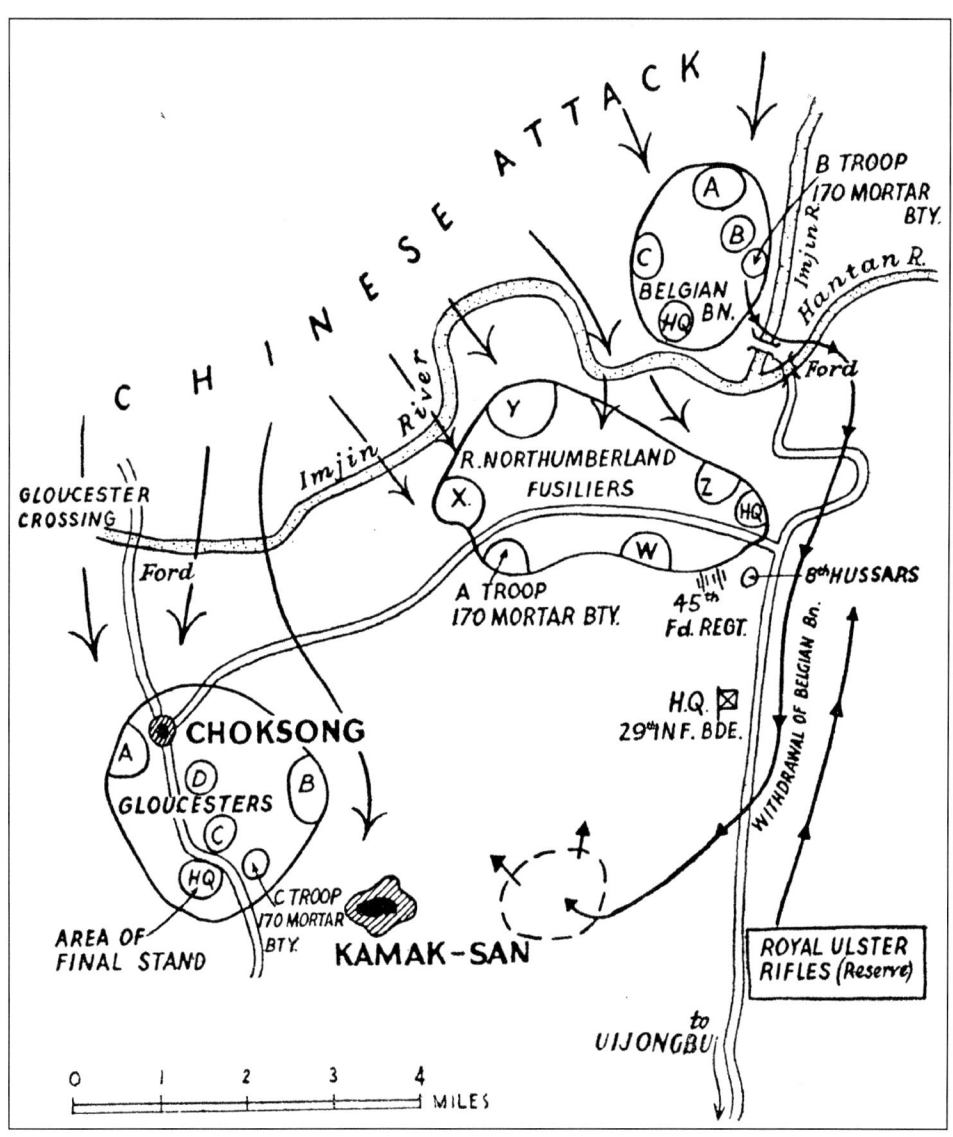

The Battle of the Imjin River, 22-25 April 1951. (Barclay, *The First Commonwealth Division*)

Lieutenant Houston Shaw-Stewart gets the MC ribbon. (Mervyn McCord)

Major Shaw (*Belfast Telegraph*)

Now both officers peered suspiciously into the darkness north of the Imjin moving forward under the starlight. In the distance they could make out the noise of engines and the rattle of tracks moving on the northern bank, but they couldn't make out what exactly, something was afoot, but what? The only way to find out was to cross the Imjin. The Patrol had just driven on to the northern bank of the river when the enemy opened fire.

Two of the carriers were hit immediately and went up in flames from ruptured fuel tanks. Kavanagh recorded what happened next, "Flames, rockets, yells, a thousand Cup Final rattles. Guy Fawkes, one of the carriers in front of us goes up. Fifty of us have run into a bloody army!" With red tracer flying around them the men fled for cover whilst Kavanagh shouted after them to "Come back!" A few did, while others disappeared into the darkness and were never seen again. Kavanagh's training kicked in and he ordered, "Lie down. Face your front and return fire!" Gunfire spat back from the Riflemen into the darkness. Kavanagh spotted something missing, "Get that Bren going," he hissed into the night. The response was an Irish voice, "There's something wrong with it, Sorr". Without a thought of what was wrong with it, or how the Rifleman was to achieve it, he snapped back, "Mend it." Whilst the rifle fire continued the Irish voice again called out, "I can find nothing wrong with the Bren, Sorr, known to God or to man." This somehow reassured Kavanagh as he told himself, "Oh, the Irish, the irresistible cadence, un-resisted," as he also opened fire. [9]

23 April
At 0203hrs on 23 April a lone Oxford carrier, driven by Rifleman Tailor, returned to the Battalion area, roaring up to the Headquarter tent at near full speed. The driver

9   Kavanagh, *The Perfect Stranger*, London, 1966.

THE BATTLE OF THE IMJIN

(Top): A shot taken from the verandah of Naafi's "Northlands" Roadhouse. A tank going forward to the battle front is at odds with the gay garden sunshade in the foreground.
(Centre): A helicopter view of the "Newcastle" Roadhouse.
(Bottom): This picture of "Northlands" shows the thatched roof and attractive architecture, features common to all of these famous and popular rendezvous.

NAAFI, the official canteen organisation for H.M. Forces at home and abroad, in peace and war, is proud to have served shoulder-to-shoulder with the men of the Commonwealth Forces in Korea — and proud to continue that service to those who have returned to the U.K.

NAAFI canteens, clubs, grocery shops, sports shops, wines and spirits supplies for Messes, special caterings for reunions and other celebrations, and specialist printing of die-stamped stationery and greetings cards represent a few of the hundred-and-one activities in which Naafi is engaged exclusively for British sailors, soldiers and airmen everywhere.

NAAFI
THE OFFICIAL CANTEEN ORGANISATION FOR HER MAJESTY'S FORCES
Imperial Court, Kennington Lane, London, S.E.11   Telephone: REliance 1200

NAAFI in Korea. (RUR Museum)

informed Major Rickcord that as the patrol arrived at the crossing it had been ambushed by enemy troops that had already crossed the river.[10]

Back at the Imjin it had quickly become apparent to Lieutenant Craig that his position was untenable; he was outnumbered and outgunned. Retaining a section of ten men he ordered Lieutenant Kavanagh to lead the remainder of the patrol back to Headquarters. The Riflemen were outnumbered by at least ten to one by the Chinese, yet they appeared to allow the survivors to withdraw. Lieutenant Craig, wounded in the shoulder and drifting in and out of consciousness, provided covering fire to Kavanagh and five Riflemen who pulled back. Lady luck was smiling and they managed to escape back across the river.

Dawn was breaking when Kavanagh and his five Riflemen, all wounded, staggered into camp, confirming the situation at the river. Kavanagh's wounds would see him evacuated to hospital in Japan; the Britcom General Hospital at Kure.[11] The war he had volunteered for had lasted just twenty four hours.[12] At the Hospital the nurses discovered most of the men's wounds were crawling with "the nightmare of maggots" … "inside plasters and under scalps and even the first colostomy dressings produced thousands of these horrors."[13] Kure was situated on the island of Honshu, close to Hiroshima. This hospital was equipped with a thousand beds and had been built by the Japanese prior to the Second World War, forming part of a secret naval base. It was here that two of the largest battleships of the War, the *Yamato* and *Musashi*, had been built and was believed by some to have been the intended target for the dropping of the first atomic bomb.[14]

Back with the Battalion Major Rickcord immediately ordered D Company to prepare to advance to the bridge as soon as daylight permitted safe movement. Before this could happen an order was received from Brigade that the entire Battalion, less B Company, was to advance to the Fusilier's position and from there to clear the enemy from the area around Ulster Crossing. The task allotted to B Company was to take up position on the saddle at Hwangbang-Ni where it would remain under Brigade control.

By dawn three Chinese divisions were attacking approximately 6,000 British troops along a seven mile wide front. The Chinese plan was to cut off the individual battalions and then destroy them piecemeal, a task which was made easier thanks to the Brigade's deployment. Within the Northumberland Fusiliers there were gaps of up to two miles between units of the Battalion.

Brodie's four infantry Battalions were dug-in on the invasion route to Seoul and the Chinese knew it was a matter of prestige to capture the Korean capital yet again, and that it would also be prime propaganda against America and the capitalist world.[15]

0520hrs saw a grey half-light false-dawn break and by this light the Rifles took up positions on the road behind the Northumberland Fusiliers. It was soon obvious that the original plan was not going to be possible. One company of the Fusiliers had been forced to withdraw during the hours of darkness after suffering heavy casualties. On the right side of the valley, where the track turned towards the crossing, the Northumberlands' D

---

10 The spelling of Tailor as per the War Diary.
11 *Quis Separabit*, 1951.
12 Potts, 'The Battle of the Imjin', *President's Newsletter* 2001/2002, p.37.
13 McNair, *A British Army Nurse in the Korean War*, Stroud, 2007.
14 McNair, *A British Army Nurse in the Korean War*, Stroud, 2007.
15 Halberstam, *The Coldest Winter*, Oxford, 2008.

Bren Gun in action. (RUR Museum)

Company situated on Hill 257 were under severe pressure, numerous casualties had been suffered and they were soon pushed back.

With daylight came air support and as the fighters strafed the known enemy positions they also hit those men of the Battle Patrol who had been taken prisoner. Fearing an escape attempt the Chinese at once opened fire on the captives. Among those killed was Lieutenant Keith Eastman of the Royal Engineers. Lieutenant Craig and his batman, who had been lying hidden, made their way down to the river. Despite his wounds Craig and his batman were able to swim the river and return to the Battalion lines.[16]

At the head of the valley the 25pdr guns of 45 Field Regiment were firing over open sights at hordes of enemy as the swarmed over the nearby hillsides.[17] A battery of American 155mm guns had joined in and was taking a heavy toll on the enemy. Both these units were in turn taking intense mortar and small arms fire from the high ground surrounding Hill 257

Major Rickcord, against advice, moved forward to carry out a personal reconnaissance. He returned about twenty minutes later pursued by a shower of enemy mortar bombs. Rickcord could see that the task of clearing the hills to the east of the road was too much for his remaining three rifle companies. Nevertheless, something had to be done and done quickly. Before any further action could be taken a message came from Brigade ordering the Rifles C Company to be detached and return to B Company's position. Here Major Shaw would take command and prepare to move to the west to reinforce the

---

16 Farrar-Hockley, *The British Part in the Korean War Volume II*, London, 1995.
17 45 Field Regiment fired an average of 1,000 rounds per gun in this action. Catchpole, *The War in Korea*, London, 2000.

Glosters, who were having a very bad time of it. After a short but frustrating wait this order was rescinded, B Company remained on its blocking position at Hwang-Ni and C Company marched off to rejoin the Battalion. Rifleman O'Kane recalls that this move was hard work, with practically all extra equipment having to be carried by the men.

To the right of the road and about 1,500 yards south of Hill 257 was Hill 398, a feature allegedly topped by a ruined castle that completely dominated the entrance to the valley.[18] A report from the Northumberland Fusiliers told of large numbers of the enemy approaching Hill 398 from the north-east. Major Rickcord ordered A and D Companies along with one section from the Medium Machine Gun Platoon to occupy the hill. He also moved his Tactical Headquarters on to the hill and called up his reserve ammunition supply with a request for extra hand grenades. By aggressive patrolling along the spurs running north and east Rickcord hoped to prevent any outflanking movement by the enemy. It was discovered that the hilltop was the site of an old fortification with walls between ten and fifteen feet high and in reasonably good condition that covered an area seventy five yards long by thirty yards wide. The southern end of the ridge was the highest and was surmounted by a stone wall between ten and fifteen feet high in reasonably good condition. This in turn completely surrounded the crest and enclosed a natural depression. Three main spurs ran north from the fort. The first, to the north-west, which ended in a rocky crag overlooking the road below, the second to the north, sloping gently down to a smaller hill about 1,000 yards forward. The third spur ran to the east overlooking an area of narrow valleys and paddy fields due south of 'Ulster Crossing'.

As D Company set to with a will digging slit trenches and machine-gun positions, A Company began a sweep forward along the central spur. This advance was met with sporadic small arms fire and several enemy soldiers were flushed from their hiding places and dealt with. About noon the leading platoon had reached the end of the spur and was able to look across the valley towards Hill 257, which was fully occupied by the enemy. A patrol of A Company went forward for a distance and in the process lost four men, who fortunately turned up a short time later at the Regimental Aid Post. Enemy troop sightings were numerous in front of the Company positions and they were engaged by the mortars of 170 Battery.

Fearful that A Company would be cut off by the encroaching enemy when darkness fell Major Rickcord ordered them back to the north-western spur to dig in for the night. A short time later C Company reached the top of the hill after a stiff climb up the rocky heights and was placed in a tight perimeter along with D Company and Tactical Headquarters on the crest of Hill 398.

Back in the valley the Main Battalion Headquarters was coming under pressure from enemy fire, the cinema screen had been torn to pieces by Chinese machine-gun fire, and it was forced to move further south for about 1,000 yards. Here they set up alongside Headquarters of the Fusiliers on a small knoll beside the road, protected by the remnants of the two Fusilier companies that had been previously forced back from their positions.

By nightfall the position of 29 Brigade at the head of the main valley was fairly stable. On the left flank the two remaining Fusilier companies were holding fast on the western ridgeline, albeit 1,000 yards apart. On the right the Rifles, less their B Company,

---

18 Castle or wall, reports are conflicting from various sources. Captain John Lane in an audio recording recalls a stone wall 10-12 feet high.

were well dug-in on and around Hill 398 with a secure perimeter. Throughout the battle the resupply of ammunition and rations was maintained by the Battalion Porters, who continued to toil up and down hill through shot and shell. With ammunition and rations brought forward and safely delivered quite often the porters then carried casualties back to the rear.

However, on the Brigade's left flank the situation was more serious. The Glosters were under near constant attack by at least a regiment that was more than adequately supported by mortars and machine-guns. It should be stressed that a Chinese regiment was the equivalent of a British brigade. Groups of Chinese were also infiltrating around their flanks, taking advantage of the large gap between the Glosters and the Fusiliers.

On the north-western spur A Company of the Rifles continued to suffer probing enemy attacks throughout the afternoon and evening. It was only with constant artillery support from artillery and 4.2" mortars that the enemy was stopped from launching a concerted attack on the Company. Captain John Lane, second-in-command, was concerned about the supply of hand grenades and ammunition of the 2" mortars. Drinking water was also running low; nothing creates a greater thirst than being in combat!

At dusk a battalion of the US 24th Regiment, described in the 1953 history as 'Negro troops',[19] arrived by road from the south, deployed and launched an attack against Hill 257 and its surrounding features. Despite a gallant effort the 24th Regiment was forced to call off the attack after some two hours and they were withdrawn back along the valley.

That evening the Belgians had withdrawn across the Imjin supported by fire from two platoons of American tanks and an air strike. The last Belgian unit across the river was a squad of men in two armed jeeps commanded by Second Lieutenant Henri Wolfs. As they crossed the pontoons to the southern bank they came across a broken-down ambulance and stopped to render assistance. While they helped, Wolfs had his men brew a pot of coffee to help calm them down – never was coffee drunk more quickly.

By 2200hrs, the Belgian Battalion had successfully crossed the Imjin and Han Rivers, the entire operation had taken forty five minutes.

There was little sleep for the Rifles that evening. The enemy kept up an endless barrage from his artillery and mortars interlaced with streams of red and green tracer from the machine-gun fire that swept across the hill on a regular basis.

24 April

At 0215hrs on 24 April an alert sentry in the forward platoon of A Company spotted the enemy forming up for an attack. With much shouting and blowing of bugles the Chinese surged forward, only to be met with steady fire from the platoon's Bren guns and .303's. The attack was driven off without loss to the Rifles. Just before dawn a second attack was launched, this time the entire Company was involved at ranges close enough for hand

---

19 The US 24th Regiment had been formed in 1869, mostly from veterans of Federal Coloured Troops that had fought for the Union in the American Civil War (1861-65). Originally known as the 'Buffalo Soldiers' due to their curly hair, their service included fighting Indians in the West, action in Cuba in 1898, the Philippine War of 1899 and Mexican Revolution, 1916. In the Second World War they served in the Pacific. In Korea the Regiment had two recipients of the Medal of Honour and continues to serve today in the Gulf.

Hill 398. C and D Coys were at the top. A Coy was on a (hidden) spur running off north-west. (RUR Association)

grenades to be used in prodigious numbers. Captain Lane estimated that approximately seventy grenades had been thrown in the previous attacks. With support from the artillery and a section from the MMG Platoon delivering 600 rounds per minute per gun, the attack was held. It was during his action that A Company got to use the newly issued 'bazooka' for the first time. While initially an anti-tank weapon, its 3.5" rocket was found to be ideal for dealing with small groups of enemy hiding in the rocks. Lance Corporal Joe Farrell recalled seeing bits of bodies "flying all over the place."[20]

Daylight showed the Battalion was vulnerable to attack from the south-east. Major Rickcord contacted Brigade and requested the return of B Company. This was refused and C Company was dispatched to a ridge some 800 yards south east of Hill 398, the location of the Battalion Tactical Command Post, to protect the Battalion from an outflanking move by the enemy.

At 1025hrs an air strike was called in on the low ground to the Battalion's front, an obvious enemy 'forming-up point'. Aircraft from the US Fifth Air Force, including the F80, arrived at such a low level that mortar fire had to be curtailed during the airstrike. Despite plastering the ground with a mixture of napalm and high explosive bombs, the enemy could not be silenced. Intense machine-gun fire was immediately directed towards A Company and for the third time the enemy charged. Once again marksmanship and a steady nerve kept the enemy at bay and would continue to do so during a further fifteen attacks. At 1415hrs, the Chinese set fire to the scrub covering the hillside below A Company's position. Fearful that the fire could preclude an attack a quick harassing fire programme was arranged with the Battery Commander of 176

---

20 Salmon, *To The Last Round*, London, 2009.

Battery and the 4.2" mortars. Lieutenant Gordon Potts, commanding No 1 Platoon, ordered his men to lie in the bottom of their slit trenches and allow the fire to burn over them. As the fire passed Potts' men took up their firing positions and were able to see the enemy forming-up below and about to charge. Once again accurate fire from the Bren guns proved most effective when combined with the shells from 176 Battery and the mortars. A short time later Potts attention was drawn to an enemy 'O' Group getting into position about a thousand yards distant. Using his binoculars Potts could see approximately twenty soldiers complete with maps gathered together for a briefing. Telling his Vickers gunners to hold their fire until the enemy group had settled down, Potts patiently waited. When the order to open fire was given the two Vickers poured a stream of bullets across the hillside and the enemy rapidly dispersed. Through his binoculars Potts counted eight dead and numerous wounded. Major Rickcord's worry about a flanking attack was unfounded and no effort was made to carry this out, although numerous enemy soldiers were observed moving in the valleys and hills to the east. As darkness descended Lieutenant McCord and his signals party struggled to keep the Battalion's communications working. It was then that an eerie sight was observed from their position – what appeared to be a Chinese with long black hair and dressed in a flowing cloak was leading a party of enemy soldiers up a distant hillside. As this 'phantom' was out of small arms range no one opened fire and he/she was given the sobriquet 'The Black Widow', or 'The Witch'.

While the right flank of the Brigade was holding firm and the enemy had been stopped, the situation on the left was serious. During the hours of darkness the Glosters had been forced back from the original positions and the remnants of the Battalion was now ensconced on Hill 235. Here they had dug-in and were putting up a stalwart defence. A message received from the Glosters informed Brigade that at least an enemy regiment had bypassed them during the night, they were now completely surrounded and no further supplies could now reach them. They also reported that the enemy was in possession of Hill 675, Kamak-San, between the Glosters and the remainder of the Brigade.

It was decided to launch an attack to relieve the Glosters using the 10th Battalion Combat Team (Philippines)[21] supported by Centurions of C Squadron of the 8th Hussars. A reconnaissance showed that the track leading to Hill 235 was virtually impossible for the tanks even without opposition. The Filipino Battalion had in the vanguard three M24 Chaffee tanks and these led the Centurions forward. The first tank, a Chaffee of the Reconnaissance Company, was knocked out, blocking the road, and an attempt by the second Chaffee to push it clear was unsuccessful. Two of the Centurions then came forward and using their 20 pounders and Besa machine-guns gave covering fire to allow the crew of the disabled tank to escape.

The advancing infantry remained too close to the road and failed to climb the sides of the track to keep the Chinese anti-tank weapons out of range of the remaining tanks. Added to this was the difficulty the Centurions were experiencing in getting forward on

---

21 The 10th Battalion Combat Team was part of the 7,500 strong Philippine Expeditionary Forces To Korea (PEFTOK). They had arrived in the country in August 1950 and were the fourth largest force under the UN Command and consisted of 64 officers, 1,303 other ranks, a company of medium tanks (Sherman), a reconnaissance company of light tanks (Chaffee), a battery of self-propelled artillery and relevant armoured cars.

what was little more than a goat track. The positions and firepower of the enemy could not have been overcome by the infantry on their own, and the attack was called off.[22]

If the Brigade were to hold its position south of the Imjin, Kamak-San would have to be retaken. Throughout the day numerous air strikes were called in against the hill, but the Chinese were well dug-in and despite bombs, napalm and cannon fire from the jets, they continued to bring more troops on to the hill. Added to this the road to the rear of the Rifles and Northumberland Fusiliers was continuously harassed by groups of Chinese infantry that had come down from the south-eastern slopes of Kamak-San.

At 0130hrs on 25 April, A Company, on Hill 398, was again attacked and once again the Chinese troops of the 188th Division were met by disciplined small arms fire, hand grenades and the 'Bazooka'. For the next one and a half-hours fighting continued, with a further attack launched against No 11 Platoon of D Company situated at the western end of the perimeter itself. In the initial onslaught the Platoon positions were almost overrun with Chinese troops inside the perimeter and star shells were fired to spot the enemy. This resulted in very close fighting with the bayonet and hand grenades until first light, when the enemy withdrew leaving behind at least nine dead, three severely wounded and one man taken prisoner. Men in A Company saw more wounded being dragged away and it was obvious that heavy casualties had been suffered in the attack, but men was not something the Chinese were short of. The Vickers of Support Company had also been in action and Corporal 'Doc' Halliday had directed his guns to scythe into the attacking lines of Chinese with deadly effect. He recalled that 'many Chinese had no weapons, only grenades, these men subsequently picked up the rifles and sub-machine-guns of the fallen.'

Soon it was the turn of C Company to face what appeared to be human waves of attacking enemy. Illuminated by flares, both British and Chinese, the enemy managed to get in close to the Company positions using the scrub for cover. At such close range the bolt action .303 was not the best weapon, but all ranks had adequate numbers of hand grenades and these were thrown by the dozen. Lieutenant Peter Whitamore was too busy giving fire orders to use his own weapon and the cry "Fire for effect" rang out from both him and his senior NCOs, maintaining command under such circumstances was vital. Eventually, after some forty minutes of continuous action, the Chinese retired, driven off by the combination of grenades and bullets. There was no time for relaxation as magazines were reloaded, the wounded seen to and more hand grenades primed. Many of the Bren gunners and their number two's had suffered from burns to their hands from changing red hot barrels during the action and all ranks were desperately thirsty. Rifleman 'Topper' Brown, a Reservist from Lancaster, was hit in the knee by a shell fragment. This was dressed by Mark McConnell of No 8 Platoon, who used a sock to form a ring pad around the wound. Brown had served as a Chindit in Burma during the Second World War and, being a non-swimmer, had crossed the Chinwin River holding on to the tail of a mule. For his actions in Burma he had been awarded the Military Medal. Despite the treatment Rifleman Brown died of his wounds

Four miles to the rear B Company situated on Hwangbang-Ni, was having its share of action. During the previous day, Captain 'Dickie' Miller the Company commander, had observed small groups of Chinese gathering on Kamak-San (Hill 675) to the north-west. In consequence of this he sent out a fighting patrol to clear the enemy from the

---

22 Hastings, *The Korean War*, London, 1987.

lower slopes of the hill. This had not been fully successful as during the hours of darkness B Company came under very heavy mortar and machine-gun fire from these slopes and casualties were suffered, especially in the left flank platoon. Captain Miller had under his command a section from the 3" Mortar Platoon, a section from the MMG Platoon, a troop of 4.2" mortars from 170 Mortar Battery and for good measure a troop of Centurion tanks from 'C' Squadron of the King's Royal Irish Hussars. With this combined firepower B Company held their ground despite more casualties, but the enemy's losses were greater and the road remained open.

The Centurions of C Squadron spent the remaining hours of darkness in close leaguer a short distance behind B Company. At first light, despite a thick mist that filled the valley, they started their Rolls Royce Meteor 12-cylinder engines and trundled forward to take up station along the road between the saddle and the forward battalions. For the remainder of the morning the Centurions engaged targets of opportunity in the paddy fields, ditches and lower slopes of Kamak-San. The tank's 20pdr gun was particularly accurate and several enemy machine-gun positions were removed with almost surgical precision at up to a thousand yards range.

At 0630hrs, on 26 April, B Company was still suffering casualties from the Chinese on the high ground, with their left flank platoon to the west taking most of the fire. The Company had in support a troop of the 4.2" mortars, a section of the Battalion's 3" mortars, two tanks and a section of Medium Machine Guns, but despite all this they still suffered casualties.

On the same day, behind Chinese lines Henry O'Kane and his fellow prisoners were being kept on a hill, concealed from those UN aircraft engaged in destroying the Centurion tanks that had been abandoned on the battlefield. Previously they had been given some watery soup and rice. There was no medical treatment available for the wounded, but Corporal Jock Calder, a Medical Orderly from B Company, did his best with what was available. O'Kane remembered seeing Captain Docker, the acting CO of C Company, Lieutenant Nicholls, Corporal Baxter and Rifleman Crawford, Maher and Brierley, also of C Company, as they prepared to march off the hill. In the days to come Crawford, a well-known Belfast boxer, would help keep up the men's spirits with tunes played on his harmonica.

Major John Shaw, acting as Battalion second-in-command, had been called to Brigade Headquarters that morning to receive orders on behalf of Colonel Carson. On returning at 0800hrs, he informed the Battalion that the Brigade was to withdraw immediately as the penetration achieved by the Chinese on the left flank had reached a point that threatened to surround the entire Brigade.

Therefore, 29 Brigade was to retire from the Imjin and take up new positions north of Seoul. The plan, as passed to the Rifles, did not please Major Rickcord, which required his companies to leave the high ground and use the valley road. It would make more sense to retire along the ridgelines, keeping the enemy below them. Taking the high ground is one of the first objectives in battle and willingly giving it up to the enemy can lead to disaster. From experience gained in India Rickcord knew of the dangers in using the road, but the British were a 'road-bound nation' and Rickcord requested an alternative route from Brigade Headquarters, fearing that Headquarters had grossly underestimated the enemy strength. However, Brigadier Brodie ordered otherwise and it would cost the men of 29 Brigade a fearful price.[23]

The Glosters were completely surrounded and all attempts to reinforce them had met with failure. Therefore, they had been ordered to form small groups and break out as best they could. The Belgian Battalion, having successfully fought its way clear previously, had come south and was now in position across the southern end of the Glosters' valley. Here they were already engaged against enemy forces attempting to move south-east. Specific orders for the Rifles were, in conjunction with the Northumberland Fusiliers, to withdraw immediately down the road. They were then to pass through B Company's roadblock and on in a south-easterly direction towards the main Uijongbu Road and hopefully meet up with the waiting transport.

Both Battalions would move as a joint force under the command of Lieutenant Colonel Kingsley Foster, the Northumberland Fusiliers commanding officer. This would have to be carried out with all haste; enemy troops were closing in from the direction of Kamak-San and the gun lines of 45 Field Regiment were already under small arms fire. The orders were passed by telephone from Battalion Headquarters to Major Rickcord at his Tactical Headquarters on Hill 398. When Rickcord passed the withdrawal order on to the men there was widespread disappointment. In the past 48 hours of the battle the Battalion had lost one man killed, ceded no ground to the enemy, seen off sixteen enemy attacks and caused innumerable casualties. Although very tired and missing their tea, they were confident they could continue the fight and stop the enemy in his tracks. Those men who had taken part in the previous action of 3-4 January knew that a withdrawal under fire was difficult at the best of time, with the enemy pressing so close it was going to be more difficult still.

Brigade had ordered a withdrawal down the road, which may have been a sensible order when issued, but the situation had deteriorated badly and Chinese troops now occupied the lower slopes of Kamak-San in great strength and many more were positioned in the paddy fields lining the road. Major Rickcord would have preferred to move his command along the ridge towards C Company and passing through them move down into the valley. At 1100hrs, the two Fusilier companies arrived in the Rifles position after successfully breaking contact with the enemy. After a few moments of exchanging information and cigarettes they continued on the way southwards.

By 1200hrs, the Major Rickcord had assembled his command in preparation for the move off the hill and back towards Brigade Headquarters. All vehicles, with the exception of two carriers belonging to the Mortar Platoon, had been ordered back and the Rifles prepared to carry their remaining heavy weapons. The porters were there to assist and would in turn suffer casualties including their commander, Lieutenant Dunlop; he was killed during the withdrawal. The Battalion interpreter, Lee Kyung-sik, was also moving back with this group and remembered the bullets hitting the paddy fields like rain drops. He was one of the lucky ones to escape.[24]

The order of March was C Company, one platoon of A Company, Tactical Headquarters, remainder of A Company, Main Headquarters, along with approximately fifty porters and D Company acting as rearguard. Unfortunately C Company was hit by 'friendly fire' as it moved to its rendezvous area and suffered four casualties. A

---

23 Audio recording held in the Royal Ulster Rifles Museum, Belfast.
24 Salmon, *To The Last Round*, London, 2009.

Major John Shaw, Battalion HQ, Imjin on the last morning of the Imjin Battle. He was killed 30 minutes later. (Mervyn McCord/RUR Association)

mortar bomb, one of several being fired to cover exploded in a trench being used by No 8 Platoon and four men were seriously wounded by shell fragments. These men could not be moved, so Lieutenant Max Nichols and a medical orderly, Corporal J. Taylor, volunteered to remain behind to care for them and a call was made to Brigade Headquarters to request a vehicle to evacuate the wounded men. This call was received and the RAMC armoured half-track was sent forward driven by Corporal J. Hough, only to be knocked out as it made its way up the hill.

As Major Rickord and his command descended into the valley it was remarkably quiet, save for the noise of gunfire coming from the saddle, still held by B Company. In turn B Company had watched the two companies of the Fusiliers pass through the block and was resolved to hang on until the remainder of the Rifles arrived. Back up the valley the Rifles were now having a very hard time of it. Large volumes of automatic fire began to sweep the valley floor emanating from the slopes of Kamak-San. Elsewhere groups of Chinese hidden in the paddy fields alongside the road added their fire to the general chaos. The Riflemen were in the open with scant cover being offered by the odd bush and occasional paddy bund. Casualties began to mount and movement was reduced to short dashes from cover to cover. C Company and the leading platoon of A Company had gone ahead a short distance and turned to fire back at the enemy, but were still moving south.

The Headquarters group was driven to cover by a particularly heavy burst of fire and the men became separated. Wireless communication, up until that point good, broke down completely as bullets and shrapnel knocked out both men and wireless sets.

Henry O'Kane.
(Henry O'Kane)

Grave of Major Shaw, United Nations Memorial Cemetery, Pusan, Korea. (RUR Association)

The two Oxford carriers of the Mortar Platoon skidded to a halt and Lieutenant John Mole, operating from Battalion Headquarters, ordered the section of two 3" mortars into action. The other two mortars were busily helping B Company in its own fight. Within a few minutes bombs were thudding off towards the lower slopes of Kamak-San and elsewhere, searching out the enemy machine-gunners. In some reports it states that while Riflemen fired the mortars they were being loaded by prisoners. It is possible that this was misidentification and it was some of the Battalion porters doing the job. Despite the accuracy of this bombardment Chinese fire still swept the valley floor.

From B Company's position on the saddle a Troop of Centurion tanks of the King's Own Irish Hussars lent weight to John Mole's fire, despite losing two tanks, one set on fire from a 'Molotov cocktail'[25] while a second lost a bogie to a Chinese suicide anti-tank squad. This squad of three men had rushed up to the tank carrying a long pole on the end of which was a cluster of hand grenades. Ramming the pole into the front of the tank's tracks the charge had exploded, killing all three men and disabling the Centurion.[26]

Finally a part of Tactical Headquarters and most of C Company reached the saddle and the welcome protection of B Company and the tanks. Lieutenant Peter Whitamore was one of those from C Company who did not make it. He had initially been able to climb aboard a withdrawing Centurion and had watched in horror as men were shot off the tanks to fall under the tracks of those following behind, there being no time for the drivers to avoid them. Eventually Whitamore's Centurion was hit by a phosphorous

---

25 A glass bottle containing a mixture of petrol and sugar, or other thickening agent, fitted with a cloth fuse. The name comes from their use during the Russo-Finnish War. It was named after Vyacheslav Molotov, the Soviet Foreign Minister.
26 Those Centurions left on the battlefield were later attacked by American aircraft dropping napalm to prevent them being taken by the Chinese. At this time certain components of the tank were still classed as secret.

US M40 155mm self propelled guns and Bofors firing in support of the RUR attack, April 1951. (Mervyn McCord)

grenade and had its engine knocked out. With his battledress on fire Whitamore jumped from the burning tank and ended up in a ditch, being captured a few minutes later. Major Rickcord and the remainder of his Headquarters ended up on a small hill to the east of the saddle and found Lieutenant Tony Trevor-Roper with his platoon, now reduced to twelve men. The Lieutenant was conferring with Captain Millar in regard to a further withdrawal.

Still in the valley, A Company, less one platoon, Battalion Headquarters and D Company had moved into the hills to the east and were moving up on to the ridgeline in a long snaking column. Behind them the Chinese was swarming down the slopes of to the west in a seemingly unending wave. Major Rickcord and the remaining twenty to thirty men of B Company had also turned south-east and moved up into the hills with all possible speed. Lance Corporal Norman Sweetlove was with Battalion Headquarters and as he and the others made their way down the slope he heard the enemy shouting, "Stop! You are fighting America's war!" While it was easy for the Chinese to shoot down at the Riflemen, shooting back was nigh impossible and Sweetlove ran on towards the MSR where he was lucky enough to be picked up by a passing American ambulance.

Rifleman Varley had his Bren in action when an enemy bullet clipped the bipod and sent fragments of metal into his eye. He went to the RAP where he was treated and told to return to his unit, there being no way of evacuating him. Varley's platoon was one of those still holding the high ground and as he made his way back he saw Chinese troops everywhere. The order "Every man for himself" was then given and the platoon scattered. Varley and his mate, Rifleman Robinson, a National Serviceman from Bristol, made their way down the hill towards the road. Robinson was half-carrying another Rifleman who had a shattered arm, who pleaded to be left behind. As they continued

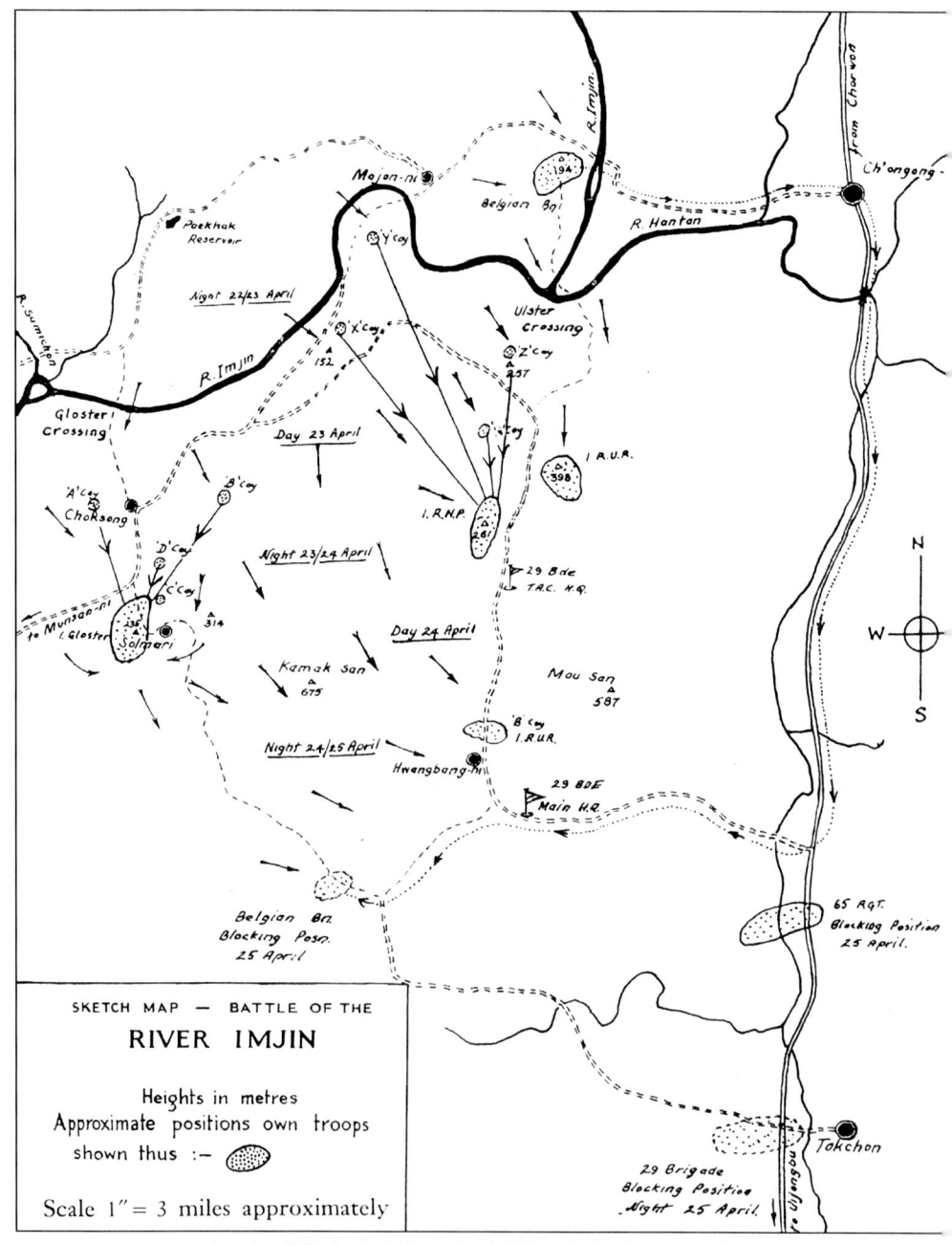

Battle of the Imjin River, April 1951. (RUR Association)

The view north from the B Coy block. The Rifles and RNF were ambushed by the enemy in the hills to the left of the photograph whilst withdrawing south along the valley floor. (RUR Association)

down the hill Varley turned every few steps and fired a burst from the Bren gun back into the pursuing Chinese. As they reached the road they were able to clamber on to the back of a passing Centurion. Varley, his ammunition exhausted, stripped the gun and threw the various pieces into the ditches on either side of the track. In the event of capture at least the enemy would not get his weapon.[27]

The Centurions, many by now out of ammunition and with their decks laden with wounded and exhausted men, turned south and roared off the saddle as quickly as their engines would permit. For the drivers steering was made that little bit more difficult by the amount of men draped over the front of the tanks as well as the engine decks.

Rifleman Dyer was also making his way back and saw a Centurion pass, its decks loaded with wounded and the Chinese scrambling around it like ants as they attempted to climb aboard the speeding tank. Many of the Chinese had no weapons and were simply running at the tank trying to pull the men from the vehicle. In turn those men aboard the Centurion were shooting and clubbing where possible and many of the Chinese disappeared under the tracks. Dyer was lucky to make it to the rear where he was picked up by members of the Indian Field Ambulance and carried to safety.[28]

Lance Corporal Erreagar of the Hussars also noticed the lack of weapons among the attacking Chinese. As a nineteen year old who had a short time previously been working in a shop, he now found himself scrambling out of his damaged tank, surrounded by hordes of the enemy. He saw dead and wounded Riflemen being robbed of their weapons

---
27 Hastings, *The Korean War*, London, 1987.
28 Audio interview with Brigadier Mervyn McCord.

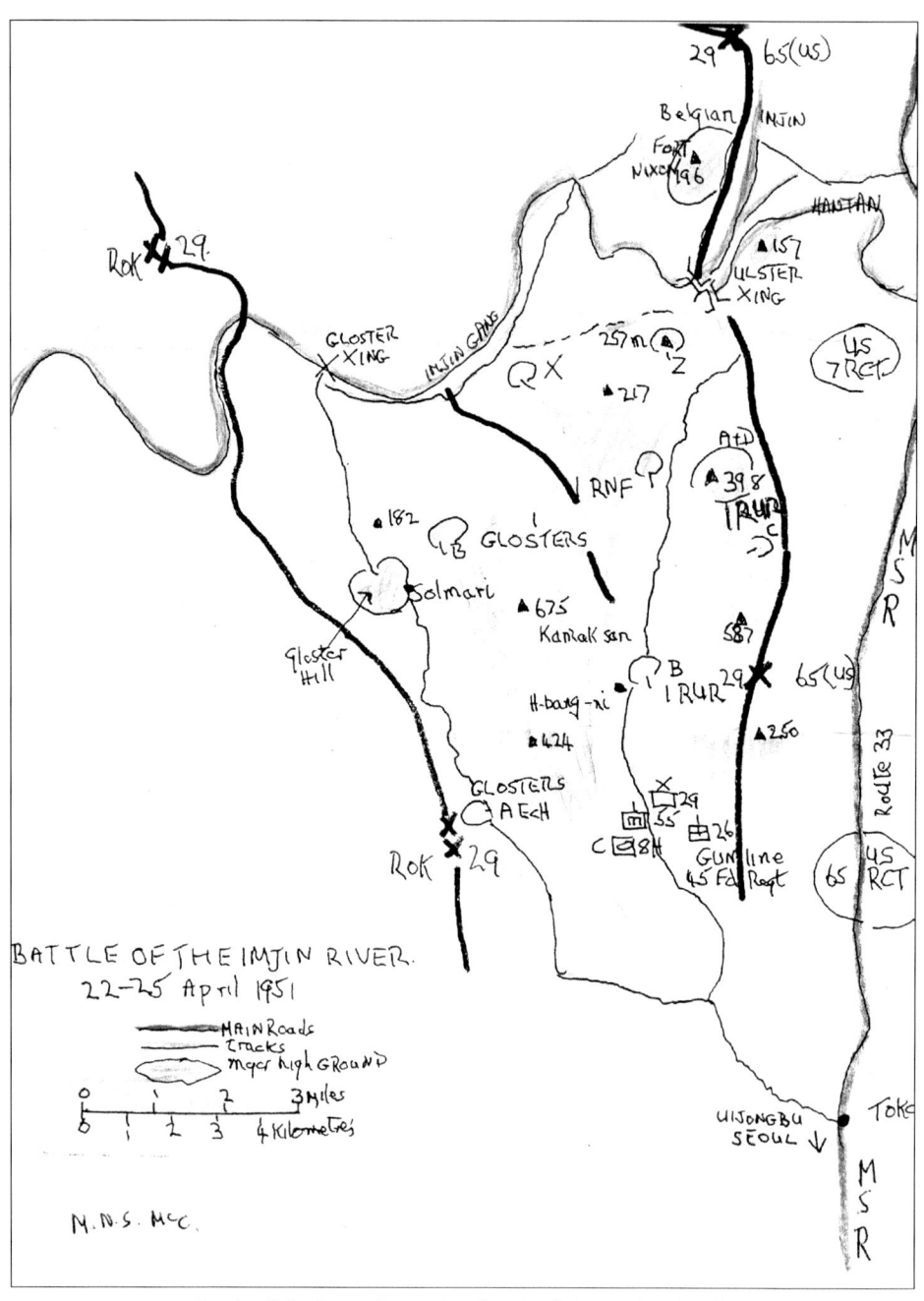

Battle of the Imjin River, April 1951. (Mervyn McCord)

Combined 1 RUR/1 RNF/ 170 Bty (4" Mortars) mortar lines on the last morning of the Imjin Battle April 1951 after expending ammo at a rapid rate – the Chinese were on the hills in the background. Mervyn McCord's 'slit' (ammo box riveted) as Signals Officer. (Mervyn McCord)

Expending mortar ammunition on the last morning of the Imjin battle. (Mervyn McCord)

Rifleman Chris Spiers.

and soon he was surrounded by men that were now armed! Having a pistol and six rounds of ammunition there was little resistance he could offer and he was soon made a prisoner.

The journey south from Hwangbang-Ni was a veritable gauntlet for the first mile and a half. The countryside seethed with Chinese, all making their way in the same direction. Every bank, ditch and house had been turned into a fortified position armed with machine-guns and mortars. Amidst all this Sergeant Bill McConnell was driving a three-tonner loaded with the Battalion's reserve supply of ammunition, determined that it was not going to fall into enemy hands. He made it back safely to the MSR.

As the Centurions sped along enemy soldiers would run out and attempt to throw hand grenades onto the decks of the vehicles or ram satchel charges into the tracks. Where possible the men on the tanks would throw the grenades among the Chinese running alongside, causing many casualties. Every now and again a fountain of blood and bone would indicate where an enemy soldier had been dragged under the Centurion's tracks and turned into a gelatinous mess, but nothing would deter the attacks. On one Centurion, commanded by Sergeant Cadman, a Chinese soldier was attempting to prise open the turret. The Sergeant directed the tank through the wall of a house to knock him off. On emerging he found an enemy machine-gun post directly in front and drove straight over it.[29]

The British did not have it all their own way, machine-guns and mortars firing from the flanks and rear caused many casualties to the men lying unprotected on the engine decks and clinging to the turret sides. Some of the wounded lost their grip and fell from the speeding vehicles and had to be left behind.

This charge to the rear cost the Troop two Centurions lost to successful attacks by enemy using pole charges, but the remainder, carrying their loads of dead, dying and wounded arrived safely in the Brigade Headquarters area.

In the hills to the east of the saddle the survivors of A and D Companies along with Battalion Headquarters, approximately two hundred men, had halted for a brief rest and to reorganise. After a few moments the column continued on its way south. From

---

29 Napier, *From Horses to Chieftains*, Arundel, 1992.

the valley floor small groups of Chinese made their way up the slope, but steady fire and well-thrown grenades kept them at bay.

The column reached the escarpment overlooking the lateral valley in the afternoon, possibly about 1400hrs. The view had both its good and bad points. Two miles to the east ran the MSR (Main Supply Route) and on the low hill through which the road passed an American regiment was dug-in.

On the valley floor a long column of infantry was nearing the MSR. Using binoculars they could be identified as Northumberland Fusiliers, Rifles, Belgians and a Company of American infantry. Behind the column, guarding their rear, stood two lonely Centurion tanks, their guns pointing to the west, facing a literal human wave of Chinese. The two Centurion's 20pdrs and Besa machine-guns poured fire into this mass, but were not slowing it down in the least.

On the escarpment the Riflemen had now come under fire from Chinese that had successfully climbed up behind them. There was no alternative but to climb down into the valley as fast as possible. At the base of the escarpment was a small village and as the Riflemen ran through the streets they came under extremely heavy fire from both mortars and machine-guns. There was no point in stopping to find cover; the best defence was to keep running. As the remnants of A Company, D Company and Tactical HQ, led by Captain Lane made their way back they came under fire from a barrage of phosphorous shells that fell some two hundred yards to their left. Before Lane could order the men to take avoiding action his Signaller Corporal Scully informed him that this was American fire being directed by Sergeant Prettyjohn, a US Forward Observer. As Prettyjohn had previously been attached to A Company Corporal Scully was able to make himself known and after several 'exchanges of pleasantries' the fire was called off![30]

Lieutenant McCord was crossing the eastern hills with the Chinese some forty to fifty yards behind and closing quickly. However, this was no panicked retreat. The command moved back by bounds, with one group firing to cover the other while it moved. Nevertheless, there was a degree of urgency and when one Rifleman decided to make off on his own McCord was forced to use his rifle butt to knock some sense into the man. In the confusion a number of prisoners captured earlier escaped, but there was nothing to be done, all was confusion with shooting and exploding grenades going off continuously. Seeing the absolute inferno that was the valley below McCord and his men made their way along the ridge. When they could go no further it became a matter of charging down the slope and making their way across the paddy fields towards a Centurion. As McCord made his way down the hill he brought with him an Artillery FOO who had lost his glasses and was hanging on the Lieutenant's webbing like grim death. McCord made his way towards the tank and as he approached it he recognised the commander as being Major Henry Huth. Bringing his men in behind the Centurion McCord shouted his thanks as the Centurion moved off.

The two Centurions were retiring in turn, while continuing to keep up a steady fire on the advancing Chinese. As the column of Riflemen passed between the tanks some of those wounded who were at the rear of the column were helped onto the engine decks and carried the last few yards to safety. Another of those grateful to Major Huth was Captain John Lane and his Signaller. As Huth spotted Lane approaching he stopped his tank for a few seconds to allow the Rifles officer to climb aboard.

30 Audio recording by Captain John Lane.

A scene during the concluding stages of the Imjin River battle. Men of the 29th British Brigade rest by the roadside during the withdrawal on 25 April 1951. (RUR Museum)

Once again Lance Corporal Joe Farrell was one of the last Riflemen to leave the battlefield. Having lost contact with his own Company he was following D Company along the hillside when he noticed a huge Chinaman following him in close pursuit. Turning, Farrell fired his Sten gun, but it only discharged one round, the magazine was empty. His target fell and rolled down the hill and Farrell tossed a couple of grenades after him just to make sure. Throwing away the now empty Sten gun Farrell ran on until he came across the body of a British soldier. From this he removed a rifle and bandolier of ammunition and continued on. On reaching the bottom of the hill he made towards the south across the paddy fields only to have a squad of enemy break cover and charge towards him. Dropping prone he shouldered the .303 and began to fire. Suddenly a voice behind him yelled 'Hubba hubba!' and Farrell turned to see a Centurion stop directly behind him. In a split second the Rifleman was up on the hot engine decking and being carried to safety, his war over for that day.[31]

Rifleman Henry O'Kane was hit in the leg and after crawling into a paddy field he dumped all his equipment save for his rifle and managed to keep moving. As he moved back he passed a number of Royal Engineers who were fighting as infantry and using a disabled Centurion as cover. Passing two more tanks that were burning he saw one of the Battalion's Oxford carriers by the roadside, its crew dead, the name painted in the vehicle was Ballymacab.

O'Kane was later taken prisoner. He had been riding on one of the Centurions when it lost a track and slewed off the road and into a paddy field. Dazed from concussion and bleeding from ears and nose he staggered on to the road to be met by three Chinese

---

31 Salmon, *To The Last Round*, London, 2009.

Destroyed Bren Carrier. (RUR Museum)

Ulster Crossing to Fort Nixon. (Mervyn McCord)

soldiers dressed in shoddy cotton uniforms who handed him and several other Riflemen safe conduct passes. An officer told them that "for you the war is over" and "Good fight!" They were then disarmed and marched back towards the Imjin. Those wounded who were left behind were never seen by O'Kane again. It was about this time that O'Kane met up with an old 'mucker', Rifleman Tommy Spiers, a former Inniskilling and Irish Fusilier who had served post-war in Austria, Trans Jordan and Egypt. At a rest stop and in what Spiers described as "an ideal place for an execution", he produced a battered packet of Philip Morris cigarettes, all that remained from an American 24-hour C Ration pack. Assuming that they would be shot out of hand O'Kane, Spiers and the others felt that there was no sense in wasting tobacco and they sat down and smoked the cigarettes – as their confinement would last a long time that tobacco would be sorely missed in the months to come. Before marching on each man was given some small green branches cut from the fir trees and when aircraft flew overhead the men were ordered to kneel and hold the branches over their heads. During these occasions many men took the opportunity to pray. It was not unknown for British or American aircraft to attack these columns, as they were unable to distinguish between prisoners and enemy troops.

An hour later the battle was over, with the last of 29 Brigade including the two Centurions safely behind the Main Supply Route. Major Huth, C Squadron commander, in his tank 'Cameronian', was the last to leave the battlefield. One of his tank commanders, Richard Napier, recalled, "after about three hours of continuous firing, my machine-gun barrels needed changing; my recoil system was so hot it wouldn't run back and my loader/operator Ken Hall, had fainted with the continual hard work and fumes."[32] The Centurions were a macabre sight, their turrets and hulls smeared with blood, their tracks dripping with intestines, skin and pieces of ragged uniforms, both Chinese and British.

It was the general opinion among the survivors of the Brigade that Major Henry Huth should have received the Victoria Cross for his actions. In the Rifles, Major Rickcord, acting Commanding Officer, stated that Huth was an absolute professional and master of his job "The man of the match and if one more VC was deserved for this action it should have gone to Huth!"[33]

As for the Rifles, Gerald Rickcord noted that not an inch of ground had been ceded on the Imjin, prior to the order to withdraw.

The men of 29 Brigade rallied, formed into a column and with the two tanks once again defending the rear began the march south towards Uijongbu.

After a four-mile march the Brigade reached the crossroads at Tokchon. A much relieved Brigadier Brodie visited Major Rickcord and expressed surprise that B Company, who had acted as rearguard, had made it. He then informed Rickcord that the Battalion must expect to fight another battle and they must begin to dig in at once. Rickcord recalled that it was odd to hear the clink of picks and shovels going again. When the roll call was made in the Rifles, it showed a total strength of fourteen officers and 240 other ranks.

---

32 Napier, *From Horses to Chieftains*, Arundel, 1992.
33 Audio recording held in the Royal Ulster Rifles Museum, Belfast.

11

The War grinds on

Tokchon 26 April – In conjunction with the Rifles, the Northumberland Fusiliers and Belgian Battalion began to dig in, a difficult task with few entrenching tools available to already exhausted men. A hot meal, the first since breakfast, did something to relieve flagging spirits.

The Brigade was only to hold this position until 2200hrs, when it was due to be relieved by The US 15th Regimental Combat Team, US 3rd Division.[1] As it was this unit did not arrive until 2330hrs, when the Battalion, in concert with the remainder of the Brigade staggered to its feet and once again exhausted men began marching south After about five or six miles the Brigade was met by a section of troop transports, which carried the men south throughout the night to Yongdungpo, on the south bank of the Han River.

It was just before dawn on 27 April when the men dismounted in a disused Japanese Ordnance depot, the same one that the Battalion had left previously when it had moved up to the Imjin. Here the men received another hot meal before immediately falling asleep.

The Battle of the Imjin was over. Although the Chinese would continue to within five miles of Seoul, the momentum could not be sustained and the casualties caused in the fighting on and below the Imjin were, for the time being, irreplaceable.

Major Rickcord came away from the Imjin battle,

> …feeling devastated. I believed that we had lost the battle, had suffered a disaster. But I was afterwards assured that it was by no means a disaster. The morning after we came out, the soldiers were singing Irish songs, playing the banjo. I told the Quartermaster to get them a bath and their green tropical uniforms. He said: 'It's much too cold for that.' But I said – No, go on, do it. It'll make all the difference in the world to them to get a change of clothes.' And forty-eight hours later, they were fit to fight again, which was a wonderful feeling. I think they felt very proud of the fight they had put up. We felt no particular animosity toward the Chinese. Indeed, I think we felt great respect, even liking for them. But the regiment's old motto – *Quis Separabit* – was something we felt very strongly about.

Subsequent reports showed that the full weight of the attack had been made against 29 Brigade with the 30,000 strong 64th CCF Army, attacking with its three Divisions in column.

While the Glosters were virtually destroyed and all other Battalions, along with the King's Royal Irish Hussars, suffered heavy casualties, those of the Chinese 64th Army were horrendous. For some time afterwards the 64th Army was rendered ineffective.

---

1   Regimental Combat Team was referred to in the RUR War Diary as a battalion.

Shown here shortly after the battle of the Imjin River, in which they played an active part are six Belfastmen, who all served with 1st Battalion, The Royal Ulster Rifles. From left they are - Rifleman David Kielty, Western Street, Shankill Road; David Fisher, Downing Street, Shankill Road; Sergeant Jack Simpson, Divis Street, Falls Road and Rifleman Robert Church, Little Sackville Street, Shankill Road. Kneeling are, George McClare, Grove Street East, Beersbridge Road and Samuel Elliott, Rockland Street, Donegall Road.

The Glosters, along with 170 Mortar Battery, were later awarded the United States Presidential Citation in recognition of their gallantry.

The Royal Ulster Rifles and the Northumberland Fusiliers had fought with equal determination against overwhelming odds and whilst the majority were able to escape their isolated positions their rear guard was cut off with about two hundred killed or captured.[2] Many of the injured died of the wounds during the next three days.[3]

Above all, the stand by 29 Brigade allowed the remainder of 1st Corps to withdraw and secure the line of the Han River, including Seoul, the prize for which the Chinese had gambled and lost! *The Times* newspaper of London published a full report of the battle which concluded with the words,

> The Gloster's, for what they had done now and what had went before it, deserve to be singled out for honourable mention, but they did not stand alone. The Northumberland Fusiliers and the Royal Ulster Rifles along with other

---

2 Cunningham, *No Mercy, No Leniency*, London, 2000.
3 Cunningham, *No Mercy, No Leniency*, London, 2000.

Commonwealth units, each with a past to live up to, shared with the Glosters in this most testing of all hazards on the battlefield, attacked by overwhelming numbers of the enemy. The fighting 5th wearing St George and the Dragon and the Irish Giants with the Harp and Crown have histories that they would exchange with no one as pride, sobered by mourning for the fallen, observes how well these young men have acquitted themselves in remotest Asia. The parts taken by the regiments may be seen as a whole. The motto of the Royal Ulster Rifles may have the last word – *Quis Separabit*. (Who shall separate us?)[4]

For Lieutenant Peter Whitamore 26 April was his first full day as a prisoner of war. He, along with other prisoners, had spent the previous night lying close to a disabled Centurion listening to the moaning of the wounded. That morning an American F-80 had screamed in at low level and bombed the tank, destroying it completely. Due to its gun stabiliser, the Centurion was still considered to be a 'secret' weapon and could not be allowed to fall into Soviet or Chinese hands. This attack left the already scorched Whitamore with more burns to carry north towards the prison camps.

Over the next two days there was little activity in Yongdungpo as debilitated men sought little else but sleep. On 27 April Colonel Carson returned to the Battalion from Japan and resumed command. The total casualties to the Battalion were ten officers and 176 'other ranks', many of who were 'missing' and presumed to be prisoner of war. With regards to weapons and equipment, things were serious. In the withdrawal many weapons had been abandoned when ammunition had run out or the crew killed or wounded, Bren guns, 2" mortars and wireless sets were all in short supply. However, the Base Organisation in Japan worked miracles in packing replacements, which were flown directly from airfields in Japan to all units in the Brigade. The men were issued with new uniforms, while an American bath unit provided copious amounts of hot water to allow all ranks a hot bath or shower, which did wonders to restore morale.

Casualties to the Brigade exceeded a thousand men, the Glosters, even with reinforcements, could only muster one company. On 29 April, the Brigade, consisting of Rifles, Northumberland Fusiliers and the Belgian Battalion, returned to the line. On the same day that Colonel Carson had returned a replacement draft of two officers and ninety men arrived, which allowed the companies to be brought back up to a reasonable strength. One of those replacements was Rifleman Christopher Spiers, who was posted to B Company as a Bren gunner. Chris had been working on a farm in County Fermanagh when he decided on an army career and had enlisted in the Royal Inniskilling Fusiliers at Omagh on 11 November 1947. He had served with the Inniskillings in Gibraltar and been posted to the Royal Irish Fusiliers in Egypt for a time before going to the Rifles in Korea. While with the Inniskillings in Gibraltar he had been appointed as 'Silverman', in his own words 'a cushy billet'. This duty involved him being responsible for the regimental silver and when pieces were required for a specific dinner of other occasion, it was his job to see that it was cleaned and presentable, which it always was. In Korea he would be as conscientious with his Bren gun.

The new United Nations front ran along the line of the Han River, except at Seoul, which was on the northern bank in a deep bend in the river, was held by the US 1st

---

4 http://royalirishrangers.co.uk/korea.html

The Mortar Platoon dug-in. (RUR Museum)

Corps. Seoul itself was defended by the 1st (ROK) Division, the 1st Cavalry Division and the 25th Division, whose flanks rested on the Han River. This was known as 'Line Golden'. Further to the east the line was held by the IX Corps, who again held the southern bank of the Han where it flowed out of the central mountain ranges. The tide that was the Chinese Spring Offensive washed against this line like an impotent force and eventually it began to turn and then ebb.

On the left flank the Han River flowed to the north-west towards the Yellow Sea and here lay the Kimpo Peninsula. This flat area was considered to be the most fertile in South Korea and its northern tip was held by the 5th (ROK) Marine Battalion, who relied on aggressive patrolling as opposed to fixed defences. In the centre of the Peninsula was Kimpo Airfield and on 28 April the Brigade moved into the Kimpo area and took up positions across the Peninsula. The Belgian Battalion ensconced itself on some hills that overlooked the Han about half way up the Peninsula, just to the north of where 'Line Golden' met the riverbank. The Northumberland Fusiliers took up a position opposite the Line, with one Company forward on Hill 131 on the riverbank and the remainder concentrated just behind, about a mile from the Airfield.

The river below Seoul was about four hundred yards wide and ran deep at high tides, while at low tide a number of sandbanks became exposed and offered several points where the river could be forded.

Initially the Rifles were placed in reserve, their billet being a chemical factory at Sosa-Ri, on the main Seoul-Inchon road. This spot was the most attractive ever occupied

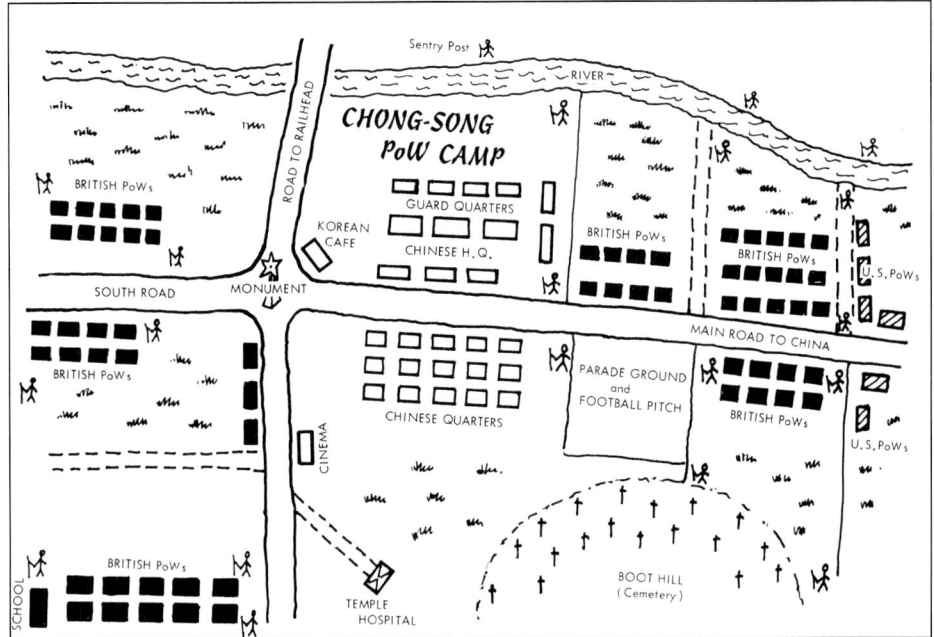

Chong-Song prisoner of war camp. (Henry O'Kane)

by the Rifles in the entire campaign. The factory provided dry shelter with hot water and was pleasantly laid out with green lawns, surrounded by orchards. The weather was agreeably warm, the trees were in blossom and there was a football pitch!

While reconnaissance patrols of the Peninsula were carried out on a regular basis a good deal of time was available to the men for recreational purposes. Inter-company football matches were organised and at Inchon a pre-war bathing lido was discovered and put to good use by all companies in turn. Given the experiences of the fighting on the Imjin it was decided that the Battalion's firepower would benefit from the inclusion of more machine-guns. Therefore a number of men, mostly Bren gunners, were went to the Americans for course on the Browning machine-gun. One of these was Rifleman Chris Spiers, who spent a day being instructed in the use of the .30cal Browning machine-gun, belt-fed, air-cooled weapon capable of 500 rounds per minute. This was an ideal weapon for defence and while most effective with a crew of two it could be used by one man. While Chris was impressed with the gun, it was the lunch provided that really made an impression – fresh bread, fresh fruit, roast meats, cream cakes, fruit juice, ice cream and of course limitless coffee. "Never seen so much food before, shame the course only lasted one day."[5]

Brigade Headquarters established contact with a US Marine unit stationed at Inchon. 'A' Company of this unit operated tracked amphibious vehicles and operated water patrols on the Brigade's left flank. A close liaison was set up with the Marines and several joint patrols were carried out. Chris Spiers did not like these patrols, he felt very exposed as they cruised the river where in many places their route was overlooked by

---

5   Interview with Rifleman Chris Spiers.

Lieutenant Gordon Potts in Korea, September 1951. (*Quis Separabit*)

high ground. Chris claimed that had they come under fire the 'metal boxes' would have become death traps.[6]

On the morning of 5 May, a warning order was received for a long-range patrol to make a reconnaissance as far north as Kaesong, which was situated just south of the 38th Parallel. Lieutenant Terry of C Company was to command the patrol, all of which were volunteers. Terry was briefed that the patrol would cross the Han near the mouth of the northern tip of the peninsula and would start out from an area held by the 5th (ROK) Marines. At this point the river was a mile or more wide, with a further eight miles of ground to be covered before reaching their objective. The crossing was timed to take place at 0200hrs on 8 May. Intelligence sources informed Lieutenant Terry that enemy resistance was deemed to be light as most of the patrol would be carried out well behind Chinese lines.

When the patrol and its supporting arms arrived at the designated crossing point on 7 May it was obvious that the enemy were very active on the northern bank. It was discovered that this was the result of a raid the day before by a unit of the ROK Marines, which had been carried out at the Rifles intended crossing place, of which the Rifles had not been informed. As a result of this the patrol was cancelled and all ranks returned to Sosa-Ri. The Rifles Sniper Section, who had established an OP on the riverbank, came under mortar fire as it withdrew from its cover position on the riverbank. No casualties were caused.

---

6   Interview with Rifleman Chris Spiers.

On 9 May the Battalion moved out of Sosa-Ri to take over the positions of the Northumberland Fusiliers on the riverbank. At the same time Colonel Carson assumed command of the Brigade while Brigadier Brodie went on a short leave. In the Colonel's absence Major Rickcord assumed command of the Battalion. For the next fourteen days the Rifles remained on the riverbank, with one company being rotated forward on Hill 131. In addition to the patrols and the guarding of the various crossing points, men were detailed for the construction of defences across the peninsula a few miles to the north.

The daily routine consisted of observation from the forward D Company position, combined patrolling in the amphibious vehicles with the US Marines and working parties digging trenches and laying barbed wire along the new defence line.

Across the Han River enemy activity was infrequent and patrols sent out from the 1st ROK Division found little sign of enemy activity and only brief contact with enemy forces, few bigger than a battalion. On 17 May the Battalion carried out an exercise in which two companies manned the defences of Hill 171 and two remained in reserve. This proved successful and in future the two forward and two in reserve became the norm. The month of May also saw the arrival of further reinforcements, including Major W.E. Brooks MC (and Bar) and Captain John Beamish MC. Brooks was from the London Irish Rifles and Beamish from the Royal Irish Fusiliers; they took command of B and A Companies respectively.

William Edwin Brooks had been commissioned into London Irish Rifles in August 1939 and served with them throughout the Italian Campaign in the Second World War earning and MC and Bar. His first award was earned on the night of 17 July 1943, during an attack on a German position south of Catania Airfield. The Bar to the MC was earned for his actions between 10-14 February 1944, at the 'Factory' near Caracetto, Anzio.[7] This was followed by service with Force 136 and the Special Operations Executive in the Far East. On arrival in Korea he was described by a battle-hardened Sergeant Major as "a lovely man", one of the highest compliments one Irishman can pay another.[8]

John Beamish had earned his MC on the night of 1 December 1944, near the Anzellara Ridge while serving with the 1st Battalion Royal Irish Fusiliers. Here Beamish, with a section of fourteen men, had fought his way through an enemy minefield, captured a German strongpoint, later discovered to be held at platoon strength and killed a large number of enemy soldiers. Beamish, who had enlisted in October 1939, had transferred to the Rifles from service with BAOR in Germany.[9]

On 20 May the Rifles, now practically back to normal strength and fighting efficiency, were inspected by Major General A.J.H. Cassels CBE DSO. He found no fault with the Riflemen and congratulated them on their performance so far. Later in the summer Cassels would take command of the newly-formed Commonwealth Division.

Two days later Operation 'Detonate' commenced. The 1st (ROK) Division, 1st US Cavalry and the 25th Division was to advance against the Imjin line. Nevertheless, there was no intention that 'Line Golden' should be abandoned entirely.

On 23 May 29 Brigade moved into the western suburbs of Seoul as Corps reserve, with the task of manning these defences should a counter-attack be mounted by the enemy. By 1200hrs the Battalion was comfortably established in the grounds of Seoul

---

7   WO 37/3/3.
8   *Blackthorn Magazine* Volume 50, No 27, 1991.
9   *Faugh-A-Ballagh Gazette*, 1969.

Members of the RUR Association Comforts' Fund Committee making up parcels of books and woollens. L to R - Miss June Charley, Mrs Cussans, Mrs H.R. Charley and Mrs Emily Reade.

University situated in a beautiful tree-covered park. For the first time some of the billets offered to the Rifles consisted of stone-built European-type two-storey houses. One room was particularly grand and the Officers' Mess hosted a very successful cocktail party for the other officers of the Brigade.

The following day it was business as usual and an extensive reconnaissance was carried out along 'Line Golden'. On 27 May a skeleton manning exercise was carried out in the old 1st (ROK) Division sector. At 1830hrs orders were received for a further move and it was goodbye to a short-lived lifestyle.

The advance of Operation 'Detonate' had been successful and had almost reached the Imjin. Therefore, 29 Brigade was to move north on 28 May to take over positions from the 1st US Cavalry Division. These positions were in the same hills as previously fought over the month before.

At 1200hrs the following day the Battalion debussed in a chestnut orchard at the southern end of the valley that had been defended by the Glosters the previous April. During the afternoon 'Hank' Carson and his 'O' Group carried out a reconnaissance to the head of the valley and found the Greek Battalion had just occupied the heights against what was described as only moderate resistance. The Greeks had pushed out patrols to the banks of the Imjin without meeting any serious resistance.

Reveille was sounded on 30 May and at 0815hrs the Battalion began its hike up the winding tracks towards their new positions. All along the route lay the debris of the previous battle, while now and again could be caught the sweet scent of an unburied body, presumably Chinese.

Just after 1200hrs the Rifles arrived at the Greek positions. Remembered as a tough-looking bunch with dark sallow skins and bushy moustaches, they were equipped with both American uniforms and weapons and proved to be most hospitable. As Colonel Carson was introduced to the Greek commander, Lieutenant Colonel Darboujis, he noticed the OP signpost featured prominently the name 'Garry Owen', together with the 1st US Cavalry Division's crest. It later transpired that the Greeks were permanently attached to the 7th US Cavalry Regiment, descendants of the famous regiment that had fought and died with Custer at the Battle of the Little Big Horn in 1876. The Irish contribution to that regiment was well known to the Ulster Rifles as was the fact that both units kept St. Patrick's Day as a regimental holiday.

In the course of the afternoon the Greeks moved out and the Rifles settled in to their new home. The situation was different from April. Now 29 Brigade held the ground previously held by the Glosters, while 28 British Commonwealth Brigade held the position formerly held by the Northumberland Fusiliers and Ulster Rifles.

The orders to the forces lining the southern bank of the Imjin were clear and concise. There would be no further advance at present, here they would dig in and here they would stay. The new defence position was to be known as 'Line Kansas' and was to be constructed along the hills overlooking the river.

It was now high summer and the monsoon rains were still some weeks away. The working parties toiled, stripped to the waist under a blazing sun, laying minefields and stringing miles of barbed wire. On the forward slopes of the hills on which the Battalion was sited all vegetation and scrub was cleared to provide clear fields of fire, while likely covered approaches up the numerous gullies were booby-trapped. During this time medical personnel kept a careful eye on the younger members of the Battalion, watching for tell-tale signs of sunstroke. In weapon pits and slit trenches reserve ammunition well in excess of the normal front line issue was stored close to hand. All those who had been present remembered the vast human wave attacks of the previous April.

The last days of May and the beginning of June saw intermittent enemy activity in the low ground on the northern bank. Listening posts placed along the south bank received an occasional round of mortar fire at night, usually the result of someone being careless with a flashlight or cigarette.

Any enemy movement spotted during the hours of daylight or darkness was immediately shelled by the Brigade's supporting artillery. In the words of Robin Charley, "if you saw a Chinaman on a hill you bombarded the top off the hill". Reconnaissance patrols by the Brigade found no sign of the enemy on either side of the river and the one occasion that a crossing was tried by the Chinese resulted in their boat being sunk by machine-gun fire from a Rifles listening post.

Despite the passive behaviour of the enemy Brigadier Brodie decide to dominate the far bank with a combination of strong fighting patrols ably supported by artillery and later the employment of tank/infantry task forces operating deep into enemy lines.

The Royal Engineers were tasked with opening up Gloster Crossing for both tanks and infantry. The river was still flowing high and fast from the late thaw in the central mountains and it brought with it a fair degree of rubble, tree branches and the occasional dead sheep. Wading proved to be impossible, but at the fords both tanks and the Oxford carriers were able to make their way across. This was possible only after the Engineers had repaired the earthen ramp through the cliffs, which had been demolished by explosives the previous April.

5 June saw C and D Companies of the Rifles carry out the first major crossing of the river. Their objective was a reconnaissance in strength to an area of small hills, the largest of which was the Sindae, about 1,000 yards north of the river. Here the enemy were known to have placed observation posts and standing patrols. No tank support was available as the approach ramps had yet to be completed. Battalion Tactical Headquarters

was established on the southern bank close to the crossing point and D Company was elected to cross first. This took a considerable time, as only three American-supplied assault boats were available to carry the men over.

Arriving on the northern bank D Company immediately went into a horseshoe defence a few hundred yards beyond the bank. As this was completed C Company crossed in turn, a laborious process given the small number of boats available. Once C Company had formed up it passed through D and moves towards Sindae. The Company had advanced only a few hundred yards when its leading platoon was pinned by fire from a concealed machine-gun. As the remainder of the Company attempted to outflank the position other enemy weapons joined in from the surrounding hills. As C Company returned the fire it was obvious to those back on the riverbank that a full-scale firefight was in progress.

Despite supporting fire from artillery, machine-guns and tanks C Company found themselves in a sticky position. With the situation getting more serious by the minute Colonel Carson order C Company to disengage.

At 1225hrs the Company began to work its way back, intending to pass through D Company and on to the riverbank. However, they were faced with a tenacious enemy who followed up immediately the withdrawal began. Supporting fire from D Company held them in check for a time, allowing C to successfully cross the river. D Company began to disengage by platoons and as they did so the last of the assault boats broke down. This left one platoon and D Company Headquarters stranded on the north bank and fighting for their very survival. Seeing their quandary from the south bank CSM McConville commandeered a rowing boat and with a volunteer crew rowed across under heavy fire to rescue the stranded men. For his action he was awarded the Distinguished Conduct Medal.

By 1450hrs the evacuation was complete. Despite the high volume of fire directed at the two companies casualties to the Rifles were light. One officer and one Rifleman had been slightly wounded and one man was reported missing. The Rifles claimed sixteen enemy soldiers killed and numerous others wounded, while casualties from the supporting artillery and tanks could not be ascertained.

While the operation could not claim to be in any way successful it did have an upbeat ending. A few days later the missing man, Rifleman Fahy, was recovered from the northern bank by a patrol. Fahy had spent the time lying very still in a patch of scrub waiting for the chance to escape.

For the following ten days fighting and reconnaissance patrols continued to operate on the northern bank, each battalion taking its turn in the line and working in the 'Kansas Line' defences.

On 15 June D Company supported a Belgian patrol that crossed the river to recover items of equipment that had been left behind after the debacle of 5 June. The majority of the items lay where they had been left, but each one was cunningly booby-trapped with a hand grenade. Rifleman Heavey was reported as being injured on this date.

Reconnaissance now revealed that the Chinese outpost line lay some 8,000 yards from the river and appeared to centre on a 187 metre high hill known by the codename 'Victor'. Probing patrols going north of the river would frequently meet enemy patrols, usually of no more than section strength. However, if any attempt was made to get close to the hill the resistance increased considerable.

The height of the river had dropped considerably and on 16 June orders were issued for an attack in strength to be made on 'Victor'. The raiding force was to consist of the Ulster Rifles, the Belgian Battalion and a squadron of tanks. The Belgian Battalion, with half a squadron of tanks, was to move north from 'Gloster Crossing' and work its way around to the rear of 'Victor' from the east. The Rifles were to move north-west along the hills on the right of the Samichon River and close down on 'Victor' from the west. The remaining half squadron of tanks was to go into a 'cut-off' position to the north-west. If, as was suspected, the enemy was holding 'Victor' in battalion strength or more, the raiders would not carry out an assault, but would engage it with all arms and air-strikes. The operation was given the code word 'Royal Harp' and the raiding force was successfully across the river by 0700hrs on 17 June.

On the right flank the Belgians had engaged the enemy by 1000hrs and found a stubborn defence. After suffering casualties they had pulled back to call in air strikes that were both accurate and successful. On the left flank A and C Companies of the Rifles had met resistance from small parties of enemy who had advanced out from 'Victor'. Just after 1200hrs a platoon of A Company were surprised by a group of five Chinese who stormed their position from close range in a near suicidal charge. Two were felled by small arms fire, while the remaining three retired wounded.

On the slopes of 'Victor' the enemy continued his defence from well-constructed bunkers and an entrenchment system second to none. Despite air strikes with bombs and napalm, artillery fire and direct hits from the tank guns, the Chinese held on and showed no sign of either giving up or retiring.

At 1315hrs, the Brigade Commander, who had his Tactical Headquarters in two tanks to the north of the river, gave the order to disengage. He wanted the complete force back across the river before darkness fell. As the tanks in the 'cut-off' position moved out one vehicle lost a track and as the damage was deemed repairable the infantry held their positions to provide cover while the repairs were carried out. Throughout the remainder of the afternoon the enemy made prodding attacks against both the Belgians and the Rifles, which were all seen off. The Rifles received numerous shells from a well-concealed Chinese 105mm gun on 'Victor' which continued to fire despite the air strikes and artillery support. Thankfully no casualties were suffered.

The damaged track was repaired by 1815hrs and in the gathering darkness the entire force made its way back to the river. The Rifles were the last to cross, this being completed by 2315hrs and the Chinese were left to lick their wounds. No doubt they also did a little celebrating.

On 19 June a Rifles' patrol was withdrawing back to base after being heavily mortared and on returning to their lines it was discovered that a man was missing. The patrol had been out for some time, there had been little opportunity for sleep and all ranks were suffering from exhaustion. On calling the roll it was found that Rifleman Murray was missing. As the patrol had moved out just ahead of a Chinese advance it appears that Murray did not hear the order to move and he was subsequently taken prisoner. There was rarely time for adequate sleep and nerves were constantly on edge. On one particular night all men of B Company were brought wide awake by a terrible scream from the darkness. On investigation it was discovered that one of the Korean 'boys' had previously set snares and one of these had caught a pheasant, which accounted for the noise. Despite this those who were not on guard quickly went back to sleep. The

Bivouacs at Line Kansas 1951. (Mervyn McCord/RUR Association)

The Royal Ulster Rifles Command Post on Line 'Kansas'. (RUR Museum)

nights were also disturbed by a North Korean aircraft, a biplane, that flew low and slow overhead and broadcast appeals to the Rifles that they were fighting 'America's War' and that they should go home, it also dropped leaflets basically saying the same thing. As this voice was female the aircraft was quickly dubbed 'Chinese Lil'.[10]

A few days later the rain began to fall as only it can in Korea and the level of the Imjin rose rapidly. Patrolling had to be curtailed, due not only to the difficulty in crossing the river, but the state of the paddy fields on the far bank, which were flooded and had turned into gelatinous mud.

While the British 28 and 29 Brigades held their positions on the riverbank, and continued with patrolling where possible and strengthening the 'Kansas Line', the 25th Canadian Brigade, recently arrived in Korea, took up positions to their rear. It was intended that in late July all three Brigades would merge into the 1st British Commonwealth Division, under the command of Major General Cassels.

In June peace talks had begun in Kaesong, which proved to be a mistake on the part of General Ridgway in accepting this as a suitable location. Kaesong was within the area controlled by the Communists and the air was both menacing and intimidating. The location was moved to Panmunjom in October.

On 1 July the Battalion commemorated the role of the 36th (Ulster) Division at the battle of the Somme in 1916. There were church services followed by a concert on the playing fields by the Pipes and Drums. In the afternoon there was a football match against the 3rd Royal Australian Regiment, which the Rifles won. The Brigade Concert Party entertained the men that evening and there was a fine meal of turkey and ham, washed down with an ample supply of Guinness.

Now that summer was here it would bring its own problems. July, August and September brought the monsoons with about 15" of rain per month. High humidity resulted in every piece of clothing being permanently damp and a green mould growing on boots overnight. Lethargy ruled the day and any physical activity was draining.

On 3 July 1951 the Royal Ulster Rifles dedicated a Memorial to those men who were lost during the Battle of Chaegunghyon (Happy Valley). It was positioned on the recaptured ground overlooking the battlefield, close to the village of Pulmiji-Ri. The site was declared as British soil by the South Korean government and had been prepared by the Royal Engineers. The memorial was carved from local stone by a Korean mason who travelled with the Padre whenever the Battalion moved, and was mounted on a plinth that sat on a platform of rough pink granite slabs. One face of the Memorial was dedicated to the Rifles, one to the Gunners of 45 Field Regiment RA and 170 Mortar Battery RA and one to the 8th King's Royal Irish Hussars.[11]

While from a tactical point of view the impending merger made good sense, the veterans of 29 Brigade held reservations. From the formation of the Brigade in Colchester a very strong *esprit de corps* had grown up among the units. Since coming to Korea this had only been enhanced in the trial by combat and the vicissitudes of the campaign. As far as the Rifles were concerned there was a very strong feeling of comradeship with and confidence in, the rest of the Brigade and especially with 176 Battery of 45 Field Regiment, with B Troops of 170 Mortar Battery and C Squadron of the 8th Hussars. Not to be forgotten was the 55th Field Squadron Royal Engineers, who received a warm

---

10 Interview with Rifleman Chris Spiers.
11 http://www.bkva.co.uk/ulster_mem.htm

welcome whenever they were met. It was a sorrowful contingent from the Brigade that attended a farewell parade at Divisional Headquarters on 23 July 1951. Here the Brigade lost the words 'Independent' and 'Group' from its title and became the 29th British Infantry Brigade, of the 1st Commonwealth Division. During this parade Brigadier Brodie presented medal ribbons to those officers, NCOs and men of the Brigade who had been awarded decorations in the campaign, the ceremony serenaded by the Pipes and Bugles of the Rifles.

With this excitement over, life on 'Line Kansas' continued in much the same manner as before. There was training and patrolling and gradually the Brigade settled into its new command with the Division.

Life in the prison camps was many things and tedium was one that was particularly hard to deal with. There were numerous lectures on the virtues of communism and the evils of America, many of which went on for hours. Lieutenant Peter Whitamore recalled that one, 'The Twilight of World Capitalism', was so bad it was beyond arguing with, although others tried. On 26 July another significant attempt was made by prisoners to escape captivity. The team comprised Rifleman C. Brierley and Private D. Richards. They stayed at large for the record period of ten days, convincing the Chinese in the process that they must have had outside help and not that their security could have had inherent weaknesses. [12]

At the beginning of August the monsoon rains began in earnest. Streams that had been a mere trickle in July now ran as foaming torrents, while the Imjin rose to new heights. In 29 Brigade area the Royal Engineers had provided a ferry consisting of a large raft attached to a steel cable that stretched across the river from bank to bank and this was used for the daily patrols that operated on the northern bank.

On 2 August Colonel Carson received orders for the Battalion to take part in a large-scale raid into enemy territory. Also involved would be the Belgian Battalion, two battalions of 28 Brigade and units of the 1st US Cavalry Division.[13] While the main thrust of the raid would occur in 28 Brigade and 1st Cavalry sectors, the Rifles would provide two companies to screen the left flank of the operation.

A reconnaissance was carried out on 3 August and the following day the force crossed the river. By mid-afternoon the Rifles had secured their objective without contacting the enemy. Their only worry was the persistent rain, the rapidly raising river with its increased current, which made the journey back seem doubtful. The Rifles were right to worry as later in the afternoon floating debris brought downstream by the fierce current struck the raft, destroying it completely.

Further upstream the same debris had wrecked the rafts and pontoon bridge that had been used by 28 Brigade and the Cavalry. To all intents and purposes the entire force was now marooned on the enemy-held bank of a very angry river. The two companies of Rifles and the Belgian Battalion were pulled back to a position close to the crossing point, but the surge of the river prevented any attempts to repair the ferry or launch rescue boats. The 'powers that be' had assumed that the raid would all be over in the course of daylight, so no emergency rations had been issued, nor were the men equipped

---

12 Cunningham, *No Mercy, No Leniency*, London, 2000.
13 The British 28th Brigade consisted of the King's Own Scottish Borderers, King's Shropshire Light Infantry and the 3rd Battalion Royal Australian Regiment.

Destroyed Chinese artillery in the Imjin. (RUR Association)

with blankets or ponchos. It was a miserable night, the only comfort being that the Chinese had the good sense to remain inside their warm dry bunkers.

At dawn the following day there was no let up in the rain and the fact that the river had risen another twelve feet caused more worry. Even the most optimistic could see that no crossing was going to be attempted until the river had fallen considerably. Later in the morning an Auster aircraft piloted by Captain Bob Begbie, Royal Artillery, with Captain Wetherall, BRASCO, acting as a dispatcher, flew over the Rifles position and made a limited supply drop. For supper that night each man had half a tin of 'compo', about four ounces of food, better than nothing.

Throughout the day the Royal Engineers had worked on the ferry, but without success, there was little in the way of material that could be used to build either a bridge or suitable raft.

The Rifles settled down for another uncomfortable night and again the Chinese left them alone. At 0900hrs on 6 August a supply drop was made by aircraft that had flown directly from airfields in Japan. The drops was accurate, with all panniers landing within reach of the Rifles, but on being opened they were found to contain only ammunition and boots, no rations! These things happen in war. By that afternoon a motorboat had been found and was pressed into service to deliver much needed supplies to the northern bank. While considered too fragile to ferry troops, the craft was able to take across rations, picks, shovels and ponchos. That night the Rifles settled down to a more sheltered existence. The Belgians opened fire on a suspected enemy patrol at about midnight, but again the Rifles were left alone.

The River Imjin, showing two bridges built by American engineers, over which the Commonwealth Division was mainly supplied – the low-level bridge in use and the high-level bridge under construction. It should be noted that the river was exceptionally low when the photograph was taken. (Public Relations, Headquarters, BCOF)

Representatives of all Commonwealth countries who provided units in the 1st Commonwealth Division; L to R, India, Wales, Canada, England, Australia, New Zealand, Northern Ireland and Scotland. (Public Relations, Headquarters, BCOF)

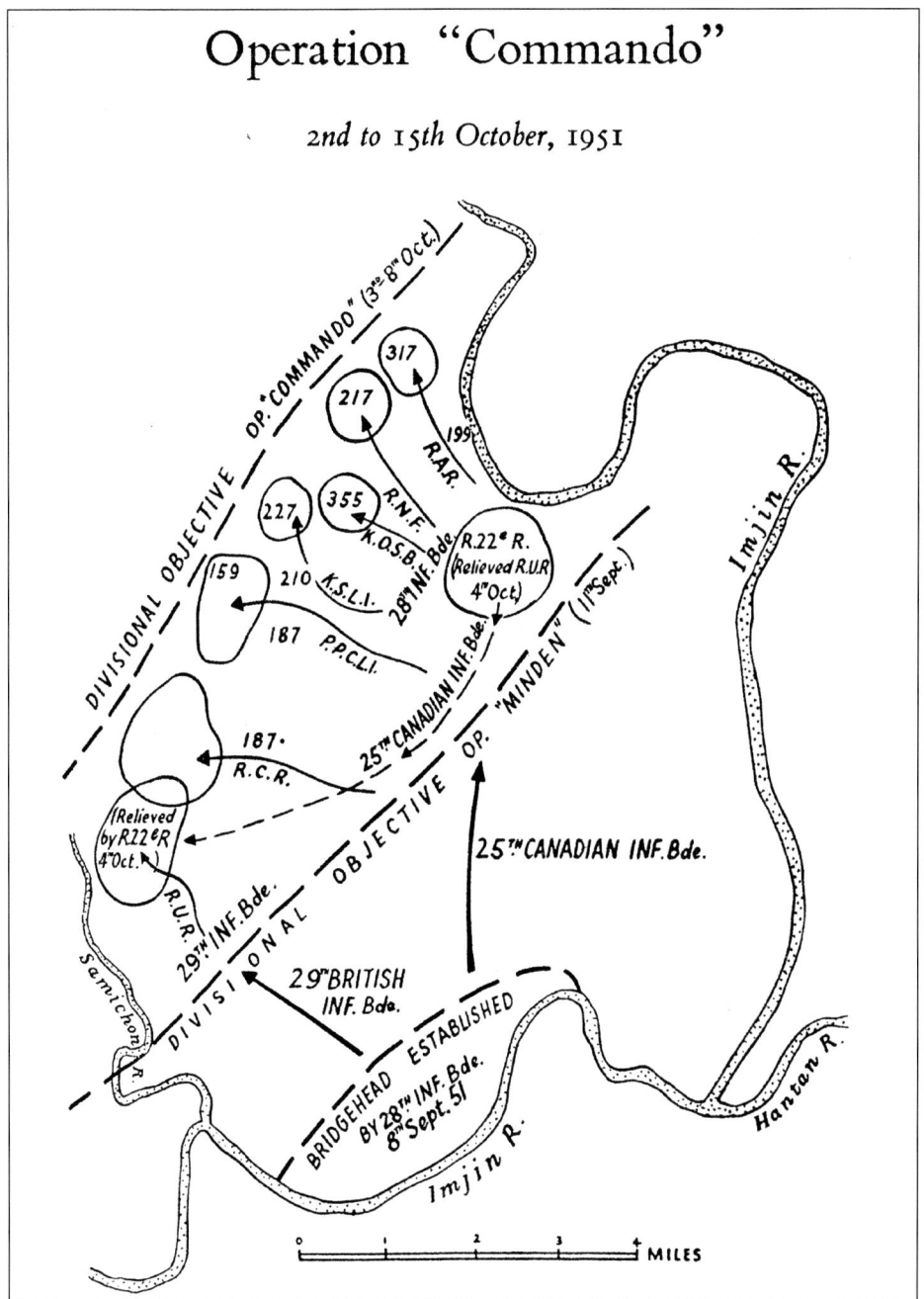

Operations 'Minden' and 'Commando'. The advance of the 1st Commonwealth Division from the line of the Imjin River, 8 September to 8 October 1951. (Barclay, *The First Commonwealth Division*)

The memorial and view looking north towards Chaegunghyon, which gives an excellent indication of the type of terrain which the Battalion fought over. (RUR Association)

The Royal Engineers had worked continuously to get a new ferry into operation and this was achieved at 1000hrs on 7 August. By nightfall the entire force had crossed to safety with no casualties being caused.

There was no alleviation in the weather and the torrential rains did great damage to the Battalion's somewhat unstable supply lines. Thankfully by mid-August the monsoon was virtually over, the rain eased, the sun came out and the river swiftly dropped back to its normal level.

Patrolling by one and two companies continued on a daily basis for the remainder of the month. There were frequent brushes with enemy patrols, but any attempts to penetrate deeper into Chinese lines met with ferocious resistance.

While the patrols suffered few casualties to enemy action, the near-constant patrolling was an unmerciful strain on the men concerned. The weather was now very hot and the going up and down the steep hillsides were both rocky and dusty, while the close-growing scrub caught at the feet of the unwary. Most patrols involved an approach march of between ten and fifteen miles and there was always the uncertainty of the river crossing, therefore a weighty load of ammunition and rations had to be carried by each man, Bren gunners and wireless operators being particularly laden.

The Royal Ulster Rifles Memorial on the heights above Happy Valley at its dedication. (Mervyn McCord/RUR Association)

Colonel Carson and Brigadier Brodie at the dedication of the Memorial above Happy Valley, 1951. (William May/RUR Museum)

Father Ryan and Lieutenant John Mole at the dedication of the Royal Ulster Rifles Memorial in Korea. (Mervyn /McCord/RUR Association)

Colonel Carson, Major Rickcord, DSO and CO 8th Hussars (centre) in conversation at the dedication service of the Royal Ulster Rifles Memorial, 1951. (RUR Museum)

Imjin Pontoon Bridge, Korea, 1951. (William May/RUR Association)

Korea, summer 1951. (RUR Museum)

RUR C Coy POWs – No 1 Camp, Intercamp Olympics, Korea. (Mervyn McCord/RUR Association)

POWs playing cards during the winter of 1952 (Henry O'Kane)

US Diamond T towing what appear to be two damaged Carriers. (RUR Museum)

Presentation of awards to the men of the 29th Brigade accompanied by the 1st Battalion, The Royal Ulster Rifles Pipe Band. (RUR Museum)

Inter-Company Sports at 'Somme Stadium', Korea. (RUR Museum)

An 'Elephant House' position for a Centurion on Yong Dong. (George Forty)

Despite all this the original objective of dominating the north bank of the river up to the Chinese main line of defence was achieved with complete success. The constant patrolling developed a good picture of the enemy's defences and the near-constant artillery barrages no doubt caused casualties and debilitated morale.

To ease the strain of patrolling every effort was made to provide recreational facilities to all ranks. The 'Kansas Line' was now finished and provided a strong defensive position against any Chinese attack. Now time and toil could be put to good use in making things a little more comfortable behind the lines.

At night the companies manned their hilltop positions, while during the day those not involved in patrolling concerned themselves with creating a 'home from home' and with the assistance of the porters straw 'bashas' were built for cookhouses, dining halls and recreation rooms. Soon the rear area resembled a small village.

The Battalion also added a rifle range, football pitch and an athletic track, all of which were put to good use. A highly organised Battalion Rifle Meeting was held on 14 and 15 August, followed by a Brigade Meeting on 19 and 19 September. The first athletics meeting was held on 6 September and proved a great success. While the field events were in progress a Chinese attack developed against a patrol base of the US 1st Cavalry Division, positioned to the east on the far side of the river. Throughout the afternoon artillery reverberated across the hills, while pillars of black smoke from napalm air strikes rose into the sky. The meeting continued as normal and news was later received that the attack had been beaten off with significant losses to the enemy.[14]

---

14 Lowe, *The Origins of the Korean War*, New York, 1986.

Constant attempts had been made to drive off the probing patrols sent across by the Commonwealth Division, but these had been unsuccessful. Aerial reconnaissance had revealed considerable activity along the Chinese lines of communication from the north and it appeared that a full-scale attack was inevitable. Intelligence sources pointed to 1st Corps being the main point of attack.

To nullify such a move, 25 and 29 Brigades were ordered to carry out Operation 'Minden'. This involved a push forward across the Imjin to occupy a line running from south-west to north-east across a ten mile wide salient, formed by the loop of the river. This would close the gap that existed between the armies and would also shorten considerably the length of front held by 1st Corps. However, this would be a limited advance and would occupy nothing more than ground that had already been thoroughly patrolled by all battalions during the previous three months.

On 10 September a reconnaissance of the north bank of the Imjin, was carried out by the Glosters, now reconstituted after their ferocious April battle.

The following day 28 Brigade, recently relieved by 25 Canadian Brigade, moved forward and established a strong screen forward of the river. The King's Own Scottish Borderers formed a bridgehead at 'Gloster Crossing', while the two other battalions, King's Shropshire Light Infantry and 3rd Battalion Royal Australian Regiment, performed similar actions at the crossings to be used by the Northumberland Fusiliers and 25 Canadian Brigade. At the same time an American Engineer Battalion came up and proceeded to construct a Class 50 pontoon bridge at 'Gloucester Crossing' to allow wheeled vehicles and tanks to cross.

It was a wet and blustery day as at 0630hrs on 12 September the Rifles, closely followed by the Glosters, filed down through a cutting between the cliffs on the southern bank of the Imjin and formed up on the shingle beach. While the day began to lighten the infantry moved to the footbridge just upstream from the pontoon where the Engineers were still at work and began to cross. As the men made their way across the river, vehicles made their way towards the now completed pontoon bridge. The first to cross was a Churchill ARV (Armoured Recovery Vehicle). As the tank began to cross its weight of forty tons damaged the bridge to such an extent that it would require six hours of repairs before it would carry tanks. There was no restriction on jeeps, but the infantry, who were due to advance on the Centurions of the 8th Hussars, had to 'hoof' it forward to their objectives.

This distance was between four and five thousand yards and by noon all companies had arrived on their objectives without meeting any opposition. Digging in commenced immediately on what would later be called 'Line Wyoming'.

On the right flank the Canadians had met with similar success and by nightfall the Division was well established. 29 Brigade was on the left flank, 25 on the right and 28 in reserve covering the bridges. In the Battalion while the Riflemen were busy constructing slit trenches and weapon pits the Quartermaster and his staff got to work with the re-supply of rations, ammunition, mines, barbed wire and sandbags, the last three items being in great demand.

The Royal Engineers had bulldozed a rough track forward up the eastern side of a narrow valley from the Imjin to the Paekhak Reservoir, which was the junction between the Rifles and the 2nd Royal Canadian Regiment (RCR), the left-hand battalion of 25 Brigade. The Rifles occupied the hills to the west of the valley, facing westwards and this necessitated the construction of a jeep track running from this track across the valley and up a narrow re-entrant to the hills.

The Battalion Porters, under the command of Lieutenant Bob Gill, had toiled long and hard on this the previous day, protected by an infantry screen provided by 28 Brigade. Even while under construction jeeps had made their perilous way up to the Battalion and as the Porters continued the track was soon able to take two-way traffic and the re-supply line was secure. As the Rifles proceeded to strengthen their positions the call for more mines, barbed wire and sandbags continued. It was obvious that the Chinese were not going to sit back and allow this to go on without interruption and soon artillery and mortar rounds were landing in the Battalion area. Digging continued, but at a slightly faster rate. That night, as weary Riflemen settled into their new homes and a welcome warm meal, the only distractions were a few rounds of mortar fire falling in front of D Company, which caused no casualties. From the Canadians came a report of an enemy patrol to their front, but no contact was made and all ranks within the Brigade managed to get some sleep.

A morning patrol was sent out from D Company on 13 September and after about four hundred yards came under fire from what was reported to be an 'aggressive enemy'. No casualties were caused. Later in the day between nine and ten rounds of 105mm artillery fire came down with commendable accuracy within the D Company area, but again no casualties were caused. The Battalion faced roughly north-west and to its front lay about 2,000 yards of broken ground and low hills covered with the inescapable scrub, before reaching the enemy line. This line centred on a spot named Hill 187. From the hill a sandy ridge ran south-west to the valley of the Samichon and was known to the Rifles as the 'Brown Bastard'. A similar feature, but this covered in thick woods, ran east almost into the forward defence line of the 2nd RCR. Both the hill and the two ridges, which formed a horseshoe, were well defended by the enemy. Deep bunkers and re-entrants were estimated to be held by at least a battalion with supporting arms, including 81mm and 60mm mortars.

12

Checkpoint 'How'

Between the two ridges and running south for 1,000 yards from Hill 187 lay a long narrow spur that ended in a conical hill. During the patrolling period prior to Operation 'Minden' this conical hill had been a Chinese outpost. Any attempts by Commonwealth patrols to encroach on this hill had met with ferocious resistance from the enemy. Nevertheless, it made an excellent observation post, commanding the entire horseshoe feature and as it was only 1,500 yards from D Company's position the Battalion was ordered to occupy it on a daily basis and in turn prevent the enemy's use of it. It was given the phonetic name Checkpoint 'How'.

Just before dawn on 14 September a patrol from B Company under the command of Lieutenant John Mole slipped quietly out of the Battalion area and, encountering no opposition, swiftly occupied Checkpoint 'How'. An Observation Post was established and the Royal Artillery Forward Observation Officer (FOO) that had accompanied the patrol established contact with his guns via wireless.

At 1015hrs Battalion Headquarters received a report from John Mole that he had identified at least four enemy tanks heavily camouflaged, in the trees on the eastern spur of Hill 187. Initially the report was queried, but the Lieutenant, backed up by the eyesight of the Forward Observation Officer, confirmed the sighting. The message was then passed back to Brigade Headquarters, where a tremor of excitement was caused. No enemy tanks had been seen on a battlefield since the initial breakthrough by the North Koreans in the summer of 1950. Intelligence had reported the presence of armour at Sibyonni, about twenty miles to the north and it was possible that this force had been brought forward with the intention of launching a combined armour and infantry assault. However, within Brigade Headquarters there was a general feeling of disbelief. Over the past several months air reconnaissance had revealed no sign of tanks or their supporting units, petrol bowsers etc.

At Checkpoint 'How' Lieutenant Mole was surprised to find himself talking directly to Brigadier Brodie who asked them for more details. Both the Lieutenant and the FOO confirmed the sighting and stated that one vehicle had been seen to move, knocking down a tree as it did so. Eventually it was decided to put a Divisional artillery shoot onto the hill, as this would, hopefully, strip the camouflage from the tanks and would be followed by a precision shoot from a battery of American 8" howitzers that were attached to the Division. This was duly carried out and after the 'Persuaders' had lobbed a dozen or more of their 200lb shells into the target area the OP reported that one tank had definitely been hit and was lying on its side minus a track.

This was not the end of the ordeal for those Chinese occupying the tree-covered ridge. Mid-afternoon an air strike was called in and a flight of US Marine Corsairs screamed over the target area delivering a combination of rockets and napalm. By this time the light was beginning to fade and further accurate observation was impossible.

Mortar Platoon dug-in. (Mervyn McCord/RUR Association)

A jeep patrol returning to base. (Mervyn McCord/RUR Association)

Two Rifleman digging in, in the winter. (RUR Museum)

At dusk the patrol moved back to Battalion lines and by 2200hrs they had arrived safe and sound.

John Mole, the RA FOO and the members of the patrol had every reason to be pleased with themselves and expressed indignation towards anyone who doubted their actions. The only people really disappointed with the day's work were the men of the 8th Hussars located down in the valley. They had been metaphorically sharpening their sabres in expectation of matching their Centurions against the Russian T34 and considered the entire business to have been grossly mishandled by the Rifles and the Gunners. That night D Company reported seeing pin pricks of light moving on the hillside where the tanks had been seen. It was later realised that these were tank exhausts and the enemy had withdrawn his vehicles well out of harm's way.

It was the turn of C Company to provide the OP for Checkpoint 'How'. As the platoon settled in it received a severe battering from enemy mortars, thankfully no casualties were caused. Throughout the day there was considerable enemy activity all around the OP, but no attacks were made and no tanks were spotted.

Early on the morning of 17 September Lieutenant Cornick was detailed to take No 11 Platoon from D Company and occupy Checkpoint 'How'. At 0400hrs the Platoon moved out of the Company position and marched towards the conical hill. They arrived at the 'lay back' position at 0500hrs and from here a Section led by Lieutenant Cornick advanced to the final objective. As the Section approached the top of the hill they were met by fire from a force of fifteen Chinese armed with an assortment of weapons

Two Riflemen examine a well believed to be the resting place of a missionary. (Mervyn McCord/RUR Association)

including light machine-guns, 'burp' guns[1] and hand grenades. The Chinese, who had moved onto the hill during the hours of darkness, had sprung a successful ambush.

The Section took cover and the Lieutenant ordered return fire as he planned a withdrawal to the Platoon position. The Bren gun was being fired by Rifleman Turner and he was seriously wounded by a Chinese with a machine-gun who had worked his way around to the right flank. Cornick then ordered the Section to fall back on the Platoon 'lay back' position and Rifleman Newport, the Bren gun No 2, immediately stood up in the open and picked up the wounded Turner and despite the heavy fire carried him the 600 yards back to the Platoon position. All this was done while under fire, not only from 'How', but from other Chinese positions firing from the west. For his actions on 'How' Newport would be awarded the Military Medal.

Once Cornick had his men into a secure perimeter he contacted Battalion Headquarters by wireless for instructions. He was ordered to hold and call down artillery fire in support. This was done and for the next few hours the platoon held their ground and reported any movement on 'How'. At approximately 1430hrs the enemy peppered the hill with mortar fire, covering his withdrawal. This movement was spotted by the Canadians, who identified a body of about fifty Chinese moving off the hill and brought

---

1   Many writers have alluded to the 'Burp' gun simply being any enemy sub-machine-gun. However research indicates that this was in fact the Russian-manufactured PPSh-41, a 7.62mm weapon of Second World War vintage, usually equipped with either a 35 round box, or more commonly 71 round drum magazine. It can still be found in use today.

Patrol briefing, Korea, 1951. (William May/RUR Association)

Battalion vehicles, Korea, 1951. (William May/RUR Association)

CHECKPOINT 'HOW' 219

Bren Carriers, Korea, 1951. (William May/RUR Association)

Machine Gun post, Korea, 1951. (William May/RUR Association)

down shellfire that caused casualties. As darkness fell Lieutenant Cornick led his platoon back to their company position.

Despite the setback of the previous day, 'A' Company's patrol reached Checkpoint 'How' without incident and apart from some intermittent mortaring experienced an uneventful day.

19 September was to be a little different. Lieutenant Gordon Potts, No 1 Platoon, 'A' Company, made an early start from the company position and arrived at the base of Checkpoint 'How' at about 0410hrs. When they had reached the halfway point towards the crest of the hill flares suddenly soared into the darkness illuminating the patrol. Raking machine-gun fire erupted from the top of the hill and the patrol threw themselves flat as tracer fire cracked over their heads. Before the enemy could lower their sights the Lieutenant called in a pre-arranged artillery strike by radio on the crest and reverse slope of the hill. When the brief, but heavy barrage had ceased, the patrol moved onto the crest and found that the enemy had retreated. The ground was clear, the enemy had taken any dead or wounded with them. Later two of them were spotted in the valley to the west and both were hit by fire from the Bren guns, despite it being at the weapon's maximum range.

As the patrol settled into its now normal, but uncomfortable routine, several rounds of mortar fire were delivered, but failed to cause any casualties. On this occasion the Chinese were not going to give up easily. As the patrol began to make its way back down the hill Gordon Potts and two Riflemen remained to provide cover. As this party was about to leave one of the Riflemen heard a sound from the reverse slope. The Lieutenant moved forward slightly and saw between ten and twenty enemy moving up the reverse slope towards the crest. He immediately opened fire with a Bren gun killing two men with the first burst and wounding two more with the second.

In the ensuing confusion Potts and the two Riflemen scrambled back down the hill and rejoined the platoon for the journey back to the Battalion. There was no attempt by the enemy to follow up. The Riflemen occupying the OP were generally left alone for the next three days with the exception of accurate mortaring and inaccurate shelling from two 105mm guns firing from somewhere to the west.

25 September was a bad day for the Battalion. C Company was providing the patrol for Checkpoint 'How' and a different arrangement was in place. Two sections under the platoon sergeant were situated on the small hill 600 yards to the south of the OP, while Second Lieutenant Ken Hodgkins, the platoon commander and Captain John Warren, the FOO, occupied the OP, protected by four Riflemen. Lieutenant Hodgkins, a South African, had joined the Battalion in April on secondment from the Border Regiment the previous April; he was considered a popular officer and a valued friend of many in the Battalion.

As daylight broke the mortaring became very heavy and at 0600hrs a bomb landed directly in the trench being used by the two officers, and both were killed outright. At the same time a platoon of Chinese, who had worked their way up the reverse slope, charged the crest, driving off the remaining men, who retired in good order under the command of Rifleman McShane, the senior man. McShane knew exactly what to do in the circumstances, having been briefed earlier by the Lieutenant. He fired a flare from his signal pistol, bringing down pre-arranged fire on the hill from a section of Vickers that were established on high ground some 400 yards from the OP.

Group and tank, Korea, 1951 (William May/RUR Association)

'Doc' Halliday. (RUR Museum)

The two Vickers, under the command of Corporal 'Doc' Halliday, poured streams of bullets into the now visible enemy on 'How' until they themselves came under attack from the north-west. The gunners quickly swivelled the guns around and a bitter firefight developed until the two machine-guns began to run low on ammunition. Eventually they were forced to withdraw towards the Battalion area, closely pursued by the Chinese. Halliday remained in the position with one of the crews and both men kept up a fire using their personal weapons. As the enemy closed in hand grenades were thrown to keep them off. Only when Halliday was sure that both Vickers guns and the patrol had made a safe return to friendly lines, did he and the Rifleman withdraw. This action earned Halliday the Military Medal. For his coolness on the hilltop Rifleman McShane received a Mention in Despatches.

The following morning Second Lieutenant Johnston, also on secondment from the Border Regiment, led a patrol out to Checkpoint 'How' and recovered the bodies of Lieutenant Hodgkins and Captain Warren. That evening a short service was held at Battalion Headquarters for the two officers who had lost their lives in what proved to be the closing days of the campaign.

13

The Closing Days

The Battalion was due to be relieved by the 1st Battalion Royal Norfolk Regiment on 28 September and a party under the command of Captain John Lane was already at work near Uijongbu on the construction of a transit camp, gloriously named 'Camp Britannia'. This would house in turn the outgoing units of 29 Brigade and their reliefs. As the end of the month drew near it as apparent that the arrival of the Norfolks was going to be delayed. Once again the war was going to interfere. On the Commonwealth Division's front the momentum of the war was increasing. Patrols, especially from the Canadian Brigade, became more frequent and more aggressive. Within the Brigade the 2nd RCR and Princess Patricia's Light Infantry began to edge forward a few hundred yards at a time.

Five miles to the north was the mountain of Kowang San, rising to a height of 357 metres. This feature overlooked the Canadian Brigade's right flank and had resisted all attacks by them and the US 1st Cavalry Division.

The mountain had been subjected to an almost continuous bombardment from artillery, both field and heavy and by frequent air strikes. To this the enemy replied with a greater volume of fire, most of which fell on the Canadian lines, although a certain amount of fire was received by the Rifles, fortunately causing no casualties. It has been estimated that more shells fell in this area than fell on the German lines at the opening of the El Alamein battle.[1]

Colonel Carson attended the Brigadier's O Group on 30 September and later the same evening the plan was revealed. A limited attack by the whole of 1st Corps was to take place with the objective of enabling the 3rd US Infantry Division and 1st US Cavalry to seize the high ground north of Chorwon. This would deny the Chinese the use of the lateral road and railway, which ran east from Chorwon across to Kumwha and then north-east to his main east coast supply route through Wonsan and would severely limit his power to mount an offensive during the coming winter. This operation, initially known as 'Cudgel' was later renamed 'Commando', with D-day to be set in early October. The full strength of 29 Brigade would be required for the operation and consequently the relief of the Rifles by the Norfolks would have to be delayed until the operation was over.[2]

The preliminary phrase of the operation began on 1 October. The Northumberland Fusiliers on the west bank of the Samichon River probed forward three or four thousand yards while making an aggressive display against the enemy. The Chinese in turn were subjected to harassing fire from artillery. The Fusiliers pulled back the same night and were relieved the following morning by a battalion from the 15th Republic of Korea

---

1 Interview with Brigadier Mervyn McCord.
2 This was to be the last battlefield assault by an Infantry Division in the history of the British Commonwealth armies.

Captain de Longueil, OC A Echelon in Happy Valley. (Mervyn McCord/RUR Association)

Regiment. They then moved back across the Imjin and on to the east to join 28 Brigade who were assembling behind the Canadian Brigade's right flank.

At 0300hrs on 3 October an extremely heavy bombardment by the Divisional artillery preceded the attack by 28 Brigade, with the Northumberland Fusiliers under command, against Kowang San.

The battle for Kowang San was visible from the Rifles position. Wireless reports revealed that both the King's Own Scottish Borderers and King's Shropshire Light Infantry in 28 Brigade were having a hard time and progress forward was painfully slow. The main enemy resistance was not on the mountain itself, but in the wooded hills surrounding its base, which provided more than adequate cover for the defenders. In the afternoon things improved slightly and by dusk the King's Own Scottish Borderers reported that they had established one of their companies on to the top of Kowang San. Observation from this company was bringing down shellfire on to the retreating enemy. In view of this it was confirmed that the Canadian attack would take place soon after first light on the following morning.

D-day for Operation 'Commando' was 4 October and the Rifles were placed under the command of the 25th Canadian Brigade. The role allocated to the Rifles was not a difficult one. 2 RCR, the left-hand Canadian Battalion, would attack Hill 187 in a pincer movement, with the main thrust along the eastern ridge and a subsidiary thrust by one company through 'How' and along the ridge from there to the main feature. This company would then swing south and occupy the 'Brown Bastard'.

When these objectives were secured, the Rifles would move up and occupy the south-west end of the ridge, overlooking the Samichon valley and in turn covering the

Canadian's left flank. The only tricky part of the operation was that 'A' Company of the Rifles were to occupy 'How' during the hours of darkness on the night of 3-4 October, in order to give 'A' Company of 2 RCR, a clean start. The entire operation was to be preceded by a heavy air strike on Hill 187 and the southern and eastern spurs.

Soon after dusk on 3 October A Company moved out to a concentration area south of the feature known as 'How'. Here the Canadian company joined them and both spent a quiet night. Just before dawn A Company quietly moved on to 'How' encountering no opposition.

The day dawned hot and misty, which took some time to clear. While patches of mist still filled the valleys, the other three rifle companies and Battalion Headquarters moved up to an assembly area a thousand yards south west of 'How'. Here they settled down to await the Canadian attack.

Fifteen hundred yards to the north the mist lifted slowly from the 'Brown Bastard', clearing also towards the right from Hill 187 itself. It was probably due to this lingering mist that the aircraft due to carry out the air strikes were late in coming in. Shortly after 0900hrs, the spotter aircraft buzzing around overhead was joined by two flights of fighters, which circled, waiting to be called in on their targets. Then, suddenly bursts of pink smoke began to blossom on the enemy-held ridge as the artillery fired their target indicator shells on pre-arranged locations. A few seconds later the monotonous drone of the circling jets changed to a high pitched scream as the aircraft swooped down to deliver a combination of rockets, high explosive and the dreaded napalm. Just before 1000hrs the air strike was completed and was quickly followed by a 'rolling barrage' from the artillery as the Canadian infantry moved forward. By 1200hrs, their objectives had been

Front, L to R: Paddy Maher, Tom McCann, Bertie McIlwaine. Rear: Tommy Maher. Tommy McIlwaine is holding a stripped Thompson SMG. (Mark McConnell)

taken and the Rifles were ordered to advance. Moving with equal speed and caution the leading companies advanced by alternate bounds and by 1500hrs all objectives had been attained without meeting any resistance. Again the Chinese had refused to meet a determined attack once their flank was threatened, as it had been with the capture of Kowang San.

Nevertheless, the PPCLI (Princess Patricia's Canadian Light Infantry) had met stiff resistance from well dug-in infantry that were covering the Chinese withdrawal, while later in the afternoon the RCR found themselves facing similar resistance from delaying parties on the reverse slope. As darkness fell the Rifles began to dig in and lay protective screens of barbed wire. On their right flank fighting continued throughout the night, but the Rifles were left alone.

With daylight on 5 October activity was observed opposite the Rifles' positions and soon shells were falling on the Canadians. Those on the immediate right of A Company were hit with 155mm shells fitted with air-burst fuses.

Later in the day reconnaissance units of the Royal Vingt-Deuxième Regiment had arrived with the Rifles and it looked like relief would soon be at hand. By 1600hrs, the Rifles had been relieved by their French-Canadian counterparts and as darkness fell they marched out of the line for the last time. After some three miles they found themselves back at the Paekhak Res. Here they were to wait for the Norfolk Regiment to take over. Then they moved to Britcamp to sort themselves out before the journey to Pusan. It had been planned to hold a drinks party and Regimental dinner there for the officers and sergeants of the Brigade who were present. This had to be cancelled due to the fighting on Line Wyoming; however Brigadier Brodie managed to come and have a champagne breakfast with the Rifles before they boarded the train to Uijongbu.

The morale of the British soldier in Korea was never neglected, with each Brigade to spend three months in the line and one and a half months in reserve. Attempts to keep them warm and well fed were achieved by provision of special winter sleeping bags and clothing – string vests, mittens, warm pullovers, socks and special boots with gauze inserts and thick rubber soles, windproof jacket and trousers worn beneath a hooded parka. Food, often American C-7 rations, was supplemented by modest amounts of Japanese Asahi beer and an evening rum ration. Behind the main lines there was weapon training, tactical exercises, parades, film screenings and ENSA shows. National newspapers were flown in to the men, which supplemented the Divisional newspaper known as *Crown News*. All ranks were also entitled to three days rest and recuperation leave near Inchon and to three days at the Ebisu Hotel in Tokyo once during their tour. It was also the policy to rotate British infantry battalions to ensure that none would endure two of the harsh Korean winters and as a result sixteen British infantry battalions served in the Korea.

The Duke of Wellington's Regiment fought the British Army's last real battle of the Korean War, at 'The Hook', on 28-29 May. The Battalion lost some 149 killed, wounded and captured, one-fifth of its strength in one day, though successfully retaining control of their positions. The war itself went on for several more weeks until the Chinese realised they would never defeat the Allies to any degree and asked for a truce. The guns would thunder right up until the last moment when the truce was declared on Monday 27 July 1953.

On 11 October the Battalion boarded a train at Uijongbu, ironically the place they had arrived just twelve months before and left for Pusan. On arrival at Seaforth Barracks all ranks were to be issued with brand new kit, so as to leave the country in much the same way they had arrived. However Korean weather was to have one final go at the Rifles. A ferocious typhoon hit Pusan and much of the camp and the new kit was ruined in the high wind and torrential rain. Despite widespread damage there were no major injuries in this the final battle with the elements.

At the final parade prior to sailing a message from General Steele was read out to the men:

> I, as Colonel of the Regiment, send all ranks a personal message of thanks on the occasion of the Battalion leaving Korea on completion of its tour of duty on active service there.
>
> It is just about a year ago that the unit embarked at Liverpool on the beginning of a foreign tour. The experience of that year has been momentous for the Battalion and for everyone who has served in it of whatever rank. You have had to contend with very severe and variable climatic conditions and to adjust your training and operational methods to overcome novel types of opposition. I have been much impressed and gratified by the personal reports of visiting officers who have seen

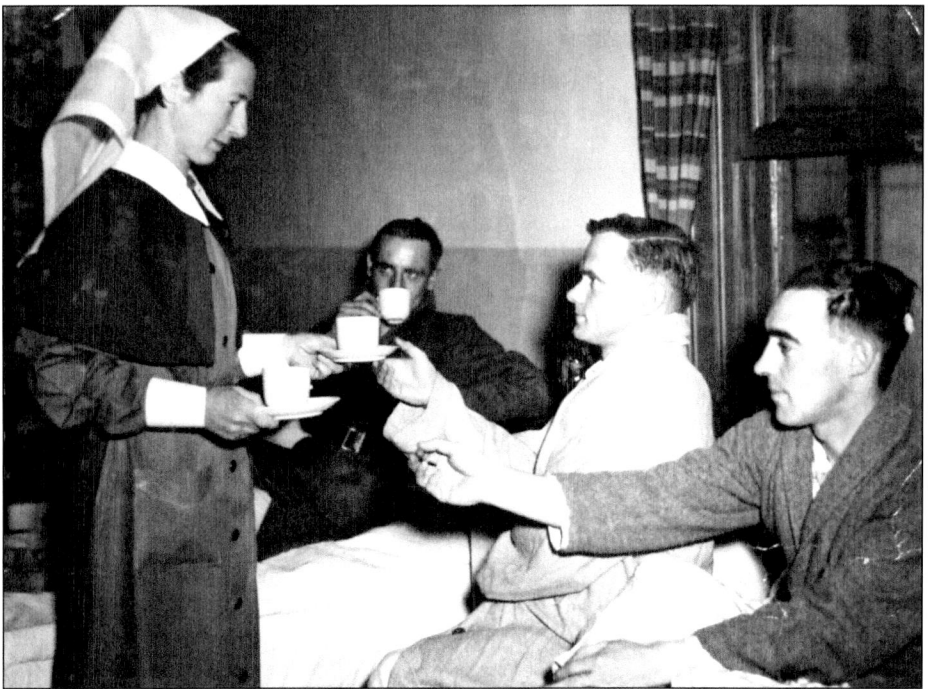

Captured the same day, taught Communism in the same Korean school, released by the enemy at the same time, these three British soldiers were still together at the BCOF hospital Kure, Japan. Left to right, Gunner Hill Slade, Wimbledon, London, Sergeant Jimmy Rankine, Belfast and Lance Corporal Stan Harris, Liverpool. Sister Ranson of Australia is distributing the tea. (RUR Museum)

This street scene in Hiroshima gives a good impression of the fascinating things to be seen while on R&R in Japan. (George Forty)

The Colonel of the regiment, General Steele, welcoming home members of the 1st Battalion, The Royal Ulster Rifles who had served in Korea. (RUR Museum)

The Boxing Team, Hong Kong, 1951. (William May/RUR Association)

Range practice in Hong Kong. (RUR Museum)

Pipe practice at Battalion Headquarters. (Mervyn McCord/RUR Association)

HMT *Empire Halladale*, used as a troopship to take the Royal Ulster Rifles to Hong Kong from Korea, 1951. (Roger Gladin)

THE CLOSING DAYS 231

Bunks onboard HMT *Empire Halladale*. (Roger Gladin)

Killing time, playing cards on board HMT *Empire Halladale*. (Roger Gladin)

A 'Girls' Opera' at Takarazuka, Japan 1951, playing to the biggest stage in the world. (Stan Packer)

A wet night in Hong Kong, all the servicemen are sheltering in the bars!

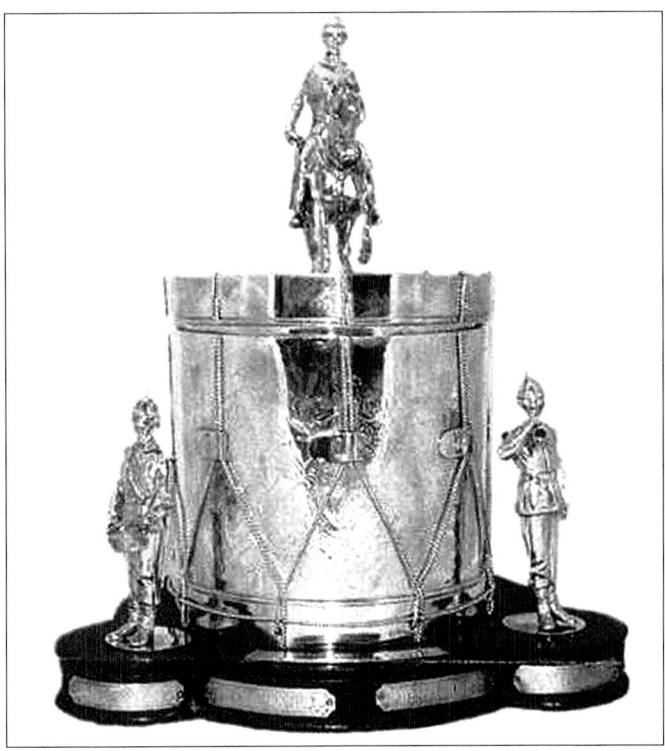

This Victorian silver biscuit barrel in the shape of a drum was originally presented by the 1st Battalion of the Royal Ulster Rifles to HMS *Belfast* at her launching in March 1938. There are four silver statuettes of Royal Ulster Rifles personnel, a mounted Officer on the lid and on the base stand a Drummer, a Bugler and a Rifleman. (Mervyn McCord)

Main street of Sasebo, Japan during the Korean war, 1950-52. (Stan Packer)

The Freedom of Belfast, band and bugles of the 1st Battalion, The Royal Ulster Rifles. (Henry O'Kane)

you either in action or at rest. Your doing will be read with pride both now and in the future, you have written another glorious chapter in the annals of the regiment.

To those who have been with the Battalion throughout, I send a special word of thanks. To all others present on leaving Korea, I send my sincere thanks; I think particularly of those who have laid down their lives serving with you, I greatly appreciate the Memorial which has been raised to them in Korea.

To you, Colonel Carson, and to your whole command, I send my best wishes for the future, and may you have a happy service in Hong Kong.

On 22 October the Rifles sailed aboard the Troopship HMT *Empire Halladale* bound for Hong Kong, where they would serve for the next two years. The voyage to Hong Kong gave the men of the Battalion the opportunity to wind down from the stress of the battlefield. There were proper meals at proper times, there was a bar, games to play, books to read and the time to relax. The men of the Battalion left Korea with mixed feelings, but most of all pride in a job well done and the sense that they had played their part in proving to the world that the Free Nations would fight, if need be, for the principles in which they believed, and this being so, would fight well.

The HMT *Empire Halladale* docked in Hong Kong harbour on 27 October 1951, tying up to a warm sunlit quay on which stood the Band and Pipes of the Argyll and Sutherland Highlanders sounding out a welcome. Also present was Lieutenant General Evans, the Commander British Forces and Major Rickcord, who commanded the Advance Party. The Battalion disembarked for a march past and, after a refreshing cup of tea courtesy of the YMCA, the Rifles entrained for their barracks in the New Territories. On the journey all ranks commented on the change from Korea – so clean and civilised, dust-free and with good paved roads. One of the first things Colonel Carson did was to relieve Captain Hugh Hamill from his post as Adjutant and task him with writing the history of the Battalion in Korea. This was subsequently published in Belfast in 1953.

Epilogue

Their departure from Korea was not the last time that the Royal Ulster Rifles and Korea were to be 'reunited'. As the city of Seoul expanded during the 1960s it was moving closer to the site of the memorial dedicated near the village of Pulmiji-Ri overlooking the battlefield of Chaegunghyon, better known to the soldiers as the Battle of Happy Valley. The original intention was that the Memorial should remain permanently in Korea, like the Gloster's Memorial at Solma-Ri near the Imjin, however the British Ambassador recommended that, as the Memorial could no longer be properly protected it should be repatriated to a location in the United Kingdom.

Somewhat appropriately the Memorial was brought home on board HMS *Belfast*, arriving in Northern Ireland in 1962 and was re-erected at The Royal Ulster Rifles Regimental Depot in Ballymena, County Antrim. It was rededicated in 1964 and as the only Memorial in Ireland to the Korean War it served as a focus for an annual Imjin Remembrance parade and service for the Korean Veterans Association of Ireland.

With the news that the Regimental Depot in Ballymena was to shut as part of the Government's demilitarisation of Northern Ireland and other military reforms steps were taken to secure a new home for the Korea Memorial. As the Royal Ulster Rifles are Freemen of the City of Belfast moves were made to ask the Lord Mayor and the Council for permission to re-site the Memorial inside the precincts of the City Hall

HMS *Belfast* at Hong Kong, Christmas 1950. The white building at the stern of the ship is the 'Old China Fleet Club'. (Stan Packer)

EPILOGUE 237

September 1953, Sergeant Ted Balfour being flown back from Korea to Japan after being a POW for two years and eight months. (RUR Association)

Ex-POWs celebrate on their way home: Reg Budden, Glosters, Henry O'Kane, RUR, Ben Baough, 8th Irish Hussars, Stan Lea, Glosters, Gerry Hassett, RUR. (Henry O'Kane)

The Memorial at St Patrick's Barracks, Ballymena. (Mervyn McCord)

General Sir James Steele, Colonel of the Regiment, laying a wreath at the Ballymena War Memorial on Remembrance Day 1953. (RUR Museum)

along with other regimental memorials. The expected costs of the move were in the region of £20,000 and an appeal was raised to assist with the funding.[1]

The Memorial was finally relocated to the west of the City Hall, beside the Garden of Remembrance, in 2008 with the re-dedication scheduled for September 2009. However in the intervening period the Korean veterans continued with their traditional short private Remembrance Service on the anniversary of the Happy Valley battle fought on 4 January.[2]

British Defence Attaché Brigadier Matthew O' Hanlon, late of The Royal Irish Regiment, visited the site of the Happy Valley battle in February 2010; the battlefield where the Royal Ulster Rifles had losses of 157 men. Interviewed for the *Korea Times* newspaper he explained that he believed that the Korean War and, in particular, individual battles, tend to be forgotten in the western world. "Many, many battles are forgotten and it's a chance of fate for those that get remembered; this is important for my regiment," he said. "The Korean War was very much at a time when people wanted to forget about war. And I think that is an element of why people in the UK tend to forget about it. And (Korea) is a very, very long way away. Very few Britons today are aware that the Korean War remains the bloodiest conflict (for Britain) since World War II," he said. "In Afghanistan, you hear reports of one or two soldiers dying – just imagine if we lost 157 men in one night."[3]

Remember …

> It is the soldier, not the reporter,
> Who has given us the freedom of the press.
> It is the soldier, not the poet,
> Who has given us the freedom of speech.
> It is the soldier, not the campus organiser,
> Who has given us the freedom to demonstrate.
> It is the soldier,
> Who salutes the flag,
> And whose coffin is draped by the flag,
> Who allows us the protester to burn the flag.

(Verse from The Korean Anniversary Brochure – 2003)[4]

---

1 http://www.bkva.co.uk/ulster_mem.htm
2 *Sunday Life*, 4 January 2009.
3 *Korean Times*, 3 February 2010. http://www.koreatimes.co.kr/www/news/special/2010/03/139_61683.html
4 *Quis Separabit*, 2003/2004.

'Morning Calm' – a 'fish eye' view of the Korean War Monument commemorating the 50th Anniversary of the signing of the armistice agreement. The monument was unveiled on 27 July 2003 in the pouring rain, but no mud. (Derek M. Slattery/RUR Museum)

Between 23-30 July 2003 a party of The Royal Ulster Rifles, Korean War Veterans attended the Korean War Armistice commemorations in Korea. They were Major Joe Lavery, Thomas McConkey, Martin Vance and Henry Kane, who all served as prisoners of war at No.5 Camp Pyucyon. The group are seen here photographed outside the Korean National War Memorial in Seoul. (*Quis Separabit*)

EPILOGUE 241

Colonel Robin Charley (left) and Sergeant Joe Farrell in front of the memorial at Belfast City Hall, 4 January 2009. (*Belfast Telegraph*)

The band of The Royal Irish Regiment lead the parade at the rededication of Korea Memorial, Belfast City Hall, 25 April 2010. (David R. Orr)

Veterans parade after the rededication of Korea Memorial, Belfast City Hall, 25 April 2010. (David R. Orr)

Spencer McWhirter at the rededication of the Korea Memorial, Belfast City Hall, 25 April 2010. (Mark Ramsay)

The Korea Memorial adorned with wreaths following the rededication at Belfast City Hall, 25 April 2010. (David R. Orr)

Korean Memorial Garden, National Arboretum. (Mervyn McCord)

Appendix I

Order of Battle

Units of 29 Brigade
Apart from the Rifles the Brigade contained two other infantry battalions. The Royal Northumberland Fusiliers (Fifth of Foot) had been raised as the 'Irish Regiment' at Bois le Duc in Holland by Viscount Clare in 1674. The Regiment saw widespread action in Europe and America during the 17th Century and served in the Peninsula during the Napoleonic Wars. During the Indian Mutiny the 1st Battalion earned three awards of the Victoria Cross, while both the 1st and 2nd Battalions served in the Boer War. In the Great War the 1st Battalion fought at Mons, while the 2nd first saw action at Ypres in 1915. In the Second World War both battalions fought in Italy. In Korea the Battalion was to be commanded by Lieutenant Colonel Kingsley Foster. The Gloucestershire Regiment (28th of Foot) was raised in Portsmouth in 1694 by Colonel John Gibson. In keeping with the Northumberland Fusiliers, it saw service in both Europe, the Americas and the Peninsula, with the 2nd Battalion fighting at both Quatre Bras and Waterloo. During the Great War the 1st Battalion served in France and Flanders, while the 2nd Battalion moved to Macedonia in 1915 and then served in Bulgaria, Armenia and Russia. During the Second World War the 1st Battalion fought in Burma and India, while the 2nd fought in France in 1940, was evacuated from Dunkirk and returned to Europe on D-Day. The two battalions amalgamated in 1948. In Korea the Battalion was led by Lieutenant Colonel Carne.

Without supporting units no Infantry Brigade could operate and this support consisted of artillery, signals, engineers and those units that made everyday life bearable.

170 Independent Mortar Battery Royal Artillery was equipped with eighteen of the M2 4.2" mortar. This weapon, derived from the American-built M1, which had first come into service in 1928. The M2 had, in turn, first seen action with US forces in the Sicilian Campaign when some 35,000 rounds had been fired in support of troops attacking over rough terrain. The mortar was capable of firing three types of ammunition – high explosive, smoke and chemical rounds. The HE shell was filled with 3.64kg of TNT and had a range of 4,023 yards; the smoke round was filled with white phosphorus and had a range of 3,932m. There is no evidence of chemical rounds being used by the Battery in Korea.[1]

The 11 (Sphinx) Anti-Aircraft Battery Royal Artillery consisted of three troops, each of six quick-firing 40mm Bofors Guns. This weapon was of Swedish design and fired a 2lb shell at theoretical rate of 120 rounds per minute, although a more practical rate was between 80-100 rounds, depending on the elevation of the barrel, as gravity played a part in the reloading of the five round clips, which were fed by hand. It had a ground range of approximately 4,000 yards. During the Second World War the Bofors gained

---

1   In May 1951 the Communists claimed that the US had used bacteriological weapons in Korea and in March 1952 this claim was expanded to cover germ warfare. No use has so far been proved and the argument continues. Bailey, *The Korean Armistice*, London, 1992.

fame with their role of firing tracer shells horizontally to mark safe paths across German minefields at El Alamein in October 1942. On D-Day a battery of Bofors of the 92nd (Loyals) Light Anti-Aircraft Regiment landed with the British 3rd Infantry Division on Sword Beach and provided protection for the vital crossing on the Caen Canal and Orne river, being credited with shooting down seventeen enemy aircraft during the ensuing days. In Korea the vast majority of their tasks would involve ground targets.

The British would deploy a number of tanks in Korea and the majority of these were from the 8th King's Royal Irish Hussars. This regiment had been raised in Londonderry, Ireland, in 1693, as Henry Conyngham's Regiment of Dragoons. It was disbanded twice in its history, from 1714 to 1715 and from 1716 to 1719, in both cases being reformed without loss of precedence. In 1751 it formally became the 8th Regiment of Dragoons, being re-designated as Light Dragoons four years later. In 1777 the regiment was renamed as the 8th (King's Royal Irish) Regiment of (Light) Dragoons, but by 1861 this had been simplified to the 8th (King's Royal Irish) Hussars. The Regiment's service included The War of the Spanish Succession, The '45, Jacobite Rebellion in Scotland, India during the Napoleonic Wars, where Colonel Robert Rollo Gillespie joined the Regiment, gaining a reputation as one of the most audacious soldiers to have served with them. In the Crimea they formed part of the Light Brigade, charging under the command of Lieutenant Colonel Sherwell in the second line during the charge at Balaclava. During the Indian Mutiny the Regiment gained four awards of the Victoria Cross. They served during the final year of the Second Afghan War and during the Boer War formed part of the 4th Cavalry Brigade. During the Great War the Regiment did not take part in the Retreat from Mons and went into the line on 9 December 1914 as part of the 1st Indian Cavalry Division, with their first action being Givenchy. In 1921 the Regiment was re-titled the 8th King's Royal Irish Hussars and in 1934 had their horses replaced by Ford V8 15cwt lorries armed with Vickers machine guns. In 1938 they became part of the Matruh Mobile Force, which in turn became the 7th Armoured Division, better known as the Desert Rats. After service in North Africa the Regiment returned to the UK and was equipped with Cromwell tanks. They landed on Gold Beach in Normandy on 9 June 1944 and served throughout the campaigns in France, Belgium, Holland and Germany. Post-war the Regiment was equipped with the new Centurion tank, probably the most dependable tank in the world.[2] Six prototypes had been sent to Belgium in January 1945, but arrived too late to see any action and by 1950 the Mk 3 had been introduced, sixty four of which would be sent to Korea. The Centurion, with a crew of four men, was armed with a 20pdr main gun, a .3" Besa machine gun fitted co-axial and another fitted to the commander's copula. The Mk 3 was also fitted with a fully automatic stabilisation system that allowed it to fire accurately while on the move. Ammunition carried included sixty-two rounds of 20prd and 9,000 rounds of .3" for the machine guns, all of which would be found necessary for service in Korea. The Reconnaissance Troop of the Hussars was comprised of six Cromwell tanks, veteran vehicles of the Second World

---

2   In 1953, an Australian Army Mk 3, with its engine running, was placed 500 yards from ground zero at Emu Field as part of Operation Totem. After the atomic blast it was found that the tank had been pushed along the ground some five feet, antennas and the armoured side plates were missing and the only reason the engine had stopped was due to lack of fuel. Nicknamed the 'atomic tank' it later served in Vietnam and in total had a service life of 23 years, of which fifteen months was on operational deployment. It can be found today at Robertson Barracks in Palmerston, Northern Territory, Australia.

War that had been borrowed from 7 Royal Tank Regiment. The troop was commanded by Captain Donald Astley-Cooper and they, along with the remainder of the Hussars, would be of great assistance to the Rifles in Korea. The Hussars were also equipped with three Centurions fitted with 'bulldozer' blades, three Churchill ARVs, three Churchill bridge-layers, four Universal Carriers and eighteen scout cars. All vehicles were ordered to be painted in Colour No 15 Olive Drab and those not painted in time would be shipped and painted immediately on arrival. All vehicles were to have a five-pointed white star painted on tops and sides to be as large as possible as available space would allow. All fuel for the tanks, in fact all fuel for all vehicles, from all nations, that served in Korea was supplied by the American Army.

Another tank unit present was C Squadron, 7th Royal Tank Regiment, which was equipped with the Churchill tank of Second World War fame. Sixteen of C Squadron's tanks were fitted with the apparatus that converted them into mobile flamethrowers known as the 'Crocodile'. While the fuel trailers had been shipped to Korea at no time were the Crocodiles employed in the flame-throwing role. The Squadron also had two Churchill command tanks and two ARVs.

The heaviest integral artillery support for the Brigade came from the 45th Field Regiment, Royal Artillery. The Regiment consisted of three batteries, 70, 116 and 176, each of eight guns divided into two troops of four guns each. Each gun was handled by a detachment of six men and was capable of firing five shells a minute with commendable accuracy.[3] For a 'Mike Target', when all guns of the regiment fired at the same target this meant 120 shells per minute. The 25pdr field gun was the heaviest artillery piece deployed by the British in Korea and would be most effective in breaking up human wave attacks. When heavier support was needed American 155mm Batteries could be called on. The Regiment also had six Cromwell tanks fitted out as mobile observation posts.

29th Independent Brigade Signal Squadron was responsible for communications within the Brigade, while the 360 men of the 55th Field Squadron, Royal Engineers undertook major tasks such as bridging rivers, recovering damaged vehicles and building defences. The 57th Company and 26th Field Ambulance Royal Army Medical Corps provided treatment over and above that provided by the Regimental Aid Posts. 29th Ordnance Field Park Royal Army Ordnance Corps was responsible for the supply of ammunition and the repair or replacement of weapons. The role of the 29th Mobile Laundry and Bath Unit RAOC is self-explanatory.

The 10th Infantry Workshops, Royal Electrical and Mechanical Engineers, pronounced by all military types as 'Reemee', had the responsibility of maintaining and servicing almost every piece of electrical and mechanical equipment in the British Army, ranging from tanks to dentist's drills. Formed in 1942, they had been granted the 'Royal' prefix from their formation. Prior to this the tasks carried out by REME were the responsibility of the RAOC, RE, Royal Corps of Signals and RASC. However, the vast increase and complexity of equipment during the Second World War required a specific branch to deal with the myriad problems that arose during wartime. In Korea the REME would well live up to their motto 'Arte et Marte', 'By Skill and By Fighting'. The 29th Light Aid Detachment, REME, would carry out light repairs in the field, while

---

3   The guns of the Royal Artillery have detachments, while the guns of the Royal Navy have crews.

the 249th General Headquarters Provost Company, Royal Corps of Military Police, would, when necessary, enforce discipline within the Brigade.

The 904th Field Security Section Intelligence Corps was tasked with both collecting and disseminating the strength and location of enemy units and worked closely with the 104th Air Photographic Interpretation Section. The 208th Field Cash Office, Royal Army Pay Corps, was present with the Brigade because everyone likes to be paid for what they do and to have cash in hand for the rare leaves to Japan.

Appendix II

Honours and Awards

The Distinguished Service Order
Major Hugh Montgomery Gaffikin (No 149563)
In the early hours of 3rd January 1951, Major Gaffikin's Company was surprised and attacked by a strong force of Chinese from different directions at the same time. The forward platoon's position was in danger of being overrun when Major Gaffikin, who was with the platoon at the time, rallied the men, he picked up the platoon 2" mortar, and standing in the open fired it from the hip at point blank range into the enemy. He then successfully commanded the orderly withdrawal of the platoon. During the action he personally killed three of the enemy with his pistol although he was himself wounded. His courage and disregard for his personal safety saved a dangerous situation and prevented the infiltration of the enemy into the Battalion's main position.

That night, when the Battalion was withdrawing through a defile the column was ambushed. Under heavy fire Major Gaffikin gathered up his Company and continually led them forward. When most of the Company were through the ambush he went back to gather up stragglers and to warn the Company following of the position. Attaching himself to this Company he led them and some vehicles through the ambush and out to safety. Throughout the two actions Major Gaffikin's courage and his example to his men was of the highest order, inspiring confidence in all around him.

Major John Kirkpatrick Hay Shaw MC (No 69180)
At Chaegunghyon, Korea, on the night of 3-4 January 1951, during the withdrawal of his Battalion, Major Shaw, Support Company Commander, was with his Company when the enemy opened very heavy fire in a defile. He attempted to extricate his column, which consisted of carriers and wheeled vehicles, at great personal risk. After vain attempts to get the column through the defile, he organised the men in the vicinity into a party, and by skilful handling extricated them from a very dangerous position, leading them over the hills into our own lines. Throughout the action, which took place in darkness, at close quarters and in great confusion, he acted with great courage and resourcefulness, and was an inspiring influence on all men under his command. It is considered by responsible members of the party that but for the presence of Major Shaw many of those who escaped from the defile would not have survived.

OBE
Lieutenant Colonel R.J.H. Carson

MBE
Captain W.E. Anderson MC

Bar to the Military Cross
Captain William Ellery Anderson MC (No 148939)
Captain Anderson was attached to the G3 Division of the 8th Army Headquarters in February 1951. Hitherto the Miscellaneous Section had been concerned with gaining information through Koreans put ashore from island bases off the enemy-held coast.

Captain Anderson's task was to form an Airborne Section which would be capable not only of collecting and passing back intelligence, but also of striking the enemy L of C with the dual object of harassing the enemy and forcing him to deploy troops in his rear area. Owing to the inexperience of his staff Captain Anderson had personally to train the men in demolitions, sabotage and intelligence, and at the same time plan and organise actual operations against the enemy. Operation Spitfire was launched on 18th June. For the operation the Section was divided into an advance party and a main body. Captain Anderson insisted on leading the Advance party himself. This was by far the most dangerous part of the whole operation. The Advance Party had to jump blind in an extremely mountainous area, about which we had no intelligence. The object of the Advance Party was to carry out a reconnaissance for a soft drop zone for the main body and to find a suitable place to set up a base camp. They carried a radio, pistols, and seven days rations. Just before take-off on 18th June Captain Anderson severely burned his hand and arm, he jumped with his arm in a sling. On the jump the interpreter was badly injured and unable to move. To reconnoitre the Drop Zone and camp site it was necessary to carry out daylight patrols. This is a very risky undertaking for a white man behind the lines in Korea. Captain Anderson left his two American Sergeants in a safe hiding place and did these patrols on his own. During one of these patrols he spotted, and directed, an airstrike on a Chinese Battalion with excellent results. Captain Anderson was successful in finding the drop zone and arranged the reception party for the main body, which dropped on 25th June. The success of Operation Spitfire was due primarily to Captain Anderson whose personal courage, tenacity and cheerfulness are a constant source of inspiration to his men and a credit to the British Army.[1]

The Military Cross
Second Lieutenant Mervyn Noel Samuel McCord (No 407952)
On the morning of 3rd January 1951, Second Lieutenant McCord led his platoon in a successful counter-attack to restore positions from which his own Battalion had been forced to give ground. At night when the Battalion was ambushed as it commenced to withdraw from its positions, he did everything in his power to extricate Mechanical Transport trapped on the track, rallied scattered vehicles and men and fought them forward under fire. He was preparing a counter-attack to extricate his Company Headquarters when stopped by his company commander. He assisted in another attack to break out of the ambush, and finally assisted a wounded man over the mountains to safety. During this, his first action, which took place at night, at close-quarters and in considerable confusion Second Lieutenant McCord showed throughout great powers of leadership and disregard for personal danger. His actions undoubtedly assisted in the extrication of a number of men from a situation where they would otherwise have been killed or captured.

---

1 Obituary, *Daily Telegraph*, 21 December 1992.

Second Lieutenant Huston Mark Shaw-Stewart (No 406701)
At first light on 3rd January, 1945¹, Second Lieutenant Shaw-Stewart was commanding a platoon in an exposed position on some paddy field, at Chaegunghyon, Korea. The platoon was attacked by a number of Chinese whose leading men were disguised in Korean peasant dress. Second Lieutenant Shaw-Stewart successfully and coolly held off this attack inflicting several casualties on the enemy. Later on, the enemy, in strength, occupied the foothills dominating his platoon in the paddy field below and he was ordered to withdraw. As the platoon withdrew it came under very heavy machine gun fire and was pinned down. Second Lieutenant Shaw-Stewart, completely disregarding the enemy's fire, got his platoon moving section by section and successfully extricated them. He made several journeys back to the abandoned position under heavy fire personally to ensure that no men or equipment had been left behind. On the night of 3rd-4th January 1951, Second Lieutenant Shaw-Stewart's platoon was with the rearguard company when the Battalion was ambushed in a defile. The platoon came under very heavy machine gun and mortar fire and a number of men were killed or wounded. Second Lieutenant Shaw-Stewart, again completely ignoring the enemy's fire, stood up and coolly organised his Platoon; he then fought his way forward killing several of the enemy in hand-to-hand combat. Second Lieutenant Shaw-Stewart's complete disregard for his own safety and his extraordinary coolness under heavy fire was such an inspiration to his men and all who saw him that a very dangerous situation was avoided and a large number of men who would otherwise have been cut off were enabled to fight their way out to safety.

Lieutenant Anthony Dacre Trevor-Roper (No 402905)
On 25th April 'B' Company 1 RUR were holding a layback position to cover the withdrawal of the Northumberland Fusiliers and the remaining companies of 1 RUR. The Company was attacked at about 0330hrs, on the 25th April and from then on almost continuously until its withdrawal in the early afternoon. Lieutenant Trevor-Roper's platoon was the only one that had a clear view of the enemy, but the platoon was badly overlooked, and under constant mortar and machine gun fire. Shortly after first light the enemy started to move along the ridges on our left flank in very large numbers, Lieutenant Trevor-Roper successfully engaged with small arms fire from his platoon and from two medium machine guns located in his area. The company had a troop of 4.2" mortars in support, but no Forward Observation Officer, and the only method of fire control was from Lieutenant Trevor-Roper to company headquarters by 88 set, and then to Brigade HQ by telephone. It was here that Lieutenant Trevor-Roper was outstanding, although under heavy mortar and machine gun fire, he remained in an exposed position and observed the fall of the bombs thereby enabling heavy concentrations of bombs to be brought down on the enemy. Shortly after midday, when the Northumberland Fusiliers were withdrawing through the company position, an enemy mortar bomb fell in the centre of Lieutenant Trevor-Roper's platoon, knocking out one machine gun and wounding eight men – in spite of the resulting chaos, Lieutenant Trevor-Roper successfully evacuated his casualties, put the second machine gun back into action and continued to hold his position until ordered to withdraw. He then led his platoon to safety across the mountains to the last. There is no doubt that by his zeal, courage and determination Lieutenant Trevor-Roper greatly contributed to the withdrawal of many men and both guns.

Lieutenant Colin MacNicol (No 385955)
On Saturday 14 April 1951 Chinese Communist forces attacked an isolated Company position of the 1st Battalion The Royal Ulster Rifles. The main enemy assault was directed at the platoon commanded by Lieutenant Colin MacNicol. Repeated attempts were made by the enemy to overrun the position between 2359hrs on 14 April and 0400hrs on 15 April. Although the forward section was penetrated and every grenade in the platoon was used Lieutenant MacNicol rallied the platoon and regained the posts temporarily lost. It was due to his coolness and disregard for his own personal safety that the enemy were dispersed leaving dead, wounded and prisoners behind.

During the period 0900hrs 23 April until 0030hrs on 26 April when the Battalion withstood the main assault of the enemy across the Imjin, Lieutenant MacNicol displayed the greatest coolness in the command of his platoon and in the face of enemy fire. Quite unheeded he constantly moved about in the open encouraging his men and repositioning them as the occasion demanded. His bearing and manner throughout was most exemplary.

The Distinguished Conduct Medal
Company Sergeant Major Andrew McConville (No 7010702)
On 5th June 1951, D Company 1st Battalion The Royal Ulster Rifles, of which CSM McConville was a member, was engaged on a reconnaissance in force across the Imjin River near Sindae. On completion of the reconnaissance, the Company was ordered to withdraw, but the enemy maintained close contact, bringing heavy small arms and mortar fire to bear on the crossing place itself. One Platoon and part of Company Headquarters was still on the enemy bank of the river, when the last boat with an outboard engine capsized. CSM McConville, who had already reached the home bank, and who had been ordered to withdraw still further, immediately organised a rowing party, and, whilst under fire, took a boat across the river to rescue the stranded Platoon. At the time the river was unfordable and there was a strong current flowing. The enemy, who had approached to within 150 yards of the far bank, were keeping up a constant fire on the river. Had it not been for CSM McConville's leadership and initiative, over thirty men would have been lost, but by his action all were recovered and the Company successfully withdrawn from a precarious situation. Previously on 25th April 1951 during an action near Nungnae the Battalion had been ordered to withdraw to escape encirclement by the Chinese. D Company had been under heavy fire from both sides of the route of withdrawal. CSM McConville collected over fifty men of various companies and led them in an organised body through the Chinese ambush to the next defensive line some five miles further back. CSM McConville has on all occasions maintained a perfect example of coolness and courage when under fire and his leadership and initiative have been second to none.

The Military Medal
Sergeant Harry Campbell (No 22243358)
During the night of 3rd-4th January 1951, at Chaegunghyon, Korea, Sergeant Campbell was with the rearguard Company of his Battalion, when it withdrew through a defile from defensive positions. This force was ambushed at close range in a riverbed and in the confusion of the attack men and vehicles were scattered. Sergeant Campbell displayed

great coolness and leadership, organising and controlling his men throughout the action. He personally stalked two light machine gun positions which were blocking the escape and put them out of action with hand grenades. He later gathered a party of men, and led them to break out of the ambush. His coolness and courage throughout this action, which took place at night, at close quarter and in considerable confusion, undoubtedly contributed to the escape of a large part of the trapped force.

Sergeant Daniel Cooke (No 7011531)
On the night of 3-4 January 1951 Sergeant Cooke's company was with the Battalion when it was ambushed in a defile. The marching column was scattered by heavy fire at close range, but Sergeant Cooke rallied his platoon and led them forward. He gathered the men together under heavy fire and went along helping the wounded and personally ensured that they were carried off, although still under fire.

Later in the night while the action continued Sergeant Cooke went out alone to rescue a Rifleman taken prisoner by the Chinese; in doing so he shot dead two of the enemy, again being under heavy fire throughout. Sergeant Cooke's behaviour throughout this action was of the highest order and his courage and coolness were an inspiration to his company.

Corporal William McWilliam Halliday (No 22229648)
For gallantry, coolness and complete disregard for his own safety, Corporal Halliday, on 25th September 1951, was commanding a Machine Gun Section which formed the firm base for an outpost Platoon some 600 yards ahead.

During the afternoon the outpost and the Machine Gun position came under heavy mortar fire. The Officer and the Gunner OP of the outpost Platoon were both killed and the remainder were compelled to withdraw by the enemy attack. Corporal Halliday on seeing the Platoon withdrawing, immediately gave covering fire and engaged the enemy at range of about 500 yards.

He carried on firing until both guns ran out of ammunition, when he sent the guns back, but remained with one other man and carried on the fire with small arms, until the Platoon had successfully withdrawn through his position.

By his devotion to duty and gallantry there is no doubt that this action enabled the Platoon to withdraw without further loss. At one time the enemy approached so close that he was compelled to throw grenades.

Rifleman John Frederick Newport (No 22337903)
On 17th September 1951, 11 Platoon "D" Company were engaged on a Patrol Task, to a feature 2,500 yards forward of our F.D.L's. The Platoon arrived at its 'lay back' position at 0500hrs, and a Section under the Platoon Commander, advanced to the finals objective. Approaching the top of the feature, this Section was engaged by some fifteen dug in Chinese with Burp guns, L.M.G's and grenades. Number One of the Bren gun, 22404529 Rfn Turner J., was seriously wounded by a bullet fired from a light automatic, three yards to his right, and fell to the ground. The Section was ordered to pull back to the 'lay back' position.

22337903 Rfn Newport J., the Number Two on the Bren gun, immediately stood up in the open, went forward to Rfn Turner, picked him up, and although continually

Major Sir C.J. Nixon, Bart, MC and Sergeant J. Knight in conversation in 'A' Company Area at Pyontaek. (RUR Museum)

under heavy automatic fire, carried Rfn Turner from the feature back, 600 yards, to the 'lay back' position. During this carry Rfn Newport not only was fired on from the feature he had left, but also from a feature some 600 yards to the west.

Rfn Newport showed extreme bravery, coolness, initiative, and he had complete disregard for his own personal safety. Without doubt he saved Rfn Turner from being taken prisoner, and probably saved his life.

Mentioned in Despatches
Lieutenant Colonel R.J.H. Carson (44059)
Major Sir Christopher J. Nixon, Bart, MC (200407)
Captain J.E. D'O. Hinde (314806)
Captain V. de P.C. Johnson
Captain R.H.S. Sinclair, MC
Captain (QM) T.P. Smith (333558)
Lieutenant L. Cornick
Lieutenant J.J. Mole (397992)
Lieutenant G.L. Potts
C/Sergeant S. Byrne (No 7012597)
Sergeant (Acting) S. Fitzsimons (No 14190364)
Sergeant T.J. Fowler (No 7047229)
Corporal D. Bruce

Lance Corporal J. Watkinson (No 3651482)
Acting Corporal N. Hunt (No 4127146)
Rifleman J.J. McShane (No 22511803)
Rifleman E. Plews
Rifleman A.E. Varley/Varney (No 6847575)

American Silver Star
Major G.P. Rickcord, DSO

In many accounts of the RUR in Korea there has been mention of the Military Medal awarded to Lance Corporal Hanna of the Royal Ulster Rifles. Research has confirmed that Fusilier, Acting Lance Corporal W.H.W. Hanna, Royal Irish Fusiliers, was awarded the Military Medal while serving in Korea with the Royal Norfolk Regiment. As a Bren gunner he carried out several acts of unselfish gallantry during the summer of 1952, most especially on the night of 2-3 August.[2] Post-Korea Hanna was a member of the Ulster Defence Regiment serving as a weapons instructor at Gough Barracks, County Armagh. He was killed by gunmen in Lurgan, County Armagh on the night of 26 July 1975.[3]

Korea Medal 1950-1953
The Korea Medal was instituted in July 1951 by King George VI to be awarded to those members of the British Commonwealth forces who had been deployed to Korea and its surrounding waters between 2 July 1950 and 27 July 1953. The qualification period was one day for service carried out on land for all three services, or one operational sortie over Korea for the Royal Air Force, or twenty eight days sea service for the Royal Navy. The medal is made from cupro-nickel, apart from the Canadian version, which is silver and has the word CANADA below the Queen's bust, is 36mm in diameter with a fixed plain suspension. On the obverse the laureate bust of Queen Elizabeth II, with three obverse legend types noted:

Korea Medal 1950–53. (RUR Museum)

Obverse legend type:
1st   + Elizabeth II Dei Gra: Britt Omn Regina F: D.
2nd   + Elizabeth . II . Dei . Gratia .Regina F: D.
Canadian   + Elizabeth . II . Dei . Gratia. Regina. Canada.

On the reverse is Hercules fighting the nine-headed Hydra, with KOREA in exergue. The British-issued medal is impressed in small sans serif similar to the General Service Medal 1918-62, while the Canadian and Australian medals are impressed with

---
2 *Faugh-a-Ballagh, The Regimental Gazette of The Royal Irish Fusiliers*, July 1953.
3 Dillon, *The Dirty War*, London, 1992.

taller sans serif capitals with no unit or rank shown. The ribbon is yellow with two wide blue stripes.

The United Nations Korea Service Medal 1950-1954

This medal was instituted by the United Nations General Assembly on 12 December 1950 and authorized for wear by the British Commonwealth Forces on 6 November 1951 and was awarded for one or more days of service. Visits of inspection required thirty days aggregate service to qualify. The qualifying area extended beyond that of the Korean Peninsula and surrounding waters to included adjacent territories such as Japan and Okinawa. Recipients of the Queen's Korea medal qualified for this award, but as the United Nations medal could be awarded for service after the armistice and had a larger geographical catchment it could therefore be awarded without the Queen's Korea Medal.

The United Nations Korea Service Medal 1950–54. (RUR Museum)

The medals are in a copper coloured bronze alloy measuring 36mm in diameter, with a fixed suspender with an integral fixed 'KOREA' bar. On the obverse is the United Nations emblem, while the reverse bears the inscription FOR SERVICE IN DEFENCE OF THE PRINCIPLES OF THE CHARTER OF THE UNITED NATIONS.

The other nations involved have their own language versions of this medal: Amharic, Dutch, French, Greek, Italian, Korean, Spanish, Thai, Turkish, and Tagalog.

The medal was issued unnamed apart from the Canadian issue, which was impressed in san serif capitals. The ribbon is comprised of nine blue and eight white stripes.[4]

---

4 *The Medal Year Book*, Honiton, 1998.

Appendix III
Nominal Roll

Rank	Number	Surname	Forenames	Awards	Company	Platoon	Notes
Sapper		Adair	Robert McA.				Wounded.
Corporal	7013974	Adair	William				Aged 31 years from Newtownards, he joined the Army in 1938. No known grave. Commemorated on UN Wall of Remembrance, Pusan, Korea. Listed missing 3 January 1951 believed dead.
Rifleman		Addis	J.				Ex-Royal Inniskilling Fusiliers. Listed in *The Times* as missing 20 January 1951 and later as a POW 6 October 1951.
Rifleman	7013478	Agnew	Thomas				
Rifleman		Agnew	Thomas				From Andersonstown, Belfast.
Rifleman	7020881	Aicken	A.				Listed in *The Times* as missing 20 January 1951 and later as a POW 13 October 1951.
Rifleman	780018	Akid	E.				Listed in *The Times* as missing 20 January 1951.
Lance Corporal		Alberts	P.				The Wiltshire Regiment (Duke of Edinburgh's) attached to The Royal Ulster Rifles. Listed as wounded in *The Times*, 28 April 1951.
Rifleman	4546387	Alexander	J.T.				Listed in *The Times* as missing 20 January 1951. POW 4/5 January 1951.
Rifleman	22286894	Altimas	Albert				Joined the Royal Irish Fusiliers in August 1949, transferred to The Royal Ulster Rifles, January 1950. Captured 25 April 1951. Listed in *The Times* as missing 3 May 1951 and later as a POW 29 September 1951. There is a Fusilier Altimas listed as transferring from the Royal Inniskilling Fusiliers Signal Platoon to the RUR in Korea.
Rifleman	6979990	Anderson	James Richard				Ex-Royal Inniskilling Fusiliers, served in Italy with the Lancashire Fusiliers. Taken POW 25 April 1951. Listed in *The Times* as missing 12 May 1951 and later as a POW 6 October 1951.

Rank	Number	Surname	Forenames	Awards	Company	Platoon	Notes
Rifleman	19041520	Anderson	N.				Taken POW 24 April 1951. Listed in *The Times* as missing 4 May 1951 and later as a POW 13 October 1951.
Captain		Anderson	William 'Bill' E.	MC and Bar, MBE			Joined the Royal Ulster Rifles in March 1944. Captured 3 January 1951. Listed in *The Times* as missing January 1951 and later as a POW finally released.
Rifleman	14446447	Anderson	William Cecil				Initially listed as missing and then killed 3 January 1951 during the Battle of Seoul 2-4 January 1951. Buried UN Memorial Cemetery, Pusan, Korea: Plot 17, Row 4, Grave 731. Aged 30.
Lance Corporal	4915090	Ashton	W.J.				Ex-Royal Inniskilling Fusiliers, King's Commendation for Brave Conduct 13.1.42.
Sergeant	4452723	Ashworth	Robert		Support	MMG	From County Antrim.
		Atkinson	John		B		Killed aged 21 years, 3 January 1951. Buried UN Memorial Cemetery, Pusan Korea: Plot 24, Row 5, Grave 1750.
Rifleman	22511192	Austin	D.S.				On secondment from the Manchester Regiment.
Lieutenant		Axeford	A.		C		Missing in action 31 March 1951.
Rifleman		Baird	J.				The Royal Irish Fusiliers attached to The Royal Ulster Rifles. Taken prisoner 3/4 January 1951.
Rifleman	19047364	Baird	J.				
Lieutenant		Baker	J.				The Suffolk Regiment attached to The Royal Ulster Rifles. Died of wounds 20 February 1951. Buried UN Memorial Cemetery, Pusan, Korea, Plot 4, Row 3, Grave 136, aged 28.
Captain	233033	Balders	N.A.M. Nigel				Captured 4/5 January 1951 and then as POW 16 June 1951. He was a prisoner for two years eight months.
Sergeant	7012253	Balfour	N.E. 'Ted'				From Belfast.
Bugler		Balway	William				

Rank	Number	Surname	Forenames	Awards	Company	Platoon	Notes
Rifleman		Bannan	Harry				From St Albans, Herts. Recalled to the Army in September 1950 with only one week of his Reserve Service remaining. He was initially reported as missing then wounded in action.
Rifleman	4272132	Bannon	H.M.				Wounded in action.
Corporal	22271021	Barbour	Hugh				Ex-Royal Inniskilling Fusiliers, from Templemore, Londonderry. Captured 4/5 January 1951. Listed as missing 20 January 1951 and then as a POW 25 August 1951.
Rifleman		Barnett	T.				Wounded 3 February 1951.
Rifleman	22231332	Barr	M.				Ex-Royal Inniskilling Fusiliers, attached to 1 RUR.
Rifleman	3599213	Bartlett	J.R.				Captured 4/5 January 1951, listed as missing in action 20 January 1951.
Corporal	21125860	Baxter	John		C		From Belfast. Captured 25 April 1951. Listed as missing 3 May 1951 and then a POW 13 October 1951. He was held in Camp 1, 'Chongsong'.
Rifleman		Bayliss	J.L.				Wounded 10 March 1951.
Captain		Beamish	John Patrick Fulcher	MC	A		
Lieutenant		Beckett	J.A.				From Cheshire. The Lancashire Regiment attached to The Royal Ulster Rifles. Previously listed as missing, but later re-joined 23 December 1950.
Rifleman		Bell	L.				Listed as missing 20 January 1951 then missing believed to be a POW 17 January 1953 then listed as died as POW 13 June 1953.
Rifleman	3857697	Bell	Lawrence				Initially listed as missing then died as a prisoner of war, 23 June 1951. Buried UN Memorial Cemetery, Pusan, Korea: Plot 70, Row 9, Grave 7837. Aged 30.
Private		Bennett	K.				
Lieutenant		Benson	R.		D		Wounded 20 January 1951.
Rifleman	22243556	Bergin	J.				Listed as POW 4/5 January 1951 also shown as killed in action 20 January 1951.

Rank	Number	Surname	Forenames	Awards	Company	Platoon	Notes
Rifleman		Berry	P.T.				Listed as wounded 3 May 1951.
Rifleman		Bickle					Attached to Battalion HQ.
		Biggar	James 'Jimmy'				From County Antrim.
		Biggar	Matthew 'Matt'				From County Antrim. He was the brother of Jimmy Biggar.
Private		Black	I.N.				The Royal Ulster Rifles attached Duke of Wellington's Regiment (West Riding). Initially listed as missing, 13 June 1953 and then killed in action 11 July 1953. May be Rifleman N Black, 22219604.
Rifleman	22219604	Black	Norman				The Royal Ulster Rifles attached Duke of Wellington's Regiment (West Riding). UN Memorial Cemetery, Pusan, Korea: Plot 70, Row 2, Grave 7758. Died 29 May 1953. Aged 21years.
Major	52575	Blake	Charles Anthony Howell Bruce				Died 3 January 1951, aged 39. Buried in the UN Cemetery within Plot 17, Row 1 Grave 690. Previously served with the 1st Airborne Division at Arnhem.
Fusilier		Blow	Harold Henry Douglas.				Died 24 June 1951, aged 27 years. Buried Hodogaya Cemetery, Yokohama, Japan, Plot B, Row C, Grave 15. The Royal Lincolnshire Regiment attached to The Royal Ulster Rifles.
Rifleman		Bockins	N.				The Gloucestershire Regiment attached to The Royal Ulster Rifles. Listed as wounded in *The Times*, 4 August 1951.
Rifleman	6284458	Bowers	E.				Wounded, reported in *The Times* 20 January 1951. Aged 19 years from Belfast. The Royal Irish Fusiliers attached to The Royal Ulster Rifles. Taken prisoner 25 April 1951. Listed as missing 3 May 1951 and then as a POW 13 October 1951.
Rifleman	22307006	Boyd	Robert				
Rifleman	21127056	Boyle	G.				The Royal Irish Fusiliers attached to The Royal Ulster Rifles. Wounded in action 15 June 1951.
Corporal		Boyle	J.				

A NEW BATTLEFIELD

Rank	Number	Surname	Forenames	Awards	Company	Platoon	Notes
Piper		Bradford			Band		Known to be officially listed as dead. Missing presumed killed during the Battle of Imjin, 22-25 April 1951. Aged 24. No known grave, Commemorated on UN Wall of Remembrance, Pusan, Korea.
Rifleman	22525626	Brannan	Thomas				From Northants he was captured 25 April 1951. Listed as missing in *The Times* 3 May 1951 then as a POW September 1951. Initially held in Camp 1, 'Chongsong' he later ended up in No.2 Penal Camp as result of his escape attempts.
Rifleman	21069205	Brierley	Charlie S.		C		Captured 4/5 April 1951. Listed as missing in *The Times* 20 January 1951 then as a POW June 1951.
Rifleman	3386814	Brodie	F.				Ex-Royal Inniskilling Fusilier, Signal Platoon, attached.
Rifleman		Brogan					Wounded November 1951. Royal Ulster Rifles attached to the King's Own Scottish Borders.
Rifleman		Brooke	R.H.				
Major		Brooks	William Edward	MC and Bar	B		Wounded in action.
Rifleman		Brown	C.W.				Aged 31 years. Missing presumed killed 25 April 1951. No known grave, commemorated on UN Wall of Remembrance, Pusan, Korea.
Rifleman	3711805	Brown	D.	MM			The Gloucestershire Regiment attached to The Royal Ulster Rifles. Listed as wounded in *The Times*, 2 May 1951.
Lance Corporal		Brown	E.				Wounded, reported in *The Times* 2 May 1951.
Rifleman		Brown	S.				Ex-Royal Inniskilling Fusiliers, from Londonderry. Wounded, reported in *The Times* 20 January 1951.
Rifleman	22309882	Brown	Thomas Walter				Ex-6th and 2nd Royal Inniskilling Fusiliers. Served in the Second World War in North Africa, Sicily and Italy. A reservist, he signed on and later became a Colour Sergeant. MID for the Imjin battle.
Corporal		Bruce	Davy	MID			Listed as missing, 20 January 1951 and then as a POW 25 August 1951.
Lieutenant		Bruford-Davies	E.R. 'Robin'		D		

NOMINAL ROLL

Rank	Number	Surname	Forenames	Awards	Company	Platoon	Notes
Rifleman	22308421	Buckley	J.J.				The Royal Irish Fusiliers attached to The Royal Ulster Rifles. Taken prisoner 4/5 January 1951.
Sergeant		Buckley	T.J.		B		Wounded, reported in *The Times* 3 May 1951.
Rifleman	6290618	Bunby	M.B.				Listed as missing January 1951 then as a prisoner. Died as a POW 27 July 1951, aged 36. No known grave. Commemorated UN Wall of Remembrance, Pusan, Korea.
Rifleman		Burcher	J.				Died as POW.
Lieutenant	397829	Burke-Gaffney	Michael Anthony Bowes		Support	Anti-tank	Ex-Royal Inniskilling Fusiliers attached to the Royal Ulster Rifles, ex-ranker, No19043060, attended Sandhurst 15.8.47.
Rifleman	4758240	Burrow	L.				Captured 23 April 1951. Listed as missing in *The Times*, May 1951 then as a POW September 1951.
Rifleman	4694588	Burton	H.				Captured 25 April 1951. Listed as missing in *The Times*, 20 January 1951 then as a POW.
Rifleman	6914122	Burton	J.C.				Captured 4/5 January 1951. Listed as missing in *The Times*, 20 January 1951 then as a POW September 1951.
Rifleman	14466141	Bustard	J.C.				Listed as missing, then as a POW, eventually dead, 15 January 1951 aged 23 years. No known grave. Commemorated on UN Wall of Remembrance, Pusan, Korea.
Rifleman	4454278	Butcher	J.				Listed as missing, then as a POW, eventually dead, 22 February 1951, aged 31 years. No known grave. Commemorated on UN Wall of Remembrance, Pusan, Korea.
Lance Corporal	4127206	Buxton	W.				Taken POW 4/5 January 1951. Listed as missing in *The Times*, 20 January 1951.
Sergeant		Byrne	C.		A		
Lance Corporal		Byrne	Patrick 'Bunker'		B		From County Tipperary.
Colour Sergeant	7012597	Byrne	S.	MID	D		CQMS.
Rifleman		Byrne	Terry				From Liverpool. Wounded, reported by *The Times* 2 May 1951.

262 A NEW BATTLEFIELD

Rank	Number	Surname	Forenames	Awards	Company	Platoon	Notes
Rifleman		Cain	R.				Wounded, reported by *The Times* 20 January 1951.
Corporal		Calder	Jock		B		He was the MO Corporal for B Company. He was held as a POW in No 1 Camp, "Chongsong".
Rifleman	21182116	Callaghan	J.P.				Wounded, reported by *The Times* 20 January 1951.
Rifleman		Cam	R.				Wounded in action.
Sergeant	22243358	Campbell	Harry	MM	B		From Belfast. He was in the battle patrol.
Rifleman	22219086	Canavan	Bernard				From Belfast. Captured 3 January 1951. Listed as missing in *The Times* 20 January 1951 and then as a POW, 1 December 1951.
Corporal		Canning					The North Irish Brigade, ex-Royal Inniskilling Fusiliers, attached to The Royal Ulster Rifles.
Rifleman	22523757	Canning	Leonard				Wounded in action 17 July 1951. From Londonderry.
Rifleman	3712554	Cannon	H.W.				Wounded and reported in *The Times*, 20 January 1951.
Sergeant	22534017	Carlin	John				Provost Sergeant, Ex-Royal Inniskilling Fusiliers from Londonderry, attached from 10 October 1951. GSM Middle East, AGSM for Kenya.
Rifleman	3188874	Carlyle	A.				Wounded and reported in *The Times*, 20 January 1951.
Rifleman		Carr	R.				Wounded and reported in *The Times*, 2 May 1951.
Lieut-Colonel	144059	Carson	R.J. 'Hank'	OBE MID			Wounded and reported in *The Times*, 20 January 1951.
Lance Corporal		Carter	J.				
Rifleman	1438925	Cartledge					Taken POW 4/5 January 1951. Reported missing in *The Times* 20 January 1951.
2nd Lieutenant		Casey	J.				Royal Irish Fusiliers attached to The Royal Ulster Rifles.
Captain		Charley	Robin				
Rifleman		Charters	F.J.				Wounded and reported in *The Times*, 20 January 1951.

Rank	Number	Surname	Forenames	Awards	Company	Platoon	Notes
Rifleman		Church	Robert				From Shankill Road.
Rifleman	14218335	Clancy	Stephen Patrick				Ex-General Service Corps and Royal Inniskilling Fusiliers, from County Sligo, GSM Malaya. Wounded and reported in *The Times*, 20 January 1951.
Rifleman	22330924	Clark	L.F.				Ex-Royal Inniskilling Fusiliers/ The Royal Irish Fusiliers attached to The Royal Ulster Rifles. Taken prisoner 23 April 1951. Listed as missing in *The Times*, 2 May 1951 and then as a POW 29 September 1951.
Rifleman	14122252	Clarke	Charles David				Ex-Royal Inniskilling Fusiliers. Missing presumed killed on or after 25 April 1951. No known grave. Commemorated on the UN Wall of Remembrance, Pusan, Korea.
Rifleman	22420635	Clarke	G.				The Royal Irish Fusiliers attached to The Royal Ulster Rifles. Killed 18 November 1951.
Rifleman	3314511	Clarke	H.G.				Wounded and reported in *The Times*, 20 January 1951.
Rifleman	22511801	Clarke	K.				Taken POW 4/5 January 1951. Reported missing in *The Times*, 20 January 1951.
Corporal		Clarke	W.				One of 100 Royal Ulster Rifles sent out together to Korea.
Rifleman	4747718	Clayton	L.				The Royal Inniskilling Fusiliers/The Royal Irish Fusiliers attached to The Royal Ulster Rifles. Taken prisoner 25 April 1951. Reported missing in *The Times* 3 May 1951.
Corporal	14190267	Clayton	Victor Keith				Aged 19 years, captured 4/5 January 1951. Listed as missing in *The Times*, 20 January 1951 and then as a POW 22 October 1951.
Rifleman	21181051	Clifford	R.S.				Wounded and reported in *The Times*, 20 October 1951.
Rifleman		Clugston	R.J.				

Rank	Number	Surname	Forenames	Awards	Company	Platoon	Notes
Captain	180164	Cocksedge	G.W.H.	MC			The Royal Inniskilling Fusiliers attached to The Royal Ulster Rifles. Listed as wounded in *The Times*, 10 February 1951.
Rifleman		Colborn	Geoff F.				Commanded a patrol in the Oxford Carriers. Wounded and reported in *The Times*, 3 May 1951.
Corporal	3712478	Colleton	W.				Listed as missing in *The Times*, 20 January, then re-joined later wounded.
Colour Sergeant		Collins	K.J.				Battalion HQ's Orderly Room Sergeant.
RQMS		Connell	R.W.				Battalion HQ.
Rifleman	14191184	Conner	James				Captured 25 April 1951. Listed as missing in *The Times*, 3 May 1951 and then as a POW 6 October 1951.
Rifleman	14184573	Connolly	Patrick				From Londonderry, The Royal Inniskilling Fusiliers/The Royal Irish Fusiliers attached to The Royal Ulster Rifles. Suffered a battle accident 24 August 1951.
Corporal		Connor					Ex-Royal Inniskilling Fusiliers, attached. Had served in the Anti Tank Platoon from the days of 2pdrs to 17pdrs.
Private	22530176	Cook	R.B.				The Gloucestershire Regiment attached to The Royal Ulster Rifles. Missing presumed killed 23 April, during the Battle of Imjin, 22-25 April 1951. No known grave. Commemorated on the UN Wall of Remembrance, Pusan, Korea.
Sergeant	7011531	Cooke	Daniel	MM	A		Wounded and reported in *The Times*, 20 October 1951.
Sergeant		Copping	G.S.		B		
Rifleman	6914177	Cordery	H.J.				Initially listed as missing then killed in action during the Battle of Imjin, 22-25 April 1951. Aged 30. Buried UN Memorial Cemetery; Pusan, Korea. Plot 17, Row 3, Grave 718.
Rifleman	6850050	Cordner	S.				Captured 25 April 1951. Listed as missing in *The Times*, 3 May 1951 and then as a POW 13 October 1951.

Rank	Number	Surname	Forenames	Awards	Company	Platoon	Notes
Lieutenant		Cornick	L.	MID			The King's Regiment attached to the Royal Ulster Rifles.
Rifleman	22546494	Corrigan	E.T.				Ex-Royal Inniskilling Fusiliers, attached from 10 October 51. AGSM Kenya.
Rifleman	3599021	Coupe	J.				Captured 25 April 1951. Listed as missing in *The Times*, 3 May 1951 and then as a POW 29 September 1951.
Lance Corporal		Cowan					Attached to Battalion HQ.
Lance Corporal		Cowap					Attached to Battalion HQ.
Rifleman	22431399	Cowell	J.				Captured 3 November 1951.
Rifleman	6980155	Coyle	James				From Londonderry, ex-Royal Inniskilling Fusiliers, attached from 5 November 1950 to 13 March 1951.
Rifleman	21187640	Coyle	William				From Templemore, Londonderry, The Royal Inniskilling Fusiliers/ Royal Irish Fusiliers attached to The Royal Ulster Rifles. Wounded in action 17 July 1951.
Rifleman	949422	Coyne	P.J.				Captured 25 April 1951. Listed as missing in *The Times*, 3 May 1951 and then as a POW 6 October 1951.
Lieutenant		Craig	A.C.				Commanded the Battle Patrol in April 1951.
Lieutenant	413746	Craig	Hedley J.M.		Batt HQ		A member of the Royal Army Medical Corps, he was a National Serviceman.
Rifleman	21127508	Craig	R.				Missing presumed killed 4/5 January 1951, initially listed as dead, aged 23 years. Reported in *The Times*, date of death 25 June 1951. No known grave, commemorated on the UN Wall of Remembrance, Pusan, Korea.
Rifleman	6985614	Crawford	David 'Big Davy'		C		The Royal Inniskilling Fusiliers/The Royal Irish Fusiliers attached to The Royal Ulster Rifles. Taken prisoner 25 April 1951. He was held in Camp 1, 'Chongsong'. Reported as missing in *The Times*, 3 May 1951.

266 A NEW BATTLEFIELD

Rank	Number	Surname	Forenames	Awards	Company	Platoon	Notes
Rifleman	22204982	Crilly	Francis				Aged 26 years he joined the Royal Ulster Rifles three years previously. Before joining he was a brass moulder in Harland and Wolff. Captured 4/5 January 1951 and listed as missing in *The Times*, 20 January 1951 and then as a prisoner of war, 20 September 1951.
Rifleman	6980687	Crompton	James Alexander				From Baronscourt, County Tyrone, he had been a Forester prior to enlisting in the Royal Inniskilling Fusiliers on 7.11.'39. Battle accident.
Lance Corporal	3530798	Cruickshanks	C.R.				Killed in action when a Scout Car overturned. Died, 27 November 1950, aged 32 years. Buried UN Memorial Cemetery, Pusan, Korea. Plot 70, Row 6, Grave 7808.
Lance Corporal		Cunningham					Attached to Battalion HQ.
Rifleman	22219766	Cunningham	R.				Died 17 August 1951, aged 25 years. Buried UN Memorial Cemetery, Pusan, Korea. Plot 24, Row 6, Grave 1764.
Corporal		Cunningham	S.				Wounded and reported in *The Times*, 20 January 1951.
Rifleman	1470442	Cunningham	William Hamilton				From Glendermott, Londonderry, ex-Royal Inniskilling Fusiliers. Previously served with the 216th Searchlight Regiment (RA) 1940-44 and Loyal Regiment 1945. Captured 25 April 1951. Listed as missing in *The Times*, 3 May 1951, then as POW, 13 October 1951.
Corporal	6980105	Cushing	Thomas Joseph, Tommy				A native of Tipperary, enlisted in the Royal Inniskilling Fusiliers, POW at Dunkirk, interned in Stalag VIIIB. Transferred to Royal Irish Fusiliers 1947.
Corporal		Daly	J.				Wounded and reported in *The Times*, 20 January 1951.
		Daly	R.				
Captain	105620	Dane	H.S.				Ex-Royal Inniskilling Fusiliers, attached, but served with HQBC Sub Area. GSM Cyprus, AGSM Kenya.

NOMINAL ROLL

Rank	Number	Surname	Forenames	Awards	Company	Platoon	Notes
Captain		Daniels	Ivor G.		B		Platoon commander and then B Company 2 i/c.
Lance Corporal	22373543	Daves	S.				Battle accident.
Corporal	14190507	Davidson	William				Listed missing presumed POW, 4/5 January 1951. Later listed as missing presumed killed in *The Times*, 20 January 1951 aged 24 years. An Army Historical Branch Roll of Honour records date of death 1 June 1951. No known grave. Commemorated on the UN Wall of Remembrance, Pusan, Korea.
Rifleman	3712680	Davies	William Owen				Initially listed as missing then killed in action during the Battle of Seoul, 2-4 January 1951 aged 32 years. Buried UN Memorial Cemetery, Pusan, Korea. Plot 17, Row 7, Grave 763.
Rifleman		Davis			A		
Rifleman		Davis	E.W.				Wounded and reported in *The Times*, 23 December 1950.
Private		Davis	P.J.				The Royal Ulster Rifles attached to King's Shropshire Light Infantry. Killed in action 17 November 1951.
Rifleman	14181143	Davison	J.				The Royal Irish Fusiliers attached to The Royal Ulster Rifles. Taken prisoner 3 January 1951. Listed as missing in *The Times*, 20 January 1951, then as POW, 8 December 1951.
Rifleman		Davison	Joseph				His brother John was serving in the Royal Irish Fusiliers whilst his other brother was serving on HMS *Belfast* during the Korean War.
Rifleman		Dawson			C	Stores	
Colour Sergeant		Dawson	S.		B		B Company CQMS.
Rifleman		Day	E.				Wounded and reported in *The Times*, 2 May 1951.

268　A NEW BATTLEFIELD

Rank	Number	Surname	Forenames	Awards	Company	Platoon	Notes
Major		de Longueuil	J.C. Stuart G.	MC			Major the Baron Stuart de Longueuil died on the 2nd December 1990 in France where he had been living in retirement for many years. His elder brother is the eleventh Baron de Longueuil — the only title in the Peerage of Canada, which was created by Louis XIV in 1700 and received recognition by Queen Victoria in 1880. He was born in California, and was educated in France and Guernsey before going to Sandhurst in 1937. He was commissioned in The Royal Ulster Rifles in 1938 and joined the 2nd Battalion at Parkhurst Barracks, Isle of Wight, on their return from Palestine. He was appointed Carrier Platoon Commander and took part in the campaign leading up to the evacuation from Dunkirk. As officer commanding 'C' Company he landed in Normandy on D-Day and led his company during the campaign in France, Belgium, Holland and Germany. He was awarded the Military Cross for gallantry during the crossing of the Meuse-Escaut Canal on the night of 18/19 September 1944. He acted as second-in-command of the 2nd Battalion for a time during operations in Belgium and Holland in early 1945, and on conclusion of the war joined the British Military Mission to Greece.
Rifleman		Dean					Wounded and reported in *The Times*, 2 May 1951.
Captain		Decker	P.G.				Captured 3/4 January 1951.
Lance Corporal		Dempster					Bandsman.
Rifleman		Devereaux					Ex-Royal Inniskilling Fusiliers Signal Platoon, attached.
Rifleman	19044465	Devey	P.J.				The Royal Irish Fusiliers attached to The Royal Ulster Rifles. Suffered a battle accident 31 May 1951.
Rifleman	6979415	Dickenson	Thomas Stanley Reid				Ex-Royal Inniskilling Fusiliers, attached 5 November 1950 to 16 September 1951.

NOMINAL ROLL

Rank	Number	Surname	Forenames	Awards	Company	Platoon	Notes
Sergeant		Dixon					REME attached to the Royal Ulster Rifles for their entire tour.
Captain		Docker	Paul G.		C		He was acting Compnay Commader of 'C' Coy. Reported as missing in action 2 May 1951 then as a POW 6 October 1951. He was held in Camp 1, 'Chongsong'.
Captain		Dockert	G.				Listed as missing in *The Times*, 2 May 1951, then as POW, 6 October 1951.
Rifleman	14450175	Dodd	R.				Captured 4/5 January 1951. Listed as missing in *The Times*, 20 January 1951.
Rifleman	14188897	Doherty	James				Ex-Royal Inniskilling Fusiliers, enlisted at Ballykinlar on 27 March 1946. Captured 4/5 January 1951. Listed as missing in *The Times*, 20 January 1951, then as POW, 10 November 1951.
Lance Corporal		Doherty	James				Previously served in the Royal Inniskilling Fusiliers for six years, later transferred into the Royal Ulster Rifles. From Londonderry he was reported missing, aged 28, being due to be demobbed the following month.
Rifleman		Dolan	P.				
Rifleman	3856357	Dolley	N.				Captured 25 April 1951. Listed as missing in *The Times*, 20 January 1951, then as POW, 8 December 1951, then later released in 1953.
Private		Done	J.				The Gloucestershire Regiment attached to The Royal Ulster Rifles. Listed as wounded in *The Times*, 2 May 1951.
Private	190404457	Donnelly	J.				Initially listed as missing then killed in action during the Battle of Seoul, 3 January 1951, aged 21 years. Buried UN Memorial Cemetery, Pusan, Korea. Plot 17, Row 7, Grave 762.
Rifleman	22523389	Doran	J.				Killed in action 3 May 1951.
Rifleman		Dougan	M.				Wounded and reported in *The Times*, 3 February 1951.

Rank	Number	Surname	Forenames	Awards	Company	Platoon	Notes
Lieutenant		Dove					Member of the Battalion shooting team. He was an avid bird watcher. He accidently drowned in Lough Neagh post-war.
Rifleman	22540209	Dovey	T.				The Royal Irish Fusiliers attached to The Royal Ulster Rifles. Suffered a battle accident 26 August 1951.
Rifleman	14185692	Dowrie	James				The Royal Inniskilling Fusiliers/The Royal Irish Fusiliers attached to The Royal Ulster Rifles. Captured 25 April 1951 aged 23 years. Listed as missing in *The Times*, 3 May 1951, then as POW, 6 October 1951. He was held in No.3 Camp of the "Democratic People's Republic of Korea", Peking. Also served in Malaya and awarded GSM 1918-62.
Rifleman		Doyce	J.T.				Killed in action 10 March 1951.
Rifleman	22289926	Doyle	J.T.				Killed 19 February 1951, aged 21 years. Buried in UN Memorial Cemetery, Pusan, Korea. Plot 4, Row 3, Grave 140.
Rifleman		Doyle	M.R.				The Royal Ulster Rifles attached to the King's Shropshire Light Infantry. Wounded and reported in *The Times*, 15 December 1951.
Rifleman	19034701	Doyle	M.R.				The Royal Irish Fusiliers attached to The Royal Ulster Rifles. Wounded in action 17 November 1951.
CSM		Drumgoole	J.		B		
Captain		Dungavel					In the Royal Army Medical Corps. He replaced Captain Ferrie.
Lieutenant	314166	Dunlop	Victor Alexander			Defence	The King's Regiment (Liverpool) attached to The Royal Ulster Rifles. O/c the porters. Missing presumed killed, 25 April 1951, aged 31 years. No known grave. Commemorated on the UN Wall of Remembrance, Pusan, Korea.
Rifleman	3773135	Dunne	P.				Captured 25 April 1951, Reported as missing in action in *The Times*, 3 May 1951.
Corporal		Dunwoody					See Corporal J.D. Gibson.

NOMINAL ROLL

Rank	Number	Surname	Forenames	Awards	Company	Platoon	Notes
Rifleman		Dunwoody	'Vimpo'				He was a Battalion sniper.
		Dyer	John				
		Dysart					Initially listed as missing then killed in action during the Battle of Seoul, 2-4 January 1951, aged 25. Buried UN Memorial Cemetery, Pusan, Korea. Plot 24, Row 5, Grave 1746.
Lance Corporal	14514364	Dytor	F.				Reported as wounded in *The Times*, 20 January 1951.
Rifleman	21029074	Edwards	A.				The Gloucestershire Regiment attached to The Royal Ulster Rifles. Listed as wounded in *The Times*, 2 May 1951.
Private		Edwards	L.C.				Attached to Battalion HQ.
Lance Corporal		Ellingham					
Lieutenant	365684	Elliot	J.D.		Batt HQ		MTO.
Rifleman	14471610	Elliott	L.				Captured 4/5/ January 1951. Listed as missing in *The Times*, 20 January 1951.
Rifleman		Elliott	Samuel				From Donegall Road.
Rifleman	3654831	Ellsmore	S.F.				Initially listed as missing presumed killed, aged 31 years. He died from wounds, 5 January 1951. Buried UN Memorial Cemetery, Pusan, Korea, Plot 17, Row 1, Grave 693.
Rifleman	6980243	English	Edward				From County Laois, he joined the Royal Inniskilling Fusiliers on 21 February 1939 at Omagh. He served in Italy, Burma and Sicily and was demobbed on 3 April 1948. He was recalled to the Army in August 1950. Taken POW 4/5 January. Listed as missing in *The Times*, 20 January 1951 then as a POW 15 September 1951.
		Esam	W.S.				
Lance Corporal	22271508	Evans	R.				The Royal Irish Fusiliers attached to The Royal Ulster Rifles. Taken prisoner 4/5 January 195 he was listed as missing in *The Times*, 20 January 1951.

Rank	Number	Surname	Forenames	Awards	Company	Platoon	Notes
Captain	159355	Farrell	Donald Patrick				Ex-Royal Inniskilling Fusiliers, then to RUR and Brigade Major in Korea. Served in Burma during the Second World War and received an MID, GSM for Palestine and Cyprus. MBE for Korea (LG 24.4.53). Murdered by the IRA on 23 April 1974.
Lance Corporal		Farrell	J.W. 'Joe'		D		An ex-boxer from Belfast, the last man in D Company to escape from Happy Valley. Post-war he organized boy's boxing clubs in Belfast.
Rifleman	6914264	Farrow	C.H.				Captured 24 April 1951. Listed as missing in *The Times*, 3 May 1951.
C Sergeant		Fay	William				Officers' Mess Steward in Korea.
Captain		Ferrie	A.M.				Captured in January 1951.
Captain	333875	ffrench	J.R.M.	MC	Batt HQ		
Rifleman		Fisher	David				From Shankill, Belfast.
Rifleman	5019250	Fitlpatrick	J.D.				Listed as wounded in *The Times*, 20 January 1951. The Royal Irish Fusiliers attached to The Royal Ulster Rifles. Died 23 April 1951. Listed as missing in *The Times*, 2 May during the Battle of Imjin 22nd-25th April 1951 aged 20 years. Buried UN Memorial Cemetery, Pusan, Korea, Plot 24, Row 6, Grave 1753.
Rifleman	22366119	Fitzgerald	F.G.				Killed on 3 January 1951 while on attachment to the Royal Northumberland Fusiliers. UN Memorial Cemetery Pusan, plot 17, row 6, position 2, grave serial 755. However, those who served in Korea remember him being shot by a sniper on 30 December 1950, as he crossed a schoolyard being use by the Fusiliers as a billet.
2nd Lieutenant	361803	Fitz-Gibbon	Gerald M.				From Eire.
CSM	14190364	Fitzsimons	Sean	MID	C		
Lance Corporal	3130672	Flanagan	T.				Captured 4/5/ January 1951. Listed as missing in *The Times*, 20 January 1951 then as a POW 6 October 1951.
Rifleman	3393270	Fleming	E.				Listed as wounded in *The Times*, 20 January 1951.

NOMINAL ROLL

Rank	Number	Surname	Forenames	Awards	Company	Platoon	Notes
Rifleman	5251687	Fletcher	K.				Initially listed as missing then killed in action 25 April 1951, during the Battle of Imjin, 22-25 April 1951 aged 30 years. Buried UN Memorial Cemetery, Pusan, Korea. Plot 17, Row 12, Grave 817.
Rifleman		Fletcher	W.J.				Listed as wounded in *The Times*, 2 May 1951.
Rifleman	22232408	Fogarty	C. Ray				Captured 4/5 January 1951. Listed as missing in *The Times*, 20 January 1951.
Rifleman	22440889	Foley	J.				Died aged 20 years, 1 October 1951. Buried UN Memorial Cemetery, Pusan, Korea, Plot 24, Row 11, Grave 1816.
Rifleman	22294763	Forbes	J.J.				Ex-Royal Inniskilling Fusiliers, attached from 29 April 51 to 3 April 52. Listed as wounded in *The Times*, 23 June 1951.
Sergeant		Forrester			B		
Rifleman	5383656	Foster	Mark				Initially listed as missing then killed in action during the Battle of Seoul, 2-4 January 1951. Buried UN Memorial Cemetery, Pusan, Korea. Plot 17, Row 4, Grave 725. The headstone of the grave location given by the Army's Roll of Honour entry above as that of Rifleman M. Foster is in fact that of an Unknown Soldier. The explanation is, presumably, that the identification of a body previously buried as Rifleman Foster's was rescinded, and it is now the view of the Ministry of Defence that it could not be established with certainty that the grave is that of Rifleman Foster. However, some records were not amended, and the register of graves at the UN Memorial Cemetery as well as the Roll of Honour still show the grave as that of Rifleman Foster. This explanation is supported by the fact that Rifleman Foster's name has been added to the end of Plaque 8 out of alphabetical order.
Sergeant	7047229	Fowler	T.J.	MID	D		

Rank	Number	Surname	Forenames	Awards	Company	Platoon	Notes
Rifleman	19032321	Fry	W.G.				From Gilford, County Down, served as a cadet, enlisted in Royal Inniskilling Fusiliers on 19 September 1946. The Royal Irish Fusiliers attached to The Royal Ulster Rifles attached to King's Shropshire Light Infantry. Listed as wounded in 17 November 1951 and in *The Times*, 8 December 1951.
Rifleman	6086731	Fuller	J.				Battle accident.
Rifleman	6980659	Fulton	D.				Captured 4/5 January 1951. Listed as missing in *The Times*, 20 January 1951 then as a POW 29 October 1951.
Sergeant		Furlong	J.		B		
Lieutenant		Furney	D.K.				The Royal Irish Fusiliers attached to The Royal Ulster Rifles.
Captain	149563	Gaffikin	Hugh Montgomery	DSO OBE			From Knock, Belfast the son of the late Mr R.M. Gaffikin, JP, of Belfast he was a pupil at Campbell College and in 1939 was a member of Queen's University O.T.C. Commissioned to The Royal Ulster Rifles in 1940 and joined the 2nd Battalion. He took part in the D-Day landings in Normandy on 6 June 1944, commanding the Carrier Platoon in Support Company and being wounded by shrapnel to his left arm on 7 June while at 'farm gazelle'. He was evacuated, but returned to duty the following day. He was present at the crossing of the Meuse/Escaut canal in September '44, the crossing of the River Rhine in March 1945, and was in one of the final battles of the war in the amphibious assault on Bremen. Listed as wounded in *The Times*, 20 January 1951.
Sergeant		Gair	D.				Listed as missing in *The Times*, 3 May 1951.
Lance Corporal		Gales	Harry W.				From Brackley, Northants, England. Listed as wounded in *The Times*, 6 January 1951.
Lance Corporal		Galloway			Band		

NOMINAL ROLL

Rank	Number	Surname	Forenames	Awards	Company	Platoon	Notes
Rifleman		Galway					The Royal Engineers attached to the Royal Ulster Rifles. Wounded aged 24 years.
Sapper		Gamble	J.				Captured 25 April 1951. Listed as missing in *The Times*, 3 May 1951 then as a POW 29 September 1951.
Rifleman	7019607	Gamble	J.				Missing presumed killed 4 January 1951. Died during the Battle of Seoul 2–4 January 1951 aged 32 years. No known grave. Commemorated on the UN Wall of Remembrance, Pusan, Korea.
Rifleman	3857481	Garner	Herbert William				Ex-Royal Inniskilling Fusiliers, enlisted on 1 January 1935 until 29 March 1946, then to Army Reserve. Missing presumed killed aged 34, 25 April 1951 during the Battle of Imjin. No known grave. Commemorated on the UN Wall of Remembrance, Pusan, Korea.
Sergeant	6977940	Gaw	David				
Rifleman	4279145	Gerrens	W.				Listed wounded in *The Times*, 20 January 1951.
Rifleman		Gibson	E.G.				Listed wounded in *The Times*, 2 May 1951.
Corporal	7011783	Gibson	J.D.				Ex-Royal Inniskilling Fusiliers. Died 29 November 1950 aged 36 years in a battle accident. Buried UN Memorial Cemetery, Pusan, Korea, Plot 70, Row 9, Grave 7840. Real name Dunwoody.
Rifleman	22287008	Gibson	W.A.				The Royal Irish Fusiliers attached to The Royal Ulster Rifles. Captured 25 April 1951. Listed as missing in *The Times*, 3 May 1951 and then listed as POW, 13 October 1951. GSM with clasp Arabian Peninsula. Listed as Corporal in Museum records.
Corporal	22219133	Gilchrist	R.J. 'Joe'				Ex-Royal Inniskilling Fusiliers and Second World War veteran, from Castlederg, County Tyrone. GSM with clasp for Cyprus.
Lance Corporal	3450830	Gill	A.				Captured 4/5 January 1951. Listed as missing in *The Times*, 20 January 1951.
Lieutenant		Gill	G.D.C.		B	6	

276 A NEW BATTLEFIELD

Rank	Number	Surname	Forenames	Awards	Company	Platoon	Notes
Lieutenant	369169	Gill	R.S.		Support		From the Manchester Regiment.
Rifleman	7014319	Gillespie	J.			Assault Pioneer	Captured 4/5 January 1951. Listed as missing in *The Times*, 20 January 1951 and then listed as POW, 13 October 1951.
Sergeant	6979315	Glendenning	Victor				Ex-Royal Irish Fusiliers/Royal Inniskilling Fusiliers, also served in Provost Staff Corps, attached to The Royal Ulster Rifles. GSM Malaya. AGSM Kenya.
Rifleman		Glendon	D.				From Durham.
CSM		Gordon	F.		HQ		HQ's Company from October 1951.
Rifleman	3857031	Gore	R.				Captured 3 January 1951. Listed as missing in *The Times*, 20 January 1951 and then listed as POW, 8 December 1951.
Rifleman	22511756	Gorman	T.				Listed as wounded in *The Times*, 19 May 1951.
Rifleman	22233422	Gouldsborough	Cornelius		C		Missing presumed killed, 25 April 1951. Died during the Battle of Imjin, 22-25 April 1951. No known grave. Commemorated on the UN Wall of Remembrance, Pusan, Korea.
Rifleman	3604615	Grace	G.				Taken POW 4/5 January 1951. Listed as missing in *The Times*, 20 January 1951.
Rifleman		Graham	S.				Listed as missing in *The Times*, 20 January 1951 and then listed as POW, 15 December 1951.
Rifleman	19043956	Graham	S.J.				The Royal Irish Fusiliers attached to The Royal Ulster Rifles. Taken prisoner 3 January 1951.
Rifleman	22219821	Gray	W.J.				The Royal Irish Fusiliers attached to The Royal Ulster Rifles. Battle accident 21 August 1951.
Rifleman		Green	A.				Listed as wounded in *The Times*, 28 April 1951.
Rifleman	6967874	Green	R.				Captured 4 January 1951. Listed as wounded in *The Times*, 20 January 1951.
Rifleman	22231234	Greene	P.				Ex-Royal Inniskilling Fusiliers, attached 19 February 1951 to 20 March 1951.
Lance Corporal		Greene	P.				Listed as wounded in *The Times*, 20 January 1951.
Rifleman		Greenwood	Joe				From Somerset.

NOMINAL ROLL

Rank	Number	Surname	Forenames	Awards	Company	Platoon	Notes
Rifleman		Greer	Joseph				From Belfast, he joined the Royal Ulster Rifles in 1946, he was transferred to the Royal Irish Fusiliers. After 2nd Batt, RUR was disbanded he joined 1st Batt, RUR before they left for Korea.
Rifleman	14457219	Greer	Samuel Henry				He joined the Regular Army in December 1944 and served in the Middle East and Austria with the Royal Ulster Rifles and the Royal Irish Fusiliers before going to Korea. His cousin was CSM Henry MM also serving in Korea. Captured 4/5 January 1951. Listed as missing in *The Times*, 20 January 1951 and then listed as POW, 22 September 1951.
Sergeant		Grey	'Dolly'		Support	Mortar	
Rifleman		Griffiths	E.				Listed as missing in *The Times*, 20 January 1951.
Lance Corporal		Grimble	M.				Listed as wounded in *The Times*, 20 January 1951.
Rifleman	22372583	Haggarty	S.				The Royal Irish Fusiliers attached to The Royal Ulster Rifles. Battle accident 21 August 1951.
Sergeant		Haines	R.		A		A Company from October 1951.
Rifleman		Hall					
Rifleman		Hall	M.				The Royal Ulster Rifles attached to Kings Shropshire Light Infantry. Killed in action 8 December 1951.
Rifleman	22436444	Hall	M.J.				The King's Shropshire Light Infantry attached to The Royal Ulster Rifles. Killed 17 November 1951. Buried UN Memorial Cemetery, Pusan, Korea, Plot 23, Row 8, Grave 1634, aged 19.
Sergeant	22229678	Halliday	William 'Doc' McWilliam	MM	Support	MMG	
Captain	314775	Hamill	Hugh		Batt HQ		Adjutant.
Rifleman		Hankinson	C.				Listed as wounded in *The Times*, 23 December 1951.
Lance Corporal	22542579	Hanna	William Henry Wilson	MM			The Royal Norfolk Regiment attached to The Royal Ulster Rifles.

Rank	Number	Surname	Forenames	Awards	Company	Platoon	Notes
Corporal	7014308	Hannaway	J.				During the Second World War he served with the Airborne Division. Captured 3/4 January 1951. Listed as missing in *The Times*, 27 January 1951.
Rifleman	14452980	Hannon	Thomas James				Ex-Royal Inniskilling Fusiliers, from County Sligo, he enlisted on 27 September 1944, attached to The Royal Ulster Rifles from 5 November 1950 to 28 November 1951. Listed as wounded in *The Times*, 2 May 1951.
Lance Corporal	3909598	Hardacre	S.J.				Captured 25 April 1951. Listed as missing in *The Times*, 3 May 1951 and then listed as POW, 29 September 1951.
Rifleman		Harding	J.				The Royal Ulster Rifles attached Kings Own Scottish Borderers. Wounded 17 November 1951.
Rifleman	4691329	Harper	F.				Captured 4/5 January 1951. Listed as missing in *The Times*, 20 January 1951 and then listed as POW, 13 October 1951.
Lance Corporal	3655261	Harris	S.				Listed as missing in *The Times*, 20 January 1951.
Rifleman	22305897	Hassett	Jeremy 'Gerry'				The Royal Irish Fusiliers attached to The Royal Ulster Rifles. Taken prisoner 25 April 1951. Listed as missing in *The Times*, 3 May 1951.
Lieutenant	392302	Hassett	John 'Jack'				Ex-Royal Inniskilling Fusiliers, attached, served in Guard Company, Pusan and HQ Britcom Sub Area. Also served in Kenya, commissioned as Major with 1st Inniskillings 10.7.60. OBE Civil as Sec TAVRA NI.
Rifleman	3598814	Healey	S.				Missing presumed captured 4/5 January 1951, aged 30 years. Listed as missing in *The Times*, 20 January 1951. No known grave. Commemorated on the UN Wall of Remembrance, Pusan, Korea. Listed as died 4 January 1951.
Rifleman	2889823	Heaney	W.				Captured 4/5 January 1951. Listed as missing in *The Times*, 20 January 1951 and then listed as POW, 23 June 1951.
Rifleman	3857092	Heath	H.				Listed as wounded in *The Times*, 20 January 1951.

Rank	Number	Surname	Forenames	Awards	Company	Platoon	Notes
Captain	268142	Heather	Charles J.				Ex-Royal Inniskilling Fusiliers, MID (LG 19.7.45), attached to The Royal Ulster Rifles, HQ 28 Brigade 17 August 1951-15 May 1952. Relinquished his commission and granted the honorary rank of Captain. Died 12 April 1988.
Rifleman	22524597	Heavey/Heavy	H.				The Royal Irish Fusiliers attached to The Royal Ulster Rifles. Wounded in action 15 June 1951. Listed as wounded in *The Times*, 30 June 1951.
Rifleman		Henderson	J.D.				Listed as wounded in *The Times*, 3 May 1951.
Lance Corporal		Hennessy	P.		A		Listed as wounded in *The Times*, 2 May 1951.
CSM		Henry	Sam	MM	Support		The Battalion boxer. Reported to have been a POW.
Sergeant		Herbert	R.		C		
Private	22341857	Heward	J.D.				The Gloucestershire Regiment attached to The Royal Ulster Rifles. Died 19 February of wounds 10 March 1951 from the Battle of Hill 327, 16-20 February 1951. Buried UN Memorial Cemetery, Pusan, Korea, Plot 4, Row 3, Grave 138, aged 21.
Rifleman	3386259	Hibbert	J.				Captured 4/5 January 1951. Listed as missing in *The Times*, 20 January 1951 and then listed as POW, 9 May 1953.
Lance Corporal		Hickey	M.				From Limerick.
Rifleman	4802166	Higginson	S.				Captured 4/5 January 1951. Listed as missing in *The Times*, 20 January 1951.
Lieutenant	397279	Hill	Alan E.		Support	3" Mortar	
Rifleman	14447894	Hill	Albert 'Bert' Norman				Missing presumed killed 3 January 1951 aged 24 years. No known grave. Commemorated on the UN Wall of Remembrance, Pusan, Korea.
Lieutenant		Hilton	R.		A	3	
Rifleman	4691197	Hinchcliffe	A.				Initially listed as missing then killed in action during the Battle of Imjin, 22-25 April 1951 aged 29 years. Buried UN Memorial Cemetery, Pusan, Korea. Plot 17, Row 3, Grave 717.
Captain	314806	Hinde	J.E.D'O.	MID	Batt HQ		Intelligence Officer.

Rank	Number	Surname	Forenames	Awards	Company	Platoon	Notes
Rifleman	22420640	Hobbs	A.				Missing believed killed, 4/5 January 1951. Later listed as dead.
Rifleman	22511760	Hobson	George L.		C		A Bren gunner he was captured 25 April 1951. Listed as missing in *The Times*, 3 May 1951, then as a POW, 20 April 1953, being finally released.
2nd Lieutenant	P/407881	Hodgkins	Kenneth Gordon				A South African educated at St Bees and Sandhurst he was commissioned into the Border Regiment. Attached to The Royal Ulster Rifles from April 1951. Died of wounds, 23 September 1951. Buried UN Memorial Cemetery, Pusan, Korea, Plot 24, Row 11, Grave 1814, aged 22. Listed in *The Times* as wounded, 13 October 1951.
Rifleman		Hollingdale	A.				The Royal Ulster Rifles attached to the King's Own Scottish Borderers. Listed as wounded in *The Times*, 17 November 1951.
Rifleman	14470172	Holmes	Thomas John				The Royal Irish Fusiliers attached to the Royal Ulster Rifles. Taken prisoner 3 January 1951, listed as missing in *The Times*, 20 January 1951, then as a POW, 22 December 1951.
Rifleman	3197359	Hooke	J.				Listed as wounded in *The Times*, 3 May 1951.
Rifleman	3531617	Hope	H.				Listed as wounded in *The Times*, 20 January 1951.
Rifleman	3857040	Horan	J.				Listed as wounded in *The Times*, 20 January 1951.
Rifleman	4802847	Horrobin	J.				Captured 4/5 January 1951. Listed as missing in *The Times*, 20 January 1951.
Rifleman	3598090	Horton	T.H.				Captured 25 April 1951. Listed as missing in *The Times*, 3 May 1951 and as a POW 6 October 1951.
Sergeant		Howarth	Harold				Captured 25 April 1951. Died 7 September 1951 aged 35 years. Listed as missing then as a POW, whether he died as a POW or afterwards is not known. No known grave. Commemorated on the UN Wall of Remembrance, Pusan, Korea.
		Hughes					The Royal Army Pay Corps.
Rifleman	2251185	Hughes	J.				Listed as wounded in *The Times*, 20 January 1951.

NOMINAL ROLL

Rank	Number	Surname	Forenames	Awards	Company	Platoon	Notes
Rifleman	4127149	Hull	J.				Captured 25 April 1951. Listed as missing in *The Times*, 3 May 1951 and then as a POW, 6 October 1951.
Corporal	4127146	Hunt	N.	MID			Listed as wounded in *The Times*, 20 January 1951.
Sergeant		Hunter			Support	Mortar	Mortar Fire Controller.
Sergeant	3387126	Hunter	J.R.				Captured 25 April 1951. Listed as missing in *The Times*, 3 May 1951.
Rifleman	22511772	Hurren	V.P.				Initially listed as missing in *The Times*, 3 May 1951 and then killed 26 April 1951, age 22 years. Buried UN Memorial Cemetery, Pusan, Korea. Plot 17, Row 5, Grave 734.
		Hutchenson	W.				
Corporal		Hyndman	Cecil				Served as a commando during the Second World War. Listed as wounded in *The Times*, 20 January 1951.
Sergeant		Ingram	Sid				A member of the Battalion shooting team.
2nd Lieutenant	407923	Ions	E.		Support	3" Mortar	The Border Regiment attached to The Royal Ulster Rifles.
Rifleman	22805335	Ireland	W.				Ex-Royal Inniskilling Fusiliers, The Royal Ulster Rifles in Korea, then to 1 King's 14 March 1953-23 June 1953.
Lance Corporal		Irvine					Ex-Royal Inniskilling Fusiliers Signal Platoon, attached.
Rifleman	7020094	Johnson	Desmond Henry				From Belfast. He was batman to Major Shaw. Died 4 January 1951 aged 28 years. Buried in UN Memorial Cemetery, Pusan, Korea, Plot 17, Row 4, Grave 722.
Lance Corporal	4032637	Johnson	F.				Initially listed as missing in *The Times*, 20 January 1951 then wounded in hospital, 27 January 1951.
Captain	103104	Johnson	V. de P.C.	MID			
Rifleman	1469658	Johnson	W.				
Corporal		Johnson	Y.				Wounded and listed in *The Times*, 20 January 1951.

Rank	Number	Surname	Forenames	Awards	Company	Platoon	Notes
Rifleman		Johnston					Ex-Royal Inniskilling Fusiliers Signal Platoon, attached.
Rifleman	3531681	Jones	E.				Listed in *The Times* as wounded, 20 January 1951.
Rifleman	22511812	Jones	H.				Captured 25 April 1951. Listed as missing in *The Times*, 3 May 1951 and then *The Times* as a POW, 10 November 1951.
Rifleman	14414293	Jones	Harold H.				Initially listed as missing 3/4 January 1951, later as date of death 29 June 1951, aged 26 years. Buried UN Memorial Cemetery, Pusan, Korea. Plot 70, Row 8, Grave 7831.
Rifleman	888356	Jones	L.				Captured 25 April 1951. Listed as missing in *The Times*, 3 May 1951 and then *The Times* as a POW, 13 October 1951.
Rifleman		Joyce			A		
Corporal		Joyce	K.				
Sergeant		Kane	R.		Support	Mortar	Mortar Fire Controller.
Lance Corporal		Karsley	S.				Listed as wounded in *The Times*, 3 May 1951.
Sergeant	14190918	Kavanagh	Lawrence				Missing presumed killed 4/5 January 1951, aged 33 years. Date of death recorded as 4 September 1951. No known grave, commemorated on the UN Wall of Remembrance, Pusan, Korea.
2nd Lieutenant		Kavanagh	P.J.G.				Royal Inniskilling Fusiliers attached to The Royal Ulster Rifles. Wounded 10 February 1951, listed in *The Times* as wounded 2 May 1951.
Rifleman	4468247	Kay	J.				Captured 25 April 1951.
Rifleman	4125575	Kay	J.				Captured 25 April 1951. Listed as missing then there are two J. Kay's reported as POW's – they may be the same person.
Sergeant		Keen	W.H.				The Essex Regiment attached to The Royal Ulster Rifles. Listed as wounded in *The Times*, 10 March 1951.
Lance Corporal		Keenan					Attached to Battalion HQ.
Rifleman		Keilty	David				From the Shankill Road, Belfast.

NOMINAL ROLL 283

Rank	Surname	Forenames	Number	Awards	Company	Platoon	Notes
Lance Corporal	Keith						Attached to Battalion HQ.
Rev	Kelly	J.G.M.					Church of Ireland Padre to the Battalion.
Rifleman	Kelly	L.J.	7043349				The Royal Inniskilling Fusiliers/Royal Irish Fusiliers attached to The Royal Ulster Rifles. Taken prisoner 4/5 January 1951.
Rifleman	Kelly	P.G.	22538854				Battle accident.
Private	Kelly	T.J.	5569911				The Gloucestershire Regiment attached to The Royal Ulster Rifles. Died from wounds 13 February 1951 from actions during the Battle of Hill 327, 16-20 February 1951. Buried UN Memorial Cemetery, Pusan, Korea, Plot 4, Row 1, Grave 114, aged 24.
Rifleman	Kelly	Tommy					From Liverpool.
Sergeant	Kennedy	Nat					From Belfast. Served in B Company; he was wounded on 24 March 1945. Later served as RSM to 6 RUR (TA) and in Korea.
Rifleman	Kennedy	Thomas	14187325				From Ligoniel. Killed in action, aged 25 years, 3 January 1951. No known grave. Commemorated on the UN Wall of Remembrance, Pusan, Korea.
Rifleman	Kerr	J.J.	6846356				Listed as missing in *The Times*, 20 January 1951 and then as a POW and finally as killed in action. Died, 19 July 1951, aged 35 years. No known grave. Commemorated on the UN Wall of Remembrance, Pusan, Korea.
Rifleman	Kewin	E.					Originally listed as missing, but subsequently found to be reported in error.
Sergeant	Killelea	Joseph Patrick	19030262				Ex-Royal Inniskilling Fusiliers, from County Roscommon attached to The Royal Ulster Rifles. GSM and MID for Malaya.
Sergeant	Killen				B		
Lance Corporal	King	A.	446395				Killed in action 3 January 1951, aged 21 years. Buried UN Memorial Cemetery, Pusan, Korea. Plot 23, Row 9, Grave 1647. Originally listed in *The Times* as a Private.

Rank	Number	Surname	Forenames	Awards	Company	Platoon	Notes
Private	14456265	King	D.W.				The Gloucestershire Regiment attached to The Royal Ulster Rifles. Died 25 April 1951 during the Battle of Imjin, 22-25 April 1951. Buried UN Memorial Cemetery, Pusan, Korea, Plot 17, Row 10, Grave 804, aged 23.
Corporal		Knight	J.				
Sergeant		Knight					
Rifleman		Knox	T.C.				The Royal Ulster Rifles attached to the King's Own Scottish Borderers. Listed as wounded in *The Times*, 17 November 1951.
Rifleman	22289439	Knox	Thomas Knox				From County Tyrone, he served in the Royal Inniskilling Fusiliers/The Royal Irish Fusiliers attached to The Royal Ulster Rifles. Wounded in action 20 November 1951.
Captain		Lane	J.B.		A		2 i/c of A Company, a prisoner of war.
Rifleman	3530122	Langan	J.				Captured 3 January 1951. Listed as missing in *The Times*, 20 January 1951 and then as POW, December 1951.
		Lannie	A.				
		Laverty	T.				
Rifleman	22219762	Lavery	C.				The Royal Inniskilling Fusiliers/The Royal Irish Fusiliers attached to The Royal Ulster Rifles. Wounded in action 17 July 1951. Reported to have been a POW.
Corporal	14187870	Lavery	Joseph S.		Support	Mortar	From Belfast, he married five days before leaving for the Far East. Captured 4/5 January 1951 whilst covering the retreat of the Royal Ulster Rifles with the Mortar Platoon. Listed as missing in *The Times*, 20 January 1951.
		Lavery	Tommy				From the Shankill Road, Belfast he was a Bugle Major.
Rifleman		Law	Samuel James				Listed as wounded in *The Times*, 2 May 1951.
Sergeant		Lawler			A		No 3 Section.

NOMINAL ROLL   285

Rank	Number	Surname	Forenames	Awards	Company	Platoon	Notes
Lieutenant		Lawlor					Ex-Royal Inniskilling Fusiliers, attached.
Inperpreter		Lee Kyung-Sik					Korean Interpreter for the Royal Ulster Rifles and later other British Regiments in Korea.
Sergeant	6983626	Lennon	Francis				The Royal Inniskilling Fusiliers/The Royal Irish Fusiliers attached to The Royal Ulster Rifles. Killed in action, 25 April 1951, aged 29 years. Buried UN Memorial Cemetery, Pusan, Korea. Plot 23, Row 8, Grave 1643.
Rifleman	22223925	Leolie	R.J.M.				Ex-Royal Inniskilling Fusiliers, attached.
Corporal	5383778	Lewis	J.O.				Buried UN Memorial Cemetery, Pusan, Korea, Plot 24, Row 6, Grave 1759, killed aged 31, 25 April 1951 during the Battle of Imjin, 22-25 April 1951. Killed in action, reported in *The Times*, 2 May 1951.
Rifleman		Lewis	'Taffy'				From Wales. He was a bandsman and medic.
Rifleman	4453504	Liddle	H.				Buried UN Memorial Cemetery, Pusan, Korea. Plot 17, Row 11, Grave 810. Killed 25 April 1951, aged 31, during the Battle of Imjin, 22-25 April 1951. Initially listed as missing but later as killed during the Battle of Imjin.
Rifleman	3393512	Liggett	W.H.				Captured 3 January 1951. Listed as missing in *The Times* 20 January 1951, then as a POW, 15 December 1951
Rifleman	926722	Lodge	Walter 'Wally'				From Speke, Liverpool. Captured 4/5 January 1951. Listed as missing in *The Times* 20 January 1951, then as a POW, 15 September 1951.
Captain	184753	Long					Ex-Royal Inniskilling Fusiliers, awarded MC in Italy, (LG 21.9.44). HQ British Commonwealth FMA 19 August 1951. Relinquished his commission and granted honorary rank of Captain.
		Long	H.				
Rifleman	21188152	Lorimer	Thomas W.				Brother of William Lorimer. From Ballymena. Captured 3 January 1951. Listed as missing in *The Times* 20 January 1951, then as a POW, 22 December 1951.

Rank	Number	Surname	Forenames	Awards	Company	Platoon	Notes
Corporal	7015373	Lorimer	William				Brother of Thomas Lorimer. From Ballymena. Buried UN Memorial Cemetery, Pusan, Korea, Plot 24, Row 1, Grave 1703. Killed 25 April 1951 aged 33 years, during the Battle of Imjin, 22-25 April 1951. Initially listed as missing but later as killed in action.
C/Sergeant		Lowry	S. 'Dekko'		A		CQMS of A Company, he had previously served with the 1st (Airborne) Battalion on Operation Varsity.
Rifleman	19046440	Lutton	W.T.				Ex-Royal Inniskilling Fusiliers attached to The Royal Ulster Rifles.
Rifleman		Lynch	William				From Falls Road, Belfast.
Rifleman	14465525	Lyons	E.B.				Died as a prisoner of war 1 August 1951 on or after, aged 26 years. No known grave. Commemorated on the UN Wall of Remembrance, Pusan, Korea.
Rifleman	3599032	MacCurrie	P.				Died as a prisoner of war, 26 February 1951, aged 34 years. No known grave. Commemorated on the UN Wall of Remembrance, Pusan, Korea. Listed as missing 4/5 January 1951 then as a POW.
Lieutenant	385955	MacNicol	Colin	MC	D		Awarded MC for his actions while patrolling with D Company over the Imjin.
Rifleman		Magee	J.				Originally listed as missing but subsequently re-joined.
Rifleman	21012612	Magill	Andrew				Captured 25 April 1951. Listed as missing in *The Times* 4 May 1951 and then as a POW, 13 October 1951.
Rifleman	22307155	Maguire	R.W.				Captured 4/5 January 1951. Listed as missing in *The Times* 20 January 1951 and then as a POW, 10 November 1951.
Rifleman	19033341	Maher	Daniel				From Tipperary. Enlisted in the Royal Inniskilling Fusiliers 7.10.46. Attached to The Royal Ulster Rifles, he was a brother of P. Maher. Missing presumed killed 25 April 1951. Other sources show him as missing presumed killed 28 September 1951. No known grave. Commemorated on the UN Wall

NOMINAL ROLL 287

Rank	Number	Surname	Forenames	Awards	Company	Platoon	Notes
Rifleman	22233423	Maher	P.		C		From Tipperary. Captured 25 April 1951. He was held in Camp 1, 'Chongsong'.
Captain		Major	C.J.				Served with The Royal Ulster Rifles.
Captain		Majury	James H.S.				Listed as missing in *The Times* 20 January 1951 then as a POW 25 August 1951. Later Major-General, Colonel of The Royal Irish Rangers.
Rifleman	22243439	Mallet	A.W.				The Royal Irish Fusiliers attached to The Royal Ulster Rifles. Captured 25 April 1951. Listed as missing in *The Times* 3 May 1951 then as a POW 13 October 1951.
Sergeant		Mann	Terry				From Worcestershire.
Corporal		Mark	S.				
Lieutenant		Marsh	H.J.		D		The South Lancashire Regiment (The Prince of Wales's Volunteers) attached to The Royal Ulster Rifles. Reported missing in *The Times*, 2 May 1951, then as a POW, 6 October 1951.
Rifleman	7043193	Martin	P.				Listed in *The Times*, 20 January 1951 as wounded. Later listed as missing in action 22 April 1951.
Rifleman	7014112	Martin	Robert				Missing presumed killed, 22 April 1951 during the Battle of Imjin, aged 31 years. No known grave. Commemorated on the UN wall of Remembrance, Pusan, Korea.
Lieutenant		Mason	J.		HQ		Assistant Signals Officer.
Lance Corporal		Massey	Richard F. 'Dick'		Support		From the Shankill Road, Belfast. Listed as missing in *The Times*, 3 May 1951.
Rifleman	22202796	Massey	W.				The Royal Irish Fusiliers attached to The Royal Ulster Rifles. Captured 3/4 January 1951.
Lance Corporal		Masters	G.C.				Originally wounded, later reported in *The Times* as missing, 20 January 1951, then as a POW, 23 June 1951.
							Listed as wounded in *The Times*, 20 January 1951.

Rank	Number	Surname	Forenames	Awards	Company	Platoon	Notes
Rifleman	7043323	May	Paddy				The Royal Inniskilling Fusiliers/The Royal Irish Fusiliers attached to The Royal Ulster Rifles. Captured 4/5 January 1951. Listed as missing in *The Times*, 20 January 1951 and later as a POW, 29 October 1951.
Rifleman		Mayne	Herbert				From Dublin, he joined the Regiment post-Second World War.
Rifleman	22257327	McAlonen	E.R.			Signals	Captured 25 April 1951. Listed as missing in *The Times*, 3 May 1951 and later as a POW, 29 September 1951. From Omagh, his father was Sergeant McAlonen, who served for 21 years with the Inniskillings and later with the USC.
Rifleman	14452927	McArdle	K.B.				From Belfast he had served as a paratrooper during the Second World War. Listed as wounded in *The Times*, 20 January 1951
Rifleman		McBurnley	W.				Listed as wounded in *The Times*, 2 May 1951.
Rifleman		McCaigue	T.P.				Listed as wounded in *The Times* 30 June 1951.
Rifleman	6980733	McCain	Robert John				From County Tyrone, enlisted in the Royal Inniskilling Fusiliers on 18 November 1939, to Army Reserve on 3 March 1947. Buried UN Memorial Cemetery, Pusan, Korea, Plot 24, Row 5, Grave 1745, aged 36 years. Killed during the Battle of Seoul, 2-4 January 1951.
T/Captain	365708	McCallan	Arthur J.		Support		Listed as wounded in *The Times*, 20 January 1951.
Rifleman	22213117	McCann	Tommy			MMG	From Shankill Road, Belfast. Captured 25 April 1951. Listed as missing in *The Times*, then later as a POW, 6 October 1951.
Rifleman	22287499	McCartan	John P.				He had served in the Royal Inniskilling Fusiliers but was transferred to the Royal Ulster Rifles in order to get to the Far East. Buried UN Memorial Cemetery, Pusan, Korea, Plot 17, Row 2, Grave 707, aged 22. Killed during the Battle of Imjin, 22-25 April 1951.
Rifleman		McClare	George				From Beersbridge Road.

NOMINAL ROLL 289

Rank	Number	Surname	Forenames	Awards	Company	Platoon	Notes
Rifleman	22511757	McClelland	S.J.				Listed as wounded in *The Times*, 20 January 1951.
Rifleman	6980303	McCloskey	Bernard James				From County Antrim. The Royal Inniskilling Fusiliers/The Royal Irish Fusiliers attached to The Royal Ulster Rifles. Suffered a battle accident 16 August 1951.
Rifleman	21187826	McCloskey	J.				Listed as wounded in *The Times*, 20 January 1951.
Rifleman		McColl	W.				Listed as wounded in *The Times*, 3 May 1951.
Rifleman	14190213	McConaghy	T.				From Belfast. Captured 3 January 1951. Listed as missing in *The Times*, 20 January 1951 and then later as a POW, 22 December 1951.
Corporal		McConnell	Mark		C	No.8	From County Antrim, he was the brother of Sergeant William 'Bill' McConnell.
Sergeant	7021702	McConnell	William 'Bill'		HQ's	MT Section	Later RSM of the 6th Battalion, The Royal Ulster Rifles. He was from County Antrim.
Corporal	7020064	McConnell	William John 'Tex'				From Ballyclare, he died from Beriberi while a POW. Buried UN Memorial Cemetery, Pusan, Korea. Plot 24, Row 5, Grave 1752, aged 28 years. Initially listed as missing in *The Times*, 20 January 1951 and later as killed in action during the Battle of Seoul 2-4 January 1951.
RSM	7010702	McConville	Andrew	DCM	D		From County Tyrone, enlisted in the Royal Inniskilling Fusiliers on 13 February 1928. He became RSM after the Imjin.
2nd Lieutenant	407952	McCord	Mervyn NS	MC	Batt HQ		A/Signals Officer. Awarded MC for his action in January 1951.
Rifleman	19036024	McCormick	R.J.				The Royal Irish Fusiliers attached to The Royal Ulster Rifles. Buried UN Memorial Cemetery, Pusan, Korea, Plot 17, Row 4, Grave 727, aged 22 years. Initially listed as missing in *The Times*, 20 January 1951 and later as killed in action during the Battle of Seoul 2-4 January 1951.

Rank	Number	Surname	Forenames	Awards	Company	Platoon	Notes
Rifleman	14471900	McCracken	Henry				Ex-Royal Inniskilling Fusiliers. Missing believed killed 25 April 1951. Buried UN Memorial Cemetery, Pusan, Korea, Plot 17, Row 12, Grave 824, aged 23 years.
L/Corporal	7014124	McCracken	R.J.				Missing presumed killed 4 January 1951, aged 31 year, during the Battle of Seoul 2-4 January 1951. Commemorated on the UN Wall of Remembrance, Pusan, Korea.
CSM		McCrory	Joe	BEM	A		Served in Normandy, the Ardennes and on 'Operation Varsity', during the Second World War where he was wounded four times and took command when Lieutenant Robertson was fatally wounded.
Sergeant		McCrory	Joe 'Bash On'				Battle accident.
Rifleman	22307864	McCullough	J.				Captured 4/5 January 1951. Listed as missing in *The Times*, 27 January 1951 and then as a POW, 13 October 1951.
Rifleman	22271585	McDonagh	J.				Listed as wounded in *The Times*, 3 May 1951.
Rifleman		McDonald	F.				Captured 25 April 1951. Listed as wounded in *The Times*, 3 May 1951.
Rifleman	4858994	McDonald	R.J.A.				Army Catering Corps attached to The Royal Ulster Rifles. Missing presumed killed 4 January 1951. No known grave. Commemorated on the UN Wall of Remembrance, Pusan, Korea.
Private	13111735	McDonnell	Patrick John				
		McDowell	W.J.				From County Londonderry, enlisted in the Royal Inniskilling Fusiliers at Omagh, to Army Reserve on 23 July 1946. Buried UN Memorial Cemetery, Pusan, Korea, Plot 24. Row 5, Grave 1747, aged 30 years. Killed 4 January 1951. Initially listed missing in *The Times*, 20 January 1951 and then killed in action, 8 September.
Corporal	6980078	McGeoghegan	Patrick				

Rank	Number	Surname	Forenames	Awards	Company	Platoon	Notes
Rifleman	14008061	McGivern	Thomas J.				From Belfast he had formerly served the first four years of his Army career in the Royal Irish Fusiliers. Buried UN Memorial Cemetery, Pusan, Korea, Plot 17, Row 3, Grave 719, aged 29. Died during the battle of Imjin, 22-25 April 1951.
Sergeant		McGoldrick	R.		A		
Rifleman	6980310	McGrath	Samuel				From Londonderry, ex-Royal Inniskilling Fusiliers, attached 5 November 1950 to 23 October 1951. The Royal Irish Fusiliers attached to The Royal Ulster Rifles. He was a prisoner of war during the Second World War. Captured 25 April 1951. Listed as missing in *The Times*, 3 May 1951, then as a POW, 13 October 1951.
Rifleman	14218381	McGuigan	John				He had served in the Royal Inniskilling Fusiliers in 1945, being demobbed in 1948. Rejoining in 1948 he was transferred to the Royal Ulster Rifles. Prior to enlistment he was employed as a machinist by James Mackie & Sons. Aged 24 years. Taken POW 3 January 1951. Listed as missing in *The Times*, 20 January 1951, then as a prisoner of war, 1 December 1951.
Rifleman	22271061	McHaffey	Thomas Beattie				Enlisted in 1948. Wounded in action 25 April 1951. Listed as wounded in *The Times*, 3 May 1951.
		McIlvar	J.				
Corporal	22034304	McIntyre	J.				From Belfast, he served throughout the Second World War, being recalled to the Colours, September 1950. Aged 29 years and attached to the Royal Ulster Rifles from the Gloucestershire Regiment he was killed in action.
Rifleman		McKee	Henry				
Rifleman		McKenna	H.				Listed as wounded in *The Times*, 2 May 1951.

292 A NEW BATTLEFIELD

Rank	Number	Surname	Forenames	Awards	Company	Platoon	Notes
Rifleman	22275061	McKenzie	Samuel				From County Tyrone, enlisted in The Royal Inniskilling Fusiliers 22 March 1949. Then Royal Irish Fusiliers attached to The Royal Ulster Rifles. Captured 4/5 January 1951. Listed as missing in *The Times*, 20 January 1951, then as a POW 29 September 1951.
Rifleman		McKeown	Alex				From Belfast he was sent out as part of reinforcements to the Royal Ulster Rifles.
Corporal		McKeown	P.				From Holywood.
Piper		McKerr			Band		
Fusilier?		McKie	J.				Listed as wounded in *The Times*, 19 May 1951.
Rifleman		McKinley	G.				Listed as wounded in *The Times*, 2 May 1951.
		McKinley	J.M.				From County Fermanagh, an ex-Royal Inniskilling Fusilier, he had enlisted on 22 February 1950. Listed as wounded in *The Times*, 20 January 1951.
Rifleman	22308423	McKinley	Thomas James				From Muff in County Donegal.
		McKinney	Lawrence				From County Donegal, enlisted in the Royal Inniskilling Fusiliers on 17 November 1945.
Rifleman	14475306	McLaughlin	C.				Captured 25 April 1951. Listed as wounded in *The Times*, 3 May 1951, then as a POW, 29 September 1951
Rifleman		McLean	W.J.				Listed as wounded in *The Times*, 3 February 1951.
Rifleman		McLoghlin	R.F.				Listed as wounded in *The Times*, 2 May 1951.
Rifleman		McLoughlin	C.				From Castlefin, County Donegal.
		McMeekin	J.				
Rifleman	22307082	McMillan	Frederick				Captured 25 April 1951. Listed as missing in *The Times*, 3 May 1951, then as a POW, 13 October 1951.
Rifleman	22233425	McMullan	J.				Captured 3 January 1951. Listed as missing in *The Times*, 27 January 1951, then as a POW, 13 October 1951.

NOMINAL ROLL

Rank	Number	Surname	Forenames	Awards	Company	Platoon	Notes
NCO	19032664	McNabb	Andrew 'Andy'				From County Londonderry, ex-Royal Inniskilling Fusiliers/ Royal Irish Fusiliers attached to The Royal Ulster Rifles. Taken prisoner 4/5 January 1951. Listed in *The Times* as missing, 20 January 1951. A former heavyweight boxer, he had fought Henry Cooper as an amateur.
Rifleman	22305359	McNally	J.N.				Captured 4/5 January 1951. Listed as missing in *The Times*, 20 January 1951, then as a POW. Later returned.
Rifleman		McNamara	M.				The Royal Ulster Rifles, attached to King's Shropshire Light Infantry. Listed as wounded in *The Times*, 8 December 1951.
Rifleman	22538966	McNamara	M.				The Royal Irish Fusiliers attached to The Royal Ulster Rifles. Wounded in action 17 November 1951.
Rifleman	22243062	McNaughton	A.J.				Buried UN Memorial Cemetery, Pusan, Korea, Plot 24, Row 4, Grave 1734, aged 25 years. Initially listed as missing then killed in action, 23 April during the Battle of Imjin 22-25 April 1951.
Rifleman	22511803	McShane	J.J.	MID			Initially listed as missing, The Time, 20 January 1951 then as killed in action during the Battle of Seoul 2-4 January 1951. Buried UN Memorial Cemetery, Pusan, Korea, Plot 17, Row 5, Grave 744, aged 31 years.
Rifleman	6980027	McSherry	Michael				
Rifleman	22526893	McWhirter	Spencer				Missing presumed killed 4/5 January 1951. Also recorded as killed 12 April 1951. No known grave. Commemorated on the UN Wall of Remembrance, Pusan, Korea.
Rifleman	7043191	McWilliams	W.				
Rifleman	5733709	Meanley	A.J.				Captured 4/5 January 1951. Listed as missing in *The Times*, 20 January 1951.
Rifleman	22219701	Megoran	J.				Captured 4/5 January 1951. Listed as missing in *The Times*, 27 January 1951.

Rank	Number	Surname	Forenames	Awards	Company	Platoon	Notes
		Mehaffy					
Rifleman	22511863	Mellor	J.B.				Captured 25 April 1951. Listed as missing in *The Times*, 3 May 1951 then as a POW, 13 October 1951.
Rifleman	21012524	Mercer	William B.				Captured 25 April 1951. Listed as missing in *The Times*, 3 May 1951 then as a POW, 13 October 1951.
Major		Miller	Dickie				
Captain		Miller	H.D.		B		Listed as wounded in *The Times*, 3 May 1951.
		Milligan	H.				
Corporal		Mills	W.				
Rifleman	21023448	Mitchell	David George				Ex-Royal Inniskilling Fusiliers, from County Tyrone, enlisted on 12 August 1947. Captured 4/5 January 1951. Listed as a POW in *The Times*, 4 January 1951 then later released, April 1953.
Lieutenant		Mole	John J.	MID	A	1	Commanded No 1 Platoon, A Company, awarded MID.
Lieutenant		Monro	J.		D		
Rifleman	19035551	Montgomery	P.				The Royal Irish Fusiliers attached to The Royal Ulster Rifles. Taken prisoner 25 April 1951. Listed as missing in *The Times*, 3 May 1951.
Rifleman	22511786	Montgomery	Samuel				From Londonderry, ex-Royal Inniskilling Fusilier. Missing presumed killed during the Battle of Imjin, 22-25 April 1951, aged 25 years. No known grave. Commemorated on the UN Wall of Remembrance, Pusan, Korea.
Rifleman	19030033	Mooney	Andrew F.				From Belfast, aged 24 years. Captured 25 April 1951. Listed as missing in *The Times*, 3 May 1951, then as a POW, 6 October 1951.
2nd Lieutenant		Moore	B.				The Royal Norfolk Regiment attached to The Royal Ulster Rifles. Listed as wounded in *The Times*, 12 July 1951.

Rank	Number	Surname	Forenames	Awards	Company	Platoon	Notes
Rifleman	3712482	Moore	F.				Captured 3 January 1951. Listed as missing in *The Times*, 20 January 1951, then as a POW, 8 December 1951.
Rifleman		Moore	J.				Listed as wounded in *The Times*, 10 March 1951.
		Moore	T.A.				
Corporal	6980318	Moore	William Alexander	MM			Awarded the Military Medal for action in Sicily (LG 18.11.43). Buried in UN Memorial Cemetery, Pusan, Korea, Plot 17, Row 4, Grave 729, aged 35 years. Originally listed as missing in *The Times*, 20 January 1951, then as killed in action 4 January, during the Battle of Seoul 2-4 January 1951.
		Moorsom					The Royal Inniskilling Fusiliers attached to the Royal Ulster Rifles from April 1951.
Rifleman	7043376	Morgan	P.				The Royal Irish Fusiliers attached to The Royal Ulster Rifles. Taken prisoner 4/5 January 1951. Listed as missing in *The Times*, 20 January 1951.
Rifleman		Morris			A		The Gloucestershire Regiment attached to The Royal Ulster Rifles. Buried UN Memorial Cemetery, Pusan, Korea, Plot 24, Row 2, Grave 1713, aged 19 years. Originally reported missing in action, subsequently confirmed killed in action 25 April during the Battle of Imjin, 22-25 April 1951.
Private	22315901	Morris	D.G.				
Lieutenant		Morrison	R.O.C.		A		A Company from October 1951.
		Morrow	A.				
Rifleman	3712359	Moxham	F.				Captured 4/5 January 1951. Listed as missing in *The Times*, 20 January 1951, then as a POW, 15 September 1951.
Rifleman	22203111	Mulhall	C.				Buried UN Memorial Cemetery, Pusan, Korea, Plot 70, Row 11, Grave 7867, aged 26 years. Listed as missing during the Battle of Imjin 22-25 April 1951 but as he has a grave presumably his body was found.
Lance Corporal		Mulholland					Attached to Battalion HQ.

Rank	Number	Surname	Forenames	Awards	Company	Platoon	Notes
Rifleman	19038016	Mullahey	J.V.				The Royal Irish Fusiliers attached to The Royal Ulster Rifles. Suffered battle accident 24 August 1951.
Rifleman	22219421	Mullan	Samuel Bill				Missing presumed killed during the Battle of Imjin, 22-25 April 1951, aged 19 years. No known grave. Commemorated on the UN Wall of Remembrance, Pusan, Korea.
Rifleman	22204254	Mullen	J.				The Royal Irish Fusiliers attached to The Royal Ulster Rifles. Wounded in action 15 June 1951. Listed as wounded in *The Times*, 30 June 1951
Rifleman	22002307	Mulligan	B.A.				Buried UN Memorial Cemetery, Pusan, Korea, Plot 17, Row 11, Grave 816, aged 22 years. Listed as missing during the Battle of Imjin, 22-25 April 1951 but as he has a grave presumably his body was found.
Major		Mulligan	J.H.W.		B		Company Commander.
Corporal		Mulligan	Joe			MT	
Rifleman	21126705	Murray	C.C.				Buried UN Memorial Cemetery, Pusan, Korea, Plot 17, Row 5, Grave 742, aged 21. Initially listed as missing then killed during the Battle of Seoul 2-4 January 1951.
Rifleman	19034072	Murray	G.				The Royal Irish Fusiliers attached to The Royal Ulster Rifles. Taken prisoner 19 June 1951. Listed as missing in *The Times*, 7 July 1951.
Rifleman	6983997	Murray	James William				Aged 34 years, ex-Royal Inniskilling Fusiliers, missing presumed killed during the Battle of Seoul, 2-4 January 1951. No known grave. Commemorated on the UN Wall of Remembrance, Pusan, Korea.
Corporal		Murray	Joe			MT	
Corporal		Murray	Tom			MT	From Wiltshire.
Rifleman		Neehan	F.				Listed as wounded in *The Times*, 3 May 1951.
Major	203156	Neely	K.	MBE	Support		Signals Officer.

NOMINAL ROLL

Rank	Number	Surname	Forenames	Awards	Company	Platoon	Notes
Rifleman	22306116	Neeson	P.				The Royal Irish Fusiliers attached to The Royal Ulster Rifles. Taken prisoner 25 April 1951. Listed as missing in *The Times*, 3 May 1951.
Rifleman	22511833	Nelder	J.				Captured 25 April 1951. Listed as missing in *The Times*, 3 May 1951, then as a POW, 13 October 1951.
Rifleman		Nesbitt	Thomas				Wounded in both legs.
Rifleman	22511802	Newman	A.J.				Buried UN Memorial Cemetery, Pusan, Korea, Plot 17, Row 4, Grave 728, aged 27. Initially listed as missing then killed in action during the Battle of Seoul 2-4 January 1951.
Rifleman	22337903	Newport	John Frederick	MM			
Rifleman	3450092	Newton	L.				Listed as wounded in *The Times*, 20 January 1951.
		Nichols	A.				
Lieutenant		Nicolls	V.M.C. 'Max'		C		Listed as missing in *The Times*, 2 May 1951, then as a POW, 17 November 1951. He was held in Camp 1, 'Chongsong'. He had remained behind with the wounded in April.
Major		Nixon	Sir Christopher J.	Bart MC MID			Reported as wounded twice in *The Times*, 10 March and 2 May 1951.
Rifleman		Norman	R.				Initially reported in *The Times* as missing, 3 May 1951 but corrected to wounded 12 May 1951.
Sergeant	7013525	Nugent	Frank				Served with the Airborne Division during the Second World War. Missing presumed died 18 April 1951 whilst a POW, aged 28 years. No known grave. Commemorated on the UN Wall of Remembrance, Pusan, Korea.
Rifleman	22511859	Oakley	S.				Captured April 1951. Listed as missing in *The Times*, 3 May 1951, then as a prisoner of war, 13 October 1951.
Rifleman	3530903	Oates	H.				Captured 4/5 January 1951. Listed as missing in *The Times*, 20 January 1951.

298 A NEW BATTLEFIELD

Rank	Number	Surname	Forenames	Awards	Company	Platoon	Notes
Father		O'Brien	Jack				Served as the Battalion Roman Catholic Padre, from Normandy to the Baltic and later in Palestine. Killed by the North Koreans in Tiajom in October 1950.
Rifleman	19031778	O'Connor	T.A.				The Royal Irish Fusiliers attached to The Royal Ulster Rifles. Captured 25 April 1951. Listed as missing in *The Times*, 3 May 1951, then as a POW, 13 October 1951.
Lance Corporal		O'Connor	W.				Listed as wounded in *The Times*, 2 May 1951.
		O'Donnell	Daniel				From County Donegal.
Rifleman	22202007	O'Gorman	J.				Buried UN Memorial Cemetery, Pusan, Korea, Plot 4, Row 3, Grave 139, died 19 February 1951 aged 21 years.
Rifleman	7014134	O'Hanlon	Felix				Ex-Royal Inniskilling Fusiliers and Lancashire Fusiliers. Captured 3 January 1951. Listed as missing in *The Times*, 20 January 1951, then as a POW, 22 December 1951.
Sergeant	14456352	O'Hara	William Patrick Michael				From London he was a member of the Battle Patrol. Captured 4/5 January 1951. Listed as missing in *The Times*, 20 January 1951. After the war he was decorated for his actions whilst a POW.
Rifleman		O'Kane	Henry				From Londonderry, ex-Royal Inniskilling Fusilier.
Rifleman	19046591	O'Kane	Henry				From Londonderry, ex-General Service Corps and Royal Inniskilling Fusilier. Captured 25 April 1951. Listed as missing in *The Times*, 3 May 1951, then as a POW, 13 October 1951.
Corporal		O'Neill	E.J.				Listed as wounded in *The Times*, 2 May 1951.
Corporal		O'Neill	J.				
Corporal		O'Reilly			A		
CSM		Orr	C.		HQ		From Belfast.

NOMINAL ROLL

Rank	Number	Surname	Forenames	Awards	Company	Platoon	Notes
Rifleman	19041502	Orr	Joseph				The son of a Rifleman from County Londonderry, he served in the Royal Inniskilling Fusiliers/The Royal Irish Fusiliers attached to The Royal Ulster Rifles. Captured 25 April 1951. Listed as missing in *The Times*, 3 May 1951. Reported as POW 17 November 1951. He was the first British solider to survive the notorious 'death house' at Camp 1, "Chongsong".
Rifleman	3712417	Ostle	T.				Buried in UN Memorial Cemetery, Pusan, Korea, Plot 17, Row 4, Grave 721, aged 29 years. Died during the Battle of Seoul 2-4 January 1951.
2nd Lieutenant	414936	Owen	D.G.				From Sandhurst to the Royal Inniskilling Fusiliers and then directly to The Royal Ulster Rifles in Korea. Later served with the King's Own Scottish Borderers, relinquished his commission on 1 July 1959.
Rifleman	22203926	Palmer	T.C.				Ex-Royal Inniskilling Fusiliers, attached.
Rifleman	22246875	Parker	J.				Captured 4/5 January 1951. Listed a missing in *The Times*, 20 January 1951, then as a POW, 29 October 1951.
Rifleman	3393930	Parkinson	F.				Battle accident.
Rifleman	3606891	Parkinson	S.				Captured 25 April 1951. Listed as missing in *The Times*, 3 May 1951, then as a POW, 13 October 1951.
Rifleman		Partlow	D.				Listed as wounded in *The Times*, 10 March 1951.
RSM		Patterson	Alex				Reported as a POW.
Rifleman	22787011	Patterson	Thomas Alexander				From County Tyrone, enlisted in the Royal Inniskilling Fusiliers on 14.12.1951. Later served with the King's Regiment.
Rifleman		Patterson	W.				From Belfast he was sent out as part of reinforcements for the Battalion.
Rifleman	4389335	Payne	H.				Captured 4/5 January 1951. Listed as missing in *The Times* 20 January 1951, then as a POW, 16 June 1951.

Rank	Number	Surname	Forenames	Awards	Company	Platoon	Notes
Rifleman	3772061	Peach	E.				The Royal Irish Fusiliers attached to The Royal Ulster Rifles. Taken prisoner 3 January 1951.
Corporal		Pearce	'Dutchey'				Served on the North-West Frontier 1935-37 and North-West Europe 1944-45, retired in the 1960s as a CQMS.
Corporal		Phillips	E.				Prisoner of war.
Corporal		Pierce	F.J.				Listed as wounded in *The Times*, 20 January 1951.
Lieutenant	376162	Pigot	E.W.		Batt HQ		The Royal Irish Fusiliers attached to The Royal Ulster Rifles. A/Adjutant.
Rifleman	468637	Pinder	C.A.				Captured 4/5 January 1951. Listed as missing in *The Times*, 20 January 1951.
Rifleman	5587159	Plant	S.F.				Buried UN Memorial Cemetery, Pusan, Korea, Plot 17, Row 4, Grave 726, aged 29 years. Initially listed as missing then killed in action during the Battle of Seoul 2-4 January 1951.
Sergeant		Platt			B		
Rifleman	6980391	Plews	Ernest	MID			The Royal Inniskilling Fusiliers attached to the Royal Ulster Rifles, he came from County Londonderry.
Rifleman		Pole	E.I.A.				Listed as wounded in *The Times*, 3 May 1951.
Rifleman	6206665	Pollard	W.G.				Captured 4/5 January 1951. Listed as missing, then as a POW, later finally released.
Rifleman	19030458	Pollock	George				From Belfast. Reported as wounded twice in *The Times*, 20 January and 10 March 1951.
Rifleman	3857019	Porter	E.				Captured 25 April 1951, later released under the Communist 'Leniency Policy'.
Rifleman	6979710	Porter	James				Ex-Royal Inniskilling Fusiliers. Missing presumed killed during the Battle of Imjin, 22-25 April 195, aged 32 years. No known grave. Commemorated on the UN Wall of Remembrance, Pusan, Korea. Served with the Inniskillings during the Second World War and was taken prisoner at Dunkirk. Interned in Stalag XXA.

NOMINAL ROLL 301

Rank	Number	Surname	Forenames	Awards	Company	Platoon	Notes
Rifleman		Porter	R.				Captured 6 January 1951 and repatriated 24 April 1951.
Captain		Porter	T.A.		HQ		HQ Company from October 1951.
Lieutenant	413609	Potts	Gordon L	MID	A	No.1	Ex-Royal Inniskilling Fusiliers. Served in Malaya with the Devons, GSM and later in Kenya. AGSM. Served with the Kenya Police and 7th King's African Rifles.
Rifleman		Pratt	J.				
2nd Lieutenant	P/403657	Prescott-Westcar	George Villiers Beeston				Buried UN Memorial Cemetery, Pusan, Korea, Plot 17, Row 5, Grave 740, aged 21 years. Initially listed as missing then killed in action during the Battle of Seoul, 2-4 January 1951.
Lance Corporal	3653860	Prior	R.				Captured 25 April 1951. Listed as missing in *The Times*, 3 May 1951, then as a POW, 29 September 1951.
Rifleman	3600500	Pritt	W.R.				Captured 25 April 1951. Listed as missing in *The Times*, 3 May 1951, then as a POW, 29 September 1951.
Lieutenant		Proctor	E.				
Rifleman	4546937	Quinn	A.T.E.				Captured 4/5 January 1951. Listed as missing in *The Times*, 20 January 1951, then as a POW, 23 June 1951.
Rifleman	22511761	Rainey	J.				Buried UN Memorial Cemetery, Pusan, Korea, Plot 17, Row 6, Grave 756, aged 26 years. Initially listed as missing then killed in action during the Battle of Seoul, 2-4 January 1951.
Colour Sergeant		Rainey	R.	MM			CQMS in HQ Company.
Rifleman	22307187	Ramsay	Charles				From Londonderry. The Royal Irish Fusiliers attached to The Royal Ulster Rifles. Killed 3/4 January 1951. Buried UN Memorial Cemetery, Pusan, Korea, Plot 24, Row 5, Grave 1749, aged 20 years.
Sergeant	7021349	Rankin	S.J.H.				Ex-Royal Inniskilling Fusiliers. Reported as missing in action, January 1951, but later re-joined.
Rifleman	6143268	Rea	R.				Listed as wounded in *The Times*, 20 January 1951.

Rank	Number	Surname	Forenames	Awards	Company	Platoon	Notes
Rifleman	19044697	Regan	D.				The Royal Irish Fusiliers attached to The Royal Ulster Rifles. Wounded in action 17 July 1951. Listed as wounded in *The Times*, 4 August 1951.
Rifleman	6979786	Reidy	Michael				Ex-Royal Inniskilling Fusiliers. Missing presumed killed, 2 August 1951, aged 31 years. No known grave. Commemorated in the UN Wall of Remembrance, Pusan, Korea.
Rifleman	3387588	Reynolds	F.				Captured 4/5 January 1951. Listed as missing in *The Times*, 20 January 1951 then as a POW, 13 October 1951.
Major	62664	Rickcord	G.P.	DSO American Silver Star	Batt HQ		Served in Normandy, the Ardennes and on Operation 'Varsity'. He was wounded in action but continued to command his Company. He commanded the 1st Battalion post-Second World War in Palestine, being awarded the DSO in 1945. This was followed by command of the 6th Airborne Division Battle School, before a return to Palestine as CO of the 3rd Parachute Battalion. Between Palestine and going to Korea, he held appointments GSO2 HQ N. Ireland District and Brigade Major, 107 (Ulster) Independent Infantry Brigade Group (TA). Served in Korea from January 1951, when he took over as 2 i/c after the death of Tony Blake.
Rifleman	3856991	Riding	G.				Missing presumed killed during the Battle of Imjin, 22-25 April 1951 aged 30 years. No known grave. Commemorated on the UN Wall of Remembrance, Pusan, Korea.
Rifleman		Riley	T.				Listed in *The Times* as wounded, 2 May 1951.
Rifleman	21182664	Ritchie	George				The Royal Inniskilling Fusiliers/The Royal Irish Fusiliers attached to The Royal Ulster Rifles. Captured 25 April 1951. Listed as missing in *The Times*, 2 May 1951 then as POW, 6 October 1951.
Lance Corporal		Robb	D.L.				Listed as wounded in *The Times*, 20 January 1951.
Rifleman	6914267	Roberts	R.F.				Captured 3 January 1951. Listed as missing in *The Times*, 20 January 1951, then as a POW, later

NOMINAL ROLL

Rank	Number	Surname	Forenames	Awards	Company	Platoon	Notes
Rifleman	2232083	Robinson	Samuel				Died as a prisoner of war, 4 July 1951. Buried UN Memorial Cemetery, Pusan, Korea, Plot 70, Row 7, Grave 7813, aged 20 years. Listed as missing in *The Times*, 20 January 1951 then as a POW.
Rifleman	3655149	Robinson	W.H.				Captured 25 April 1951. Listed as missing in *The Times*, 4 May 1951.
Rifleman	14403852	Robshaw	J.				The Royal Irish Fusiliers attached to The Royal Ulster Rifles. Captured 25 April 1951. Listed as missing in *The Times*, 3 May 1951, then as a POW, 13 October 1951.
Rifleman	22522036	Ross	E.				The Royal Irish Fusiliers attached to The Royal Ulster Rifles. Captured 25 April 1951. Listed as missing in *The Times*, 3 May 1951, then as a POW, 13 October 1951.
Father		Ryan					Roman Catholic Padre to the Battalion.
Rifleman		Ryan	A.C.				Listed as wounded in *The Times*, 2 May 1951.
Major		Ryan	M.D.G.C. 'Joe'	MBE			Commanded A Company. Listed as missing in *The Times*, 20 January 1951 then as a POW, 25 August 1951. He was decorated after the war for actions whilst being a POW. Post-war joined the church.
Rifleman	22204446	Ryan	P.				Captured 3 January 1951. Listed as missing in *The Times*, 20 January 1951 then as a POW, 8 December 1951.
Rifleman		Sainsbury	G.		A		Wounded in action, shrapnel to groin and left hand.
Rifleman		Schofield					
		Scully					
Rifleman	7014292	Shannon	James				A Reservist from Ballymena, County Antrim. Buried UN Memorial Cemetery, Pusan, Korea, Plot 17, Row 4, Grave 732, aged 30 years. Initially listed as missing in *The Times*, 20 January 1951, then as killed in action during the Battle of Seoul, 2-4 January 1951.
Rifleman	14412324	Shaw	A.				Captured 25 April 1951. Listed as missing in *The Times*, 3 May 1951, then as a POW, 29 September 1951.

Rank	Number	Surname	Forenames	Awards	Company	Platoon	Notes
Major	P/69180	Shaw	John Kirkpatrick Hay	DSO MC	Support		Born at Simla, India, on 23 October 1916, he was educated at Boxgrave Preparatory School and Malvern College. He passed through Sandhurst and was commissioned into the Regiment in 1936. The following year he was posted to the 1st Battalion at Rawalpindi and saw service on the North-West Frontier. On 1 April 1940, he was promoted to Captain and returned to the UK with the Battalion. He married Marian Maud Wray of Harpenden and they had three children. In 1941 he transferred to the 18th Battalion, Royal Fusiliers and saw action with Paiforce in Iraq. When the Battalion was converted to the 100 Light Anti Aircraft Regiment he was promoted to Acting Major in December 1941. A desire for a more active role saw him accompanying 'Trotsky' Davies to Force 133 in the Mediterranean and Albania, where he was awarded the Military Cross. Later still he was part of Force 136 in Burma where he remained until the surrender of the Japanese. After a spell in England he accompanied the advance party to Korea in October 1950 as part of the 29 Independent Infantry Brigade. He was awarded the DSO as a result of his gallant leadership and bravery when bringing out the remnants of the Battalion after it had been ambushed by the Chinese to the north of Seoul on the night of 3–4 January 1951. On 25 April 1951, at the height of the Imjin River battle the Battalion was ordered to withdraw and during this time Major Shaw received a fatal wound. His body was not recovered for some weeks. Buried UN Memorial Cemetery, Pusan, Korea, Plot 24, Row 1, Grave 1701, aged 34. Initially listed as missing in *The Times*, 2 May 1951, then killed in action.
Rifleman	22274708	Shaw	J.W.				Captured 4/5 January 1951. Listed as missing in *The Times*, 20 January 1951, then as a POW, 13 October 1951.

Rank	Number	Surname	Forenames	Awards	Company	Platoon	Notes
Lieutenant	406701	Shaw-Stewart	Houston Mark	MC	A		Wounded in action.
Rifleman	6979731	Shelly	Roy				Ex-Royal Inniskilling Fusiliers, captured 3 January 1951.
Rifleman		Shelly or Shelley	A.				Listed as missing in *The Times*, 20 January 1951 then as a POW, 8 December 1951.
Lance Corporal	4130452	Shields	W.				Captured 25 April 1951. Listed as missing in *The Times*, 3 May 1951, then as a POW, 6 October 1951. Buried UN Memorial Cemetery, Pusan, Korea, Plot 17, Row 12, Grave 818, aged 19 years.
Rifleman	22372596	Short	L.				Initially listed as missing in *The Times*, 3 May 1951 then as killed in action during the Battle of Imjin, 22-25 April 1951.
Rifleman		Shute	J.F.				Listed as wounded in *The Times*, 2 May 1951.
Sergeant		Simpson	Jack				From Falls Road, Belfast.
Captain		Sinclair	R.H.S.	MID			
Rifleman	6980298	Sinclair	Robert				Ex-Royal Inniskilling Fusiliers, attached from 5 November 1950 to 31 January 1951.
Rifleman	21012085	Sinclair	William				From Belfast, he was married a week before leaving for Korea. Listed as wounded in *The Times*, 20 January 1951.
Rifleman	6980926	Sloan	Edward				Ex-Royal Inniskilling Fusiliers, attached. Previously served with the Cameronians and Royal Scots Fusiliers.
Rifleman	21038124	Small	A.S.				Captured 4/5 January 1951. Listed as wounded in *The Times*, 20 January 1951.
Rifleman		Smith	E.				Wounded in action by gunshot.
Rifleman		Smith	E.R.				Listed as wounded in *The Times*, 10 February 1951.
Rifleman		Smith	F.A.				
Rifleman	4748240	Smith	G.W.				Captured 4/5 January 1951. Listed as missing in *The Times*, 20 January 1951.

Rank	Number	Surname	Forenames	Awards	Company	Platoon	Notes
Rifleman	3857001	Smith	H.				Captured 4/5 January 1951. Listed as missing in *The Times*, 20 January 1951 then as a POW, 29 October 1951.
Lance Corporal	3909362	Smith	J.				Buried UN Memorial Cemetery, Pusan, Korea, Plot 24, Row 6, Grave 1760. Killed 25 April 1951, aged 30 years.
Rifleman		Smith	L.				Listed as wounded in *The Times*, 2 May 1951.
Lance Corporal		Smith	R.				Listed as wounded in *The Times*, 20 January 1951.
Lance Corporal	5437816	Smith	Reginald A.				Missing presumed killed 18 July 1951, aged 30 years. No known grave. Commemorated on the UN Wall of Remembrance, Pusan, Korea.
Captain	333558	Smith	Tom P.	MID	Batt HQ	QM	Quartermaster.
Lance Corporal	14191501	Spence	John 'Jack', 'Blind'				From Ballycastle. Captured 4/5 January 1951. Listed as missing in *The Times*, 20 January 1951. He suffered from blindness as a side effect of vitamin deficiency whilst a POW.
Rifleman	3654393	Spencer	E.F.				Captured 4/5 January 1951. Listed as missing in *The Times*, 20 January 1951, then as a POW, then released.
Rifleman	21128738	Spiers	Christopher		B		From County Antrim, he was ex-Royal Inniskilling Fusiliers. He was a Bren gunner. The Royal Inniskilling Fusiliers/Royal Irish Fusiliers attached to The Royal Ulster Rifles.
Rifleman	14471989	Spiers	Thomas James				Captured 25 April 1951. Listed as missing in *The Times*, 3 May 1951, then as a POW, 13 October 1951. From County Antrim, Prisoner of War at Camp No 1, North Korea, brother of Rifleman Christopher Spiers.
Lieutenant		Squires	R.F.				
Lieutenant		St.C.Alcock	B.		C		He was 2 i/c of the battle patrol.
Sergeant		Stafford			B		
Sergeant		Stafford	Jimmy		B		He was on the Battalion shooting team.

NOMINAL ROLL

Rank	Number	Surname	Forenames	Awards	Company	Platoon	Notes
Rifleman	14471238	Stephens	W.J.				The Royal Irish Fusiliers attached to The Royal Ulster Rifles. Captured 4/5 January 1951. Listed as missing in *The Times*, 20 January 1951, then as a POW, 22 September 1951.
		Stevens	W.				
Rifleman	21181083	Stevenson	J.				Captured 4/5 January 1951. Listed as missing in *The Times*, 30 January 1951.
Sergeant		Steward	J.		D		Listed as wounded in *The Times*, 2 May 1951. From Belfast.
Rifleman		Stewart	R.				
Rifleman	22233418	Stewart	S.				Captured 25 April 1951. Listed a missing in *The Times*, 12 May 1951.
Rifleman	22352068	Stoner	B.				Listed as wounded in *The Times*, 2 May 1951.
Rifleman	864660	Street	W.				Captured 4/5 January 1951. Listed as missing in *The Times*, 20 January 1951.
Rifleman	1712407	Stroner	W.				Captured 25 April 1951. Listed as missing in *The Times*, 3 May 1951, then as a POW, 13 October 1951.
C/Sergeant		Sturgeon	Tommy		Support		
Porter		Suk Bum Yoon					
Rifleman	22308131	Sullivan	J.				Captured 4/5 January 1951. Listed as missing in *The Times*, 20 January 1951.
Rifleman	3856975	Sutton	W.				Missing presumed killed 11 March 1951, aged 33 years. No known grave. Commemorated on the UN Wall of Remembrance, Pusan, Korea.
Lance Corporal		Sweeney					Attached to Battalion HQ.
Rifleman	22247149	Sweeney	A.				Ex-Royal Inniskilling Fusiliers.
Lance Corporal		Sweetlove	Norman			Signals	Attached to Battalion HQ.
Rifleman	5449284	Swindells	V.				Captured 4/5 January 1951. Listed as missing in *The Times*, 20 January 1951 then as a POW, 6 October 1951.

Rank	Number	Surname	Forenames	Awards	Company	Platoon	Notes
Rifleman	14470450	Taggart	A.				The Royal Irish Fusiliers attached to The Royal Ulster Rifles. Captured 4/5 January 1951. Listed as missing in *The Times*, 20 January 1951 then as a POW, 22 September 1951.
Rifleman	5674078	Tague	G.				Listed as wounded in *The Times*, 20 January 1951.
Rifleman		Tailor	J.				
Sergeant		Talbot					
Rifleman	5726316	Tanner	L.G.				Captured 3 January 1951. Listed as missing in *The Times*, 20 January then as a POW, 1 December 1951.
Corporal		Taylor	J.				Royal Army Medical Corps, missing presumed POW.
Lieutenant	379573	Terry	M.J.		Support	MMG	The Royal Irish Fusiliers attached to The Royal Irish Fusiliers.
Lance Corporal	22264498	Thomson	A.J.				Listed as wounded in *The Times*, 19 May 1951.
Rifleman	14417408	Tice	A.E.				Listed as missing presumed killed 28 May 1951, aged 30 years. No known grave. Commemorated on the UN Wall of Remembrance, Pusan, Korea.
Rifleman	3864530	Timmons	H.				Listed as wounded in *The Times*, 20 January 1951.
Rifleman	3655385	Tompson	W.H.				Captured 25 April 1951. Listed as missing in *The Times*, 3 May 1951.
Rifleman	21187572	Tosh	George Earl				Ex-Royal Inniskilling Fusilier from County Londonderry. Listed as wounded in *The Times*, 20 January 1951.
CSM		Towler	T.		C		
Rifleman	3857105	Traynor	R.				Captured 4/5 January 1951.
Rifleman		Traynor	T.				Listed as missing in *The Times*, 20 January 1951, then as POW 6 October 1951.
Lieutenant	402905	Trevor Roper	Anthony Dacre	MC	B	5	Awarded the MC.
Private		Tucker	H.				
Sergeant		Tuley	C.		C		Listed as missing in *The Times*, 2 May 1951.

NOMINAL ROLL

Rank	Number	Surname	Forenames	Awards	Company	Platoon	Notes
Rifleman	14190665	Tumilson	William				The Royal Irish Fusiliers attached to The Royal Ulster Rifles. Captured 25 April 1951. Listed as missing in *The Times*, 2 May 1951, aged 23 years. He was held in No.3 Camp of the "Democratic People's Republic of Korea", Peking.
Sergeant		Turmey	'Ginger'		C	No.8	A Reservist from Yorkshire.
Corporal	6460598	Turner	A.				Buried UN Memorial Cemetery, Pusan, Korea, Plot 17, Row 7, Grave 760, aged 31 years. Initially listed as missing and then killed in action during the Battle of Seoul, 2-4 January 1951.
Rifleman	22404529	Turner	J.A.				The Royal Irish Fusiliers attached to The Royal Ulster Rifles. Wounded in action 17 September 1951. Listed as wounded in *The Times*, 6 October 1951.
Rifleman	14186737	Tweedie	John				From Ballyclare. Missing presumed killed during the Battle of Imjin, 22-25 April 1951 aged 22 years. No known grave. Commemorated in the UN Wall of Remembrance, Pusan, Korea.
Rifleman	22230958	Twomey					From Eire.
Rifleman		Tyass	Albert				Captured by the Chinese, 25 April 1951 at the Imjin. Held captive for two years.
Rifleman		Valler	E.J.				Originally listed as missing in *The Times*, 3 May 1951 then corrected to wounded, in *The Times*, 12 May 1951.
Lance Corporal	14412184	Vance	Martin				He joined the regiment in 1941 and served in Palestine and Austria and took part in the Normandy landings. He was also with the Airborne for a time. Captured 4/5 January 1951. Listed as missing in *The Times* and then as prisoner of war, 22 September 1951.
Rifleman		Varley	A.E.	MID			Also listed as Varney.
Corporal	21124032	Vincent	P.A.				The Royal Irish Fusiliers attached to The Royal Ulster Rifles. Wounded in action 15 June 1951. Listed as wounded in *The Times*, 30 June 1951.

310 A NEW BATTLEFIELD

Rank	Number	Surname	Forenames	Awards	Company	Platoon	Notes
Sergeant		Vyse				Intel Section	
Rifleman	22306871	Waide	Joseph				From Ballymena, listed as missing aged 21 years. Captured 4/5 January 1951. Listed a missing in *The Times*, 20 January 1951.
Sergeant		Walker	'Hooky'				Wounded in the head at Happy Valley.
Rifleman	7043334	Wallace	Samuel Gerald				The Royal Irish Fusiliers attached to The Royal Ulster Rifles. Died as a prisoner 20 March 1951, aged 36. Missing presumed killed. Buried UN Memorial Cemetery, Pusan, Korea, Plot 22, Row 4, Grave 1451, aged 36. Although listed as missing presumably his body was found as he has a grave.
Rifleman		Walsh			Support		Believed to be the oldest British solider in Korea and Battalion cobbler.
Rifleman		Walsh	G.				Listed as wounded in *The Times*, 2 May 1951.
Rifleman	22523389	Walshe	J.				Buried UN Memorial Cemetery, Pusan, Korea, Plot 17, Row 2, Grave 706. Died 25 April 1951, aged 20 years.
Rifleman	22247233	Ward	M.O.				Captured 25 April 1951. Listed as missing in *The Times*, 3 May 1951 then as a POW, 6 October 1951.
Corporal	6980166	Waring	Daniel Charles				Ex-Royal Inniskilling Fusiliers, attached from 10 May 1951. Also served in Kenya and awarded AGSM.
Rifleman	3598562	Washer	R.S.W.				Buried UN Memorial Cemetery, Pusan, Korea, Plot 24, Row 6, Grave 1761. Died 25 April 1951, aged 29 years.
Rifleman	22203078	Waters	P.				Battle accident.
Corporal	3651482	Watkinson	J. 'Ginger'	MID			Ex-King's Regiment and Chindit, a reservist, awarded MID.
Sergeant		Watt					Ex-Royal Inniskilling Fusiliers, attached.
Major		West	T.J.	MC			The Royal Irish Fusiliers attached to The Royal Ulster Rifles.
Corporal	7012933	Wheeler	E.				Buried UN Memorial Cemetery, Pusan, Korea, Plot 17, Row 7, Grave 759. Killed 3/4 January 1951, aged

Rank	Number	Surname	Forenames	Awards	Company	Platoon	Notes
2nd Lieutenant		Whitamore	V.P.C. 'Peter'		C		The Loyal Regiment (North Lancashire) attached to The Royal Ulster Rifles. Reported as missing in *The Times*, 2 May 1951, then as a POW, 6 October 1951
Rifleman		White	H.				From Yorkshire. Listed as wounded in *The Times*, 10 March 1951.
Rifleman	4866540	White	Mark				Brother to Rifleman Thomas White.
Rifleman		White	S.				Listed as wounded in *The Times*, 20 January 1951.
Rifleman	3655126	White	Thomas				From Larne. Missing presumed killed 2 February 1951. Buried UN Memorial Cemetery, Pusan, Korea, Plot 24, Row 5, Grave 1714, aged 29 years. Although listed as missing presumably his body was found as he has a grave.
Rifleman		Whiteside	William				From Belfast he was formerly wounded twice during the Second World War - first at Dunkirk and later in Normandy. Worked as a professional boxer prior to being recalled to the Colours. Listed as wounded in *The Times*, 2 May 1951 he was treated for back wounds in a military hospital in Japan.
Rifleman	1439092	Wilcox	W.				Missing presumed killed during the Battle of Seoul, 2-4 January 1951, aged 29 years. No known grave. Commemorated on the UN Wall of Remembrance, Pusan, Korea.
Captain		Williams	A.B.				
Rifleman		Williams	G.				
Corporal	22243665	Williams	P.F.P				Captured 4/5 January 1951. Listed as missing in *The Times*, 20 January 1951, then as a POW, 30 June 1951.
		Wilson	Andy				He was a piper.
Corporal		Wiseley	W.J.				Listed as wounded in *The Times*, 3 February 1951.
Rifleman	5672255	Woodhouse	Wilfred John				Missing presumed killed during the Battle of Seoul, 2-4 January 1951 aged 30 years. No known grave. Commemorated on the UN Wall of Remembrance, Pusan, Korea.

Rank	Number	Surname	Forenames	Awards	Company	Platoon	Notes
A/Sergeant		Woods					
Rifleman	3770892	Woods	E.F.				Captured 25 April 1951. Originally wounded later missing in action, later in the same report, 6 October 1951, he was listed as a POW and still missing - still unclear which is accurate.
Reverend		Woods	R.		HQ		HQ Company from October 1951.
Pipe Major		Woods	T. 'Lakari'				'Lakari' is the Hindustani word for wood. Attached to Battalion HQ.
		Wright	M.				
Rifleman	7013336	Wright	Thomas				From Larne. Buried UN Memorial Cemetery, Pusan, Korea, Plot 17, Row 4, Grave 730. Killed 3/4 January 1951, aged 28 years.
		Wynn	William		Support	Mortar	
Rifleman	22273215	Young	W.J.				Captured 25 April 1951. Listed as missing in *The Times*, 3 May 1951, then as a POW 29 October 1951.

NOMINAL ROLL

Corporal Tommy Cushing.

Rifleman McNabb, missing in action.

Rifleman J. Stevenson, missing in action.

Rifleman Francis Crilly, missing in action.

Rifleman Lodge, missing in action.

Rifleman Thomas Beattie McHaffey, missing in action.

Lieutenant G. Fitz-Gibbon, killed in action.

Rifleman Graham, missing in action.

Rifleman Andrew Aicken, missing in action.

Rifleman T. Kennedy.

Rifleman Desmond Henry Johnston.

Rifleman Thomas Wright.

Rifleman William Sinclair.

Corporal E. Phillips, captured by the Chinese. (RUR Museum)

Sergeant J. Talbot, Chinese prisoner. (RUR Museum)

Corporal W. Mills returning from an anti-guerilla patrol. (RUR Museum)

Rifleman A. Ryan returning from an anti-guerilla patrol. (RUR Museum)

Rifleman T. Agnew (*Belfast Telegraph*)

NOMINAL ROLL 315

Rifleman S.H. Greer.

Rifleman Joseph Davison.

Rifleman B. Canavan.

Rifleman Thomas W. Lorimer.

Appendix IV

Operation 'Spitfire'

'Spitfire' was launched on 18 June, the 136th Anniversary of Waterloo and its success can be laid at the door of an Ulster Rifleman, Captain William Anderson. To quote the citation for Anderson's Bar to the Military Cross:

For the operation the Section was divided into an advance party and a main body. Captain Anderson insisted on leading the Advance party himself. This was by far the most dangerous part of the whole operation. The Advance Party had to jump blind in an extremely mountainous area, about which we had no intelligence. The object of the Advance Party was to carry out a reconnaissance for a soft drop zone for the main body and to find a suitable place to set up a base camp. They carried a radio, pistols, and seven days rations. Just before take-off on 18th June Captain Anderson severely burned his hand and arm, he jumped with his arm in a sling. On the jump the interpreter was badly injured and unable to move. To reconnoitre the Drop Zone and camp site it was necessary to carry out daylight patrols. This is a very risky undertaking for a white man behind the lines in Korea. Captain Anderson left his two American Sergeants in a safe hiding place and did these patrols on his own. During one of these patrols he spotted, and directed, an airstrike on a Chinese Battalion with excellent results. Captain Anderson was successful in finding the Drop Zone and arranged the reception party for the main body, which dropped on 25th June.

The success of Operation Spitfire was due primarily to Captain Anderson, whose personal courage, tenacity and cheerfulness are a constant source of inspiration to his men.

Appendix V

Korean Lament

There's blood on the hills of Korea, it's the blood of the brave and the true,
Where the nations they battled together, 'neath banners of white and pale blue,
As they marched over the fields of Korea to the hills where the enemy lay, they remembered the Brigadier's orders, those hills must be taken today.
And forward they went into battle, with faces unsmiling, and stern, for they knew as they charged up that hillside there were many would never return.
Some thought of their wives and their mothers and some of their sweethearts so fair, and some as they plodded and stumbled were softly saying this prayer,
"There's blood on the hills of Korea, it's the blood of the freedom we love, may our names live in glory forever, and our souls rest in heave above."
And boys, when you go back to Belfast, when this War is over and done,
Just think of the ones left behind you out in the Korean sun.

Mark B. McConnell
RQMS (W.O.1)

Rifleman McCormick at Sinujui about 80 miles south of Yalu River. Rifleman McCormick was later missing presumed killed during the Battle of the Imjin. (RUR Museum)

Bibliography

Unpublished material
RUR Museum Archives
Derrick Gibson Harries, *The Royal Ulster Rifles in Korea* (unpublished manuscript)

Newspapers and journals
Daily Telegraph
Belfast Telegraph
Korean Times
Sunday Life
The Times
Blackthorn Magazine
Faugh-A-Ballagh: Regimental Gazette of the Royal Irish Fusiliers
Newsletter of The Royal Ulster Rifles Officers' Club
President's Newsletter
Quis Separabit: The Magazine of the Royal Ulster Rifles

Books and articles
Anonymous [Capt. H. Hamill], *The Royal Ulster Rifles in Korea*, Belfast, 1953
Bailey, S.D., *The Korean Armistice*, Basingstoke, 1992
Barclay, Brig. C.N., *The First Commonwealth Division – the story of British Commonwealth Land Forces in Korea, 1950-1953*, Aldershot, 1954
Barker, A.J., *Fortune Favours The Brave. The Battle of the Hook, Korea, 1952-53*, London, 1974.
Bayly, C. & Harper, T., *Forgotten Wars – the end of Britain's Asian Empire*, London, 2008
Bellis, Malcolm A., *The British Army Overseas, 1945-1970*, Wistaston, 2001
Catchpole, Brian, "The Commonwealth in Korea", *History Today*, November 1998
Catchpole, Brian, *The Korean War*, London, 2000
Cunningham, Cyril, *No Mercy, No Leniency. Communist mistreatment of British prisoners of war in Korea*, Barnsley, 2000
Dillon, Martin, *The Dirty War*, London, 1988
Doherty, R, *The Sons of Ulster. Ulstermen at War from the Somme to Korea*, Belfast, 1992
Dungan, Myles, *Distant Drums. Irish Soldiers in Foreign Armies*, Belfast 1993
Durney, James, *'The Far Side of the World'. Irish Servicemen in the Korean War 1950-53*, Naas, County Kildare, 2005
Farrar-Hockley, Anthony, *The British Part in the Korean War, Volume I: A Distant Obligation*, (London, 1990)
Farrar-Hockley, Anthony, *The British Part in the Korean War, Volume II: An Honourable Discharge*, (London, 1995)
Forty, George, *At War in Korea*, London, 1997

Gaston, Peter, *Korea 1950-1953, Prisoners of War, The British Army*, Glasgow, 1976
Halberstam, David, *The Coldest Winter – America and the Korean War*, London, 2008
Halliday, J. & Cumings, B., *Korea, the unknown war*, London, 1990
Hastings, Max, *The Korean War*, London, 1993
Jackson, Robert, *Air War over Korea*, London, 1973
Kavanagh, P.J., *The Perfect Stranger*, London, 1966
Kershaw, Robert, *'It Never Snows in September'. The German view of Market-Garden and the Battle of Arnhem, September 1944*, Shepperton, 1995
Linklater, Eric, *Our Men In Korea*, London, 1953
Lowe, Peter, *The Origins of the Korean War*, New York, 1986
MacDonald, C., *Korea – The War Before Vietnam*, London, 1986
McNab, C., *Twentieth Century Small-Arms*, Hoo, 2001
McNair, E.J., *A British Army Nurse in Korea*, Stroud, 2007
Napier, Richard, *From Horses to Chieftains. The true story of an original 'Desert Rat'*, Arundel, 1992
O'Kane, Henry, *O'Kane's Korea*, Kenilworth, 1988
Ryan, Cornelius, *A Bridge Too Far*, London, 1975
Salmon, Andrew, *To The Last Round, the epic British stand on the Imjin River, Korea, 1951* London, 2009
Shipster, Col. J.N., *The Die-Hards in Korea*, n.p., 1975
Thomas, Graham, *Furies and Fireflies over Korea*, London, 2004
Wheal, E.A. & Pope, S., *The Macmillan Dictionary of the Second World War*, London, 1989
Whiting, Charles, *Battleground Korea, The British in Korea*, Stroud, 1999

Websites

http://palacebarracksmemorialgarden.org/korea.htm
    Palace Barracks Memorial Garden – Korea 1951 to 1952
http://www.nationalarchives.gov.uk/battles/korea
    National Archives – British Battles – Korea 1951
http:/royalirishrangers.co.uk/korea.html
    The Royal Irish Rangers – Korea 1950-53
http:/www.britains-smallwars.com/korea/roh-korea/rur.hmtl
    Britain's Small Wars – Roll of Honour, Korea – The Royal Ulster Rifles

Index

116 Battery, RA, 68, 71
116 Division, People's Communist Volunteers, 95
117 Light Anti Aircraft Regiment, 121
139 Heavy Battery, RA, 37
170 Mortar Battery, RA, 77, 96, 118, 132, 145, 168, 173, 181, 188, 199, 244
175 Battery, RA, 96
176 Battery, RA, 71, 77, 170, 171, 199, 246
17pdr guns, 43, 61, 73, 77, 79, 80, 264
25th Canadian Brigade, 199, 224
26 Field Ambulance, 49, 52, 93, 152
27th Commonwealth Infantry Brigade, 74, 136, 156
29th British Infantry Brigade, 74, 75, 76, 78, 80, 89, 104, 115, 116, 119, 145, 147, 149, 156, 184, 200, 209
29th Independent Brigade Signal Squadron, 246
29th Light Aid Detachment, REME, 246
29th Mobile Laundry and Bath Unit, RAOC, 246
29th Ordnance Field Park RAOC, 246
2nd Royal Canadian Regiment, 212
3rd Battalion Royal Australian Regiment, 200, 212
45 Field Regiment, 35, 54, 71, 90, 92, 143, 158, 167, 174, 199
55th Field Squadron, 93, 147, 162, 199, 246
60th Indian Field Ambulance, 76, 81, 179
65th (Puerto Rican) Regiment, 143
65th Regimental Combat Team, 144
8th King's Royal Irish Hussars, 35, 77, 87, 90, 106, 130, 131, 135, 141, 143, 145, 147, 149, 151, 171, 173, 176, 179, 187, 199, 206, 212, 216, 237, 245, 246

Acheson, D., 25
Addis, J., Rfn, 53, 256
Advanced Dressing Station (ADS), 93
Afghanistan, 239, 245
Agnew, T., Rfn, 256, 314
Aicken, A., Rfn, 256, 313
Alberts, L/Cpl, 149, 152, 153, 256
Alexander, G., Lt, 101
Anderson, W.E., Capt, 248, 249, 316
Andrep, Col, 113
Andrews, Rear-Admiral, 27
Anti-Tank Platoon, Royal Ulster Rifles, 43, 79, 80, 93, 133, 264
Anyang-Ni, 122
Argyll and Sutherland Highlanders, The, 27, 157, 234
Arctic Oil, 106
Assault Pioneer Platoon, Royal Ulster Rifles, 44, 80, 126,
Astley-Cooper, D., Capt, 90, 92, 101, 246
Attlee, C., 27
Auster aircraft, 201
Axeford, A., 42, 257

Balders, N., Capt, 116, 134, 257
Ballymacab, 184
Ballymena, 32, 37, 43, 107, 108, 236, 238, 285, 286, 303, 310
Baough, B., 237
Bartlett, J.R., Rfn, 112, 258
Battle Patrol, 74, 80, 81, 83, 89, 93, 96, 98, 99, 101, 102, 127, 132, 134, 149, 162, 167, 262, 265, 298, 306
Baxter, Cpl, 173, 258
Bayonets, 26, 30, 99, 172
Bazooka, 45, 162, 170, 172
Beamish, J., Capt, 193, 258
Bean Camp, 112, 130
Beckett, J.A., Lt, 39, 79, 108, 258
Begbie, Capt, 201
Belfast City Hall, 241, 242
Belgian Battalion, 20, 152, 155, 158, 159, 161, 169, 174, 187, 189, 190, 197, 200
Benson, R., Lt, 42, 43, 45, 95, 258
Black, Cpl, 101
Blake, C.A.H.B., Maj, 38, 45, 75, 76, 80, 86, 89, 92, 93, 96, 97, 98, 99, 101, 104, 105, 259, 302
Bofors Guns, 244
Border Regiment, The, 116, 220, 222, 280, 281
Boyd, R., Rfn, 109
Boyle, J., Cpl, 53
Braithwaite, A., Maj, RA, 71, 72
Bren Carrier, 43, 87, 185, 219

INDEX

Bren gun, 44, 66, 94, 95, 96, 102, 167, 169, 171, 179, 189, 191, 217, 220, 252, 254, 280, 306
Brierley, C., Rfn, 173, 200, 260
Brodie, T., Brig, 35, 68, 74, 75, 83, 89, 98, 117, 118, 119, 131, 141, 145, 166, 174, 186, 193, 195, 200, 205, 214, 226
Brooks, W.E., Maj, 193, 260
Brown, 'Topper', Rfn, 65, 172
Browning MG, 191
Bruce, D., Cpl, 253, 260
Bruford-Davis, E.R., Lt, 42, 64, 67, 68, 81, 94, 97, 110, 260
Buckley, T.J., Sgt, 107, 261
Buckley, J.J., Rfn, 136, 261
Budden, R., 237
Bunby, Rfn, 106, 261
Burma, 42, 115, 172, 244, 271, 272, 304
Butler, R., Maj, 147
Byrne, CQMS, 68, 253
Byrne, J., VC, 31
Pearson, J., VC, 31
Byrne, T., Rfn, 108

C47, 99
Cadman, Sgt, 182
Cain, Rfn, 95
Calder, Cpl, 173
Campbell, H., Sgt, 63, 79, 101, 102, 104, 110, 127, 251
Canavan, B., Rfn, 262, 315
Cardwell Reforms, 34
Carlin, Sgt, 106, 262
Carson, R.J.H., Lt-Col, 20, 37, 38, 45, 47, 50, 57, 62, 69, 72, 75, 76, 80, 83, 86, 87, 89, 92, 93, 113, 116, 117, 132, 134, 135, 141, 143, 144, 145, 147, 152, 161, 173, 189, 193, 194, 196, 200, 205, 206, 223, 234, 235, 248, 253
Cassels, A.J.H., Maj-Gen, 193, 199
Centurion tank, 35, 77, 79, 80, 90, 93, 106, 117, 118, 130, 132, 134, 145, 148, 151, 153, 154, 171, 173, 176, 179, 182, 183, 184, 186, 189, 211, 212, 216, 245, 246
Chaegunghyon, 83, 85, 89, 91, 98, 100, 110, 199, 204, 236, 248, 250, 251
Chaffee tank, 171
Changdon, 82
Changu-Ri, 132
Chapman, J., Lt, 40, 107
Charley, W.R.H., Capt, 40, 45, 49, 60, 78, 79, 96, 107, 195, 241

Checkpoint 'How', 214, 216, 217, 220, 222, 224, 225
Chinnampo, 142
Chinwin River, 172
Chongchon, 76, 83
Chong-Song, 191,
Chorwon, 64, 93, 161, 223
Chosin Hotel, 83
Church, R., Rfn, 188
Churchill tank, 89, 132, 134, 212, 246
Churchill, W., 25
Clifford, Rfn, 113, 114
Coad, B.A., Brig, 27, 74
Cocksedge, G.W.H., Capt
Coforce, 117
Colchester, 20, 34, 35, 42, 62, 199
Colombo, 53, 54
Commonwealth Division, 66, 74, 102, 125, 156, 163, 193, 199, 200, 202, 203, 212, 223, 318
Compo Canyon, 83, 84, 86, 88, 89
Cook, Sgt, 107, 110, 252
Cooper, Henry, 20, 37
Cooper, Rfn, 68
Cooperforce, 85, 89, 93, 98, 99, 101, 104
Copping, Sgt, 107
Cornick, L, Lt, 216, 217, 220, 253
Cowan, W.J., 36
Crahay, A., Col, 152
Craig, H., Lt, 162, 166, 167
Crawford, Rfn, 173
Crilly, F., Rfn, 313
Cromwell tank, 89, 90, 92, 99, 101, 102, 104, 105, 245, 246
Cushing, T., Cpl, 36, 313
Cussans, Mrs, 194

Dakota, 125
Daniels, I, Lt, 96, 108, 138, 141
Darboujis, Lt-Col, 194
Davies, 'Trotsky', 42, 304
Davis, Rfn, 80
Davison, J., Rfn, 315
Defence Platoon, Royal Ulster Rifles, 71, 118, 127
Dickson, Capt, 45
Dixon, Sgt. REME, 61
Docker, Capt, 108, 173
Dolan, P., Rfn, 69
Doran, John, 36
Dorset Regiment, The, 27, 110
Drumgoole, J., CSM, 97

Duke of Wellington's Regiment, The, 226
Dungavel, T., Capt, 113, 127
Dunlop, V., Lt, 116, 121, 134, 139, 174
Dunne, Rfn, 144
Dyer, Rfn, 158, 179

East Lancashire Regiment, The, 116
Eastman, K., Lt, 162, 167
Egypt, 30, 31, 37, 38, 121, 162, 186, 189
Elliott, S., 188
Empire Halladale, HMT, 230, 231, 234
Empire Pride, HMT, 43, 46, 48, 49, 51, 52, 53, 54, 56, 57, 110
Empress of India, HMT, 54
Erreagar, L/Cpl, 179

F80, Shooting Star, 96
Fahy, Rfn, 196
Farmer Sgt, 101
Farrell, J., Cpl, 94, 102, 104, 108, 170, 184, 241
Ferrie, A.M., 38, 39, 45, 95, 110, 113, 138
ffrench, J.R.M., Capt, 41, 42, 56, 83
Filipino Battalion, 89, 171
Fisher, D., Rfn, 188
Fitch, William, Col, 30
Fitz-Gibbon, G., Lt, 313
Fitzsimons, S., CSM, 101, 106, 253
Forrester, Sgt, 107
Fort Nixon, 20, 148, 151, 155, 161, 185
Forward Defence Line (FDL), 93, 149, 150, 213
Fowler, T.J., Sgt, 95, 253
Foxholes, 45, 93
Frazer, Lt, 45
French Battalion, 28

Gaffikin, H.M., Maj, 42, 45, 68, 79, 87, 95, 108, 110, 161, 248
Gale, Sir Richard, Gen, 141, 143
Gales, Rfn, 82
Galway, Rfn, 71
Gibbon, A.H.G. 'Spud', Maj, 101
Gibson, Cpl, 75
Gill, Derek, Lt, 147
Gill, R.S., Lt, 44, 213
Gin Palace, 62
Glendon, D., Rfn, 63
Glennon, P., Miss, 109
Gloster Crossing, 158, 161, 195, 197, 212
Gloster Regiment, The, 76, 77, 93, 97, 98, 124, 125, 131, 139, 158, 159, 161, 162, 168, 169, 171, 174, 187, 188, 189, 194, 195, 197, 212, 236, 237
Glover, M., Capt, 134
Gordon, CQMS, 107
Gore, H., 56
Gorman, T., 36
Gough Barracks, 121, 254
Grace, G., Rfn, 116
Graham, Rfn, 313
Greek Battalion, 89, 194, 195
Greenwood, J., Rfn, 108
Greer, S.H., Rfn, 315
Grenades, 20, 67, 81, 94, 95, 100, 101, 102, 114, 120, 127, 147, 150, 155, 156, 161, 162, 168, 169, 170, 172, 176, 182, 183, 184, 217, 222, 252
Griffiths, Rfn, 130
Guerisse, A.M., Col, 152

Hackett, 'Shan', Brigadier, 42
Haju, 140
Halliday, W.McW., Cpl, 172, 221, 222, 252
Hamill, H., Capt, 20, 38, 45, 81, 86, 87, 92, 118, 235
Han River, 63, 64, 93, 98, 106, 110, 124, 130, 135, 136, 141, 143, 149, 150, 159, 169, 187, 188, 189, 190, 193
Happy Valley, 40, 44, 83, 84, 86, 87, 91, 105, 106, 110, 113, 114, 116, 143, 199, 205, 224, 236, 239
Harris, 'Stan', L/Cpl, 130, 227
Hassett, G., 237
Hazlehurst, Thomas, Sgt, 30
Heavey, Rfn, 196
Helicopters, 28, 81, 106, 117, 118, 149, 152, 153
Heward, Rfn, 134
Hibbert, J., Rfn, 112
Hickey, M., L/Cpl, 63
Hill 127, 96, 132
Hill 184, 150
Hill 187, 213, 214, 224, 225
Hill 194, 147, 148, 149, 151, 158, 159, 161
Hill 195, 95, 96, 107
Hill 235, 171
Hill 257, 167, 168, 169
Hill 327, 124
Hill 398, 168, 169, 170, 172, 174
Hill 630, 130, 131, 132
Hill 675, 171, 172
Hill, A, Lt, 81, 126

Hilton, Lt, 107
Hinde, J.E.D'O., Capt, 38, 56, 75, 76, 87, 127, 253
Hiroshima, 166, 228
HMS *Belfast*, 27, 138, 139, 140, 141, 142, 233, 236
HMS *Black Swan*, 27
HMS *Ceylon*, 27
HMS *Consort*, 27
HMS *Cossack*, 27
HMS *Jamaica*, 27
HMS *Triumph*, 27
HMS *Unicorn*, 27
Hodgkins, K., Lt, 220, 222
Hong Kong, 20, 27, 37, 38, 49, 121, 157, 229, 230, 232, 234, 236
Hook, The, 226
Horrabin, Rfn, 85
Hunt, N., Cpl, 110, 254
Huth, H., Maj, 183, 186,
Hwangbang-Ni, 152, 159, 166, 168, 172, 182
Hwang-Ni, 168

Inchon, 26, 136, 139, 140, 141, 157, 190, 191, 226
Jerome, H.E., VC, 31

Jikkay, 125
Johnson, V. de P.C., Capt, 253
Johnson, Y., Cpl, 53
Johnston, D.H., Rfn, 314
Johnston, Lt, 222
Joyce, K., L/Cpl, 63

K Volunteers, 34
Kaesong, 73, 80, 93, 192, 199
Kamak San, 143, 144, 145, 158, 159, 171, 172, 173, 174, 175, 176
Kansas Line, 195, 196, 198, 199, 200, 211
Kapyong River, 68, 69, 156
Kavanagh, P., Lt, 162, 164, 166
Kaye, Rfn, 144
Kelly, J.T., Rfn, 112
Kelly, Padre, 44, 45, 87
Kennedy, N., Sgt, 108, 128, 130
Kennedy, T., Rfn, 314
Killen, Sgt, 107
Kim II-Sung, 25
Kimpo Airfield, 190
King's Own Scottish Borderers, The, 157, 176, 200, 212, 224

King's Shropshire Light Infantry, The, 200, 212, 224
Knight, J., Sgt, 253
Korangpo-Ri, 88
Kowang San, 223, 224, 226
Kumwha, 64, 223
Kumyangjang-Ni, 123, 136
Kure, 141, 166, 227
Kyeruji, 117, 118

Lane, J., Capt, 40, 117, 168, 169, 170, 183, 223
Lavery, J., Maj, 240
Lavery, Joe, Rfn, 138
Lavery, J., Cpl, 43
Laving, L.F., 39
Lea, Stan, 237
Lee Enfield, 44, 106
Lee Kyung-sik, 174
Leiding, Sgt, 161, 162
'Lightning Bugs', (converted C-47 flare-droppers), 99, 104
Line Golden, 190, 193, 194
Line Wyoming, 212, 226
Liverpool, 37, 46, 47, 48, 49, 108, 227
Lodge, Rfn, 313
London Irish Rifles, The, 33, 39, 46, 193
Longueuil de, J.C.S.G., Maj, 39, 45, 87, 107
Lorimer, T.W., Rfn, 108, 315
Lowry, C/Sgt, 107
Loyal North Lancashire Regiment, The, 108
Luxemburg, 28, 152
Lynch, W., Rfn, 111
Lyons, Rfn, 128, 130

M1 carbine, 45, 106, 147, 244
MacNicol, C., Lt, 42, 95, 150, 251
Maher, P., 173, 225
Maher, T., 225
Main Supply Route, 62, 89, 183, 186
Mainwaring, Rfn, 71
Majon-Ni, 148
Majury, J.H.S., Capt, 40, 43, 79, 100, 103, 104, 110, 131
Mann, T., Sgt, 108
Mansergh, L, 28
Mark, S., Cpl, 53
MASH (Mobile Army Surgical Hospital), 28
Mason, J., Lt, 39, 117, 135
Massey, W., Cpl, 110, 111, 112, 113, 130, 135, 136
Mau San, 143, 144

May, I.A., Maj, 42, 93, 117,
Mayforce, 117, 118
McAlonan, Rfn, 80
McArthur, Gen, 25, 27
McCallan, A.J., Lt, 41, 43, 56, 86, 134, 136
McCann, T., 225
McCarthy, Joe, US Senator, 26
McClare, G., 188
McClelland, J.C., 36
McConkey, T., 240
McConnell, Mark, 42, 45, 65, 172
McConnell, William 'Bill', Sgt, 39, 51, 54, 61, 80, 81, 88, 121, 182
McConville, A., CSM, 68, 110, 196, 251
McCord, M.N.S., Lt, 20, 43, 49, 79, 88, 91, 93, 96, 97, 98, 99, 101, 102, 103, 107, 109, 110, 133, 138, 139, 140, 141, 161, 171, 179, 181, 183, 223, 249
McCormick, Rfn, 317
McCrory, C.S.M., 105, 107
McCullough, Rfn, 68
McGoldrick, Sgt, 107
McHaffey, T.B., Rfn, 313
McIlwaine, T., 225
McKeown, A., Rfn, 71
McKeown, P., Cpl, 141
McNabb, A., Rfn, 313
McShane, J.J., Rfn, 220, 222, 254
McSherry, M., Rfn, 106
McWhirter, S., 242
Memorial, RUR, Korea, 91, 143, 199, 204, 205, 206, 234, 236, 238, 239, 240 241, 242, 243
Middlesex Regiment, The, 27, 78
Miller, H.D., Capt, 42, 62, 73, 108, 109, 136, 172, 173
Mills, W., Cpl, 314
Mole, J.J., Lt, 40, 94, 95, 107, 176, 206, 214, 216, 253
Moore, J., Rfn, 63, 144
Moore, Lt, 108
Moorsom, Lt, 107
Mortar Platoon, Royal Ulster Rifles, 40, 43, 73, 79, 98, 100, 106, 107, 110, 118, 126, 142, 173, 174, 176, 190, 215
Mullgan, J.H.W., Maj, 40, 45, 108
Murray, Rfn, 197
Murray, T., Cpl, 108
Musan-Ni, 69, 143, 159
MVD (*Ministerstvo Vnutrennikh Del*, or [Russian] Ministry of Internal Affairs), 113

Neely, K., Capt, 39, 45, 125, 126
Newport, J.F., Rfn, 217, 252, 253
Nichols, Max, Lt, 42, 68, 116, 117, 139, 142, 173, 175
Nixon, Sir C., Bt, Maj, 40, 56, 60, 107, 132, 134, 148, 253
No.62 Wireless Set, 80
Nogo San, 89, 93,
Nugent, F., Sgt, 53

O'Kane, H., Rfn, 20, 58, 72, 80, 104, 105, 168, 173, 176, 184, 186, 237
O'Keefe, Rfn, 71
O'Neill, J., Cpl, 63
Onjong-Ni, 81, 82
Operation Chromite, 26
Operation Commando, 203, 223, 224
Operation Cudgel, 223
Operation Detonate, 193, 194
Operation Husky, 26
Operation Minden, 203, 212, 214
Operation Spitfire, 249, 316
Ori-Dong, 150, 152
Osan-Ni, 106, 116, 117,118, 123, 135
Otway, T.B.H., Capt, 33
Oxford Carrier, 43, 67, 73, 80, 147, 148, 149, 159, 164, 176, 184, 195
Oyaso, 125, 126, 131

Pabalmak, 123, 124
Page, J., Capt, 147
Pak's Palace/Death House, 113
Panmunjom, 26, 199
Parsons, R.M., Maj, 107
Patterson, Alex, RSM, 49, 121, 137, 141
Phillips, E., Cpl, 314
Pigot, E.W., Lt, 38, 75, 76, 81
Platts, Sgt, 107
Plews, E., Rfn, 254
Point 151, 98
Point 158, 94
Point 195, 94
Porters, 64, 73, 115, 121, 122, 123, 124, 125, 126, 134, 135, 139, 141, 148, 149, 151, 169, 174, 176, 211, 213
Potts, G.L., Lt, 107, 166, 171, 192, 220, 253
Pratt, J., Rfn, 120, 128, 130
Prescott-Westcar, G., Lt, 41, 42, 45, 54, 98, 101, 108, 143

Prettyjohn, Sgt, 183
Princess Patricia's Canadian Light Infantry, 223, 226
Provost Section, 106
Pukhan River, 136
Pulmiji-Ri, 98, 99, 100, 104, 106, 199, 236
Pusan, 26, 27, 41, 56, 57, 58, 59, 61, 62, 73, 87, 105, 152, 176, 226, 227
Pyongtaek, 106
Pyongyang, 58, 70, 73, 75, 76, 77, 78, 79, 112, 113
Pyucyon, 240

Raffles Hotel, 56
Rainey, C/Sgt, 122
Rangarai, A.G., Lt-Col, 81
Rankin, S.J.H., Sgt, 130
Rankine, J., Sgt, 227
Ranson, Sister, 227
Reade, E., Mrs, 194
Red Cross, 113
Rhee, Syngman, 25, 83
Richards, D., Pvt, 200
Rickcord, G., Maj, 121, 122, 125, 137, 138, 139, 140, 141, 147, 148, 162, 166, 167, 168, 170, 171, 173, 174, 175, 177, 186, 187, 193, 206, 234, 254
Ridgeway, Capt, 33
Ridgway, M.B., Gen, 26, 42, 115, 116, 119, 199
Riley, Rfn, 65
Robertson, H., Lt-Gen Sir, 63, 68
Rodgers, J., 65
Roosevelt, F.D., 25
Royal Army Service Corps, 35, 62, 68
Royal East Kent Regiment, The, 121
Royal Engineers, The, 35, 36, 68, 93, 104, 126, 131, 139, 147, 148, 162, 167, 184, 195, 199, 200, 204, 212, 246
Royal Inniskilling Fusiliers, The, 40, 107, 189
Royal Irish Fusiliers, The, 38, 189, 193, 254
Royal Irish Regiment, The, 33, 239, 241
Royal Norfolk Regiment, The, 121, 223, 226, 254
Royal Northumberland Fusiliers, The, 35, 77, 93, 97, 98, 125, 131, 134, 135, 136, 147, 158, 159, 161, 166, 168, 172, 174, 183, 187, 188, 189, 190, 193, 195, 212, 223, 224, 244, 250
Royal Tank Regiment, The, 132, 246
Royal Vingt-Deuxième Regiment, The, 226
Ryan, A., Rfn, 314
Ryan, Father, 45, 206

Ryan, M.D.G.C., Maj, 40, 45, 94, 101, 104, 107, 110, 113, 131, 135, 138

Sainsbury, G., Rfn, 132
Samichon River, 197, 213, 223, 224
Sasebo, 233
Scully, Cpl, 183
Seaforth Barracks, 227
Shaw, Rfn, 136
Shaw, J.K.H., Maj, 42, 45, 56, 57, 104, 110, 135, 161, 164, 167, 173, 175, 176, 248
Shaw-Stewart, H.M., 40, 60, 88, 110, 161, 164, 250
Sibyonni, 77, 214
Simpson, J., Sgt, 188
Sinclair, R.H.S., Capt, 68, 253
Sinclair, W., Rfn, 314
Sinje, 117
Sinujui, 71, 317
Slade, H., Gnr, 130, 227
Slag Heap Hill, 128
Smith, Rfn, 128, 130, 132
Smith, T.P., Capt, 39, 45, 58, 61, 62, 141, 253
Sobraon Barracks, 34, 38, 62
Solma-Ri, 236
Somme Stadium, 210
Spears, C., 182, 189, 191, 192, 199
Spiers, T., Rfn, 186
ss *Kamina*, 152
ss *Karanja*, 33
ss *Stratidore*, 61, 62
St Clair Ford, A., Capt Sir, 142
St George's Day, 161
St Patrick's Barracks, 32, 238
St Patrick's Day, 137, 141, 195
St. Alcock, B., Lt, 40
Stafford, Sgt, 107
Stalin, Josef, 25, 135
Steele, J., Gen Sir, 36, 37, 45, 49, 227, 228, 238
Sten gun, 44, 75, 76, 106, 114, 128, 142, 147, 184
Stevenson, J., Rfn, 313
Stewart, J., 36
Stewart, R., Rfn, 63, 68
Stowe, K., L/Cpl, 107
Strachey, J., Rt. Hon, 46, 49
Street, Rfn, 68
Sturgeon, C/Sgt, 126
Suan, 112, 130, 135
Suffolk Regiment, The, 134
Suk Bum Yoon, 64, 65, 121, 122

Support Company, Royal Ulster Rifles, 26, 34, 37, 42, 68, 75, 83, 98, 104, 107, 110, 118, 126, 131, 132, 144, 172, 248
Suwon, 58, 60, 61, 62, 106, 117, 123, 136
Sweetlove, N., L/Cpl, 177

T34 tank, 45, 62, 158, 216
Tailor, Rfn, 164, 166
Takarazuka, 232
Talbot, J., Sgt, 314
Tangyong-ni, 80
Taylor J., Cpl, 175
Terry, Lt, 192
Theobald, Lt, 45
Thompson sub-machine gun, 45, 106, 225
Tokchong, 186
Trevor-Roper, A.D., Lt, 108, 177, 250
Turkish Brigade, 76, 77, 115, 118, 161
Turner, Rfn, 217, 252, 253

Uijongbu/Uijonbu, 62, 64, 65, 68, 69, 70, 93, 143, 174, 186, 223, 226, 227
Ulster Crossing, 146, 151, 159, 160, 162, 166, 168, 185
US 1st Corps, 75, 76, 83, 142, 189,
US 1st Cavalry Division, 211, 223
US 7th Regiment, 125, 127, 143, 147
US 9th Field Artillery Battalion, 96, 144
US 15th Regimental Combat Team, 187
US 24th Regiment, 125, 131, 132, 134, 169
US 25th Division, 83, 104, 116, 117, 118, 122, 125, 158, 161, 190, 193
US 35th Infantry Regiment, 93
US 39th Field Artillery Battalion, 144
US 82nd Airborne Division, 115
Utting, Sgt, 118

Van Damme, A., CQMS, 162
Van Fleet, J.A., Gen, 28
Vance, M., L/Cpl, 102, 106, 107
Varley, A., Rfn, 97, 110, 177, 179, 254
Vickers MG, 43, 66, 68, 98, 99, 118, 134, 162, 171, 172, 220, 222, 245

Wagner, Capt. US Army, 76, 104,
Walker, Sgt, 85, 104
Walker, W., Gen. US Army, 87, 115
Warren, J., Capt, 220, 222
Washer, Rfn, 85
Watkinson, J., L/Cpl, 110, 254

Wetherall, Capt, 201
Whitamore, P., Lt, 108, 172, 176, 177, 189, 200
Williams, A.B., Capt, 86, 92
Williams, G., Rfn, 120
Wiltshire Regiment, The, 27
Wolfs, H., Lt, 169
Wonsan, 223
Woods, Pipe Maj, 60, 87, 88
Woolworths Brigade, 27, 78
Wright, T., Rfn, 314

Yalu River, 26, 56, 71, 72, 75, 317
Yong Dong, 211
Yongdungpo, 142, 143, 187, 189
Yulp'p-Ri, 145

David R. Orr devotes much of his spare time to the field of military research and has supplied research material and photographs for several books. A member of The Royal Ulster Constabulary GC Historical Society, Society of Friends of the Airborne Museum, Oosterbeek, Police History Society, Society of Friends, Royal Irish Fusiliers Museum and The Military History Society of Ireland, he has delivered talks to local history groups, historical societies, museums and Regimental Associations. Author of *Duty Without Glory – The Story of Ulster's Home Guard in the Second World War and Cold War* and co-author of *The Rifles are There: 1st & 2nd Battalions The Royal Ulster Rifles in the Second World War*, he is currently completing the researching and writing of the history of the Royal Ulster Constabulary Reserve Force and is working in collaboration on a history of the Ulster Volunteer Force and 36th Ulster Division. He is married with two sons, lives in Belfast and works full-time which impacts on his available time for writing and research, and which also competes with a number of other interests and hobbies.

David Truesdale opted for early retirement in 1998 and since then has written for films and television and produced two battlefield guides on behalf of the Royal Irish Fusiliers Museum, *The First Eagle: the 87th at the Battle of Barrosa and Regulars by God! the 89th at the Battle of Lundy's Lane*. He is the author of *Brotherhood of the Cauldron: Irishmen in the 1st Airborne Division at Arnhem, Angels and Heroes, the story of a machine gunner with the Royal Irish Fusiliers August 1914 to April 1915* (with Amanda Moreno), *Irish Winners of the Victoria Cross* (with Richard Doherty), and *Leading The Way To Arnhem, a history of the 21st Independent Parachute Company* (with Peter Gijbels) With David Orr he has written *The Rifles are There: 1st & 2nd Battalions The Royal Ulster Rifles in the Second World War* and is in collaboration on a history of the Ulster Volunteer Force and 36th Ulster Division, 1913-1919. For relaxation he paints in watercolours, photographs wildlife, listens to good music and drinks red wine.